D1564212

Federalism, Democratization, and the Rule of Law in Russia

FEDERALISM, DEMOCRATIZATION, AND THE RULE OF LAW IN RUSSIA

JEFFREY KAHN

OXFORD

UNIVERSITY PRESS

OXFORD
UNIVERSITY PRESS

Great Clarendon Street, Oxford OX2 6DP

Oxford University Press is a department of the University of Oxford.
It furthers the University's objective of excellence in research, scholarship,
and education by publishing worldwide in

Oxford New York

Auckland Bangkok Buenos Aires Cape Town Chennai
Dar es Salaam Delhi Hong Kong Istanbul Karachi Kolkata
Kuala Lumpur Madrid Melbourne Mexico City Mumbai Nairobi
São Paulo Shanghai Singapore Taipei Tokyo Toronto

with an associated company in Berlin

Oxford is a registered trade mark of Oxford University Press
in the UK and in certain other countries

Published in the United States
By Oxford University Press Inc., New York

© Jeffrey Kahn 2002

British Library Cataloguing in Publication Data

Data available

ISBN 0–19–924699–8

Library of Congress Cataloging in Publication Data

Data available

1 3 5 7 9 10 8 6 4 2

Typeset by Kolam Information Services Pvt. Ltd, Pondicherry, India
Printed in Great Britain by
TJ International Ltd, Padstow, Cornwall

To
My Family,

and to
LaiYee,

and in memory of
Herbert Kahn,
who would have loved the adventure,
and
Augusta Hausman Bellinoff,
no less an inspiration

Acknowledgements

One of the major goals of this book is, where appropriate, to bring together the insights of comparative law and comparative politics. The idea for this book began in an undergraduate thesis I wrote at Yale in 1993 on conceptions of sovereignty at play in the politics of building the new Russia. As I worked, Boris Yeltsin's conflict with the Russian parliament grew increasingly intense, ultimately culminating in a tank attack against the Russian White House, where the parliament was headquartered. At St. Antony's College, Oxford, I deepened my exploration of these earlier ideas in a doctoral dissertation on the problems for federalism and democratization that Yeltsin's new constitutional order—the prize of that previous conflict—presented for the struggling Russian Federation. I wrote this thesis from the vantage point of comparative politics and Russian area studies. Revision of this work for publication as this book was completed at the University of Michigan Law School. That experience added a third dimension to my previous understanding of Russia's problematic institutional palimpsest. My legal studies coincided with the proclamation by Russia's second president, Vladimir Putin, that he would create a 'dictatorship of law' in Russia. The final project, therefore, addresses subjects and problems of interest to legal scholars, comparative political scientists and specialists on Russia and the diverse peoples that comprise the Russian Federation.

With that multi-disciplinary genesis, my intellectual and personal debts to others are many and deep. Errors found in this book, however, are mine alone. This book's shortcomings are clear indications of instances when I did not follow the advice generously offered to me by others.

Sincere thanks are due to many scholars and friends, but none more so than Professor Archie Brown. The tremendous quality of his supervision was matched only by the generosity with which he gave of his time. His will always be the high academic standard by which I will measure my own work. Professor Alfred Stepan, in the capacity of an unofficial supervisor, was extraordinarily giving of his knowledge and guidance. An hour spent in his company was the equivalent of a full academic conference, but much more enjoyable. Bernard Rudden, Neil Melvin, Alex Pravda, Robert Service, and Harry Shukman all read and commented helpfully on my work in its dissertation form at Oxford. Chapters One, Two, Eight, and Nine were written while I was a law student at the University of Michigan Law School. Barbara

Anderson and John Romani provided excellent advice and warm hospitality during the final stages of this project. Juan J. Linz at Yale University, and Daniel Halberstam, Sallyanne Payton, A. W. Brian Simpson, Eric Stein, and James Boyd White at the University of Michigan Law School made helpful comments on different chapters. Suzanne Gray at the Hatcher Graduate Library provided the computer technology and patient tutorials that generated the maps in this book. The Michigan Law Library offered a quiet place to make final revisions and check legal references. I am especially grateful to Dominic Byatt, Amanda Watkins, and Georgina Klar at Oxford University Press.

Chapter Five is based upon an article I first published in *Post-Soviet Affairs*, Vol. 16, No.1 (2000), pp. 58–89. © V. H. Winston & Son, Inc., 360 Ocean Boulevard, Palm Beach, FL 33480, All Rights Reserved. This work has been used with permission.

My thoughts about this topic were refined by opportunities to present my research at university lectures and academic conferences. I am extremely grateful to Archie Brown at the Centre for Russian and East European Studies at St. Antony's College, Markku Kivinen at the Aleksanteri Institute of the University of Helsinki, Katlijn Malfliet at the Catholic University of Leuven, Martha Merritt at the Kellogg Center for International Studies at the University of Notre Dame, and William Zimmerman at the Institute for Social Research at the University of Michigan for invitations to present different facets of my research at their institutions.

The families of Shamil Valiullin in Ufa, Maksim Andreev in Kazan' and Tanya Argounova in Yakutsk were extremely kind and wonderful hosts. The Panov family, especially, gave me a home away from home in Moscow. Their warm kitchens were the embodiment of hospitality and their friendship is dear to me.

I wish to express my lasting thanks to Professor Emilia P. Hramova of Yale University.

Karen Aarre, Tim Benbow, Doug Brown, Ralph Della Cava, Steven Everts, David Hoffman, Alan Kahn, Charles King, Tamara Kovacevic, Andrew Kramer, Tomila Lankina, LaiYee Leong (who read the entire manuscript with super-human reserves of kindness, humour, and patience), Nicholas Mead, Nuala Mole, Virginia Mucchi, Andrew Smith, Craig Weller, James E. Wiggin, and Jackie Willcox all offered help at different times and places that was much appreciated. In addition to their excellent advice, their friendship and support made all the difference to me as my spirits inevitably flagged and my strength faltered.

But, above all, it is to my family that I owe the deepest and most lasting gratitude and love. This book could not be dedicated to anyone else but them.

J. D. K.

Muskegon, Michigan
December 2001

Contents

List of Tables

List of Maps and Figures

List of Abbreviations and Glossary

ASSR	Autonomous Soviet Socialist Republic
CPSU	Communist Party of the Soviet Union
Dogovor	A treaty between a region and the federal government on general principles and jurisdiction
Krai	One of six territories in the Russian Federation
Oblast	One of forty-nine provinces in the Russian Federation
Okrug	One of ten districts in the Russian Federation
Republic	One of twenty-one ethnic republics (primarily former ASSRs) in the Russian Federation
RF	Russian Federation
RSFSR	Russian Soviet Federated Socialist Republic
Soglashenie	A detailed agreement between a region and the federal government on a specific issue or issues
SSR	Soviet Socialist Republic
SZRF	Sobranie zakonodatel'stva Rossiiskoi Federatsii—Collected Legislation of the Russian Federation
Ukaz	A decree issued by either the federal executive or a regional executive
USSR	Union of Soviet Socialist Republics
Zakon	Law (statute)

1

Introduction

> I am certain that there is no simple causal relationship between federal-
> ism and freedom.
>
> *William Riker*[1]

What is the relationship between federalism, democracy and the rule of
law? It has frequently been asserted, first, that federal government is possible
in a non-democratic regime, and second, that this holds true even when
fundamental legal principles are absent. The Union of Soviet Socialist
Republics is cited as the classic example of such a state structure. I dispute
the validity of these theoretical and empirical assertions. Like a Potemkin
village—the fabled sham settlements built by the Empress Catherine's
favourite minister to deceive foreigners touring her conquered lands—the
Soviet Union was a federal façade that hardly masked the most centralized
state in modern history. This façade has had tremendous repercussions for
the subject of this book: the development of post-Soviet Russian federalism.
Unlike Potemkin's false fronts, so quickly dismantled once his *paramour* had
passed by with her court, the institutional and conceptual architecture of
Soviet 'federalism' was not so easily deconstructed following the collapse of
the Soviet monolith. The keystone republic of the Soviet Union and its
acknowledged successor—the Russian Soviet Federated Socialist Republic
(RSFSR)—was itself a multi-national state partially comprised of a score of
so-called 'Autonomous Soviet Socialist Republics', (ASSRs). When the Soviet
Union collapsed, the RSFSR retained the fundamentals of the old Soviet
superstructure, building the new Russian Federation upon its crumbling
foundations.[2] The magnitude of such an undertaking is difficult to conceive:
a new state was built almost overnight in both the real and ideological
rubble of the *ancien régime*.

---

[1] William H. Riker, *Federalism: Origin, Operation, Significance* (Boston: Little, Brown, 1964), 13–14.
[2] Between the collapse of the Soviet Union in December 1991 and the adoption of a new
constitution for the Russian Federation in December 1993, the 1978 Constitution of the RSFSR was
still law, although subject to increasing amendment.

This book is a study of Russian (i.e., *Rossiiskii*)[3] federalism, on its own terms and in comparative perspective with other federal systems. What is this 'new' Russian federalism? How have its institutions, old and new, influenced the development of Russia's new state system, its attempts at democracy, and the development of the rule of law? What effect has the division of federal and regional political agendas had on Russia's beleaguered transition from authoritarianism? Is Russia what its Constitution, in its very first words, purports it to be: a democratic, federal, rule-of-law state?[4]

This book relates to several debates in political science and law. In a departure from the classic exposition of federal theory by William Riker, I dispute the assertion that federalism is possible in an authoritarian environment.[5] The immediate implication of this approach is the rejection of the surprisingly unchallenged view of the Soviet Union as an authoritarian, yet nevertheless federal, system of government. The outward display of federal structures was just a thin veneer that masked a highly centralized state, one in which the vanguard role of the profoundly anti-federal Communist Party was enshrined at the heart of its Potemkin constitution.[6] Of course, no serious scholar would dispute the fact that the Soviet Union was an authoritarian (and, at times, terrifyingly totalitarian) state. However, although few took the claim to be a 'people's democracy' at face value, the Soviet assertion to have adopted a federal system of government was rarely the subject of critical study.

Federalism is a broad church, and 'federal' can describe a wide continuum of institutional arrangements; nevertheless, the minimum requirements of democracy and the rule of law must adhere to the term if it is not to be rendered

---

[3] A distinction, obvious in Russian but hidden in English, must be made clear. The term *Rossiiskii* denotes 'Russian' in the sense of relationship to the Russian Federation, regardless of national origin or ethnicity. *Russkii* is the adjective denoting Russian ethnicity. In such a multinational state system as Russia, it is insulting and erroneous to use these terms carelessly.

[4] See Part One, Chapter One, Article One, Section One, *Konstitutsiia Rossiiskoi Federatsii* (1993).

[5] William H. Riker, *Federalism: Origin, Operation, Significance* (Boston: Little, Brown, 1964), 38–40, 115–16, 124. William H. Riker, 'Federalism', in Fred I. Greenstein & Nelson W. Polsby, eds. *Handbook of Political Science: Volume 5. Governmental Institutions and Processes.* (Reading, MA: Addison-Wesley, 1975), 93–172.

[6] See e.g. Arts. Three and Six, *Constitution of the Union of Soviet Socialist Republics* (1977):

Article Three: The Soviet state is organized and functions in accordance with the principle of democratic centralism: all organs of state power are elected from the lowest to the highest, they are accountable to the people, and the decisions of higher organs are binding for lower organs.
Article Six: The Communist Party of the Soviet Union shall be the guiding and directing force of Soviet society, the core of its political system and of state and social organizations.

Aryeh L. Unger, *Constitutional Development in the USSR: A Guide to the Soviet Constitutions* (New York: Pica, 1981), 234–5. These articles of the USSR Constitution are reproduced verbatim in the constitutions of the 15 union republics, including that of the RSFSR. See F.J.M. Feldbrugge, *The Constitutions of the USSR and the Union Republics: Analysis, Texts, Reports* (Alphen aan den Rijn, Netherlands: Sijthoff & Noordhoff, 1979), 275.

meaningless. These minimum requirements are beyond the reach of authoritarian systems. That is why authoritarian states that have asserted a federal or quasi-federal structure are fascinating objects of study. The Soviet façade, for all its faults, was *crucially* important in the way that it framed conflict within particular institutional constraints, influenced the development of political agendas at different levels of government, and provided ready-made templates for political (and sometimes ethnic) mobilization that could be used by different elites for different objectives. This was especially true as the party-state weakened and some electoral prizes were gradually introduced. Studies that accept at face value the institutional structure of the Soviet Union as a genuinely federal structure overlook important factors that distinguish the failure of the Soviet (and imperiled Russian) federal experiments from multi-national federal states that, by various measures, are more stable and successful. In fact, the explanations this book offers for the course of Russian federal politics over the last ten years dwell more on the weaknesses and failings of ostensibly federal systems than on the strengths of 'real' federal systems.

An emphasis on the strong path-dependency of the development of the new Russian Federation out of Soviet institutions is a recurring theme of this book. The institutional shell of federal government, for so long inactive in the Soviet Union, offered enormous opportunities for political mobilization in a 'renewed' Russian Federation once the party-state structure had eroded and regional elections provided the impetus for new, more localized political agendas. Both in its philosophical formulation and in its empirical application, post-Soviet Russian federalism is also a federal façade, but one very different from that of the preceding regime. This study charts the stages in the rebuilding of federal structures after the collapse of the Soviet Union. Constitutional re-engineering progressed from early, ill-defined assertions of sovereignty—the 'Parade of Sovereignties' inspired and manipulated by the first Russian president, Boris Yeltsin—to the writing of federal 'treaties', a federal Constitution and scores of bilateral treaties all authored predominantly by old political actors creating (and contesting) new rules of a post-Soviet, post-Communist political game.

Special attention is devoted to two particularly unexplored aspects of federal theory that are among Russian federalism's most pronounced attributes: (1) extreme constitutional, unconstitutional (but *de facto*), and institutional asymmetry in federal-regional relations, and (2) the problem of establishing a consensus about the fundamental purpose of the federal compact and the importance of enforcing basic principles of legality in the drafting and functioning of that compact.

Asymmetry is not an uncommon characteristic in federal states; indeed, geographic, economic, demographic, political, and other forms of asymmetry may be incentives for federal union. However, the institutional asymmetry entrenched in the Russian Federation Constitution raises serious problems for relations between the federal centre and regional units as well as for relations among regional units themselves. Some units, for example, are governed by presidents and constitutions; others elect governors on the basis of 'charters'. These institutional differences are exacerbated by Soviet legacies of privilege for some ethnic groups over others. Invariably, these institutional differences (and there are many more) affect federal politics. The greatest casualty of this variation has been the development of democratic politics and the rule of law in many of Russia's eighty-nine federal units, weaknesses that return to haunt the federal system as a whole.

Institutional asymmetry is not just a problem for *de jure* federal relations. In many ways, asymmetric, *ad hoc* and non-transparent bilateral 'treaty' arrangements between federal authorities and individual units have *de facto* superseded the federal constitution, which promises a rule-of-law basis for equality and openness in centre-periphery relations. The exclusive control of these relations by federal and regional executive branches has thus far excluded these 'treaties' from ratification by the legislative branch of either level of government, and just as often from interpretation by the judicial branch. The exceptions and contradictions these *treaty*-based relations present to *constitution*-based federal structures are problematic. These problems are exacerbated (and partly caused) by the privileging of personal political patronage over the protections of the rule of law.

What euphemistically has been termed the 'treaty-constitutional' approach to federalism has adversely affected transitions to democracy in Russia. This is both an effect and a self-reinforcing cause of problems in Russia's federal development. *Ad hoc* bilateral negotiations that circumvent federal institutions weaken structures that already suffer from low levels of respect or even compliance. Federal authority to preserve a unified legal environment and to collect taxes for all-federal needs was drastically diminished under Boris Yeltsin. This itself would be a blow to any democratic transition. Russia's asymmetrical federalism exacerbated these difficulties by creating islands of republican authority in which the federal executive is too weak to act, and often too wary of the potential negative effect on his political future to interfere. Just as republican leaders insist that the federation is no greater than the sum of its parts, Russia's transition to democracy is threatened by a creeping authoritarianism in its constituent republics. There is a new federal façade in Russia today: behind the thin veneer of federal structures, a mass of conceptual and legal contradictions reduces federal rules into a sink of misfeasance, non-compliance and brinkmanship. Russia's second president, Vladimir Putin, has sought to re-centralize authority by strengthening what he calls the 'vertical of executive power' in the

Federation by way of a 'dictatorship of law'. His reforms, however, may turn out to be worse than the problems they seek to remedy.

The second theme of this book is the politically driven and uncritical adoption of concepts and philosophies ill-suited to the project of a 'new federalism', a project which Boris Yeltsin and the leaders of Russia's component units conceived for almost diametrically opposed purposes. While everyone used the new vocabulary of federalism—sovereignty, autonomy, separation of powers, the rule of law—few seemed to share a common understanding of the meaning of these terms. The result is the conspicuous lack of a strong consensus on the merits and design of federal government shared by Russia's leaders at different levels of government. From the start, federal political elites—the 'centre', in the lexicon of the debate—have conceived the purpose of federal relations in a manner strikingly different from regional political elites—the 'periphery'.[7] Despite rhetoric to the contrary, the centre in the guise of Yeltsin, his executive branch advisers and successor Vladimir Putin, have viewed federalism as a tool to centralize control over (if not to save) the largest piece of the Soviet empire. Yeltsin began this project, using the rhetoric of Soviet federalism to gain the allegiance of regional leaders in his struggle for the political high ground against Mikhail Gorbachev. Yeltsin's promises of a decentralized, limited federal system that privileged regional autonomy were disingenuously made and quickly broken. Regional elites—who, with hindsight, perhaps should have known better—drafted with Yeltsin a Federation Treaty that seemed to deliver all of those promises. When Yeltsin unilaterally rescinded the Treaty in favour of his own Constitution—a document that reversed many of the presumptions previously favouring local autonomy—regional elites felt the sting of betrayal. The repercussions for federal relations have lasted more than ten years and will taint centre-periphery relations for a long time to come. While some regions (desperately poor or politically impotent) quickly accepted Yeltsin's new regime, the most powerful regions stopped paying taxes, refused to recognize the supremacy of federal law, and rattled whatever nationalist or economic sabres they had to hand.

1. WHY STUDY THE REPUBLICS?

The Russian Federation is a multi-national state with a complicated federal structure. It is composed of eighty-nine units or 'subjects of the Federation', as they are called in the federal constitution. In addition to twenty-one

---

[7] Or, as federal officials in Moscow sometimes say, the *glubinka*, a term with the same slightly pejorative ring a New Yorker might lend the phrase 'Deep South'. When relations turn particularly sour, the appellation might switch to *zakholust'ye*, roughly translated as 'the back of beyond'. Thanks are due to Dr Tomila Lankina for sharpening the author's understanding of these colloquialisms.

ethnically defined republics, there are forty-nine *oblasti* (provinces), ten autonomous *okruga* (districts), six *kraia* (territories), two cities of federal significance (Moscow and St. Petersburg) and one autonomous *oblast'*. Over twenty-three million people, including over ten million ethnic Russians, live in these republics, almost one-sixth of the total population. The republics constitute roughly 28% of the total area of the Russian Federation (see Maps 1-4, and Table 1.1, showing Russian administrative divisions).

Article Five of the federal constitution declares that 'in interrelationships with federal organs of state power all subjects of the Russian Federation possess equal rights'.[8] In fact, there are very real differences in the hierarchy of federal subjects. Both *de jure* and *de facto*, republics possess more rights and advantages than other federal units. These privileges have long (if dubious) histories which have lent credence to ever-increasing demands. The result is a self-fulfilling prophecy, as *oblasti* and other units emulate republican gains and thus provide them with implicit justification. Further complicating these relations is the variation in privileges among units of the same type. This is despite constitutional assertions that all units are 'equal rights subjects of the Russian Federation'.[9] As George Orwell might have observed, all republics may be equal, but some are more equal than others.

In legal terms, republics are quite distinct from other units. A Federation Treaty signed in 1992 elevated republics to the apex of this hierarchy of federal subjects. Although this treaty was later subordinated to the 1993 Federal Constitution, republics still retain a *primus inter pares* relationship to other units. That constitution recognizes a republic, in contradistinction to all other subjects, to be a 'state' (*gosudarstvo*).[10] Republics are the only federal units that have ratified their own constitutions, most of them by mid-1994. The remaining sixty-eight units are governed according to *ustavy*, or charters, most of which were adopted after mid-1995. The chief executive of a republic is, in almost every case, called a president; governors preside in the remaining regions. Such distinctions are not merely terminological. Republics present these and other differences as hallmarks of their state sovereignty. Republics enshrine in their constitutions rights to republican citizenship, with attendant privileges and duties. There is no such thing as *oblast'* citizenship. Governorships, unlike presidencies, have only relatively

---

[8] Article 5, §4. *Konstitutsiia Rossiiskoi Federatsii* (1993).

[9] Article 5, §1. *Konstitutsiia Rossiiskoi Federatsii* (1993).

[10] Article 5, §2: 'The republic (state) has its own constitution and legislation. The krai, oblast, city of federal significance, autonomous oblast, and autonomous okrug has its own charter and legislation'. *See* introduction by M.A. Mitiukov (former first deputy chairman of the Duma), in *Konstitutsii Respublik v sostave Rossiiskoi Federatsii*, Vol. 1 (Moscow: Izdanie Gosudarstvennoi Dumy, Izvestia, 1995), 3.

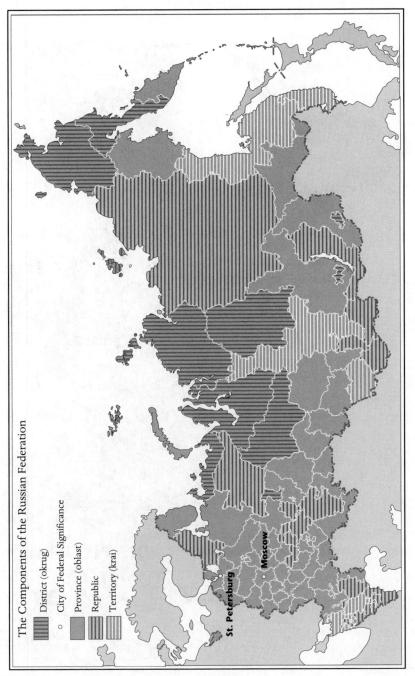

The Components of the Russian Federation

District (okrug)

○ City of Federal Significance

Province (oblast)

Republic

Territory (krai)

St. Petersburg

Moscow

MAP 1. The Components of the Russian Federation

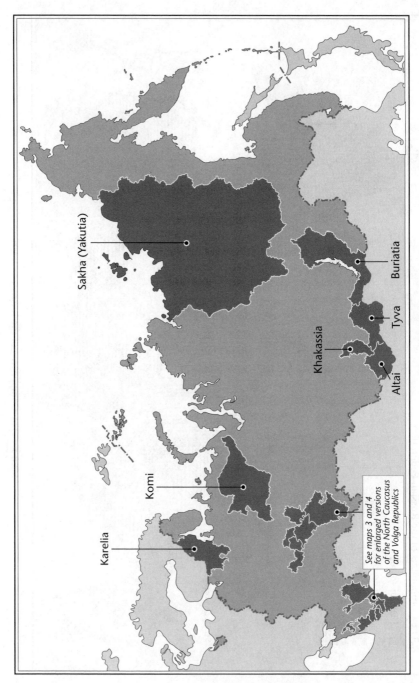

Sakha (Yakutia)

Buriatia

Tyva

Khakassia

Altai

Komi

Karelia

See maps 3 and 4
for enlarged versions
of the North Caucasus
and Volga Republics

MAP 2.   The Republics of the Russian Federation

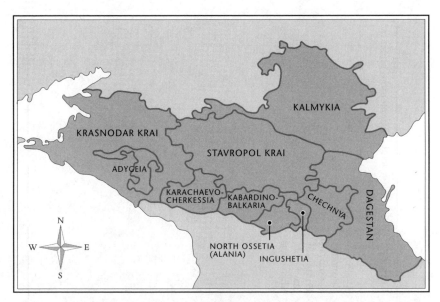

MAP 3. The North Caucasus.

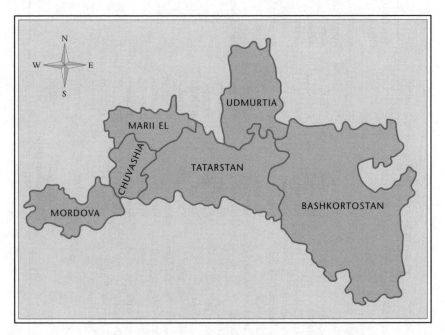

MAP 4. The Volga Region.

Table 1.1 Constituent Units of the Russian Federation

Republics (21)	Oblasts (49)		Autonomous Okrugs (10)	Krais (6)	Cities of federal significance (2)	Autonomous oblast (1)
Adygeia	Amur	Novgorod	Aga-Buryat	Altai	Moscow	Jewish
Altai	Arkhangelsk	Novosibirsk	Komi-Permyak	Krasnodar	St. Petersburg	
Bashkortostan	Astrakhan	Omsk	Koryak	Krasnoyarsk		
Buryatia	Belgorod	Orenburg	Nenets	Primorskii		
Dagestan	Briansk	Orël	Taimyr	Stavropol		
Ingushetia	Vladimir	Penza	Ust-Orda	Khabarovsk		
Kabardino-Balkaria	Volgograd	Perm	Khanty-Mansi			
Kalmykia	Vologda	Pskov	Chukchi			
Karachaevo-Cherkessia	Voronezh	Rostov	Evenk			
Karelia	Ivanovo	Ryazan	Yamal-Nenets			
Komi	Irkutsk	Samara				
Marii El	Kaliningrad	Saratov				
Mordova	Kaluga	Sakhalin				
Sakha (Yakutia)	Kamchatka	Sverdlovsk				
North Ossetia (Alania)	Kemerovo	Smolensk				
Tatarstan	Kirov	Tambov				
Tyva	Kostroma	Tver				
Udmurtia	Kurgan	Tomsk				
Khakassia	Kursk	Tula				
Chechnya (Ichkeria)	Leningrad	Tyumen				
Chuvashia	Liptesk	Ulyanovsk				
	Magadan	Chelyabinsk				
	Moscow	Chita				
	Murmansk	Yaroslavl				
	Nizhnii Novgorod					

recently become elected posts—until Autumn 1996, most governors were appointed by the Kremlin.[11] This has led to sharp political differences in the amount of control federal authorities have been able to exert over republics, as compared to other units.

From the point of view of federalism, the republics of the Russian Federation raise a number of interesting issues that the other regions do not. Following the lead of the union republics (SSRs, or Soviet Socialist Republics) that comprised the Soviet Union, the republics (then ASSRs, or Autonomous Soviet Socialist Republics) fostered with declarations of their rights as sovereign states what became known in 1990 as 'The Parade of Sovereignties'. These declarations were the basis for negotiating the principles of a new Russian Federation in 1992. Starting in 1994, republics played the vanguard role in the parade of bilateral treaties that occupy a defining position in Russian federalism.

These declarations and treaties have shaped the development of the Russian Federation. Their emphasis on sovereignty has fundamentally affected the manner in which federal relations are conceptualized in Russia. Many republican elites comprehend federalism in the most profoundly confederal terms, as the loosest of associations in which the sovereignty of constituent members is paramount. Republican elites speak about 'treaty-constitutional' federal relations and about building federalism 'from the ground up'. Their philosophy tolerates minimal federal intrusion at the same time that it demands considerable federal financial and social supports. In its starkest formulation, this doctrine is the justification republican elites use to discriminate between federal obligations they choose to honour and those that they choose to ignore. The most intransigent republican leaders have occasionally insisted upon the right to pay taxes only for the services from which they immediately benefit, rejecting the notion of a general obligation to the federation. Contrary to most theories of federalism and almost universally accepted practice in other federations, the Russian Federation is not judged by many of the leaders of its republics to be greater than the sum of its parts.

Russia is a multi-ethnic state, in which republics and enormous, sparsely populated *okruga* are named after (though rarely predominantly comprised

---

[11] One analyst reports that 'Until December 17, 1995 only 9 of the sixty-eight [governors] holding office were elected; of the sixty-eight, fifty-three were appointed by Yeltsin in the six months or so after August, 1991'. In the 49 oblasts, through December 1995, 45 governors were Yeltsin appointees. By comparison, by December 1993, 16 republics had elected presidents. Jeffrey W. Hahn, 'Democratization and Political Participation in Russia's Regions', in Karen Dawisha & Bruce Parrott, eds. *Democratic Changes and Authoritarian Reactions in Russia, Ukraine, Belarus, and Moldova* (Cambridge University Press, 1997), 148, 157.

of) particular ethnic groups. This is a remnant of the earliest Soviet nationalities policies. The republics are frequently called 'titular' republics because they are named after the ethnic groups (e. g. Tatars in Tatarstan, Udmurts in Udmurtia) for whom Bolshevik planners constructed these often artificial administrative units (according to the last census, in 1989, Russians outnumbered the titular nationality, although they rarely constituted a majority themselves, in twelve of the twenty such units that then existed). The remaining forty-nine *oblasti* are almost entirely Russian; in only five of them is the ethnic Russian population below 80 per cent (Astrakhan, Kaliningrad, Magadan, Orenburg, Ulianovsk). With only a few exceptions, only republics declared sovereignty in 1990—Russian *oblasti* did not. Likewise, although the bilateral treaty process has been extended to encompass all federal units, republics initiated the process, have set the standard and reaped the greatest benefits from this system. The importance of these ethnically defined components for the Russian Federation is immediately apparent if they are cut out of a hypothetical map of Russia *without* these units. What remains snakes crazily across eleven time zones of Eurasia, marked by holes, splits, and impossibly configured borders. Only four of the other former union republics of the Soviet Union contained any specially demarcated autonomous ethnic units—Azerbaijan (Nagorno-Karabakh and Nakhichevan), Georgia (Abkhazia, Azaria and South Ossetia), Tadjikistan (Gorno-Badakhshan), and Uzbekistan (Karakalpak). All fourteen former SSRs became unitary states, though three of the four mentioned above continue to suffer threats to their territorial integrity.

The republics also pose serious concerns for democracy. Although demographic shifts have reduced titular ethnic groups to minorities in their own republics, the privileges that accrued through titular membership in the Soviet era have not disappeared. In fact, in the new Russian Federation, republics have increased advantages for titular ethnic populations in terms of electoral representation, cultural and linguistic policies, and other benefits. Institutional legacies and new constitutionally entrenched developments have established republican parliaments that systematically privilege the titular ethnic group far in excess of its demographic position. Eligibility for high political office has been restricted by language requirements, effectively excluding Russians and other non-titular ethnic groups.

2. METHODOLOGY AND SOURCES

The nature of federal systems places special emphasis on written compacts, formal structures and institutional arrangements. This book combines a range of methodologies—most obviously those of comparative politics, federal theory, law, and post-Soviet area studies—but orients itself primarily within a legal-constitutional, institutionalist approach. That is, it seeks to combine the structuralist and legalist emphases of the 'old institutionalism' with an awareness of the influence of both individual and institutional actors, the changeable nature of formal and informal political 'rules of the game' and the interplay between state and society that are all hallmarks of the 'new institutionalism'.[12]

Comparative questions of federalism have long fascinated both political scientists and legal scholars. Amazingly, however, these two disciplines have each developed extensive scholarly literatures on the subject that scarcely acknowledge one another. The 'greats' do not engage in cross-disciplinary discussion, as even a cursory glance at the bibliographies of specialists in either field will confirm. In fact, within disciplines, the harshest criticism seems to involve insinuations that a scholar is over-employing the methodology of the other discipline.[13] The result has been a terrible loss for both areas of scholarship.[14]

One of the major goals of this book is, where appropriate, to bridge that gap, bringing together the insights of comparative law and comparative politics. American legal thinking (understandably) has focused on the specific constitutional problems uniquely experienced in the American experiment with federal government. Nevertheless, the insights developed in this field on the theoretical and philosophical nature of federalism put forward in treatises, law reviews and opinions of the federal circuit courts and U.S. Supreme Court are of tremendous value to comparative political scientists interested in all federal systems. Perhaps counter-intuitively, area-studies specialists on Russia and the post-Communist states of Eastern Europe can also benefit from this scholarship—not to mimic the American approach (a very dangerous illusion), but to adopt and adapt a rich learning experience of how to combine the rule of law with federal democracy.

[12] B. Guy Peters, *Institutional Theory in Political Science: The 'New Institutionalism'* (London: Pinter, 1999). James G. March & Johan P. Olsen, 'The New Institutionalism: Organizational Factors in Political Life', 78 *American Political Science Review*, 3 (1984): 734–49.

[13] In his suggestions for further reading at the end of his book, Riker comments on Wheare's *Federal Government*: 'It is highly legalistic in tone and displays very little understanding of political realities'. This is one of Riker's gentler criticisms. William H. Riker, *Federalism: Origin, Operation, Significance* (Boston: Little, Brown, 1964), 157.

[14] Legal scholars writing in law reviews, similarly, spare little effort on the extensive political science literature on federalism. One excellent example of legal scholarship, in over 70, 000 words and 400 footnotes, makes not a single mention of William Riker, Kenneth Wheare, or Ivo Duchacek. *See* Roderick M. Hills, Jr. 'The Political Economy of Cooperative Federalism: Why State Autonomy Makes Sense and "Dual Sovereignty" Doesn't', 96 *Michigan Law Review*, 813 (1998).

The British legal scholar Lord Dicey noted that citizens in a federation become a 'nation of constitutionalists'.[15] Post-Soviet legal scholars, at the command of newly elected (but rarely new) political elites, drafted the institutions and structures of a new legal order at a furious rate of speed. As another British legal scholar explained: 'During the last years of its life the Soviet Union turned to law like a dying monarch to his withered God... with the fervour of one who sees in legislation the path to paradise'.[16] Although this speed was not always conducive to exemplary legal drafts-manship, the phenomenon provided a bounty of new political and le-gal documents to study. Declarations of sovereignty, constitutions, bilateral treaties, and judicial opinions are the core of primary sources around which this book is structured. These documents provide a rich opportunity to compare the underlying principles of this federation with the foundations of other federal systems, as well as to examine the success of the Russian Federation in meeting its own officially documented aspirations.

Hardly any of these documents are available in English translation. Many of them have not even been compiled in Russian collections. Extensive use has been made by the author of the embassy-like 'permanent representa-tions' (*postoiannye predstavitel'stva*) that republics operate in Moscow. In addition, extended stays in many of the republics have provided access to official and unofficial periodicals and in some cases to the stenographic records of republican parliaments (in two republics, legislative sessions were observed in action).

As important as official documents certainly are, their formal prose may nevertheless conceal how institutions function in practice. As Oliver Wen-dell Holmes observed, '[t]he interpretation of constitutional principles must not be too literal. We must remember that the machinery of government would not work if it were not allowed a little play in its joints'.[17] Russian federal governance, to put it mildly, does not suffer from arthritis. Interviews with federal and republican officials, opposition politicians, judges, lawyers, legal academics, and other political actors have been used to augment written primary sources. In two cases, the presidents of republics were interviewed (Mintimer Shaimiev of the Republic of Tatarstan, and Kirsan Ilumzhinov of the Republic of Kalmykia). Interviews were conducted be-tween June 1995 and December 1998 over the course of five research trips to the far compass points of the Russian Federation.

---

[15] A.V. Dicey, *Introduction to the Study of the Law of the Constitution*, 10th Ed. (London: Macmillan, 1967), 141.

[16] Bernard Rudden, 'Civil Law, Civil Society, and the Russian Constitution', 110 *The Law Quarterly Review* (Jan. 1994): 56.

[17] *Bain Peanut Co. of Tex. v. Pinson*, 282 U.S. 499, 501 (1931).

3. STRUCTURE OF THE STUDY

This book integrates analysis of federal theory with its unique application in the turbulent post-Soviet political environment. A limited case study methodology is eschewed in favour of examination of an entire tier of the Russian federal structure—the republics. A detailed analysis of even three or four republics could not capture the dynamics of centre-periphery struggles in Russia. Study of the apex of Russia's federal hierarchy allows both generalizable conclusions about the Russian Federation as a whole and sufficient detail to shed light on some of the problems of individual republics, notably their difficult (and largely incomplete) transitions from authoritarian rule.

Readers will note that this book refers to Chechnya more often as a foil to the other republics than as a focus in its own right. Chechnya—or, the Chechen Republic of Ichkeria, as it refers to itself—has very little to offer from the point of view of the institutional development and operation of a federal system. The choices made by Chechen leaders stand in sharp contrast to the very different choices of almost all other republican leaders. After issuing one of the most belligerent declarations of the 'Parade of Sovereignties', in which the republic distinguished itself as the only ASSR actually seeking independence, not merely greater autonomy within a federal Russia, the republic approved a constitution in March 1992 and separated from Ingushetia that June. Increasing violence ultimately led, in December 1994, to a Russian military invasion. Two bloody wars have been fought and years of warlordism and anarchy have followed.[18] In August 1996, an armistice was signed, leaving determination of the republic's status until 2001. In February 1999, Chechen President Aslan Maskhadov replaced by decree the old Constitution with the Islamic law of Sharia, establishing a legislature without law-making powers and giving the president virtually unchecked authority.[19] That Autumn 1999, then Russian Prime Minister Vladimir Putin began a second bloody war against the secessionist republic. Horrifying, frequent, and flagrant violations of the most basic human rights led the Parliamentary Assembly of the Council of Europe to suspend Russia's voting privileges in April 2000. The fate of Chechnya—arguably

---

[18] For analysis of the legal implications of the Chechen war, see William E. Pomeranz, 'Judicial Review and the Russian Constitutional Court: The Chechen Case', 23 *Review of Central and East European Law*, 1 (1997): 9–48. For a brief analysis of the Chechen elections from an OSCE observer and distinguished expert on Russian law see F.J.M. Feldbrugge, 'The Elections in Chechnia in the Framework of Russian Constitutional Law', 23 *Review of Central and East European Law*, 1 (1997): 1–7.

[19] Alla Barakhova, 'Maskhadov sdalsia shariatu', *Kommersant"-daily*, 5 February 1999, 3.

among the units best situated to secede from Russia[20]—has served as an
ominous warning to both centre and periphery over the course of Russia's
federal development.[21] The lessons of secession exhibited by the Chechen
case are lessons for all multi-national federal systems. But from the point of
view of analysis of Russia's functioning federal structure and republican
transitions from authoritarianism, Chechnya's extreme situation makes its
constitutional-legal analysis an unenlightening exercise.

This book comprises nine chapters. In Chapter Two, federal theory is
deconstructed to examine the fundamental issues of sovereignty, democracy,
and law faced by all federal systems. These themes form the backbone of
this book. The theoretical link between democracy and federalism is given
special attention in this chapter and the possibility of 'non-democratic
federalism' is disputed.

Chapter Three examines one candidate for 'non-democratic federalism'—
The Soviet Union. The origins and successive changes in the constitutional
structure of the system are assessed on the basis of the analysis of the
preceding chapter. Chapter Three also establishes the starting point for
one of the recurring themes of this book, the path-dependency from Soviet
models under which more recent institutions have struggled.

Chapter Four focuses on Mikhail Gorbachev's conceptual and policy
struggles with two 'problems': nationalities and federalism. Boris Yeltsin's
role in stimulating regional demands for autonomy, exacerbating both these
problems, and his involvement in the failed Novo-Ogarevo renegotiation of
a 'renewed' Soviet Union are closely scrutinized. Chapter Five reverses the
perspective from 'high politics' in Moscow to focus on republican reaction to
the federalism problem. The 1990 'Parade of Sovereignties', 1992 Federation
Treaty and 1993 Federal Constitution provide milestones for their changing
demands and evolving approach.

Chapter Six returns to a theoretical problem presented in Chapter
Two: institutional asymmetry in federal systems. Following a more detailed
theoretical treatment of the issues, Russian conceptions of asymmetrical
federalism are explored in detail. The most problematic application of these
theoretical and conceptual issues to centre-republican relations in Russia is
the negotiation of bilateral treaties between federal and republican executive
branches. This process is carefully examined, with special attention given to

---

[20] Alfred Stepan notes that Chechnya had the highest population percentage of everyday
speakers of the titular language, centuries of conflict with Moscow, and an external border with
a foreign state. Alfred Stepan, 'Russian Federalism in Comparative Perspective', 16 *Post-Soviet
Affairs*, 2 (2000): 170, note 45.

[21] For an analysis of the Chechen war, *see* Anatol Lieven, *Chechnya: Tombstone of Russian Power*
(New Haven: Yale University Press, 1998).

the implications for the development of a unified legal and economic space, two subjects of intrinsic importance to any federal system. The chapter concludes with a brief discussion of the effect of such a system on a transition to democratic government in Russia as a whole.

Chapter Seven continues the theme of democratic transition but again reverses the perspective from the federal to the republican level. Until the rise of Vladimir Putin, bilateral treaties were the weak backbone to Boris Yeltsin's laissez-faire federal approach to regional development, as much a function of federal impotence as political calculation. Republics had been left relatively unhindered to establish their own constitutions, citizenship, and systems of government. An examination of these intra-republican institutional developments and their effect in republican elections suggests that discussion of 'transition to democracy' in the republics is inappropriately optimistic. The chapter concludes with suggestions on how republican transitions might more fruitfully be assessed.

Chapter Eight examines the sweeping federal reforms undertaken between Summer 2000 and Autumn 2001 by Yeltsin's successor, Vladimir Putin. The establishment of presidentially appointed governors-general, reform of the Federation Council and the legislative package that strengthened the *vertikal* of federal executive power are all analysed in detail. In particular, Putin's promise of a 'dictatorship of law' is considered for its effect on both the institutional and conceptual pillars on which Russian federalism rests.

The conclusion of this book (Chapter Nine) returns again to the complex relationship between federalism and democracy in a final assessment of Russia's prospects both as a federal multi-national state and as a weakly democratic one.

2

Federal Theory

It is not by the consolidation, or concentration of powers, but by their distribution, that good government is effected.

Thomas Jefferson

In its very first breath of post-Soviet life, Russia, the largest country on Earth, declared itself to be a 'democratic, federal, rule-of-law state'.[1] Whether this is a legitimate factual assertion, a worthy aspiration, or a quixotically mistaken political path is the complex question this book aims to answer. At first glance, Russia seems to stand in good company in its claim to be a federal state: after Russia, six of the seven largest states are both federal and democratic political systems (Canada, United States, Brazil, Australia, India and Argentina).[2] What common features do these states share? Is it helpful to think of Russia as part of this international club? Consider some more first impressions:

- The correlation between size and federalism hardly seems coincidental—for states the size of continents, few other alternatives exist between dissolution and dictatorship. On the other hand, some of the world's smallest states—Switzerland, Belgium, Austria—are also federal systems. Federalism appealed to Montesquieu, who idealized small, autonomous states, but also to Madison, who considered large, federal, representative democracy to be the best bulwark against factionalism.

- What about the hinted relationship between federalism and democracy? Democratic government is professed (if not always achieved to the same measure) by all of the states listed above. Robert Dahl noted that democratic principles thrived in federal systems before they appeared in unitary systems.[3] Are these two concepts intrinsically linked or only coincidentally, and not necessarily, associated? Czechoslovakia, the Soviet Union and Yugoslavia were often identified as non-democratic federal systems. Is that a useful regime typology? Brazil and Argentina have accomplished

[1] *Konstitutsiia Rossiiskoi Federatsii* (1993), Part One, Chapter One, Article One, Section One.

[2] J. Denis Derbyshire & Ian Derbyshire, *Political Systems of the World* (Oxford: Helicon, 1996), 15–19. Omitted from this list, because neither a federal nor a democratic state, is China, ranking third.

[3] Robert A. Dahl, *Democracy, Liberty, and Equality* (Oslo: Norwegian University Press, 1986), 116.

difficult, but broadly speaking successful, transitions to democracy following periods of authoritarian rule. Russia's constitutional claim to
democracy is as earnestly asserted as its federalism. But is either assertion
particularly sound in its first post-Soviet decade?

- Is it coincidental that, with few exceptions, federal states are multi-ethnic
in composition, or are populated by citizens who possess multiple, cross-
cutting political identities (in terms of religion, linguistic group, class,
etc.)? The citizens of the Russian Federation are an extraordinarily varied
population. There are over one hundred recognized ethnic groups, scores
of languages and dialects, and a wide range of religions, cultures and
historical legacies.

Despite the prevalence of federal political systems (collectively encom-
passing half of the world's land area and more than 1.5 billion people)[4] there
is no accord in federal theory on these and other fundamental issues. One of
the most respected political scientists of his time, Harold Laski, considered
federalism a 'handicap... to governmental progress', and dismissed it as
obsolete as early as 1939![5] Professor William Riker—a giant in the field of
political science[6]—dismissed any link between democracy and federalism,
considering the 'federalism' of the Soviet Union just as genuine (and with
similar origins and limitations) as that in the United States and post-1945
Germany![7] American legal scholars, understandably, have primarily focused
their attention on the unique federal system of the United States. Comparative analysis of other federal systems almost invariably has been conducted
through the distorting prism of the American experiment (often leaving
critically understudied important issues for most federal states).[8]

---

[4] Derbyshire, 15–19.

[5] Harold J. Laski, 'The Obsolescence of Federalism', 98 *New Republic* (May 1939): 367.

[6] Robert L. Goodin & Hans-Dieter Klingemann, eds. *A New Handbook of Political Science* (Oxford
University Press, 1996), 40. Riker, a founder of rational choice theory, is cited in the index to this
work 24 times. Between 1954 and 1994, Riker published 16 articles in the *APSR* and was cited over
3,700 times, more than any other political scientist. Arthur H. Miller, Charles Tien, and Andrew A.
Peebler, 'The *American Political Science Review* Hall of Fame: Assessments and Implications for an
Evolving Discipline', *PS: Political Science & Politics* (Mar. 1996): 73–83. Thanks to Alfred Stepan for
bringing these references to my attention. *See* his 'Toward a New Comparative Politics of Federalism, Multi-nationalism, and Democracy: Beyond Rikerian Federalism', in Alfred Stepan, ed.
Arguing Comparative Politics (Oxford University Press, 2001).

[7] William H. Riker, *Federalism: Origin, Operation, Significance* (Boston: Little, Brown, 1964),
38.

[8] As K.C. Wheare put it: '... the federal principle has come to mean what it does because the
United States has come to be what it is'. *Federal Government*, 4th Ed. (London: Oxford University
Press, 1963), 11.

Fundamental issues, such as democracy, multi-nationalism, and sovereignty, are sharply disputed in the classics of federal theory. There are almost as many definitions of federalism and federal government as there are theorists to theorize about them. Varying importance is ascribed to formal versus informal institutions, processes versus structures, and variations in the degree of decentralization, representation, and pluralism permissible under the rubric of federalism. This is a broad church, indeed, and one which should be explored in greater detail for insights into the problems Russia has faced in its short experience of federalism.

1. DEFINITIONS

The plurality of approaches and definitions to federalism make the first task one of consolidation. What common ground can be agreed from the beginning? If we start with an analysis of definitions from four respected scholars, the core features of federalism become clear (Table 2.1). Three

Table 2.1 Four Scholars, Four Definitions. Federalism is . . .

Robert A. DAHL	'. . . a system in which some matters are exclusively within the competence of certain local units—cantons, states, provinces—and are constitutionally beyond the scope of the authority of the national government, and where certain other matters are constitutionally outside the scope of the authority of the smaller units.'[a]
Arend LIJPHART	'In addition to the primary federal principle of a central-regional division of power, five secondary characteristics of federalism can be identified: a written constitution, bicameralism, the right of the component units to be involved in the process of amending the federal constitution but to change their own constitutions unilaterally, equal, or disproportionately strong representation of the smaller component units in the federal chamber and decentralized government.'[b]
William H. RIKER	'The rule for identification is: A constitution is federal if 1. two levels of government rule the same land and people, 2. each level has at least one area of action in which it is autonomous, and 3. there is some guarantee (even though merely a statement in the constitution) of the autonomy of each government in its own sphere.'[c]
Kenneth C. WHEARE	'By the federal principle I mean the method of dividing powers so that the general and regional governments are each, within a sphere, co-ordinate and independent.'[d]

[a] Robert A. Dahl, *Democracy, Liberty and Equality* (Oslo: Norwegian University Press, 1986), 114.
[b] Arend Lijphart, *Democracies: Patterns of Majoritarian and Consensus Government in Twenty-One Countries* (New Haven: Yale University Press, 1984), 170–71.
[c] William H. Riker, *Federalism: Origin, . . .* , 11.
[d] Wheare, 10.

requirements of federalism can be distilled from these definitions: (1) divided government, (2) a written constitution, and (3) explicitly formulated exclusive and concurrent areas of jurisdiction. A fourth requirement, general consensus in the polity on the value of this complex federal endeavour, implicitly grounds the other three.

First, federalism requires divided government: one state is established, but not one government. Multiple levels of autonomous decision-making authorities also function. Almost always, this is accomplished via territorial division—states, provinces, cantons, or other such units carve a federal state into easily discernable jurisdictions. But physical demarcation is not a *sine qua non* of federal government. The philosophical principles behind federalism, if not actually federal institutions, have also been used to dissipate ethnic tensions in polities where ethnic groups are so intermixed that simple geographic division is not possible. The non-territorial form of representation devised by the Austro-Marxists Otto Bauer and Karl Renner to alleviate the tense relations between Czechs and Germans in the Austro-Hungarian Empire (never fully adopted)[9] was successfully implemented for similar purposes in pre-Soviet Estonia.[10] A federal system based in part on territorial division and in part on non-territorial mechanisms has existed in Belgium since 1991.[11] Belgium is an example especially worth noting both for its unusual permutation of federalism and for the more general lesson (unlearned by Russian politicians in the early 1990s): federal institutions both shape and reflect the political playing field on which they are constructed.[12] In Belgium, majority-constraining procedural rules and intricately balanced federal parliamentary and cultural councils (with executive coalitions and

[9] The proposal envisioned the creation of national councils (*Nationalrath*) with jurisdiction over each cultural community (*Kulturgemeinshäfte*), regardless of location in the pre-existing *Länder*.

[10] The 1925 Cultural Autonomy Law granted legal identity to ethnic groups with greater than 3,000 members. Incorporated groups were entitled to elect councils, levy taxes, and administer cultural issues in much the same way as proposed for Austria-Hungary. The German and Jewish minorities availed themselves of these councils until an authoritarian coup in 1934. *See* John Coakley, 'Approaches to the Resolution of Ethnic Conflict: The Strategy of Non-Territorial Autonomy', 15 *International Political Science Review*, 3 (1994): 297–314.

[11] Belgium at the time was comprised of 9 historical provinces, 4 language regions (Dutch, French, German, and bilingual Brussels), 3 ethnic regions (Flanders, Wallonia, and multi-ethnic Brussels) and three cultural communities (Dutch, French, and German), the last a non-territorial distinction. *See* Aristide R. Zolberg, 'Splitting the Difference: Federalization without Federalism in Belgium,' in Milton J. Esman, ed. *Ethnic Conflict in the Western World* (Ithaca, NY: Cornell University Press, 1977).

[12] For an early analysis of this phenomenon in Belgium (and elsewhere) by a respected Belgian jurist, *see* Koen Lenaerts, 'Constitutionalism and the Many Faces of Federalism,' 38 *American Journal of Comparative Law*, 2 (Spring 1990): 205–63.

cabinets formed on the basis of linguistic parity) could politicize issues into Flemish and Walloon sides, regardless of the subject matter.

Second, federal systems use written constitutions to assign jurisdictional authority. (Wheare, concerned in his work more with the philosophy of federalism than the empirical practice of federation, elsewhere concurs with this requirement.) As A.V. Dicey observed, federalism abolishes the principle of the supreme sovereignty of parliament, subordinated in a federal system by specially protected laws that are difficult to change. The processes for constitutional amendment are purposefully designed to be lengthy and cumbersome: the opposite of efficient government. Federalism embraces a distinction common to political systems based on written constitutions: ordinary laws may be subject to change as parliament changes its collective mind, but constitutional or fundamental laws require super-majorities in parliament, special conventions, or even popular referendum for their alteration. The power to make amendments is often not granted exclusively to the federal government, but requires subsequent ratification by a set number of units of the federation—part of the multilateralism that is intrinsic to federalism. This is one important distinction between federalism and the mere decentralization or devolution of power, under which a parliament granting greater authority to lower levels of government retains the legal right (though not always the political ability) to revoke those powers at a later date.[13]

Third, scholars largely agree that each level of government must possess some sphere of authority, some closed agenda, which is expressly its own exclusive jurisdiction; likewise, there must also exist bounded areas of concurrent jurisdiction shared by both levels of government. But how should these powers be divided? Among specific powers, for example, the power to tax and collect revenue is of tremendous importance for all levels of government, but care must be taken not to erode the environment of free trade and economic cohesion that is a primary advantage of federal association. As the Russian case strongly demonstrates, the level of fiscal autonomy of constituent units radically changes the dynamic of federal relations.

There is a fourth requirement, too, although left unmentioned by these scholars. Perhaps this is because the requirement seems so self-evident in long-established, stable federations. It is none the less crucial. As Dicey famously expressed this 'very peculiar state of sentiment', the citizens of a federation 'must desire union, and must not desire unity'.[14] Federal citizens,

---

[13] Vernon Bogdanor, *Devolution in the United Kingdom* (Oxford University Press, 1999), *passim*, especially Ch. 8 on 'federal devolution'.

[14] A.V. Dicey, *Introduction to the Study of the Law of the Constitution*, 10th Ed. (London: Macmillan, 1967), 141.

in his phrase, become a 'nation of constitutionalists', or, to express the same sentiment in less legal terms, there emerges a 'federal political culture'. Ivo Duchacek defined this condition as involving 'cognitive, emotional and evaluative orientations toward the federal nature of the political system and attitudes toward the role of self in both the general system and its federal components'.[15] Even Riker was willing to concede the importance of a sense of national loyalty that replaces loyalty to, and primary identification with, the constituent units of the federation.[16] The basic ingredient here is consensus in the polity on the value of regulating conflict in this complex and often inefficient manner.

This value system is not to be underestimated, nor considered merely concomitant to the more obvious structural features of federal systems. As Wheare argued: 'It is not enough that the federal principle should be embodied predominantly in the written constitution of a country. That is something, but it is no guarantee necessarily that a system of federal government will operate. What determines the issue is the working of the system'.[17] Still a third way of expressing this sentiment is to refer to a concept developed by Alfred Stepan and Juan Linz. The combined force of institutional and social forces should create the same sort of loyalty in citizens of a federation that Linz and Stepan detect in what they call a 'state-nation': '... multicultural, or even multinational states, which nonetheless still manage to engender strong identification and loyalty from their citizens, an identification and loyalty that proponents of homogeneous nation-states perceive that only nation-states can engender'.[18] Acceptance of multiple political identities is crucial in a federal system. It does not seem coincidental that the three examples Linz and Stepan give of 'state-nations'—the United States, Switzerland, and India—all possess entrenched federal systems of government. Juan Linz has referred to this attitude as the 'soul of a working federalism', of which the German constitutional and jurisprudential concept of *Bundestreue* (roughly translated as federal state loyalty) is indicative:

Bundestreue implies three dimensions: 1) the institutions geared to that purpose and assuring a certain solidarity between the component units of the federal state,

---

[15] Ivo Duchacek, 'Comparative Federalism: An Agenda for Additional Research,' in Daniel J. Elazar, ed. *Constitutional Design and Power-Sharing in the Post-Modern Epoch* (New York: University Press of America, 1991), 27.

[16] Riker, *Federalism: Origin*, ..., 103–10.

[17] Wheare, 33.

[18] Juan J. Linz & Alfred Stepan, *Problems of Democratic Transition and Consolidation: Southern Europe, South America, and Post-Communist Europe* (Baltimore: Johns Hopkins, 1996), 34.

2) a basic set of attitudes of majorities of the population in the federal national units and the state population as a whole, and 3) behavioral aspects that go from the specific policies of the government of the federal components and the central government, to, last but not least, the rhetoric of the political leaders, particularly in crisis situations.[19]

In other words, the component governments of a federation should consider the interests of the whole federal system, not just the singular pursuit of that component's interests. The conspicuous absence of this concept in contemporary Russian federalism is discussed in more detail in Chapter Six and in conjunction with the problem of nullification (*see below*, p. 36).

A federal state, it should now be clear, is more than the sum of its constituent parts. A well-known metaphor by Morton Grodzins makes this clear.[20] A federal system is not merely a layer cake, its governments built in tiers of authority hierarchically placed one atop the other. Federal government is a marble cake, its components easily identified but virtually impossible to separate, its governments co-ordinate and independent (to use Wheare's phrase), but not in any absolute sense prioritized. The process of federalization also serves to marbleize individual and group rights at the centre-regional level. That is, the right to abrogate the federal agreement (through secession or some such unilateral action) cannot be realized without adversely affecting the rights of other constituent units and federal citizens. The multilateral decision to create and maintain a federal system cannot be altered unilaterally without infringing the rights of all federal citizens. In the battles that Yeltsin fought with recalcitrant regions—a military contest in the case of Chechnya, political and legal struggles in the case of Tatarstan and others—precisely this controversy presented itself. The decision to create a federal system thus fundamentally reduces available mechanisms to amend strained inter-governmental relations.

2. CONCEPTS

The philosophical doctrine of federalism works profound changes on three concepts fundamental to the future of the Russian state—indeed, all federal systems. These concepts, therefore, occupy the core of this book: sover-

---

[19] Juan J. Linz, 'Democracy, Multinationalism and Federalism'. Paper presented at the International Political Science Association Meeting in Seoul, Korea, Aug. 1997, 31, 59–60.

[20] Morton Grodzins, *The American System: A New View of Government in the United States*, Daniel J. Elazar, ed. (Chicago: Rand McNally, 1966), 8.

eigny,[21] democracy[22] and the rule of law.[23] These three concepts are intertwined in multiple and complicated ways. Analysis of the doctrine of nullification, for example, involves both issues of sovereignty and law; discussion of questions of judicial review necessarily relates to both law and democracy. Recognizing the inter-relatedness of these concepts is crucial to understanding how federalism can function in a state and what different federal permutations imply for Russia's struggling transition. Each of these concepts is examined below, not only for the light each concept shines on the others, but to expose the problems, conflicts, and potential solutions that federal understandings of sovereignty, law, and democracy create.

2.1 Sovereignty and Federalism

Sovereignty is an elusive, ambiguous, and yet, paradoxically, a powerfully evocative concept—features that made it both an irresistible rallying cry for Boris Yeltsin and later a plague on both federal and regional houses of government in Russia (the focus of Chapter Four). Originally, sovereignty defined the qualities of the monarch and the realm that he personified, inviolate and indivisible in the equation of Jean Bodin. In international law, remnants of that absolutism remain: a state is sovereign in the international community if it is the subject of no other state in its domestic or foreign activity—a free actor constrained only in so far as it freely chooses to be so

[21] Sovereignty is the focus of Section 2.1 of this chapter.

[22] As a working definition, I adopt Robert A. Dahl's 8 insitutional guarantees for democracy. See Robert A. Dahl, Polyarchy: Participation and Opposition (New Haven, CT: Yale University Press, 1971), 3. I gradually expand this working definition, particularly in Section 2.2 and Ch. 7, using the five 'arenas' of a consolidated democracy, articulated by Juan Linz & Alfred Stepan. See Juan J. Linz & Alfred Stepan, Problems of Democratic Transition and Consolidation: Southern Europe, South America, and Post-Communist Europe (Baltimore: Johns Hopkins, 1996). Because a consolidated democracy presupposes many of the ideas complicated by federal theory (e.g. the rule of law, civil and political society) and because consolidated democracy is hardly a reasonable starting assumption for analysis of Russian politics, I prefer to develop this definition slowly over several chapters. In general, I consider democracy as a combination of the principles of political equality and majority rule but with rationally predetermined limitations on the latter to protect certain fundamental rights. See Robert A. Dahl, After the Revolution? Authority in a Good Society, rev. Ed. (New Haven: Yale University Press, 1990). It is immediately apparent, however, that we have already crossed a divide between 'pure' democratic theory and theories of constitutionalism.

[23] Jon Elster differentiates between the rule of law (the prospective principles that laws be stable and predictable) and the 'principle of legality' (an example of which is the retrospective principle that punishment is only tolerable for acts prohibited by law at the time of action). This book uses the phrases 'rule of law' and 'government under law' in their broader senses, incorporating both of these ideas and others. See Jon Elster, 'Introduction', in Jon Elster & Rune Slagsted, eds. Constitutionalism and Democracy (Cambridge University Press, 1988), 2–3. The relationship between law and federalism is explored in Section 2.3 of this chapter.

constrained. Sovereignty is no less than a political synonym for the state's most ephemeral but crucial quality: legitimacy.

Max Weber's famous definition of the state, 'a compulsory political organization with continuous operations...[that] successfully upholds the claim to the *monopoly* of the *legitimate* use of physical force in the enforcement of its order', expresses sovereignty's object, but not its substance.[24] That substance involves another, more abstract monopoly: the state must exercise 'control of the meanings of its mystical source of authority'.[25] When sufficiently many citizens question the legitimacy of state power over them, sovereignty is in the grip of what Linz and Stepan have identified as a 'stateness' problem.[26] Although few scholars would question the modern principle that legitimate sovereign authority in a democracy is ultimately popular authority, politicians routinely contest who precisely 'the people' are and, crucially, who is entitled to speak in their name. Monopoly control over the definition of who 'the people' are is really monopolization of the myth of sovereignty: 'Only by maintaining control over the depiction of its people can the state authoritatively claim to be the agent of its people'.[27]

As will be argued in Chapter Four, this was the mission and the misery of Yeltsin's invitation to Russian regions to 'take all the sovereignty you can swallow', in the hot summer of 1990. That chapter provides compelling evidence that serious attention to what sovereignty really means in a federal system was conspicuously and woefully absent from Yeltsin's call to arms, nor did the regional elites who made declarations of sovereignty at Yeltsin's prompting seek any deep understanding of what they were rushing to proclaim. A window of opportunity was perceived to be closing and regional political elites blindly jumped through it. Reactionary acceptance of the terminology of sovereignty was both a crucial political stratagem and a fatal flaw in the efforts of Yeltsin and his constitutional engineers to design and build what they called Russia's 'new federalism'.

As one might well imagine, federalism turns traditional conceptions of sovereignty upside down. Daniel Elazar has observed that 'the federal principle represents an alternative to (and a radical attack upon) the modern

---

[24] Max Weber, *Economy and Society.* Edited by Guenther Roth & Claus Wittich (Berkeley University of California Press, 1978), 54.

[25] Cynthia Webber, *Simulating Sovereignty: Intervention, the State, and Symbolic Change* (Cambridge University Press, 1995), 28.

[26] Linz & Stepan, op. cit., 16, 26–33.

[27] Webber, op. cit.. The same difficulty has been identified in asserted rights to self-determination and secession (see below), especially in the context of international law. *See* D.J. Harris, *Cases and Materials on International Law*, 5th Ed. (London: Sweet & Maxwell, 1998), 122.

idea of sovereignty'.[28] Federalism struck the death blow to Bodin's assertion of the indivisibility of sovereign power (a notion that had already been repeatedly weakened in successive conceptual revolutions). Federalism establishes the notion that sovereignty is something that can be discretely distributed within the state on several, inter-connected levels of governmental authority. In the domestic context, there is no longer a single sovereign.[29] Each unit relinquishes its claim to unfettered sovereignty, contributing part of its own sovereignty to the greater whole of the federation. The federation, made greater than the sum of its parts, is now the sovereign creature with which other states in the exclusive international club of states must do business. The components of a federation are not recognized as sovereign states on the world stage.

The early experience of federalism in the United States was an important—perhaps the most important—catalyst for this changed view of sovereignty. The Articles of Confederation of the early American states did not make the conceptual link between sovereignty and federalism. All sovereignty was delegated by 'the people' to one centre of power, their own individual states. These states dominated a weak central entity which possessed no executive power.[30] It was the states' unyielding retention of old notions of indivisible sovereign power that was largely responsible for the unworkability of this first arrangement. The most lasting accomplishment of *The Federalist Papers*, by Hamilton, Madison, and Jay, was to change the understanding of the term 'federalism' itself from its original meaning, which was nearly synonymous with the loose confederal union of completely sovereign states. The second attempt at constructing an American union utilized new thinking about sovereignty. Sovereignty was 'all but impossible to find in the American system of federalism. Formal sovereignty presumably inhered in the constituent authority that had created and could amend the constitution, but amendment was deliberately made cumbersome, and sovereignty, or what there was of it, was parcelled out among the three branches of the federal government and the states'.[31]

---

[28] Elazar, *Exploring . . .* , 109.

[29] In an international context, of course, the federal state is still the exclusive sovereign actor. Federal units—states, provinces, cantons, etc.—possess no sovereign standing as subjects in international law.

[30] Art. IX provided for a 'president' to preside (for no more than one year every three years) over a 'Committee of the States', a body comprised of a delegate from each state that sat when Congress was in recess. No powers were outlined for this post, which served a secretarial function for the Confederation's legislature akin to a presidium. *Articles of Confederation* (ratified 1 March 1781), reprinted in Henry Steele Commager, ed. *Documents of American History*, 9th Ed., 2 Vols. (Englewood Cliffs, NJ: Prentice-Hall, 1973), I: 114.

[31] Sanford Lakoff, 'Between Either/Or and More or Less: Sovereignty vs. Autonomy Under Federalism', 24 *Publius*, 1 (1994): 70.

The most direct and radical change federalism works on sovereignty is the destruction of the preconception that sovereignty is an absolute—an all-or-nothing quality not susceptible to variation or degree. Federalism exposes a continuum of possible expressions of sovereignty, and occupies for itself the centre of that range. Figure 2.1 expresses this continuum at its simplest. At either end of this spectrum, federalism is clearly impossible. If the relationship between governing units is one of subordination (i.e. if one body is simply the administrative branch of the other), one can hardly speak of either sovereignty or federalism. This is the relationship of Paris to its *départements*, or of Tokyo to its prefectures. These administrative demarcations have no meaningful sovereignty with regard to the metropolitan centre. Likewise, self-determination is a categorical rejection of the 'pooling of sovereignties' so characteristic of federalism. A federal unit can no more legitimately 'opt-out' of the federation than it can unilaterally alter any other aspect of the arrangement. Metaphors like 'pools of sovereignty' or 'marble cakes of federalism' make clear that, once having entered such a union, the determination to exit affects not just the seceding unit but all constituents of the federation. Self-determination is an expression of 'complete' sovereignty—surrounding states are foreign neighbours. What room, then, is left in the centre of this diagram, for the delicate relationship of subsidiarity—the fulcrum of the federal balance?

The term subsidiarity—occupying the middle ground of this continuum—has many different connotations.[32] In the federal lexicon, subsidiarity describes an approach to the distribution of powers to different levels of

Figure 2.1.   The Basic State-Sovereignty Continuum

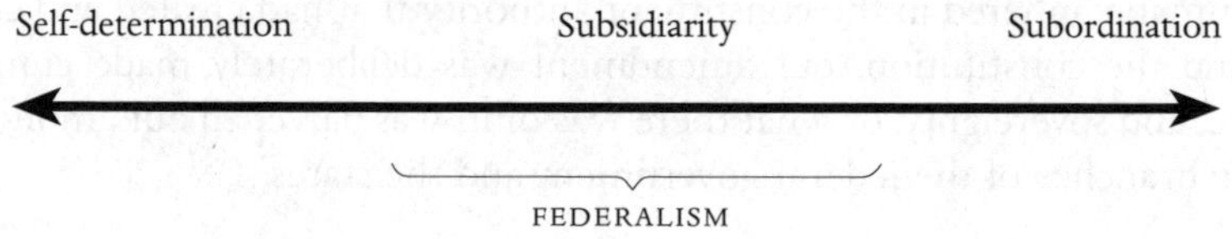

Self-determination	Subsidiarity	Subordination

⟵⟶

FEDERALISM

[32] Subsidiarity, as part of political Catholicism, is not a neutral, or even originally federal, term. For arguments in favour of its expression in 'organic-statist' models of government, see Alfred Stepan, *The State and Society: Peru in Comparative Perspective* (Princeton: Princeton University Press, 1978), 35–40. Andrew Adonis notes that this principle was originally intended to act only in strict adherence with the other parts of the Catholic triad, 'Personality' and 'Solidarity', and with strict acceptance of the Church's higher authority and right to interference. Thus, the principle as used in the papal encyclical quoted in note 35 rejects, as did its author, basic principles of democracy. Andrew Adonis, 'Subsidiarity: Theory of a New Federalism?' in Preston King & Andrea Bosco, eds. *A Constitution for Europe: A Comparative Study of Federal Constitutions and Plans for the United States of Europe* (London: Lothian Foundation Press, 1991), 65.

government, 'co-ordinate and independent'.[33] It is one of the founding principles of the European Union, elaborated in the Treaty of Maastricht.[34] Subsidiarity is the presumptive rejection of 'transfer to the larger and higher collectivity functions which can be performed and provided for by lesser and subordinate bodies'.[35] Viewed from a slightly different perspective, subsidiarity means a philosophical commitment to local government, not merely as units of administration for a higher authority but as intrinsically valuable institutions for the representation of interests at the lower level. In the United States, it is state government and state courts, not federal, that enact, interpret, and enforce the laws that most affect the everyday life of citizens: criminal law, contracts, torts, property.[36] This is the philosophy that, in part, supports the Tenth Amendment to the U.S. Constitution.[37] It is similarly an influence behind the famous *Erie* doctrine (discussed further regarding law and federalism, below) that compels federal courts in cases of 'diversity jurisdiction' (i.e. involving citizens of different states, as opposed to 'subject jurisdiction', according certain issues to federal resolution) to follow the court precedents of the relevant state.[38] As Ivo Duchacek observed:

[33] For a thorough and critical analysis of subsidiarity in the European Union and the United States, *see* George A. Bermann, 'Taking Subsidiarity Seriously: Federalism in the European Community and the United States', 94 *Colum. L. Rev.* 332 (Mar., 1994).

[34] 'Resolved to continue the process of creating an ever closer union among the peoples of Europe, in which decisions are taken as closely as possible to the citizen in accordance with the principle of subsidiarity...' Preamble, *Treaty of European Union* (Maastricht Treaty), 7 Feb. 1992. For an analysis of the 'Janus-faced' nature of this doctrine, see Jonathan Golub, 'Sovereignty and Subsidiarity in EU Environmental Policy', 44 *Political Studies*, 4 (1996): 686–703.

[35] Excerpt from the 1931 papal encyclical of Pius XI, 'Quadragesimo Anno'. See Michael Burgess, 'The European Tradition of Federalism: Christian Democracy and Federalism', in Michael Burgess & Alain-G. Gagnon, eds. *Comparative Federalism and Federation: Competing Traditions and Future Directions* (New York: Harvester Wheatsheaf, 1993), 148.

[36] William Riker perceived a 'universal rule' in the spirit of America's 'deeper unwritten Constitution' that 'decisions are to be made at the lowest level (i.e. by the smallest units) consonant with efficient operation'. Riker, *Federalism: Origins, . . .*, 92.

[37] 'The powers not delegated to the United States by the Constitution, nor prohibited by it to the States, are reserved to the States respectively, or to the people'. *U.S. Con.*, X Amend. (1791). *See* e.g. *New York v. United States*, 505 U.S. 144 (1992) (holding that although 'Congress has substantial power under the Constitution to encourage the States . . . , the Constitution does not confer upon Congress the ability simply to compel the States . . .').

[38] *Erie R. R. Co. v. Tompkins*, 304 U.S. 64 (1938) ('There is no federal general common law. Congress has no power to declare substantive rules of common law applicable in a State whether they be local in their nature or "general," be they commercial law or a part of the law of torts. And no clause in the Constitution purports to confer such a power upon the federal courts'.) *See* Laurence H. Tribe, *American Constitutional Law*, 3rd Ed., Vol. 1 (NY: Foundation Press, 2000), 470 *et seq. Erie* is even cited in the (infamous) concurrence in *Bush v. Gore*: 'In most cases, comity and respect for federalism compel us to defer to the decisions of state courts on issues of state law. That practice reflects our understanding that the decisions of state courts are definitive pronouncements of the will of the States as sovereigns'. *George W. Bush v. Albert Gore, Jr.* 531 U.S. _____ (2000) (Rehnquist, C.J., concurring).

'...the acceptance and recognition of *the right of communities to exist and make their own corporate decisions* while functioning between the state, on the one side, and the individual, on the other, seems a *conditio sine qua non* for the existence of a federal political culture'.[39]

If federal government appeals to citizens who desire union but not unity, on what basis should issues be left for decision on one level and not another? It does not necessarily follow that subsidiarity need be, or even should be, a directly justiciable issue in federal-regional controversies.[40] Attempts to evaluate particular policies according to their 'fit' with subsidiarity may well expose the highly political pressures to which this principle is suscep- tible. Subsidiarity, if not the only logical principle on which a federal framework *could* be built, is the animating principle that federal states have most often adopted. The continuum depicted in Figure 2.1 suggests the many variations possible in the day-to-day operation of a federal system. Subsidiarity is the default principle that informs this process. Were subsidi- arity not valued, what reason to preserve the complex and duplicative inter- governmental relations presupposed by federalism? This problem of pre- sumption has ramifications for questions of democracy as well. By defining an issue as a local matter—and therefore not one to concern the polity as a whole—federal citizens outside that community are excluded from decision- making. Conversely, some local majorities (e. g. a densely concentrated ethnic group) who care deeply about some issue might always remain minorities when the federation as a whole is the unit for voting. If an issue is placed on the all-union agenda for everyone to register a vote, a collective will may be imposed on that local majority but union-wide minority, who must bear the result imposed by citizens perhaps far less interested in the outcome. A majority of citizens in a federation might support nuclear power, for example, but the minority of citizens who live next to power plants may care most of all. Multiple levels of government provide a multitude of approaches to such a question. Subsidiarity, therefore, is also about determining degrees of importance (or inequality) in the representa- tion of competing interests.

It is clear that there is an inherent trade-off between subsidiarity and regional distinctiveness: differences (and a degree of inequality) may emerge among regional units as different policies and interests are developed. Subsidiarity, therefore, is not a binary concept; although present in all federal

[39] Ivo Duchacek, 'Comparative Federalism: An Agenda for Additional Research', in Daniel J. Elazar, ed. *Constitutional Design and Power-Sharing in the Post-Modern Epoch* (New York: University Press of America, 1991), 27–8.

[40] In Germany, for example, where the principle is entrenched in the Basic Law (Art. 72(2)), subsidiarity has been determined to be a nonjusticiable political question. Bermann, 393.

systems, it may be emphasized to different degrees in different federations, as the continuum in Figure 2.1 implies. The Federal Republic of Germany specifically outlines the principle (although not by name) in its constitution.[41] Switzerland is a federation that famously operates with a very high level of respect given to the local government of its cantons. The United States also employs the principle, though to a much lesser extent.[42] All three, however, adhere to the philosophical basics of the presumption. How could a federal polity preserve its citizens' desired union, but not centralizing unity, if the animating principle of subsidiarity (leaving aside variation in its everyday operation in different areas) were absent? Would this not result in the 'undesired unity' citizens sought to avoid in the first place? On the other hand, excessive fealty to the principle can descend into crude localism, sending federal intentions spiralling into confederation or even into disassociation via a Calhounian presumption for nullification or interposition against undesired federal laws (these important concepts are discussed on p. 36–40).

Another problematic issue of autonomy is the appropriate level of interference by central authorities in the government of constituent units. Interference by the federal government in the legislative prerogatives of states is usually prohibited, triggering often lengthy adjudication by a third authority, usually a constitutional or supreme court. But consider the emergency powers of the federal constitution of India, which permit the central

[41] See Art. 72(2): 'The Federation shall have the right to legislate in these matters to the extent that a need for regulation by federal legislation exists because: 1. a matter cannot be effectively regulated by the legislation of individual Lander, or 2. the regulation of a matter by a Land statute might prejudice the interests of other Lander or of the whole body politic, or 3. the maintenance of legal or economic unity, especially the maintenance of uniformity of living conditions beyond the territory of any one Land, necessitates such regulation'. *Basic Law for the Federal Republic of Germany of 23 May 1949*, reprinted in S.E. Finer, Vernon Bogdanor & Bernard Rudden, eds. *Comparing Constitutions* (Oxford: Clarendon Press, 1995), 157.

[42] In fact, the term is barely used in scholarly and judicial writing. For a contrary view, see Bermann, 406–7: 'I conclude first that, like its foreign-sounding name, subsidiarity is foreign to the law and practice of federal legislation'. However, even if Congress provides no more than conclusory justifications for federal action, the mere fact that such an unsolicited justification is somehow deemed necessary suggests the underlying presumption of subsidiarity at the heart of American federalism. Even Bermann, it seems, would concur on this point, at 414 (notes omitted): 'This of course is not to say that Congress shows no respect for subsidiarity in its exercise of federal legislative power.... Whatever the degree of precision or strictness of the standards that it ultimately adopts, Congress can, and very often does, leave the states conditionally free to select the means they prefer to implement them.... Though the term is of course never used, subsidiarity may also be built directly into the structure of federal legislation. Many statutes specifically allow the states to enact their own regulatory programs, provided they meet certain minimum federal criteria'. And at 423: 'I have thus far argued that subsidiarity, as understood by the Europeans, is not a judicially enforceable constitutional norm in the United States, but rather a value whose fortunes are essentially left to the political forces'.

government on the recommendation of a state governor (himself appointed by the central government) to dismiss that constituent state's chief minister and cabinet and to suspend its legislative Assembly. Attempts to subordinate emergency powers to judicial review are *de facto* inherently limited since 'it is well-nigh impossible to restore an already dismissed Assembly to power....'.[43] Use of this 'President's Rule' steadily increased until about 1992 and has been increasingly challenged since then.[44] Such a practice poses concerns for the autonomy promoted by subsidiarity: the constituent units are subordinated to the centre in ways not strictly enumerated and therefore not easily anticipated. The rule is open-ended and by definition *ad hoc*, pushing constituent members of a federation toward a more administrative role. India has developed a complex matrix of consociational-consensual parliamentary mechanisms combined with strict territorial-linguistic federal divisions that serves to mitigate the threats such a practice presents to multinational India's federal system. But, to the extent that it is employed, such an emergency rule compromises through the threat of summary action the overall autonomy of the constituent states. It is worth considering the problems such powers present for federalism, especially given Russia's super-presidential constitution and the quasi-judicial authority it gives the federal president to suspend regional executive and legislative action (explored further in Chapter Five).

It is difficult to imagine a sustainable federal structure in which the subsidiarity principle is absent, although other scholars, notably William Riker, have predicted the inevitable centralization of ageing federal systems.[45] This centralization, however, is surely limited and the 'centralized federalism' which Riker foresaw might be seen as an excessive extrapolation by him based on a perceived shift in the degree of American acceptance of this principle at the time of his research. Were subsidiarity entirely absent from a political system, the other inter-connected requirements of federalism would be diminished as well; the result would not be 'centralized federalism' but merely centralized rule. One of the objectives of this study is to discern the level of institutional and political support for subsidiarity in the Russian Federation, and in so doing assess the degree of federalism in that context. Subsidiarity is a necessary, but on its own insufficient, requirement of federalism. The basic ingredient here is the consensus in the polity

---

[43] Krishna K. Tummala, 'The Indian Union and Emergency Powers', 17 *International Political Science Review*, 4 (1996): 377–9, 381–2.

[44] Douglas V. Verney, 'Federalism, Federative Systems, and Federations: The United States, Canada, & India', 25 *Publius*, 2 (1995): 91. Arend Lijphart, 'The Puzzle of Indian Democracy: A Consociational Interpretation', 90 *American Political Science Review*, 2 (1996): 264.

[45] Riker, *Federalism: Origin, ...*, 7–8.

on the value of regulating conflict; that consensus in a federal system is strongly on the side of subsidiarity.

Subsidiarity is part of federalism's philosophical foundation. The degree to which it is functionally present, however, is subject to wide variation. This fact creates a continuum of reactions to federal constraints on sovereignty, each with its own set of problems and challenges for federal systems. Figure 2.1 can now be depicted in more detail as Figure 2.2.

Just as the constituent states of a federation tend to forfeit by federal membership their sovereign status in international law, many other aspects of sovereignty are lost as well. Sovereignty usually ceases to be the primary issue for federal units (though, as will be seen, Russia is the clear exception). Disputes over sovereignty are usually replaced by the more particular question of jurisdiction over different subject matters, since no single body can claim to be the unlimited repository of sovereignty. The degree of sovereignty retained by component states fundamentally determines the nature of the system that results. The rest of this section is devoted to exploring those possibilities, located at different places on the continuum in Figure 2.2.

Secession

Secession, the most extreme expression of sovereignty, occupies the far left of the continuum in Figure 2.2. The ultimate check against the power of the centre is Albert Hirschman's famous option to exit from the system itself.[46] International documents and state practice deliberately avoid the issue of secession: the UN Charter and the International Covenant on Civil and

Figure 2.2.   The Sovereignty-Federalism Continuum Expanded

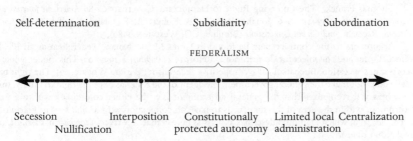

Note: Of course, more and different details could be included: government structures, variation in enumerated and reserved powers in inter-governmental relations, etc. The figure is intended to be a helpful, not exhaustive, heuristic device.

[46] Albert O. Hirschman, *Exit, Voice and Loyalty: Responses to Decline in Firms, Organizations, and States* (Cambridge: Harvard University Press, 1970).

Political Rights are careful to declare self-determination a right of peoples (with all the attendant difficulties of definition),[47] not secession a right of states.[48]

Likewise, most scholars find it difficult to defend secession as a right of federal units.[49] There is really no room for compromise between federal conceptions of sovereignty and a right to secession. To quote Abraham Lincoln (a man whose governing experience of a federation plagued with secession is probably second to none), in his First Inaugural Address: 'Perpetuity is implied, if not expressed, in the fundamental law of all national governments. . . . [N]o government proper ever had a provision in its organic law for its own termination'.[50] Mikhail Gorbachev's attempt to devise such a law in the Soviet Union (examined in detail in Chapter Three) exposed the political dangers and conceptual paradoxes of a law on secession.[51] In essence, the act of secession is a rejection of the *status quo*, a denial of established authority. This is the primary reason why secession presents such a grey area of legitimacy: the attempt is pronounced illegal by the very legal order being challenged. To some extent, the real value of a right to secede is in the negotiating power it creates. After all, secession is a single-shot weapon. The process rejects a fundamental tenet of federal theory: a component of the federation, having relinquished its claim to absolute sovereignty, cannot restore the same status via its own unilateral act.

---

[47] E.g. Croatia, in its 1991 declaration of independence from the former Federal Republic of Yugoslavia, asserted its 'inalienable right' to self-determination and 'disassociation'. The Arbitration Commission pointedly did not consider this justification in its favourable determinations and opinions on the matter. *See* D.J. Harris, *Cases and Materials on International Law*, 5th Ed. (London: Sweet & Maxwell, 1998), 122.

[48] Thomas Franck, 'The Emerging Right to Democratic Governance', 86 *American Journal of International Law*, 1 (1992): 58–9. Jonah Alexander & Robert A. Friedlander, *Self-determination: National, Regional, and Global Dimensions* (Boulder, CO: Westview, 1980), 5.

[49] Arguments to the contrary may be found in James M. Buchanan, 'Federalism as an Ideal Political Order and an Object for Constitutional Reform', 25 *Publius*, 2 (1995): 22. This model, which incorporates secession, Buchanan calls 'competitive federalism'. *See also* Wheare, 87: 'The right to secede does not make the general government the agent of the states as does the right to nullify; on the contrary it recognizes that the general government is to be either co-ordinate with a state government within the area of the state, or is to have no connection with it'. *But see The Federalist Papers*, No. 22, in which Hamilton describes as a gross heresy that 'a *party* to a *compact* has a right to revoke that *compact*, . . .'.

[50] Quoted in Cass R. Sunstein, 'Constitutionalism and Secession', 58 *U. Chi. L. Rev.*, 633 (Spring 1991).

[51] *See* Law 'On the Procedure for Deciding Questions Connected with the Secession of a Union Republic From the USSR', Law of the USSR (3 Apr. 1990), *Vedomosti SND SSSR* (1990), No. 15, item 252. Had one of the Baltic states sought to secede in strict conformity with this law, and suffered only one major controversy, thus triggering one of the repeat series of referendums required by the law (an optimistic hypothesis), I calculate that secession would have taken 32 years!

Revolutionary America, France, and Russia all declared rights of secession only subsequently to count among the fiercest opponents of the idea (though secession remained a nominal right in Soviet constitutions long after *de facto* use was inconceivable).[52] Secession, like sovereignty, is a concept that confers power to those who wield it successfully. Secession subordinates one government to another. If the right is exercised, the federation is torn apart; if it is merely threatened, coercion and brinkmanship become accepted methods of conflict resolution. Cass Sunstein contends that a 'right' to secession would hold federal government (indeed any form of government) to ransom, subordinating its role under the ominous threat of departure from the union.[53] The mirror image of the right of states to secede from a federation, the right of the federal authority unilaterally to expel unwelcome members, is obviously inconsistent with federalism for the same reasons outlined above for secession.

The problem secession poses for federalism on these lines lies primarily in its inherent unilateralism.[54] The question of secession rests on the assumption that there is a universal right to localized self-government. Convenience, utility or efficiency aside, it is more difficult than often thought to find a universal entitlement of a minority to overrule a majority on the issue of general government.[55] As Robert Dahl argues, any satisfactory answer must

[52] Alfred Cobban, *The Nation State and National Self-Determination* (New York: Thomas Y. Crowell, 1969), 136. Ivo Duchacek notes how malleable are the ideological roots for secession: 'This author has always been awed by the astonishing capacity of the Americans, especially north of the Mason-Dixon Line, to celebrate within the span of ten days in February both the symbol of successful ideological secession and that of successful suppression of ideological secession: on February 22 the secession of Englishmen from England is lauded on George Washington's birthday, while ten days before, on February 12, Abraham Lincoln is remembered for his suppression of Southern secession'. Duchacek in Elazar, *Constitutional Design . . .* , 38–9, note 8.

[53] Cass Sunstein makes a strong case against the right to secession (with considerable attention paid to Eastern European events then unfolding), which is based largely on the 'precommitment strategies' that support his approach to the theory of constitutionalism. Cass R. Sunstein, 'Constitutionalism and Secession', 58 *U. Chi. L. Rev.*, 633 (Spring 1991). Among his reasons to reject a right of secession: 'To place such a right in a founding document would increase the risks of ethnic and factional struggle; reduce the prospects for compromise and deliberation in government; raise dramatically the stakes of day-to-day political decisions; introduce irrelevant and illegitimate considerations into those decisions; create dangers of blackmail, strategic behavior, and exploitation; and, most generally, endanger the prospects for long-term self-governance. Constitutionalism, embodying as it does a set of precommitment strategies, is frequently directed against risks of precisely this sort. Political or moral claims for secession are frequently powerful, but they do not justify constitutional recognition of a secession right'. Sunstein, 634.

[54] *Multi-lateral* secession (i.e. an agreed process involving all members of a federation in assessing and ruling on the desire of one member to exit) would seem to conflict less with federal theory. Some would argue that such a process would be qualitatively different from secession by virtue of its inclusiveness.

[55] Dahl, *Democracy, . . .* , 121.

be tied to a question of what constitutes the proper unit of democratic governance.

Fortunately, secession, like demands to change internal state borders, has not been a serious problem for the Russian Federation.[56] The utility of the threat seems to have been exhausted by the Soviet Socialist Republics against the Soviet Union. Of all of the declarations of sovereignty made by regions within the Russian Federation, only one unit—Chechnya (now self-styled the Chechen Republic of Ichkeriia)—pursued its claim to sovereignty further, to a declaration of independence, naturally meaning secession. The result—calamitous for all parties—has not raised *federal* questions, either in Moscow or in the capitals of other units. All seem to have accepted that, either for reasons of *Realpolitik* or acceptance of the federal pooling of sovereignty, that secession was not an option. These questions are discussed in greater detail in Chapter Four.

Nullification and Interposition

The doctrine of nullification interprets a constitution to be a *political* compact or treaty adopted by multiple, equally sovereign signatories, not as a higher *law* for the foundation of a single new state (which derives its sovereignty, in part, by draining its components of some of their previously untapped sovereign authority). Nullification is located to the right of secession on Figure 2.2, although in this respect, it presents even greater potential problems to federal relations. A federal government's sole legitimate role is understood by this doctrine to be only as an *agent* of the component sovereign states. Thus, states may selectively reject federal laws (or their agency) when these are judged by state legislatures or specially convened state conventions to be unconstitutional encroachments on state powers. The individual states-signatories assert the right to interpret and renegotiate the compact as their interests change.

The core difference between the nullifier and the federalist is in their different understandings of what type of document a federal constitution really is. For the nullifier, the constitution is more a political document than a legal one. Disputes over the distribution and separation of state and federal

---

[56] Serendipitously, and despite sometimes bizarrely drawn boundaries, both Russia's federal and regional politicians have almost all adhered to the doctrine of *uti possidetis juris*, the general rule that existing borders should be left unaltered. *See* Zakon RF 'Ob ustanovlenii perekhodnogo perioda po gosudarstvenno-territorial'nomu razgranicheniiu v Rossiiskoi Federatsii' (3 July 1992) *Vedomosti S''ezda narodnykh deputatov RF i Verkhovnogo Soveta RF*, No. 32 (13 Aug. 1992), item 1868, 2397–8. The only significant exception, the border between Ingushetia and Chechnya, has a long and complex imperial and Soviet history behind it. That dispute is the subject of a 'treaty' between the two republics, although war has largely etiolated the meagre solutions that document proposed.

powers are unavoidably highly politicized issues. To leave such interpretative matters to the federal judiciary is thus 'tantamount to inviting any other form of federal political control over the states'.[57] For the federalist, these disputes are questions of law, to be resolved by courts that although federally created can be trusted to be neutral forums to resolve federal-state disputes. State legislatures or *ad hoc* conventions, reflecting and beholden to the popular temper of the moment, are improper tribunals to decide matters that affect the entire federation.[58] Their sheer multiplicity, compared to the unified legal space federal courts create, would pockmark the union with the parochial interests of each state *qua* tribunal.

Interposition is the weaker cousin of nullification. This is the argument that *state* courts have the authority (indeed, the obligation) to strike down a federal law on the grounds that it violates the *federal* constitution, and that their decision is final. Thus, rather than a state legislature or state convention declaring a federal action null and void because unconstitutional— nullification—the state judiciary possesses that same power.[59]

Because these doctrines played such a central role in the events leading up to the American Civil War,[60] the experience of nullification in the United States is worth considering in some depth. This excursus, however, is not meant to lend support to the fallacy that systems incongruent with the American model are therefore of some lesser federal quality. While admitting the tremendous influence the American experience has had on the development of federal theory, such an approach would erroneously deny the continuum of different federal approaches that this chapter has been devoted to studying. The American struggle with nullification, rather, is interesting for the light it sheds for a general comparative study of federalism

[57] Keith E. Whittington, 'The Political Constitution of Federalism in Antebellum America: The Nullification Debate as an Illustration of Informal Mechanisms of Constitutional Change', 26 *Publius*, 2 (1996): 9.

[58] In the United States, the constitutional foundation for this view is Article III (establishing a federal judiciary), Article VI (establishing the supremacy of federal Constitutional law and binding state judges to uphold that hierarchy) and §25 Judiciary Act of 1789 (concretizing U.S. Supreme Court appellate jurisdiction over state supreme courts on issues of the federal constitutionality of both federal and state laws).

[59] For a sharp rejection of this view in the American constitutional system, *see* Alexander M. Bickel, *The Least Dangerous Branch: The Supreme Court at the Bar of Politics*, 2nd Ed. (New Haven: Yale University Press, 1986), 9–10.

[60] In fact, the very language used to describe that war indicates the substantial difference in conceptions of sovereignty under federalism. 'Civil War', used by the federal victors, suggests sovereignty possessed by one unit—the United States—split in two. The Southern sobriquet, 'War Between the States', strongly implies the view held by southern nullifiers: each state possesses sovereignty in the name of its own people, and is entitled to fight to defend the same. This insight is made by Calvin R. Massey, 'State Sovereignty and the Tenth and Eleventh Amendments', 56 *U. Chi. L. Rev.*, 61, 92 (note 161) (Winter 1989).

and, in particular, the study of Russian federalism (where the underlying tensions of this doctrine have frequently been at the heart of federal-regional conflicts).

The question whether state or federal forums should determine the constitutionality of federal action was a point of contention from the start of the United States. It was not uncommon for states to reject unpopular decisions made on the federal level. Thus, following the decision of the Supreme Court, in *Chisholm v. Georgia*[61] (holding that a citizen of South Carolina could sue the state of Georgia for payment of a debt) an outraged Georgian legislature flatly refused to comply with the Court's decision, passing legislation providing that persons attempting to enforce the ruling would 'suffer death, without the benefit of clergy, by being hanged'.[62] The matter ultimately was resolved in favour of state sovereign immunity by the adoption of the Eleventh Amendment and the Supreme Court's subsequent related jurisprudence.[63] This was not the only federal ruling to provoke hostile state reactions: angry legislative resolutions and even executive orders to state militias not infrequently followed rulings by the federal courts.[64] Federal legislation could have the same result. Among the many

---

[61] 2 U.S. 419 (1793).

[62] Don E. Fehrenbacher, *Constitutions and Constitutionalism in the Slaveholding South* (Athens, GA: University of Georgia Press, 1989), 39.

[63] 'The Judicial power of the United States shall not be construed to extend to any suit in law or equity, commenced or prosecuted against one of the United States by Citizens of another State, or by Citizens or Subjects of any Foreign State'. *U.S. Con.*, XI Amend. (1798).

[64] The history of school desegregation in the American South provides a number of recent examples of state governors and legislatures attempting to reject federal authority in what was considered by them to be an area of exclusive jurisdiction, the public schools. Consider this response, by a unanimous Supreme Court, in *Cooper v. Aaron*, 358 U.S. 1, 18–19 (1958):

Every state legislator and executive and judicial officer is solemnly committed by oath taken pursuant to Art. VI, cl. 3, 'to support this Constitution'. Chief Justice Taney, speaking for a unanimous Court in 1859, said that this requirement reflected the framers' 'anxiety to preserve it [the Constitution] in full force, in all its powers, and to guard against resistance to or evasion of its authority, on the part of a State...'. *Ableman v. Booth*, 21 How. 506, 524.

No state legislator or executive or judicial officer can war against the Constitution without violating his undertaking to support it. Chief Justice Marshall spoke for a unanimous Court in saying that: 'If the legislatures of the several states may, at will, annul the judgments of the courts of the United States, and destroy the rights acquired under those judgments, the constitution itself becomes a solemn mockery...'. *United States v. Peters*, 5 Cranch 115, 136. A Governor who asserts a power to nullify a federal court order is similarly restrained. If he had such power, said Chief Justice Hughes, in 1932, also for a unanimous Court, 'it is manifest that the fiat of a state Governor, and not the Constitution of the United States, would be the supreme law of the land; that the restrictions of the Federal Constitution upon the exercise of state power would be but impotent phrases...'. *Sterling v. Constantin*, 287 U.S. 378, 397–398.

The parallels with the nullifying and interposing actions of regional units of the Russian Federation against federal executive, legislative as well as judicial orders is striking, to say the least.

proposals to establish ultimate interpretive authority in *ad hoc* conventions organized by states, rather than the federal judiciary, perhaps the most well-known are the Kentucky and Virginia Resolutions (drafted by Thomas Jefferson and James Madison, respectively) attacking the Alien and Sedition Acts.[65]

Probably the most ardent advocate of the doctrine of nullification was the antebellum U.S. Senator from South Carolina (the first state to secede from the Union), John C. Calhoun. As he expressed his view:

> The great and leading principle is, that the General Government emanated from the people of the several States, forming distinct political communities, and acting in their separate and sovereign capacity, and not from all of the people forming one aggregate political community; that the Constitution of the United States is, in fact, a compact, to which each State is a party, in the character already described; and that the several States, or parties, have a right to judge of its infractions; and in case of a deliberate, palpable, and dangerous exercise of power not delegated, they have the right, in the last resort, to use the language of the Virginia Resolutions, 'to interpose for arresting the progress of evil, and for maintaining, within their respective limits, the authorities, rights, and liberties appertaining to them'. This right of interposition, . . . be it called what it may,—State-right, veto, nullification, or by any other name,—I conceive to be the fundamental principle of our system, . . . If those who voluntarily created the system cannot be trusted to preserve it, who can?[66]

This doctrine found its application in an 'Ordinance of Nullification' passed by a special state convention in South Carolina convened in opposition to a debilitating federal tariff. The Ordinance declared the federal law to be contrary to the federal constitution and therefore 'null, void, and no law'.[67] Its enforcement was declared unlawful in the state, appeals from

---

[65]   The text of these resolutions is reprinted in Commager, I: 178–86. In the words of Jefferson's Kentucky Resolution (16 November 1798): '. . . the [federal] government created by this compact was not made the exclusive or final judge of the extent of the powers delegated to itself; since that would have made its discretion, and not the Constitution, the measure of its powers; but that as in all other cases of compact among parties having no common Judge, *each party has an equal right to judge for itself, as well of infractions as of the mode and measure of redress'*. Crucially, however, these resolutions, while declaring the Alien and Sedition Acts they protested void and of no force, ultimately called for no more than their repeal at the next session of Congress. Many other states, it should be noted, rejected the state-right of legislative nullification in favour of adjudication by the courts.

[66]   Address on the Relations of the States and Federal Government (1831), reprinted in *Reports and Public Letters of John C. Calhoun*, 7 Vols. Richard K. Cralle, ed. (New York: D. Appleton, 1856), VI: 60–1, 68.

[67]   South Carolina Ordinance of Nullification, November 24, 1832, reprinted in Commager, I: 261.

state courts to the U.S. Supreme Court were prohibited, and all state officials (but not legislators), including judges and even sometimes jurors, were compelled to swear a special oath to obey and enforce the will of the convention. The Ordinance concluded by warning the federal government that any attempt to force obedience to the tariff was also unconstitutional and would lead South Carolina to consider itself 'absolved from all further obligation to maintain or preserve their political connexion with the people of the other States, and will forthwith proceed to organize a separate Government, and do all other acts and things which sovereign and independent States may of right to do'.[68]

A very similar doctrine has had a profound effect on Russian federalism (as will be examined more closely in Chapter Six), one that cannot be overemphasized. Nothing could be further from Yeltsin's and Putin's view of the federal constitution than Calhoun's exposition of nullification. Conversely, nothing could be closer to Calhoun's theory than the 'treaty-constitutional' view of key republics in the Federation—notably, Tatarstan, Bashkortostan, and Sakha-(Yakutia)—which have been the most active in the repudiation of federal authority.

Centralization

Concern over the *'vertikal'* of executive power in the Russian Federation, particularly in the guise of President Vladimir Putin's sweeping federal reforms, is really concern about a return to a centralizing past. Centralization, at the far right of Figure 2.2, results in the subordination of one level of government to the other. When the federal government overwhelms the authority of the component units, the result is centralization; the reverse situation, when regional governments subordinate the authority of the central government, may result in the problems of interposition, nullification, or even secession described above. William Riker perceived a centralizing trend in all existing federal systems, in which 'the rulers of the federation can overawe and overrule, but not annihilate, the rulers of the constituent units'.[69] Many legal scholars have noted pendulum swings in the United States, toward increasing federal powers unprecedented before the New Deal and 'activist' Supreme Courts of the last fifty years, and, more

---

[68] Commager, I: 262. For President Andrew Jackson's indictment of this ordinance and the doctrine of nullification in general, *see* his Proclamation to the U.S. Congress of December 10, 1832, reprinted in Commager, 262–8. *See also* the Kentucky Resolution of 1799, in which, further protesting the unconstitutionality of the Alien and Sedition Acts, the state asserted its sovereign right to nullification but refused to exercise it, instead registering its protest against the Acts while promising allegiance to the federal union it had joined. Commager, I: 183–4.

[69] Riker, *Federalism: Origins,* ..., 50.

recently, decisions by the Rehnquist Court tending toward a rollback to states' rights.[70]

Constitutionally Protected Autonomy versus Limited Local Administration: Getting the Balance 'Right'

The remaining two markers on the continuum framed in Figure 2.2 require only brief mention. The federal distinctions between the two are by now familiar. Federalism *is* the constitutional protection of selected areas of autonomy in different governmental jurisdictions. This protection is founded on belief in the inherent value of multiple levels of authority, entrenched in a written constitution, and grounded in the consensual acceptance of federal citizenship and sense of *Bundestreue*. It is different from the devolution or delegation of authority to local administrations by a unitary state's government. Unitary, centralized states are quite capable of qualitatively deep and quantitatively extensive decentralization or devolution of power. Analytically and empirically speaking, it is obviously possible to have decentralization without federalism. However, the decentralization of power by unitary states is not permanent in the way that federal distribution of power is. The federal compact uniquely protects jurisdictional authority over certain issues against reclamation by the central government. In a federal system, the sovereignty component units give up to form a new federal state cannot be redeemed; the authority distributed in that state between federal and constituent units cannot be unilaterally redistributed.

2.2 Democracy and Federalism

Democracy and federalism are political philosophies and theories of government process, but they operate on different levels. Federalism describes the particular institutional arrangement of a category of non-unitary polities; democracy is a more general political typology, sometimes normatively conceived as an end in itself, and one which is viable in both unitary and non-unitary polities. One can speak of federal government as a subset of democratic systems but, as this section argues, it is meaningless to speak of democracy as a subset of possible approaches to federalism. Surprisingly, given the requirements for federalism outlined above, this is a point of considerable contention; Riker insisted that one fallacy about federalism is 'the assertion that federal forms are adopted as a device to guarantee freedom. Numerous writers on federalism, so many that it would be invidious to pick out an example, have committed this ideological fallacy'.[71]

---

[70] See e.g. *Bd of Trustees of the University of Alabama v.Garrett*, 121 S.Ct. 955 (2001).
[71] Riker, *Federalism: Origin, . . .* , 13.

Definitions of democracy, like the etymology of the word itself, extend back to ancient times. A rigorous treatment of this enormous subject is neither intended nor necessary. Beyond normative philosophical treatments, democracy has been studied as sets of decision-making processes, rights and rules for association, institutions, and social conditions.[72] Democracy requires a state and institutions in which to operate, norms and attitudes by which to be preserved, and procedures and practices through which to ensure fairness, reliability and (for the long-term) a modicum of loosely defined success for citizens.[73] Among the 'arenas' of a modern consolidated democracy, Linz and Stepan count vibrant civil, political, and economic societies, a healthy respect for rule-of-law arrangements and a state bureaucracy with a rational-legal base of authority. These arenas interact and saturate a stable democratic system along multiple and complex matrices. Giuseppe DiPalma concludes on a note with a distinctly federal ring to it: 'It is better to say that, though it is no longer the harbinger of instant material progress, democracy has gained dramatically for delivering something else: mutual security in diversity'.[74]

Federal Problems for Democratic Government

What does federalism *do* to a democracy? Does the application of federal templates result in a polity that is more or less democratic? There are three related criticisms commonly made of democracy in federal systems: first, that it results in gross over-representation of some units at the expense of others; second, that its legislative and judicial structures permit counter-majoritarian defiance of the popular will (usually due to a combination of judicial review and the heightened protection against quick amendment given to constitutional laws); third, that federalism results in asymmetry of various forms among units of the federation.

Does federalism result in over-representation? By some measures, absolutely. Almost by definition, federalism rejects the notion that a simple majority of voting citizens is the source of sovereignty for the state. A territorial basis of representation (instead of one based on equal representa-

---

[72] Robert A. Dahl, *Democracy and its Critics* (New Haven: Yale University Press, 1989), 6–8.

[73] The terminology and qualifiers for the five 'arenas' of democracy are from Linz and Stepan, ch. 1. Since their work both encompasses a detailed understanding of existing scholarship on the prerequisites of democracy, and deliberately focuses on the comparative problems of transition and consolidation to democracy, I have adopted their nomenclature.

[74] Giuseppe DiPalma, *To Craft Democracies: An Essay on Democratic Transitions* (Berkeley: University of California Press, 1990), 151. In addition, it is interesting to hear the ring of subsidiarity in one 'pragmatic principle' suggested by Dahl: 'If a matter is best dealt with by a democratic association, seek always to have that matter dealt with by the smallest association that can deal with it satisfactorily'. Robert A. Dahl *After the Revolution?* . . . , 79.

tion of populations) is the typical (but not ubiquitous) method of organizing the upper chambers of federal bicameral parliaments. This may lead to gross distortions of traditionally calculated proportional representation. Table 2.2 surveys the extreme over-representation of which federal systems are capable, using data for the upper chambers of eight federal legislatures. Because each unit is equally represented in the upper chamber regardless of variance in population, the least populated units are quantitatively better represented than the most populous units. For example, in the United States, the vote of a senator from the least populous state is worth sixty-six times that of the most populous state's senator. A summation of these results working upwards from the least populated states (e. g. Wyoming + Vermont + Alaska, etc.) reveals that 10 per cent of the population is accorded almost 40 per cent of the representation in the Senate. The extreme over-representation displayed by the Russian Federation is due to even greater differences in the populations of its constituent units.

Many theorists proclaim this tendency of federalism to over-represent sparsely populated units as a democratic heresy. If majoritarian democracy finds its classic embodiment in a Westminster-style parliamentary system,

Table 2.2   Over-representation in the Upper Chambers of Eight Federations[75]

Ratio of best to worst represented federal unit (based on population)	Belgium	Spain	India	Germany	Canada	U.S.A.	Brazil	Russia
	2:1	10:1	11:1	13:1	21:1	66:1	144:1	370:1

Percentage of seats held by the best represented 10% of the total population	Belgium	India	Spain	Germany	Canada	Russia	U.S.A.	Brazil
	10.8	15.4	23.7	24.0	33.4	35.0	39.7	41.3

[75] In Table 2.2, data for India provided by Cindy Skach; for Russia by Jeff Kahn; for remaining federations by Alfred Stepan and Wilfried Swenden. Table designed by A. Stepan. A more detailed version of this table, including coefficients for inequality, has appeared in a number of papers by A. Stepan. Its latest version may be found in A. Stepan, *Arguing Comparative Politics* (Oxford University Press, 2001), 344.

then the weighted representation promoted by federalism is a conflicting logic which seems to run counter to that tradition. Wheare admits the charge, but tempers the criticism: '. . . if federal government is really appropriate to a country, it is most likely that government by a majority of the people is not usually enough'. Riker concluded his observations on federalism on a particularly cynical note, suggesting that because minoritarian democracy holds such sway in federal systems, one should support federal government only if one supports the idea of a system that privileges a minority of its citizens.[76] Riker's critical observations were based on watching how a ruling minority of racists in the American South stymied (for a time) progressive civil rights legislation. On the other hand, others have looked at the American case (among others) and seen the utility of federalism in permitting democracy to percolate into the system 'from below'.[77] States may be 'lighthouses' for innovation and experimentation in government, first by other states and then, perhaps, by the federation as a whole.[78] Analysis of the principle of subsidiarity, so integral to federalism, supports the Madisonian concern with diffusing power to protect liberty.[79]

To indict federalism as counter-majoritarian is to contest the democratic legitimacy not only of federal divisions of power and voting populations, but of written constitutions generally and their judicial review.[80] But, fundamentally, *all* written constitutions, by creating heightened criteria for amendment, are counter-majoritarian.[81] The deliberate protection of basic rights and procedures from simple majority control is indeed the most

[76]   Elazar, *Exploring . . .* , 19; Wheare, 236; Riker, 155.

[77]   'Between the Revolution and the Civil War, there was extensive progress toward the democratization of political consent in the United States—most of it achieved through state constitutional change'. Fehrenbacher, 7.

[78]   For a criticism of the lighthouse effect and the potential for perverse outcomes due to state competititon, see Susan Rose-Ackerman, 'Does Federalism Matter? Political Choice in a Federal Republic', 89 *Journal of Political Economy*, 1 (1981): 152–65.

[79]   *See* Bermann, 341: 'To the extent that subsidiarity promotes the diffusion of authority among different levels of government within the European Community, it can serve as a similar check against political oppression and tyranny and, like self-determination, also promote individual freedom'. *See also Coleman v. Thompson* 501 U.S. 722, 759 (1991) (Blackmun, J., dissenting: 'Rather, federalism secures to citizens the liberties that derive from the diffusion of sovereign power'.)

[80]   The 'counter-majoritarian difficulty' is famously explored in Alexander M. Bickel, *The Least Dangerous Branch: The Supreme Court at the Bar of Politics*, 2nd Ed. (New Haven: Yale University Press, 1986), 17. See also Steven P. Croley, 'The Majoritarian Difficulty: Elective Judiciaries and the Rule of Law', 62 *U. Chi. L. Rev.*, 689 (1995).

[81]   Nor is a rigorous amendment process the only constitutional element open to the charge of counter-majoritarianism. Regulations and administrative decisions by unelected officials of the executive branch are no less counter-majoritarian, and probably affect more citizens on a daily basis then the negative power to declare laws unconstitutional. Term limits on elected officials may produce a short-term version of the freedom from the electorate to which life-appointees to the bench are accused.

attractive feature of a constitution. Absolute democracy has been considered no more desirable than an absolutely free market. Tempering the popular will with protections for the liberty interest of the minority is crucial to working democracies as they are valued today. This is, in large part, the work of a constitution as well as a vigilant citizenry. The requirement that a super-majority engage in a more deliberative and time-consuming process of amendment in order to change the fundamental features of the polity seems not just a reasonable democratic price to pay, but a necessary one for the stability and prosperity of the polity. Jefferson's wish for constitutional revolutions with each generation is not widely shared.[82]

Despite these valid and critical observations, there is little foundation for the argument that voting is less democratic in a federal system than in a unitary one. Constitutionally protected agendas (whether territorially or otherwise demarcated) provide local majorities (which are federation-wide minorities) opportunities to prevail locally on certain issues over federation-wide majorities. What equality is lost in one voting arithmetic must be compared to the equally valid democracies possible with different ways of dividing minorities and majorities. Ivo Duchacek briskly explains this trade-off: 'Asymmetric federalism (and they all are) violates the principle of equality of franchise . . . for the sake of the federal principle of equal representation of unequally populated territorial units'.[83] Democratic theory is internally (perhaps, eternally) incomplete: there are no grounds within democratic theory for determining the 'rightfulness of the unit itself'. Robert Dahl summarizes the result: 'Yet on that ground alone federalism cannot be judged less democratic than a unitary system, except on the premise that the proper unit in which majorities should prevail is the nation or the country. . . . [S]uch a premise is arbitrary and highly contestable. By purely theoretical reasoning from democratic principles it appears to be impossible to establish that the city-state, the country, a transnational system, or any other unit is inherently more democratic or otherwise more desirable than others'.[84]

To put this another way, federalism affects traditional interpretations of representation—just as it alters traditional conceptions of sovereignty—to create new approaches that are not necessarily less democratic. Simple

---

[82] 'Each generation is as independent as the one preceding, as that was of all which had gone before. It has then, like them, a right to choose for itself the form of government it believes most promotive of its own happiness; . . . and it is for the peace and good of mankind, that a solemn opportunity of doing this every nineteen or twenty years, should be provided by the constitution; . . .'. Letter to Samuel Kercheval, July 12, 1816, reprinted in Lance Banning, *Jefferson and Madison: Three Conversations from the Founding* (Madison: Madison House, 1995), 224.

[83] Duchacek, *Comparative Federalism* . . . , 282.

[84] Dahl, *Democracy*, . . . , 125–6.

calculations of an indivisible majority will are discarded in favour of a system that simultaneously can utilize different measures of who constitutes a majority on different levels of government. Federalism establishes the notion that sovereignty is something that can be discretely distributed to the state on several levels by the people in whom it is said naturally to reside. This definitional shift clearly also has an effect on the assumptions on which democratic procedures are based.

A third criticism levied against federalism from the point of view of democratic government relates to the various forms of asymmetry typical in federal systems. In all but a few subject areas, however, the quest for symmetry in federal democracies is a mistaken pursuit.[85] Even Westminster-styled parliamentary systems must operate under conditions of often extensive geographic, social, economic, and even political asymmetry.[86] Alaska is bigger than Rhode Island; New Hampshire is more homogenous than Texas; California is richer than West Virginia, etc. Yet all these states have equal representation in the U.S. Senate. At best, the goal is unattainable, and perhaps also undesireable: perfect symmetry would require states equalized along every measure (size, population, economic, institutional, even social and ethnic composition), a model in miniature of the larger federal whole. Likewise, perfect asymmetry would require constituent units exactly and perfectly matched to the different problems and interests in the polity. What consensus is possible in such a federation; indeed, what purpose would the units have to establish such a system in common?[87] Of course, neither of these ideals is even remotely approached in reality. *Prima facie*, it is easy to see how incompatible perfect symmetry is with political and social realities. Furthermore, such an atomized polity as the perfectly asymmetrical one, comprised of units uniquely fashioned for the issues each confronts, would seem unlikely to contain a set of interests common enough to all to require federal resolution.

The charge of voting disparities due to asymmetrical territorial divisions, distribution of wealth and other socioeconomic factors is likewise rebut-

[85] Alfred Stepan considers concern over asymmetry in federal systems legitimate in only two areas: socioeconomic asymmetry that affects inter-elite bargaining, and constitutional asymmetry that affects the fundamental 'rules of the game' in federal (indeed all) political systems. *See* Alfred Stepan, 'Russian Federalism in Comparative Perspective', 16 *Post-Soviet Affairs*, 2 (2000): 141–5.

[86] For an analysis of the political follies in pursuing strict symmetry, with reference to recent devolution reforms in the United Kingdom, *see* Archie Brown, 'Asymmetrical Devolution: The Scottish Case', 69 *The Political Quarterly*, 3 (July–Sept. 1998), especially 217: '[S]ymmetry should be left to the mathematicians and neatness to the logicians. They have little or nothing to do with politics'.

[87] '...an asymmetrical federal government is one in which political institutions correspond to the real social "federalism" beneath them'. Charles D. Tarlton, 'Symmetry and Asymmetry as Elements of Federalism: A Theoretical Speculation', 27 *The Journal of Politics*, 4 (1965): 869.

table. Many of the arguments already advanced in the above analysis of over-representation are applicable here. The very fact that a federal system seems appropriate implies that arithmetic divisions of the polity are neither possible nor desirable.

Accepting the impossibility of perfect symmetry of composition and the inevitability of a basic asymmetry of interests, long-lasting and relatively stable federal systems have, in general, tended to promote a certain symmetry in the processes used to resolve disputes. Here, the issue of *institutional* or *constitutional* asymmetry is worth serious attention. This asymmetry usually involves the creation of special channels between the federal government and a particular constituent unit that is favoured with special privileges, dispensations, and exceptions *vis-à-vis* other constituent units of the federation. Such special channels are often undemocratic and conflict with the logic of universal, constitutional-legal norms for organizing and administering the polity. Russia's unique tripartite federal structure—a Soviet-era holdover based on a system of privileges for select 'titular' ethnic groups—suffers from this form of institutional-constitutional asymmetry. Even more corrosive of federal arrangements is *aconstitutional* asymmetry—idiosyncratic (often *ad hoc*) bilateral relations between governmental levels that neither seek justification within, or even relate to, the founding document of the federal union. Given their nature outside of law, these relations often quickly descend into personality-centred intrigues, rather than iterated, predictable and above all, institutionalized procedures. Russian federalism has also been affected by this form of asymmetry. The special relationship between select regional leaders and Boris Yeltsin, often conducted in secret, generated a fog of suspicion among other units of the Federation. The *perception* of privilege—even beyond the reality—led to rumours and allegations of secret treaties and special deals, creating yet another stumbling block in the path to the expressed goal, a democratic, rule-of-law federation.

Concrete examples demonstrate these points further. Revenues and subsidies are crucial issues in *any* state; the complexities of a federal relationship serve to heighten their importance. The United States and Australia—federal systems with considerable socioeconomic disparity among regions—employ diverse, but highly public and formal methods to promote openness and a sense of fairness to federal redistributive processes.[88] If a

---

[88] The Australian Constitution requires uniformity in the distribution of federal bounties and prohibits tax discrimination or other preferential treatment by the federal government to states (see Arts. 51 [ii & iii] and 99). The United States federal government publishes annual tables of federal expenditure in the states. Cheryl Saunders, 'Constitutional Arrangements of Federal Systems', 25 *Publius*, 2 (1995): 76.

constituent unit is granted privileges above any other in its dealings with the centre, such institutional asymmetry might be minimized by the deliberate inclusion of other units, and/or the federal legislature, in ratification of this relationship. The experience with the establishment of *autonomias* in Spain is a good example of an open process involving all levels of government to dispel potential suspicion of privilege or patronage.

The bilateral treaty process in Russia provides one of the most flagrant examples of these forms of asymmetry, problems to which the arguments of this book will repeatedly be directed. There is nothing in federal theory that demands complete isomorphism in the institutional structure of constituent units of a federation, or that those units adopt the same structures of internal governance as utilized at the federal level. And it certainly goes without saying that non-institutional areas of comparison (e. g. socioeconomic, demographic, etc.) rarely exhibit much similarity. The Russian Federation exhibits an astounding degree and amount of institutional asymmetry (not to mention other forms) that poses serious concerns for the long-term stability of the Federation as a whole. These questions are addressed in Chapters Six and Seven.

The Curious Question of 'Non-democratic Federalism'

Federal government is clearly compatible with democracy. It should also be clear that many of the 'arenas' that support democracy embody principles or promote attitudes equally conducive to federal structures. The argument thus far has been that federal government is a particular subset of democratic polities. But is democracy really a prerequisite for federal systems or is it merely coincidentally associated with them? Are non-democratic federal systems theoretically possible? Are there empirical counter-examples to this argument?

One approach to finding an answer is to attempt to construct a hypothetical non-democratic federal system. Such attempts demonstrate the theoretical contradictions that result from efforts to adhere simultaneously to the fundamentals of federalism and non-democratic government. The existence through time of non-democratic polities claiming federal title is no more demonstrative proof of non-democratic federalism than the democratic centralism of the Soviet Union and Cold War 'people's democracies' of Eastern Europe was convincing evidence of genuine democracy.[89]

---

[89] This statement should be contrasted with the insistent view of William Riker: '... federalism is no more than a constitutional legal fiction which can be given whatever content seems appropriate at the moment'. Riker accepted the assertions of the USSR and Tito's Yugoslavia to be federal systems. William H. Riker, 'Six Books in Search of a Subject or Does Federalism Exist and Does it Matter?' 2 *Comparative Politics*, 1 (1969): 146.

Cheryl Saunders presents the challenge: '[W]hile federalism historically and characteristically is associated with democracy, it is theoretically possible to create a working federal system in a polity that is not otherwise democratic'.[90] Riker confidently answered: 'Only the most casual observation of, for example, the Soviet Union or Mexico demonstrates, however, that even though all the forms of federalism are fairly scrupulously maintained, it is possible to convert the government into a dictatorship'.[91] But what could a non-democratic federal system look like? An acceptable answer would require a system that was *both* non-democratic *and* federal; that is, the system would be required to sufficiently maintain the four minimum requirements of a federal system without permitting democratic regulation of conflict. Non-democratic regimes come in a variety of typological shapes and sizes. However, it is reasonable to assume that if federalism were incompatible with the least non-democratic of these, it would be incompatible with all of those ranged higher on a non-democratic continuum.

A non-democratic regime requires the active use of coercion well beyond the Weberian requirements that establish a state. Coercion excludes civil and political approaches to conflict resolution and is a method of societal control for the ruling elite. The pluralism of elites that may exist within a ruling structure does not extend sufficiently deep into the polity itself, or its development in society is restricted by the ruling clique. Non-democratic regimes rely on the ability to pre-empt or countermand choices or preferences made by citizens about their government.

Such a regime is clearly incompatible with the fundamental requirements of federalism. The unilateralism presupposed above has no more place in federal systems than unilateralism in the guise of secession or nullification. It is impossible to square the coercive methods of a non-democratic regime with the rejection of subordination in favour of co-ordination that is one of the core principles of federalism. Coercion and subordination are antonyms to subsidiarity and autonomy. From the perspective of federalism, it little matters that political scientists can detect predictability or the influence of unwritten constraints on the seemingly arbitrary actions of ruling elites in a non-democratic regime. The fact that any predictability is *de facto* and not *de jure*; that it is a predictability forced by circumstance and not by law; that it can only be expected but not enforced or reasonably ensured; such a situation is clearly not compatible with the requirements of federalism.

---

[90] Cheryl Saunders, 'Constitutional Arrangements of Federal Systems', 25 *Publius*, 2 (1995): 77.

[91] Riker, *Federalism: Origin,* ..., 14. Chapter 3 presents the counter-argument to this cavalier assertion of the scrupulous maintenance of federalism in the Soviet Union.

Wheare corroborates this view, noting that the presence of autocratic or dictatorial government, in general or regionally, '...seems certain, sooner or later, to destroy that equality of status and that independence which these governments must enjoy, each in its own sphere, if federal government is to exist at all'.[92] Whether federalism is viewed as a set of ideologies, procedures, or institutions, its philosophical source is within a western tradition of liberalism. Assessing the failure of Pakistan and the Central African Republic to develop entrenched federal governments in the early 1960s, F.G. Carnell firmly placed the blame on their 'inability to set up democratic regimes providing good government'.[93]

And yet, how should one match theory with the empirical fact of systems clearly non-democratic and ostensibly federal? A critical analysis of Soviet 'federalism' is the subject of Chapter Three. Two empirical examples will briefly be discussed here: the former Federal Republic of Yugoslavia and Brazil.[94]

The Yugoslav Constitution of January 1946 heralded what claimed to be the first 'popular democracy' in Eastern Europe. Article One proclaimed a 'Federal People's State of republican form' in a 'community of equal peoples'.[95] However, Yugoslav federalism, both under Tito and after, clearly did not constitute a genuine federal system any more than its many constitutions managed to create democracy. A brief review of some key constitutional provisions reveals a system based far more in democratic centralism than in federalism, the incompatibility of which two is beyond doubt. In the course of analysing these texts, the fact of these constitutions' historical subordination when in conflict with the particular interests of the ruling elite should not be forgotten; a fictive constitution suggests both the existence of a non-democratic regime and the absence of federalism.

The 1946 constitution of Yugoslavia developed a centralised state, a version of democratic centralism that some scholars argue was even more

[92] Wheare, 46.
[93] F.G. Carnell, 'Political Implications of Federalism in New States', in Ursula K. Hicks, ed. *Federalism and Economic Growth in Underdeveloped Countries* (London: Allen & Unwin, 1961), 47.
[94] Of course, other examples could also have been explored, for instance, Czechoslovakia. Because of its highly unusual nature as a two-unit system, I have not focused on it. For an excellent analysis of this 'federal' system, and the failed attempts at federation after 1989, *see* Eric Stein, *Czecho/Slovakia: Ethnic Conflict, Constitutional Fissure, Negotiated Breakup* (Ann Arbor, MI: University of Michigan Press, 1997). Professor Stein, who served on a highly respected international advisory group and in that capacity helped to draft a federal constitution for a new Czechoslovakia that failed to materialize, notes of the 1968 amended constitution: 'In reality, the federal aspect proved at best an administrative division, at worst a hollow sham, ...' and '...a caricature of that form of government'. Stein, at 23 and 28.
[95] Edward McWhinney, *Federal Constitution-making for a Multi-national World* (Leiden: A.W. Sijthoff, 1966), 81.

extreme than the 1936 Stalin Constitution in the USSR. The six people's republics and two autonomous regions were dependent on a federal centre that had the constitutional power to regulate the division of revenue. The centre also held the power to countermand decrees and orders of constituents without recourse to arbitration by a constitutional court; no such institution had been created. Even following the proclaimed 'Third Way' to socialist democracy after 1948—with constitutions redrawn in 1953 and 1963—promised decentralization and direct participation were circumscribed by a constricting ring of central domination.

Another case to be considered is that of Brazil. The 1964 military coup created a period of unstable authoritarian rule which, with the rise of General Ernesto Geisel to the presidency in 1974, began perhaps one of the most gradual transitions to democracy in modern history; democracy in Brazil is still considered unconsolidated.[96] Yet, throughout this period, Brazil's federal structure seems at first glance to have survived relatively unscathed. Daniel Elazar probably goes too far in his suggestion that the governors of Brazil's twenty-six states were able to muster sufficient military autonomy to counter directives from the centre.[97] However, even if his point is taken that autonomy was to be found in considerably greater proportions in Brazil than in other non-democratic cases, this still does not say very much. Governors in Brazil were not elected until 1982, but rather federally appointed, and the military police were under the direct orders of colonels or higher in the federal military. Control of natural and financial resources was centralized. To the extent that the governors' power was not overridden by any number of authoritarian decrees (the 1968 Fifth Institutional Act, the suspensions of Congress, glaring human rights abuses, etc.), each in and of themselves contrary to the four federal principles outlined above, the fact that what autonomy was maintained was preserved through brittle adversarial relations with the centre operating under the implicit threat of force clearly indicates the absence of respect for subsidiarity, reciprocity, and entrenchment.

Brazil's case is particularly interesting because of the origin and manner of liberalization and later gradual democratization after 1974: unlike other regimes in southern Europe and Latin America, Brazil's authoritarians did not engage in concerted propaganda against democracy. On the contrary, faint traces of past democratic practices were maintained during this period and some military elites asserted that their ambition was to make democracy possible again in Brazil, a paradox which in part contributed to Juan

---

[96] Linz & Stepan, 178, 187.
[97] Daniel J. Elazar, 'From Statism to Federalism: A Paradigm Shift', 25 *Publius*, 2 (1995): 16.

Linz's suggestion that what emerged in Brazil after 1964 was not an authoritarian *regime* but an authoritarian *situation*.[98] If federal structures did not completely disappear or become mere façades, neither was the normative interest in democracy completely routed from the minds of the ruling elite.[99] Just as democratic practices have enjoyed extremely turbulent, irregular but recurrent use in Brazilian history, the federal structures, first formed in one of these more liberal interludes (Brazilian federalism was established in 1891 and patterned after the U.S. Constitution two years after a bloodless revolution ended the monarchy), have varied in their strength and meaning for Brazilian politics and political arrangements.

Another reason for interest in Brazil is the development of federal relations after the promulgation of the 1988 constitution. Democratization has unleashed a decentralising trend that threatens to remove Brazil from the narrow range of practices and principles which establish federation, this time through *too much* of these principles rather than too little. The governors' veto power, ability to affect federal appointments, control over internal resources (especially banks) and other powers have resulted in a situation of iterated bilateralism as the federal centre is forced into repeated negotiations over debt restructuring and other issues with its grossly unequal (socially and economically) constituent states.[100] The previously constrained states now have too little responsibility to the centre; in this case, too much subsidiarity and autonomy can be as problematic for federalism as too little.[101]

2.3 Law and Federalism

In many ways, the relationship between law and federalism has already been suggested in the preceding sections. Questions of sovereignty are not abstract questions but controversies over jurisdiction (i.e. legal authority in a particular place over particular people and subject matter). Subsidiarity involves the recurrent problem of determining what matters should be resolved at which level of government (i.e. what authority will make the laws, enforce the standards and weigh the conflicts that inevitably arise). The question 'Who decides what is law?' is at the core of the conflict over

[98] Juan J. Linz, 'The Future of an Authoritarian Situation or the Institutionalization of an Authoritarian Regime: The Case of Brazil', in Alfred Stepan, ed. *Authoritarian Brazil: Origins, Policies, and Future* (New Haven: Yale University Press, 1973), 235.

[99] Celina Souza, *Constitutional Engineering in Brazil: The Politics of Federalism and Decentralisation* (New York: St. Martin's Press, 1997), 31–4.

[100] Souza, 105.

[101] *See* Alfred Stepan, 'Brazil: The Burden of the Past; The Promise of the Future', 129 *Daedalus*, No. 2 (2000): 145–69.

nullification as well: states that reject federal authority in a particular sphere typically do not hesitate to declare that the offending federal action is simply 'not law', even if it has been adopted in full compliance with the procedural rules of federal law-making.

When political scientists and legal scholars compare modern democracies, government under law is generally considered to be a fundamental precondition.[102] Perhaps because the expression is so commonly used today, the tremendous force of the idea of 'government *under* law' is taken for granted. The preposition in that phrase is the operative word, defining a relationship between citizen and ruler that preceded the development of modern democracies by hundreds of years. The establishment of government under law was an unprecedented act of self-restraint begun by the 12th-century kings of England (prior to that time responsible only to the god under whose authority power was claimed to flow). Assent by the monarch to bind his ministers and officers to act under laws, interpreted by royal courts, was a revolutionary event. The citizen could appeal to the law, as opposed to the personal authority of another patron, against abuses of power by those who acted in the name of the crown. This is the origin of judicial review and the conception of government as held in trust for the governed, each of whom possess an undivided interest in the system. The citizen is entitled to seek *legal* remedies for the violation of private rights by officials-trustees who misuse their public powers. Democracy simply puts the power to choose and be chosen a lawmaker in the hands of the citizen. But democracy is a *political* power, capable of only periodic exercise. Without the *legal* power to use the authority of courts to compel action, disclose information and demand the rational use of the power of the state, the force of democracy to ensure individual rights is greatly diminished.[103] Law is what makes democratic government a 'republic of reasons' and not simply majoritarian rule.[104]

English, unfortunately, does not lend itself to the distinctly different meanings telescoped into the word 'law'—a word crucially important to understanding both the philosophical underpinnings of federalism and the

---

[102] *See* e.g. Linz & Stepan, *passim*, especially 3–15.

[103] It is from English common law that the United States adopted the concept of judicial review of administrative decisions. Judicial review of legislative action, of course, is an American constitutional invention. *See Marbury v. Madison* 5 U.S. 137, 163 (1803) (Marshall, C.J., observing that 'The very essence of civil liberty certainly consists in the right of every individual to claim the protection of the laws, whenever he receives an injury. One of the first duties of government is to afford that protection. In Great Britain the king himself is sued in the respectful form of a petition, and he never fails to comply with the judgment of his court'.)

[104] 'The minimal condition of deliberative democracy is a requirement of reasons for governmental actions...the republic of reasons'. Cass Sunstein, *The Partial Constitution* (Cambridge: Harvard University Press, 1993), 20.

story of its development in Russia. Of course, law can be understood in positivist terms simply as the statutes, legislation, and rules enacted by legislatures. But law, or rather 'Law', may also connote first principles for the organization of human relations (in the American and English legal traditions, primarily developed as the common law). The state, as Harold Berman neatly phrased it, is 'not only the creator but also a creature of law'.[105] The difference between a state governed *by laws* and one ruled *by Law* is enormous. The former, what Berman called a 'law-based state', is the *Rechtstaat*: laws, that is, statutes and other legislation are the supreme authority in the state by virtue of the *process* of law-making that generates them.[106] It is the state, to paraphrase Max Weber, that exercises monopoly control over the creation of law.[107] A 'Rule-of-Law' state, on the other hand, is a state that is *not* the sole source of law. In common law countries, courts (administered by the state but distanced from the overtly political branches of state power) are the wellspring of principles of equity and other normative standards. In both common law and civil law countries, theories of natural law, the counterweight of civil society, and customary private law have served as sources of Law beyond the generative power of a state's parliament. The laws of the legislature may be declared unlawful or, rather, un-Lawful, because mere procedural accuracy is not enough to legitimate (consecrate) the law. 'While, in complying with the notion of the rule of law, the political power that governs the state is subordinated to a law that it has not directly produced, in the case of *Rechtsstaat*, the state subordinates itself to its "own" law'.[108] The self-binding notion of 'government under law' does not create the *Rechtsstaat*—not rule by laws—but the rule of Law. Cass Sunstein's characterization of deliberative democracy as 'the republic of reasons', only partially captures this meaning. English loses a distinction that is better expressed in Latin (*lex* versus *jus*), French (*loi* versus *droit*) or, for that matter, in Russian (*zakon* versus *pravo*).

To be accepted in a rule-of-law state, a law must meet certain criteria beyond procedure. 'Federalism', A.V. Dicey insisted, 'lastly, means legal-

---

[105] Harold J. Berman, 'The Rule of Law and the Law-Based State (Rechtsstaat)', in Donald D. Barry, ed. *Toward the 'Rule of Law' in Russia? Political and Legal Reform in the Transition Period* (Armonk, NY: M.E. Sharpe, 1992), 49.

[106] This notion is captured by the aphorism: '*Auctoritas, non veritas, facit legem*' [Authority, not truth, creates statutes.]

[107] As Berman rightly points out, the *Rechtsstaat* could theoretically be a fascist or dictatorial state—there is no substantive prescription beyond the positivist procedural requirements of rule by laws. Nazi Germany, the Soviet Union, and apartheid South Africa were all states rich in laws, however unjust (i.e. un-Lawful) these laws were.

[108] Gianmaria Ajani, 'The Rise and Fall of the Law-Based State in the Experience of Russian Legal Scholarship: Foreign Patterns and Domestic Style', in Barry, 3–6.

ism—the predominance of the judiciary in the constitution—the prevalence of a spirit of legality among the people'.[109] Dicey has in mind Law, not law. Valuable (if not prerequisite) to both federal and non-federal democratic systems are the core qualities of this legalism: legitimacy, predictability, stability, fairness, efficiency, and a repudiation of secrecy in promulgating laws and regulations. The role to be played by the judiciary and the legislature in attaining these objectives is a more controversial question. Fehrenbacher, commenting on the American federal system, observed: 'Thus it was in the judicial function that the two systems of government were to be connected and national supremacy secured. State legislatures were not accountable to Congress; state governors were not accountable to the President, but state courts were, in certain crucial ways, accountable to the United States Supreme Court'.[110] This arrangement helped to dampen the most contentious political disputes, by forcing their resolution into a forum based on reason, precedent, and deliberative process.[111]

Constitution-making does not imply the creation of a basic law that must remain forever unchanged. Strength does not come through stagnation; the Jeffersonian extreme of this position—encouraging redrafting every generation—is well-known. Constitution-making *does* mean the assertion of heightened respect, and therefore more difficult alteration, for the law establishing the procedural and substantive superstructure of the state. A constitution does away with the supremacy of parliament, replacing it with a self-binding document to which parliament agrees to conform its actions, or undertake the difficult and lengthy process of creating new constraints on its powers. Courts are the arbiters of this conformity. The counter-majoritarian difficulties judicial review presents for democracy have already been mentioned. There are corresponding federal difficulties as well. It does not necessarily follow that, because a constitution establishes a federal government, it establishes judicial review of the legislature's activity. As countless scholars have noted, the power of judicial review is nowhere explicitly found in the U.S. Constitution, although that is undoubtably one of the corner-

---

[109] Dicey, 175.

[110] Fehrenbacher, 37.

[111] 'The transcendent importance of the American Revolution is that it demonstrated for ever that quality of the Western European government we have called "law-boundedness". Here is a government that draws its powers from and can only act within a framework of fundamental law—the Constitution—which is itself interpreted by judges in the ordinary courts of the country. Could law-boundedness go further, could it receive a more striking affirmation?' S.E. Finer, *The History of Government: Vol. III. Empires, Monarchies and the Modern State*. (Oxford University Press, 1997), 1485.

stones of that country's federal system.[112] Its development as one of the most powerful and distinctive forces of American federalism was a slow, arduous and (even today) highly contested process.[113] While not disputing the crucial condition that some matters be 'constitutionally *beyond*' the authority of the federal government, Robert Dahl notes that judicial review does not necessarily have to be universal: 'Even in a federal system the courts might be denied the power to declare unconstitutional laws passed by the national parliament; their authority to do so could be restricted only to laws passed by the lower units. Such, in fact, is the solution adopted by the Swiss'.[114] However, it should be emphasized that in no federal system is the sovereignty of parliament, at any level of government, left completely intact. In Switzerland, the electorate, not the court, has the power to declare a law of the federal government invalid—by way of a referendum.

The relationship between law and federalism is of crucial importance to an analysis of Russian federalism. This is not just because, in the words of Bernard Rudden, '[d]uring the last years of its life the Soviet Union turned to law like a dying monarch to his withered God'.[115] Although undoubtably true that the Supreme Soviet and its successor, the Russian Duma, have engaged in a law-making campaign 'with the fervour of one who sees in legislation the path to paradise',[116] that Utopia is nowhere within reach, nor likely to be grasped by the lawyer-politician. What did Mikhail Gorbachev (incidentally, a lawyer by training) mean *exactly* when he famously expressed the need to return to a *pravovoe gosudarstvo* (rule-of-law state)?[117] Did he

---

[112] Probably none have framed the question more elegantly than Alexander Bickel: 'The least dangerous branch of the American government is the most extraordinarily powerful court of law the world has ever known. The power which distinguishes the Supreme Court of the United States is that of constitutional review of actions of the other branches of government, federal and state. Curiously enough, this power of judicial review, as it is called, does not derive from any explicit constitutional command. . . . This is not to say that the power of judicial review cannot be placed in the Constitution; merely that it cannot be found there'. Bickel, 1.

[113] The Supreme Court's power of judicial review was gradually established in several important cases: most famously, *Marbury v. Madison*, 5 U.S. 137, 177 (1803) (holding 'It is emphatically the province and duty of the judicial department to say what the law is'.); but also *Martin v. Hunter's Lessee*, 14 U.S. 304 (1816) (holding federal judicial review of state government action to be a legitimate exercise of federal power); and *Cohens v. Virginia*, 19 U.S. 264 (1821) (holding federal judicial review of state law in criminal proceedings to be a legitimate exercise of federal power); and, more recently, *Cooper v. Aaron*, 358 U.S. 1, 18 (1958) (unanimously holding, in the context of school desegregation orders contested and later enforced under threat of military force by National Guardsmen and federal troops, respectively, that the premise of the supremacy of the federal judiciary to interpret the law and Constitution is 'a permanent and indispensable feature of our constitutional system'.)

[114] Robert A. Dahl, *Democracy and its Critics* (New Haven: Yale University Press, 1989), 189.

[115] Bernard Rudden, 'Civil Law, Civil Society, and the Russian Constitution', 110 *The Law Quarterly Review* (Jan. 1994): 56.

[116] Rudden, 56.

[117] The mere use of this phrase marked a turning point in Soviet history. Labelled for seven decades a 'bourgeois' concept, the term had been proscribed from discussion of Soviet law. *See* Donald D. Barry, ed. *Toward the 'Rule of Law' in Russia?*, xiii.

mean to go beyond the Soviet *Rechtsstaat*, to rule by laws made legitimate by something beyond the unanimity of Party-controlled parliamentary assent? Did he mean a 'rule-of-law' state, a state held accountable to *pravo* (i.e. *jus*)? In May 1988 Gorbachev told a gathering which included directors from the mass media that the creation of a socialist rule-of-law state was a 'large-scale turning point'.[118] The 'Theses' published prior to the 19th Party Conference (which radically restructured electoral procedures, legislative and judicial institutions in June 1988) made reference to the importance of a division of powers in a rule-of-law state and established a constitutional review commission. In October 1988, Gorbachev asserted that this was the key to *perestroika*, political reforms that could be characterized as 'a legal revolution'.[119] The following month he promoted a 'socialist system of checks and balances'.

It became clear that Gorbachev was talking about something new for the Soviet Union. Increasingly, the relationship between state and law drew closer to conceptions of a genuine rule-of-law state. As the future USSR Minister of Justice Yakovlev explained in 1988:

The specific question is: what over what? The state over the law or the law over the state? Despite the fact that the law is born of the state, and has its sources in state institutions, the state nevertheless becomes truly law-based when it places the law above itself.[120]

The 'War of Laws' and 'Parade of Sovereignties' into which the Soviet Union descended exposed a world of newly anointed legislators who prided themselves on the quantity of their laws more than their quality. Too many politicians had tasked themselves with establishing not a *pravovoe gosudarstvo*, a state based on *jus*, but a *zakonnoe gosudarstvo* (i.e. another *Rechtsstaat* based solely on *lex*). Boris Yeltsin resolved his legislative impasse with a rebellious parliament by sending tanks to their assembly, the White House, in October 1993—a violent demonstration of law's tenuous foothold in a weakly legitimized transitional political environment. The purpose of Law was forgotten in the process of law-making. Conceptual confusion about *pravovoe gosudarstvo* did not wither away with the proclamation in a new constitution of the existence of a new 'federal, democratic, rule-of-law state'. Ten years after the collapse of the Soviet Union, the new Russian president Vladimir Putin would announce his reliance on a 'dictatorship of law' to restore stability and legitimacy to federal power.

---

[118] 'Cherez demokratizatsiiu—k novomu obliku sotsializma: Vstrecha v Tsentral'nom Kommitete KPSS', *Pravda* 11 May 1988, 1–2.

[119] 'Interv'iu M.S. Gorbacheva zhurnalu "Shpigel" (FRG)', *Pravda*, 24 Oct. 1988, 1–2.

[120] Quoted by Berman in Barry, 49.

A transition in *thinking* about law and legal abstractions is as important as the transition to the rule of law itself. It is unsurprising that, operating in the shell of a state built on the administrative use of law as tool and weapon,[121] inexperienced parliamentarians often resorted to instrumentalist Soviet legal habits. According to one scholar and early member of the Russian democratic opposition, '... while arguing for the rule of law or a law-based state, "democrats" saw law as a means of toppling the regime, as a tool that should have been directed mainly against their Communist opponents, while they themselves did not feel bound by what they considered to be outdated and unjust Communist laws'.[122] Soviet legal study had for years been steeped in the basic principles of Marxism-Leninism (e. g. law as an instrument of class domination), dialectical materialism (including the forecast withering away of all law and state administration) and the history of the Communist Party. All the while, Russian lawyers were starved of serious study of comparative law, constitutionalism, and federalism. The Soviet lawyer 'whether he be a convinced Marxist-Leninist or not, of whatever disposition, his concepts of law, its origins, role, and purpose, have been affected by this intellectual framework'.[123]

There is no common law tradition in Russia, and thus, crucially, no tradition of protecting individual rights through the judicial review of administrative acts.[124] There is no sense of government *under* law. Though the development of Russian law has a long and fascinating history, its course was profoundly different from either the civil law traditions of continental Europe (from which it mainly drew) or the common law traditions of

[121] Perhaps the most famous (and horrifying) expression of this Soviet view is that of the first Commissar of Justice, N. V. Krylenko: 'The court is, and still remains, the only thing it can be by its nature as an organ of the government power—a weapon for the safeguarding of the interests of a given ruling class ... A club is a primitive weapon, a rifle is a more efficient one, the most efficient is the court ... For us there is no difference between a court of law and summary justice. ... The court is an organ of State administration and as such does not differ in its nature from any other organs of administration which are designed, as the court is, to carry out one and the same governmental policy...'. Quoted in Vladimir Gsovski, *Soviet Civil Law*, 2 Vols. (Ann Arbor: University of Michigan Press, 1948), I: 241.

[122] *See* the Oxford doctoral thesis by Alexander Lukin, *'Democratic' Groups in Soviet Russia (1985–1991): A Study in Political Culture* (Faculty of Social Studies, Trinity Term 1997), 323. *See also* Alexander Lukin, *The Political Culture of the Russian 'Democrats'.* (Oxford University Press, 2000), 204–10.

[123] William E. Butler, *Soviet Law*, 2nd Ed. (London: Butterworth, 1988), 27. *See also* Harold J. Berman, *Justice in the USSR: An Interpretation of Soviet Law* (Cambridge: Harvard University Press, 1966).

[124] *See* Albert J. Schmidt, 'Soviet Civil Law as Legal History: A Chapter or A Footnote', in George Ginsburgs, Donald D. Barry, & William B. Simons, eds. *The Revival of Private Law in Central and Eastern Europe: Essays in Honor of F. J. M. Feldbrugge* (The Hague: Martinus Nijhoff, 1996), 45–62; *See also* Gsovski, I: 259. The right to judicial review of administrative action (and inaction) is now (nominally) guaranteed by the 1993 Russian Constitution, Art. 46, §2.

England, Scotland and the United States.[125] In the Russian Empire, prior to the Judicial Reform of 1864, judicial opinions were neither published nor circulated.[126] As legal experts from the Parliamentary Assembly of the Council of Europe concluded, in their report on Russian conformity with the fundamental principles required for full membership in the Council of Europe (human rights, the rule of law, and democratic pluralism): 'The courts can now be considered structurally independent from the executive, but the concept that it should in the first place be for the judiciary to protect the individuals has not yet become a reality in Russia'.[127] This opinion was little changed two years later, as noted by the Council's rapporteur:

... [T]he mentality towards the law has not yet changed. In Soviet times, laws could be completely disregarded—party politics and 'telephone justice' reigned supreme. While it cannot be said that laws are ignored as a matter of course in present times, they are disregarded if a 'better' solution to a particular problem seems to present itself. This assertion is valid for every echelon of the Russian state administration, from the President of the Federation ... down to local officials. . . . [I]t is very difficult to enforce the law through the courts. Often, a complaint against administrative abuse cannot even be brought to court, since the prosecutor's office is the competent state organ. But even when such cases are brought to court, and the court rules against the administration, the decision is sometimes not implemented due to the low standing courts and their decisions enjoy in public opinion.[128]

Russia's constitutional engineers, the 'founding fathers' of its new federalism, were consigned to struggle with a Soviet legal legacy with few comparative legal tools to guide them.[129] In the Soviet era, from the legal

[125] See e.g. A.H. (Archie) Brown, 'The Father of Russian Jurisprudence: The Legal Thought of S.E. Desnitskii', in W.E. Butler, ed. Russian Law: Historical and Political Perspectives. (Leyden: A.W. Sijthoff, 1977) (emphasizing the influence on Russian legal education of German, Scottish, and English scholarship). See, generally, W.E. Butler, Russian Law (Oxford University Press, 1999), ch. 2 & 3.

[126] William G. Wagner, 'Civil Law, Individual Rights, and Judicial Activism in Late Imperial Russia', in Peter H. Solomon, Jr., ed. Reforming Justice in Russia, 1864–1996: Power, Culture, and the Limits of Legal Order. (Armonk, NY: M.E. Sharpe, 1997), 32.

[127] Rudolf Bernhardt, Stefan Trechsel, Albert Weitzel, & Felix Ermacora, 'Report on the conformity of the legal order of the Russian Federation with Council of Europe standards', Doc. AS/Bur/Russia (1994), reprinted in 15 Human Rights Law Journal, 7 (31 Oct. 1994): 287. In fact, given the oversight of the judiciary by the executive branch Ministry of Justice for another two years (see note 132), 'structural independence from the executive' is unduly optimistic.

[128] Rudolf Bindig, 'Opinion on Russia's application for membership of the Council of Europe', Doc. 7463 (18 Jan. 1996) Opinion by the Committee on Legal Affairs and Human Rights, Parliamentary Assembly of the Council of Europe, Strasbourg. Reprinted in 17 Human Rights Law Journal 3–6 (15 Oct. 1996): 218–19.

[129] For an excellent and detailed examination of early Soviet legal concepts and 'discontinuity' with pre-Revolutionary legal thought, see Vladimir Gsovski, Soviet Civil Law, 2 Vols. (Ann Arbor: University of Michigan Press, 1948 and 1949), especially I: ch. 5–7.

nihilism of 'revolutionary legality' to the rigid formalism of the Stalinist bureaucratic state, one of the few constants in legal thought was the subordination of the judiciary, 'hierarchically inferior to parliament and to the executive, and both of these to the Communist Party'.[130] It was only with the adoption of the 1993 Constitution—in the aftermath of a violent confrontation between the executive and legislative branches of government—that judicial independence was, at least nominally, acknowledged.[131] Even then, it was not until passage of the 1996 Constitutional Law on the Judicial System that the traditional dependence of courts of general jurisdiction on the Ministry of Justice, which not only provided 'logistical support' but also was charged with the ordinary courts' 'oversight', officially came to an end.[132] This is a monumental problem for Russia if that country's leaders truly intend to pursue a programme of federalism that, by its very nature, is so steeped in, and so dependent on, fundamental respect for *jus* and not just *lex*, for Law and not just laws.[133]

This phenomenon was vividly on display in the republics and regions of Russia throughout the 1990s. In the republic of Tatarstan, for example, Soviet-trained lawyers held important seats in every constitutional commission and session of the new post-soviet parliament; their influence was felt in the constitution and laws they quickly drafted. Though lawyers were rarely influential in politics during Soviet times (when all decisions were first made by the Party and then rubber-stamped by state organs), they were repeatedly tapped as advisors, drafters, and legislators to the new Tatar republic. Kazan' State University is one of the oldest and most respected in Russia (Vladimir Ulianov [Lenin], was a distinguished expellee) and its Law Faculty one of its strongest departments. Boris Zheleznov, professor of law and a member of the Russian Academy of Scientists, served on the Constitutional Commission and other official advisory groups during the entire course of the Tatar transition. Even he is reserved about the value of service of which his fellow lawyers were capable:

I should say that we lawyers were, nevertheless, how does one say, apologists, freely or not freely, but we were apologists of all former laws and it was very difficult for lawyers to reconstruct themselves. Therefore, very often when lawyers came up into our higher organs, including the Constitutional Commission, disappointment

---

[130] Gennady M. Danilenko & William Burnham, *Law and Legal System of the Russian Federation* (Parker School of Foreign and Comparative Law, Columbia University: Juris, 1999), 58–9.

[131] *See* Arts. 10 (separation and independence of branches of government) and 120 (independence of the judiciary under law) of the 1993 Constitution.

[132] Danilenko and Burnham, 58–9.

[133] To be sure, it would be a tremendous transitional step forward were the Russian state to develop even a fundamental respect for the Rule of *Lex*.

would come because they were often not able to adapt to the new conditions, democratic conditions, and helped very little. And sometimes even, they were pulling back. Especially those lawyers who weren't able to manage to understand what was happening.[134]

Apparatchiks and former Party officials could scarcely be said to have been much more open to or capable of the sort of profound conceptual changes a genuine *pravovoe gosudarstvo* (rule-of-law state) required. In the transition period in Tatarstan, most of them retained their government posts while simply dropping their Party memberships. All of the political actors involved repeatedly evinced profound confusion about the concepts fundamental to the work they had taken upon themselves: sovereignty, self-determination, federalism, etc. This confusion was sometimes deliberate and sometimes genuine. Unfortunately, during a period of time when the rules of the political game were very much in flux, vagueness for whatever reason could and often did lead to serious problems with lasting legacies. The result is that many fundamental questions have been left unanswered, only deferred. And as questions mount, they have a tendency to turn into problems. Issues of the supremacy of laws, judicial review, nullification, and sovereignty have all remained unresolved problems in Russia. These issues, and the conceptual battles that have plagued attempts at their resolution, are recurring themes throughout this book.

3. APPLICATIONS

If federalism is so complex; if it requires such complicated notions of citizenship; if it is so costly, inefficient and difficult to sustain; the obvious question is, why bother to construct a federal system? Federal arrangements traditionally offer small polities the freedom to preserve their own distinctive self-government while offering the economic and defensive advantages of open internal borders, free trade, and a larger population with expanded territory. Federalism appeals to states struggling with various forms of internal disharmony, but which nevertheless value diversity within a more unitary framework. From the opposite perspective, minorities may see federalization as the only available means to cultural self-preservation short of attempts at secession. There is seldom a single motivation; a variety of factors often intermingle and co-determine the prospects for federalism.

As the materials in this chapter suggest, there are also a variety of ways in which the philosophy of federalism has been adopted into practical

---

[134] Boris L. Zheleznov, personal interview, Law Faculty, Kazan' State University, 6 June 1997.

approaches to government. Leagues, associations, confederations, federations, federacies, and other forms of government all involve some measure
of the different requirements of federalism (bifurcated government, written
constitutions, jurisdictional division and common consensus) and present
different problems of sovereignty, democracy, and law. Reconsider the original, simple diagram (Figure 2.1) presented at the start of this chapter, this
time complicated in a slightly different fashion than before (see Figure 2.3).
As this diagram demonstrates, the continuum of approaches to state structures that could reasonably be termed federal is not always clear. There is
considerable debate, for example, over the appropriate characterization of
the European Union: has its system been sufficiently constitutionalized to be
considered confederal (or even *federal*)? Even within the category 'federation'
there may be several alternative analytical approaches to distinguish state
systems (e. g. over-representation in the upper chamber). Because of the
emphasis placed in this work on constitutional structures, institutional asymmetry is the distinguishing device I have chosen. As the diagram shows, states
that are multinational and multilingual (Spain, India, etc.) tend to develop
federal systems that institutionalize higher degrees of asymmetry than
countries without those potential cleavages.[135]

Figure 2.3.   The Federal Continuum: Where does Russia Fit?

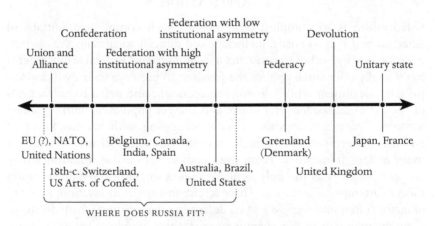

[135] I am in the intellectual debt of Professor Alfred Stepan for this observation. For an excellent
analysis of some of these issues in comparative perspective and with specific reference to Russia, *see*
Alfred Stepan, 'Russian Federalism in Comparative Perspective', 16 *Post-Soviet Affairs*, 2 (2000).

Many approaches to federal government are not only possible but prevalent in the world today. They may also overlap, with one state involved in federal relations on several different levels. The United States of America, for example, is a federation of fifty states, but it also maintains special links with Puerto Rico and the Northern Marianas islands, is involved in associated state relationships with the Marshall Islands, Republic of Palau, and the Federated States of Micronesia (as its name implies, itself a federation), and possesses numerous special territorial agreements with Native American nations displaced on to reservations but increasingly accorded greater autonomy. To suggest that the only expression of federalism is territorial federation is of little help in interpreting the myriad combinations possible in the application of federalism.

It is easy enough to discern the extremes of the continuum depicted in Figure 2.3. Independent states, attributed the highest degree of sovereignty, are confined only within the bounds of international law and are free to enter into, and exit from, international organizations. As states voluntarily increase the degree of sovereign authority they are willing to share with other states for the greater economic, military or political good, unions, and alliances of varying strictures are created. At the other extreme, as governmental units are increasingly subordinated to another authority, that unit appears more and more to be part of a unified state, outside the bounds of international law. Two types of systems, on either side of federation in Figure 2.3, are of particular salience to the Russian case. It is worth discussing confederation and one federation with a high level of institutional asymmetry, Spain, in more detail; comparison to these alternative approaches to federalism will be made in later chapters.

3.1 Confederation

'Confederation' has been discussed intermittently throughout this chapter. Only a brief word is necessary here to mark this category as one of particular interest for comparative analysis of Russian federalism. The most pronounced difference between a confederation and a federation rests in their opposite approaches to sovereignty. The American experience with confederation—ultimately an unsuccessful one—is instructive. The U.S. Constitution of 1789 was a reaction to the Articles of Confederation of 1781, virtually reversing the presumption for state sovereignty exhibited in that document, as Table 2.3 suggests. The Articles of Confederation explicitly confirm the sovereignty (and independence) of its member-units; the Constitution does not refer to state sovereignty anywhere in the document. The Articles make clear that, other than through an 'express' delegation of

Table 2.3 Jurisdictional Presumptions: Confederations and Federations

Articles of Confederation (Article II)	U.S. Constitution (X Amendment)
Each state retains its sovereignty, freedom, and independence, and every power, jurisdiction and right, which is not by this confederation expressly delegated to the United States, in Congress assembled.	The powers not delegated to the United States by the Constitution, nor prohibited by it to the States, are reserved to the States respectively, or to the people.

powers to the general government, the default holder of authority is the individual state unit; the federal Constitution ultimately adopted is not only more circumspect (the restrictive word 'express' is conspicuously absent), but specifically denies its member-states powers normally considered hallmarks of sovereignty: the restrictions found in Article I, Section 10, include prohibitions on the states from unilaterally entering into treaties, alliances, confederations, or any agreement or compact with another state or foreign power. The states are forbidden to coin money or lay any duties on imports or exports. And while the enumerated powers of federal (national) government, and the powers prohibited the state governments, do not render these two separate authorities juridically unequal, the states are in a weaker relationship *vis-à-vis* the federal government than under the Articles of Confederation. The extraordinary shift accomplished by the Tenth Amendment reserves to the states *only* that which is not either enumerated in the powers of the federal government (quite substantial powers) *and* not prohibited to the powers of the states (equally substantial).

Moving away from the American model, this change in emphasis does not exhaust the possible approaches that range in a continuum between confederation and federation. As Laurence Tribe observes, 'it is more than a logical possibility—it is a reality in some legal systems with a "federal" character—that *nothing* is retained apart from that which is expressly reserved, or that some of what is retained is *simultaneously* surrendered'.[136] The Russian experience has proven the truth of this statement, both by showing the range of possibilities between confederation and federation, and the range of extremes. At their most recalcitrant, the political elites of some constituent units of the Russian Federation have propounded philosophies of separateness and autonomy that make the Articles of Confederation look tame. Federal officials in Moscow have, likewise, sometimes expected a deference from constituent units that would make the existence of concurrent or reserved powers meaningless.

[136] Laurence H. Tribe, *American Constitutional Law*, 3rd Ed. (New York: Foundation Press, 2000), 904, note 3.

3.2 Spain

The transition to democracy in post-Franco Spain is a good example of a polity strongly affected by the emergence of federal principles in what Linz and Stepan describe as a case of negotiated and pacted democratic transition.[137] The Spanish case provides some important insights into issues of bilateralism, the rule of law, constitutional asymmetry, and *ad hoc* centre-periphery relations. All of these issues in Russia became problems that plagued Boris Yeltsin's entire presidency, and required the immediate attention of his successor, Vladimir Putin (see Chapter Six).

The Spanish transition to democracy was, in some ways, also a federal transition of sorts. In short, the Spanish approach of creating autonomous communities (*autonomías*) was a response to pressure from nationalists in the Basque Country and Catalonia in the late 1970s. The new communities that were formed won the right to provide a variety of local self-government functions.[138] Autonomous communities all maintain unicameral legislatures based on proportional representation and are headed by a prime minister. The boundaries of autonomous communities overlap part or all of (sometimes more than one) pre-existing provinces, the traditional political-administrative unit of representation (of which there are fifty) akin to French *départements*.[139] Bilateral negotiations followed by ratification procedures that included both provincial and all-Spain institutions at several stages was the process of choice by which the Spanish government established each autonomy. A fast-track for autonomy was established by the 1978 constitution for certain regions (Galicia, Catalonia, and the Basque Country), while most others followed a more ponderous process of creation.

The Russian Federation's experiment with what became known as 'bilateral treaties' between the federal centre and many of its constituent units is a highly unusual, but not unique feature, in federal systems. In comparison with the Russian Federation, the most important aspect of the Spanish approach was the role of the new constitution in this process: recognition of the right to pursue the status of an *autonomía* was contingent on the prior approval of the constitution for all of Spain. The statutes (*Estatutos*) that established an autonomous community were, as Juan Linz observed, 'not technically part of the constitution, . . . [but] derived from it and therefore

---

[137] Linz & Stepan, *Problems* . . . , 87, 111.

[138] See Art. 148–150 of the Constitution. Albert P. Blaustein & Gisbert H. Flanz, eds. *Constitutions of the Countries of the World: Spain* (Dobbs Ferry, NY: Oceana, 1997), 78.

[139] Robert Agranoff and Juan Antonio Ramos Gallarin, 'Toward Federal Democracy in Spain: An Examination of Inter-governmental Relations', 27 *Publius*, 4 (1997): 3.

occupy an important position in the Spanish political system'.[140] Only *after* the establishment of the constitution, and only *through* constitutionally enshrined procedures, could the process begin in earnest. This meant that, for most interest groups in Spain, the 'rules of the game' were in place before autonomy statutes could be negotiated. Catalonia, the Basque Country and Galicia—where political tensions initiated this approach—did not exactly follow this pattern, although the constitutionalization of the process was no less important in those regions. Negotiations entrenched the notion that autonomization could only occur via a constitutionally accepted process, meaning the Spanish constitution must be approved first. Catalonia, for example, has repeatedly expressed its location in the power matrix (eschewing even the word 'federalism') as one of *primus inter pares*.[141]

The Spanish approach was a constitutionally entrenched, multilateral process, adopted and accepted (even if reluctantly) by all parties.[142] The Spanish constitution set out a multi-step process for the creation of an autonomous community (i.e. devolution of asymmetrical power to a region). This process often (although not always) began with referendums in the provinces to be affected by the creation of a new *autonomía*, the drafting of a self-government statute by the territory's deputies and senators convened in an assembly, consensus with a Constitutional Commission of the *Cortes* on the draft, another referendum involving all provinces affected by the new statute, with a majority *in each province concerned* required for approval, and finally, a plenary session of both chambers of the *Cortes Generales* voting for ratification.[143] There are now seventeen autonomous communities spanning fifty Spanish provinces.[144]

This process integrates the notion that, as nationals inhabiting a national homeland, local self-government is a basic right, while at the same time acknowledging the obvious impact of such a change to the *status quo* to

---

[140] Juan J. Linz, 'Spanish Democracy and the Estado de las Autonomias', in R.A. Goldman, A. Kaufman & W.A. Shambra, eds. *Forging Unity Out of Diversity: The Approaches of Eight Nations* (Washington, D.C.: American Enterprise Institute, 1989), 261.

[141] For this insight, I am grateful to Alfred Stepan.

[142] Consider the state of sentiment in the Basque Country, as Juan Linz observed: 'The approval of the Estatuto, derived from the constitution and approved by the Spanish legislature, could be considered an indirect approval of the constitution, and the initial lack of support for the constitution may be due to its approval being conditioned on the acceptance of the Estatuto. Politically, although not juridically, one could say that in Euskadi the Estatuto legitimized the constitution, while in all other regions the legitimacy of the constitution was the basis for the legitimization of the autonomous communities'. Linz, in *Forging Unity out of Diversity*, 271.

[143] *See* Art. 143 & 151 of the Constitution. Albert P. Blaustein & Gisbert H. Flanz, eds. *Constitutions of the Countries of the World: Spain* (Dobbs Ferry, NY: Oceana, 1997), 78.

[144] Robert Agranoff, 'Federal Evolution in Spain', 17 *International Political Science Review,* No. 4 (1996): 387.

neighbouring citizens. From its inception, the process of autonomization was carefully circumscribed by Spanish laws which constantly reinforced the link between autonomy statutes and the constitution from which they were derived.[145] Through clever sequencing of national and regional elections, as well as the sequencing of reform itself, Spain managed a successful transition to democracy despite the almost simultaneous intensification of national and linguistic centrifugal forces.[146] Linz and Stepan note that Spain's asymmetrical federal system in many ways *created* the space to manage problems of transition.

As explored below, the Russian variant of this approach, by comparison, labours under problems of transparency, inclusion and ratification on both the federal-republican and inter-republican levels. Russia compares unfavourably with Spain in terms of the process of regionalization, stability of the federation (in terms of federal identity, legal authority and fiscal cooperation) and the transition to democracy and the rule of law. Where the process of autonomization required legislative ratification in Spain, the Russian processes of sovereignization and treaty-negotiation were often *ad hoc* and, in the negotiation of bilateral treaties, beyond the reach of both regional and federal legislatures. In fact, rumours abounded of secret, backroom deals between executive authorities on different levels.[147] Unlike the Russian case, the Spanish transition was assisted by the involvement of courts, whose rulings were obeyed. According to Alfred Stepan, 'In the first twenty years of the Spanish Constitution (1978–1998), more than a thousand cases involving center-*autonomia* jurisdictional conflicts have gone before the Constitutional Court. To date there is not one case in which either the center or an *autonomia* has refused to accept the decision of the court'.[148] In Russia, astoundingly, the decisions of courts—when a venue for dispute resolution at all—are openly flouted, ignored, or unenforced. The Spanish case is a particularly interesting counterpoint to the 'parade of treaties' that occurred in Russia in the mid 1990s. Russia's Catalonias—and there are many—have not infrequently expressed the sentiment of *primus inter pares*, or simply let their unilateral action speak for itself.

---

[145] Juan J. Linz, in *Forging Unity Out of Diversity*, 261, 269–74, 283.

[146] Linz & Stepan, *Problems . . .*, 99–107. See also, Juan J. Linz & Alfred Stepan, 'Political Identities and Electoral Sequences: Spain, the Soviet Union, and Yugoslavia', 121 *Daedalus*, No. 2 (1992): 127.

[147] Arguably, *in camera* negotiation between political elites may be a necessary part of this process, but final approval by a democratically elected body (typically the legislature) must follow to establish the legitimacy of the end product of elite negotiations.

[148] Alfred Stepan, 'Russian Federalism in Comparative Perspective', 16 *Post-Soviet Affairs*, 2 (2000): 147.

4. WHERE DOES RUSSIA FIT?

The rest of this book is devoted to exploring the range of possible answers and problems this simple question suggests. It is far from clear that Russia neatly 'fits' any one of the categories indicated in Figure 2.3. Some elements of the new Russian federalism expose the weakness of the central government; other aspects indicate a very powerful 'super-presidential' federal executive authority. The very lexicon of the debate over federalism in Russia is a contested one: is Russian federalism based on a constitution or a treaty? Does enforcement of federal laws, collection of taxes, and protection of rights rely on the courts (federal or regional), on the 'vertical of federal executive power', or on extra-constitutional bilateral relations between savvy regional elites and the federal president forced to negotiate with them as often out of weakness as out of strength? Certainly, Russia's institutional legacy and path-dependency from its Soviet past has played a powerful role. The complicated array of constituent units of the Russian Federation, and the even more complex manner in which relations have been managed between centre and periphery as well as among regions themselves also suggests that Russian federalism is an institutional system *sui generis*. That is not to say, however, that the problems of sovereignty, democracy, and law that Russia confronts with its unique brand of federalism are themselves uniquely Russian problems.

3

Soviet 'Federalism'

A constitution is fictitious when law and reality diverge; it is not fictitious when they coincide.

Lenin, 1909

Since the Soviet Union preserves all the features of federalism, the mere fact that its federalism fails to prevent tyranny should not lead to casting it out of the class of federalisms. Rather it should lead to a re-evaluation of what federalism means and implies.

William H. Riker[1]

The Soviet Union's claims to be a democracy were not considered credible by most serious scholars. Terms like 'democratic centralism' and 'people's democracy' were deemed rhetorical. The reality of the Soviet system belied any such assertions found in its constitutions or declared by its leaders. The same scepticism was far less common when it came to Soviet claims to be a federal system. 'The federalism of the Soviet Union', wrote William Riker, '... is as clearly the product of the two conditions [of the federal bargain] as are the United States and German federalisms'.[2] Riker employed a continuum of centralization in federal systems, by which he expressed the range of policy-issues on which a central government could make decisions independent of consultations with constituent units of the federation. The USSR, though at the maximum extreme of this continuum, maintained a 'unique form of federalism'.[3] Riker was not alone among scholars who, although quick to puncture sham claims to democracy, accepted at face value the 'federal' form of Soviet autocracy.

These are extraordinary assertions. They have also had an extraordinary impact on scholarship in this area. This chapter examines why this uncritical acceptance of federal form as a proxy for federal content presents serious problems for analysis of both Soviet and post-Soviet institutions and politics.

---

[1] William H. Riker, *Federalism: Origin, Operation, Significance* (Boston: Little, Brown, 1964), 40.
[2] Riker, *Federalism: Origin, . . .* , 38.
[3] William H. Riker, 'Federalism', in Fred I. Greenstein & Nelson W. Polsby, eds. *Handbook of Political Science: Vol. 5. Governmental Institutions and Processes* (Reading, MA: Addison-Wesley, 1975), 97, 102.

Demands for self-rule, decentralization, and even various forms of federal autonomy were common to turn-of-the-century political parties and intelligentsia as well as national minorities that occupied the physical and social periphery of the Russian Empire.[4] The Bolshevik faction of the Russian Social Democratic Labour Party, however, initially rejected federalism as contrary to the dialectics of history and the faction's own global vision. Lenin promised: 'Marxists will never, under any circumstances, advocate either the federal principle or decentralisation. The great centralised state is a tremendous historical step forward ... and only *via* such a state (*inseparably* connected with capitalism) can there be any road to socialism.'[5] However, influenced by the work of Austro-Marxists Otto Bauer, Karl Renner and others, and by the fact that virtually all contemporary major political parties had issued solutions to 'the national question', Lenin made a tactical reversal in support of political self-determination of peoples, a concept he soon recognized had enormous propaganda potential. Lenin cleverly promoted *proletarian* self-determination, achievable only via the dictatorship of the proletariat in the form of the Russian Communist Party. The right to secede and form independent states was granted, contingent on its prudent exercise: 'The party of the proletariat must decide the latter question quite independently in each particular case from the standpoint of the interests of the social development as a whole and of the interests of the class struggle of the proletariat for socialism'.[6] As Stalin stated with regard to the North Caucasus in 1920: 'Autonomy means not separation, but a union of the self-ruling mountain peoples with the people of Russia'.[7]

This Orwellian redefinition of concepts is one far-reaching aspect of the Soviet 'federal' legacy: autonomy, sovereignty, and self-determination took on very different meanings when used by Soviet leaders. Autonomy meant unification, not independence! Seventy-five years later, this rhetorical amphiboly was still useful. 'Take all the sovereignty you can swallow', Yeltsin's exhortation to regional politicians in the hot summer of 1990,[8] was the rhetorical progeny of Lenin's 'Release from the prison house of nations'.

[4] Richard Pipes, *The Formation of the Soviet Union—Communism and Nationalism: 1917–1923* (Cambridge: Harvard University Press, 1964), 28, 77.
[5] V.I. Lenin, 'Kriticheskie zametki po natsional'nomu voprosu' (1913) *Polnoe sobranie sochinenie*, Vol. 24 (Moskva: Gosudarstvennoe izdatel'stvo politicheskoi literatury, 1961), 144.
[6] 'Resolution of April 24–29 (May 7–12), 1917 "On the National Question"' in Zigurds L. Zile, *Ideas and Forces in Soviet Legal History: A Reader on the Soviet State and Law* (Oxford University Press, 1992), 78–9.
[7] Pipes, 248.
[8] The slight variations the reader will note in the wording of this famous phrase are due to Yeltsin's own varying uses of it and to different translations. When I use the quotation broadly—without citation—I adopt this, the most popular, version. When the exact wording matters (as in later chapters), I make a direct citation.

Once in power, Yeltsin discovered what problems such rhetoric created, especially when deprived of the terroristic methods of his Soviet predecessors.

1. FORMATION: LENIN'S CONSTITUTIONS

Following the Revolution, the old Bolshevik approach of fomenting dissent in the Russian Empire conflicted with the new task of building a socialist state from which to launch world revolution. A federation of peoples, previously rejected as regressively nationalistic, was now considered a transitional tactic. Lenin's first official statements supporting federalism, after years of opposition, were made in January 1918; in essence, the new policy was lifted directly from the Socialist Revolutionary Party. Ukraine and Russia were joined by Bolshevik fiat, and considerable violence, into a new 'federation': the Soviet Russian Republic. Armed force was required after the Ukrainian *Rada* sought to realize pre-Revolution promises of autonomy and resisted Ukrainian 'independence' under Russian Bolshevik leaders. The *Rada* leaders' attempts to remain in control exposed the contradictions of Soviet federalism for the first time.[9] It is worth pausing to note how different these origins of the Soviet state were to the precondition that Riker rightly identified for federal systems: willingness among respective government leaders to conclude a mutually beneficial bargain of union.[10] Forceful annexation is, of course, anathema to the Rikerian voluntary federal bargain. Riker glossed over the bloody origins of Soviet 'federalism' by asserting that national elites 'gladly accepted the bribe of federalism' in the face of the military threat of the Red Army.[11] Considering that this threat was the Civil War, caused by the lack of recognition by these governments and large sectors of the population of the legitimacy of the Soviet takeover, it seems strange to imagine any voluntary bargain in the grip of the Red Terror.

[9] Pipes, 115–48. For propaganda, *see* 'Resolution on the Occasion of the Proclamation of Ukrainian Independence April 3, 1918'. Zile, 78.

[10] Riker, *Federalism: Origin*, . . . , 11–12.

[11] Riker, *Federalism: Origin*, . . . , 39. Riker euphemistically notes that ruling elites in the Caucasus and elsewhere were 'persuaded' to join with Russia. When leaders of national and religious movements sought to implement self-rule, they were purged by Soviet central authorities who then installed more sympathetic local elites. The republics of Armenia, Azerbaijan, and Georgia were created in 1920–1 to crush forces opposing the Soviet regime, then unified in 1922 as the Transcaucasian Socialist Federated Soviet Republic. John N. Hazard, 'Codification of Soviet Nationalities Policies', in Henry R. Huttenbach, ed. *Soviet Nationalities Policies: Ruling Ethnic Groups in the USSR* (London: Mansell, 1990), 51.

Two distinctive aspects of Soviet 'federalism' appeared early: fusion of party and state institutions, and the manipulation of ethnic groups to establish central control over distant regions. First, the distinction between the growing Party apparatus and the state bureaucracy blurred as the Soviet state emerged from the crucible of what became known as 'War Communism'. The establishment of the world's first party-state revealed the deeply centralist assumptions behind the Bolshevik theory of federalism: there were many Soviet republics, but there could be only one Communist Party to rule them. Although Ukraine, Latvia, Lithuania, and Belorussia were accepted as separate Soviet republics, separate national communist parties were categorically rejected. Second, elites from ethnic minorities in these and much smaller groups were encouraged to serve in new Soviet institutions, part of the programme of nativization (*korenizatsiia*)— Lenin's surprisingly successful promotion of indigenous languages and local customs. Such an indigenous cadre created what Philip Roeder calls an 'institutionalised monopoly on the public expression of ethnic identity', and therefore on the ethnic group itself.[12] The seeds were planted for the institutionalized dominance of titular ethnic groups in state regional structures.

As will be argued in later chapters, years of such propaganda decreased the range of options available to ethnic republics after the collapse of the Soviet Union and elevated to the point of irresistability the idea of state sovereignty founded on a particular ethnic group. There are serious risks to minority rights and democracy inherent in what Robert Hayden calls constitutional nationalism, which 'envisions a state in which sovereignty resides with a particular nation (*narod*)' and which privileges that group above others in different ways.[13] Without making a statement about the beginnings or growth of nationalism in general across the range of Soviet nationalities, it can be said that the origins of the conceptual, legal and institutional structures associated with *constitutional* nationalism can be traced to these beginnings. By the early 1920s, seventeen republics and oblasts within the Russian Soviet Federated Socialist Republic (RSFSR) declared themselves to be, and thus acquired the prefix, *autonomous*. These units were in addition to those higher-level soviet republics (e. g. Ukraine and Belorussia) which had already united with Soviet Russia.

[12] Philip G. Roeder 'Soviet Federalism and Ethnic Mobilization', 43 *World Politics*, 2 (1991): 205.

[13] Robert M. Hayden, 51 'Constitutional Nationalism in the Formerly Yugoslav Republics', *Slavic Review*, 4 (1992): 655–6.

1.1 The Constitution of the Russian Soviet Federated Socialist Republic

Virtually every administrative post in the regime soon required the approval of the powerful People's Commissariat of Nationalities (*Narkomnats*) and its first Commissar—Joseph Stalin.[14] The Commissariat's portfolio included the maintenance of Soviet power in autonomous republics and supervision of constitutions, decrees, and laws.[15] *Narkomnats* had a pernicious effect on the new federation's structure. A constitutional commission for the RSFSR, headed by Yakov Sverdlov and Stalin (perhaps simply speaking for Lenin), rejected proposals to establish a federation based on anything other than national divisions.[16] A member of the Commissariat of Justice, Mikhail Reisner, had vigorously advocated a federation of trade unions and other socioeconomic groups in a non-territorial manner reminiscent of the old Bauer–Renner proposals. His warning against 'hidden centralism under the cover of a federal structure', was rejected by Stalin, who demanded a national-based structure.[17]

The new Constitution established a 'free union of free nations', joined in federation (Art. 2). This extremely ideological document, written at a time when a prevailing legal nihilism inspired the destruction of the tsarist judicial system, could be called 'anti-law' in that it categorically rejected legal principles of property on which the law (in Russia, as in most of Europe) had for centuries been based.[18] The document contained no provisions for the resolution of disputes between federal authority and different republics. Formal institutions were proclaimed, but not necessary infrastructure or procedures. Most of the country was in administrative chaos and the new constitution did little to alter that condition.[19] This was a federation in name only. The powers of the central authority were enormous and unchecked (cf. Arts. 49 and 81); regional institutions were administrative appendages of the centre.

---

[14] Rudolf Schlesinger, *The Nationalities Problem and Soviet Administration: Selected Readings on the Development of Soviet Nationalities Policies* (London: Routledge, 1956), 33.

[15] Robert Conquest, ed. *Soviet Nationalities Policy in Practice* (London: Bodley Head, 1967), 34.

[16] A January 1918 resolution 'On the Federal Institutions of the Russian Republic', ordered the writing of a constitution. A drafting commission was established in April. The constitution was completed by July.

[17] Pipes, 111–12.

[18] Aryeh L. Unger, *Constitutional Development in the USSR: A Guide to the Soviet Constitutions* (New York: Pica Press, 1981), 9.

[19] Schlesinger, 253–4. John N. Hazard, William E. Butler, & Peter B. Maggs argue that the Russian Republic was called a federation for no greater reason than 'to dramatize the relationship' with the small nations the Bolsheviks were intent to tie to their Russian centre. John N. Hazard, William E. Butler, & Peter B. Maggs, *The Soviet Legal System*, 3rd Ed. (Dobbs Ferry, NY: Oceana, 1977), 36.

The final draft was never intended to withstand close legal scrutiny (there is no mention in the document of *any* judicial institutions) nor was its aim long-term institution-building (Art. 9 proclaimed the constitution to be '...designed for the present transition period...'.). The state was expected to wither away. From the perspective of federalism, its great legal innovation was the notion of 'dual subordination:' each executive body was accountable both to its electorate and to the executive body immediately above it in the hierarchy of democratic centralism (Arts. 61 and 62). As Aryeh Unger remarks: 'It need hardly be emphasized that while centralism might conceivably be reconciled with democracy it was entirely incompatible with local autonomy. The administrative device of "dual subordination" obscured this contradiction but did not resolve it. By coupling "horizontal" with "vertical" subordination it seemed to grant local authorities a measure of control over local affairs; by the same token, however, it ensured that no part of such control was truly autonomous'.[20] The reader would be right to note how such a concept resonates with the 'vertical of federal executive power' asserted (although rapidly softened) by President Vladimir Putin more than eighty years later (the subject of Chapter Eight).

1.2 The Constitution of the Union of Soviet Socialist Republics

Any nominal federalism expressed in the RSFSR constitution was lost as the regime was consolidated. As noted above, social movements demanding genuine self-rule were crushed and their leaders executed or exiled. Concrete planning for the Union of Soviet Socialist Republics began in August 1922 in a special commission chaired by Stalin. A Treaty of Union was adopted in December joining the RSFSR, Ukraine, Belorussia, and the Transcaucasian SFSR. This was the basis for the constitution issued by decree of the Central Executive Committee on 6 July 1923 and given final ratification ten days after the death of Lenin, on 31 January 1924 at the Second All-Union Congress of Soviets.

The constitution which emerged from this treaty, establishing the Union of Soviet Socialist Republics, was drafted in a single week by a subcommittee chaired by the Commissar of Foreign Affairs, and then quickly passed to Stalin and Lenin. The document established national-territorial units for only a fraction of the 104 officially recognized nationalities. These units were arranged hierarchically (union republic, autonomous republic, autonomous region), implicitly rejecting the principle of equality for all ethnic groups.

[20] Unger, 19.

Only the top-tiered union republics were constitutionally guaranteed the right to secession (Art. 4), a sham promise in the light of other articles (e. g. Art. 6). The framers of this constitution did not expect it to last very long. This was still a heady, ideological atmosphere: constitutions, laws, and states were anticipated soon to whither away.[21]

This new constitution can no more be interpreted to establish a federal system than the 'federal' constitution of the preceding RSFSR. Alongside the increasing indistinguishability between Party and State, the powers given the centre made the USSR the most centralized state on earth. The first article conferred upon the centre not only the power to tax and form a state budget but the power to authorize taxes for the budgets of the constituent republics, establish and control a central economic plan for the entire economy (including location of industry), unilaterally annul republican activity deemed contrary to the constitution, control migration, and regulate the alteration of internal state boundaries. Article 20 granted the Central Executive Committee the right to suspend or annul the actions of all lower-level congresses, executive committees and other organs *without the condition of alleged unconstitutionality or any other condition or check*. Article 29 declared the Central Executive Committee's Presidium to be the highest administrative, legislative, and executive organ of power. This body had powers of suspension and annulment over every other institution (Art. 31). Union republics, to the extent that they could freely exercise the rights promised them, were favoured over autonomous republics in terms of representation and internal decision-making powers.

Lenin and Stalin increasingly disagreed about the structure of this Union. The most basic disagreement concerned the distinction between the autonomous republics already incorporated within the RSFSR and the soviet republics joined by various separate treaties to the new USSR, thereby enjoying higher institutional status. In one of the first drafts to emerge from his commission, Stalin envisioned the incorporation of the soviet socialist republics (SSRs) of Ukraine, Belorussia, Georgia, Armenia, and Azerbaijan as lower-level autonomous republics (ASSRs). This was intended both to end the accumulated piecemeal collection of treaties and to strengthen an already highly centralized structure. In response, Georgian, Bashkir, and Tatar representatives to the 12th Party Congress in April 1923 argued that the ASSRs should be permitted to secede from the RSFSR and rejoin the union independently. Others argued that only a select number of union

---

[21] Raymond Pearson, 'The Historical Background to Soviet Federalism', in Alastair McAuley, ed. *Soviet Federalism, Nationalism and Economic Decentralisation* (Leicester: Leicester University Press, 1991), 26–30.

republics (SSRs) should have deputies in the Council of Nationalities in the first place. Stalin rejected both proposals.[22]

Stalin began to enact his own changes, however, even as the draft was distributed for comment, enraging nearly every national group. Lenin, who came sick, late, and ill-informed upon Stalin's 'autonomization plan' rejected it as tactically flawed. In the end, Lenin marshalled his remaining authority to preserve the constitutional distinction between units. As Pipes concludes: 'It is likely that had he [Lenin] not suffered a nearly fatal stroke in March 1923 the final structure of the Soviet Union would have been quite different from that which Stalin ultimately gave it'.[23]

2. SYSTEMATIZATION: STALIN'S CONSTITUTION

Stalin's totalitarianism required a centralized bureaucracy with enormous powers, but one with sufficiently rigid and calcified command structures to afford complete control (and complete protection) to its increasingly para-noid creator. After more than a decade of volatile mass mobilization, but with the apex of Stalin's bloody purges still to come, Stalin's desire for stability in the aftermath of his massive industrialization and collectivization campaigns led to the drafting of a new constitution in 1936. Combined with the purging of the top tier of ethnic elites to 'unmask and liquidate' national deviations, the result further weakened once-promised federal powers by removing regional authority over natural resources, heavy industry, and fiscal planning.

The anarchy and nihilism of revolutionary legality now ossified into an increasingly conservative, legalistic, and bureaucratic regime. While the new constitution claimed to guarantee property rights and long lists of political freedoms, these were abridged by the qualification that they be exercised solely in the interests of workers and in order to strengthen the socialist system (Art. 125). It also noted, for the first time by name, the vanguard role of the Communist Party as the core of all state and social organizations (Art. 126). From the point of view of federal structure, the new constitution strengthened the existing façade while ignoring its ever-weakening founda-tions. The number of soviet socialist republics increased from six to eleven as Central Asia was divided into SSRs. The changes in the powers specifically accorded these republics were cosmetic at best. Each SSR had rights to its

---

[22] Robert Conquest, *The Nation Killers: The Soviet Deportation of Nationalities* (London: Mac-millan, 1970), 37–44.
[23] Pipes, 276.

own constitution (Arts. 16 and 60), to secession (Art. 17), and to inviolable borders (Art. 18). But these were subordinated to the principle of dual subordination (Art. 101), the total primacy of all-union legislation (Art. 20), and the unilateral central power to carve out new territories and autonomous republics in the union (Art. 14). The constitution announced that SSR sovereignty was limited within the bounds set by Article 14, the 23 sub-clauses of which stripped republics of virtually all sovereignty, including jurisdiction over civil and criminal codes, transportation, all aspects of fiscal and monetary policy, and the establishment of 'basic principles' for essentially everything else.

If the real and imagined powers of union republics (SSRs) had been denuded in the new constitution, autonomous republics (ASSRs) were weakened even more. The equivalency of representation possessed by both types of republics was terminated under Article 35: SSRs were granted twenty-five deputies in the Council of Nationalities, but ASSRs were permitted only eleven deputies, and still fewer were granted to autonomous regions (five) and national areas (one). The five articles devoted to ASSRs listed no specific rights or powers; even union republics, following in the logic of dual subordination, were given the right to suspend or annul actions of commissars and executive committees of these now officially second-class autonomous republics (Art. 82).

The deportation of entire peoples in 1941 and 1943–4 exposed the horrors possible in such a 'federal' system. In retaliation for alleged Nazi collaboration, the Chechen-Ingush, Kalmyk, Crimean Tatar, and Volga German autonomous republics were literally erased from Soviet maps: territorial-administrative borders of neighbouring units were redrawn and the ethnic populations of these regions, in a matter of days, exterminated or exiled to remote regions in Siberia and Kazakhstan.[24] As a constitutional formality, following a speech by Vyshinsky to the USSR Supreme Soviet in February 1947, Article 22 of the Constitution was retroactively amended to remove all reference to the former ASSRs. Their representatives to the Soviet of Nationalities vanished, as did citations in encyclopaedias and other publications.[25]

Stalin's death in 1953 led to a counter-movement that first haltingly ventured criticism of his cult of personality and then sought to revitalize the Soviet experiment *sans* brutal Stalinist methods. However, there would

---

[24] The territory of these former ASSRs was partitioned among the Georgian SSR, North Ossetian and Daghestan ASSRs, the provinces of Saratov, Stalingrad and Rostov, and Stavropol territory. A Kabardin ASSR and the provinces of Astrakhan and Grozny were created from scratch, also to fill the void.

[25] Conquest, 67–83.

be no Khrushchev Constitution, only ill-fated and relatively short-lived attempts at constitutional amendment and structural revision of the state bureaucracy. Khrushchev began a shift towards decentralization shortly after his secret speech to the Twentieth Party Congress in February 1956, transferring a number of enterprises from federal to republican control. At the Twenty-second Party Congress in 1961 Khrushchev softened the official doctrine on nationalities, contending that a dialectic *sblizheniia* (drawing together) would allow national cultures to flourish while a *sliyanie* (merging) would create Soviet unity. Declaring the equality of all nations in the USSR, the programme noted that internal borders between Union republics were 'increasingly losing their former significance'.[26] The programme suggested the increasing obsolescence of federal structures as the Soviet Union reached the final stage of history.

One year after Khrushchev's secret speech, the constitution was amended. Notable from the point of view of federal affairs were the laws and amendments enacted on 11 February 1957.[27] Articles in the constitution on state structure were revised to shift authority for regional and territorial-administrative structures to the jurisdiction of the union republics (Art. 28, 1957). Non-autonomous regions were deleted from the lists by one law, while another law began the process of reinstating and renaming regions for some of the now rehabilitated exiled nationalities (e.g. the Chechen-Ingush ASSR; the Kabardin ASSR again became the Kabardino-Balkar ASSR).[28] Khrushchev also announced a complete ministerial restructuring, creating 105 economic regions (overseen by Councils of Regional Economy, *Sovnarkhozy*), and eliminating twenty-five central ministries. By edict of the Supreme Soviet, the federal Ministry of Justice already had been abolished, in May 1956 'to eliminate excessive centralization in guidance of the work of the courts and legal institutions of the republics and to strengthen the role of the latter'. Ministries of Justice in the republics were abolished in 1960 and their powers transferred to supreme courts and new juridical commissions of the Council of Ministers in each republic.[29] The result, however, was often

---

[26] Programma kommunisticheskoi partii sovetskogo soiuza (XXII S''ezda KPSS), 'IV. Zadachi partii v oblasti natsional'nykh otnoshenii', *Kommunist*, No. 16 (1961): 84.

[27] E.g. 'Ob otnoshenii k vedeniiu soiuznykh respublik zakonodatel'stva ob ustroistve sudov soiuznikh respublik, priniatiia grazhdanskogo, ugolovnogo i protsessual'nykh kodeksov' and 'Ob otnoshenii k vedeniiu soiuznykh respublik razresheniia voprosov oblastnogo, kraevogo administrativno-territorial'nogo ustroistva' zakony ot 11 fevralia 1957 g. (Vedomosti Verkhovnogo Soveta SSSR, 1957 g., No. 4), in *Sbornik zakonov SSSR i ukazov Prezidiuma Verkhovnogo Soveta SSSR 1938–1961g.* (Moskva: Izdatel'stvo, 'Izvestiia Sovetov Deputatov Trudiashchikhsiia SSSR', 1961), 42–3.

[28] No longer anticipating the fall of Finland to communism, the Karelo-Finnish SSR reverted to the status of the Karelian ASSR earlier that summer.

[29] John N. Hazard, 'Statutory Recognition of Nationality Differences in the USSR', in Edward Allworth, ed. *Soviet Nationality Problems* (New York: Columbia University Press, 1971), 90.

far from genuine decentralization. The Fundamentals of Legislation enacted in 1958 and subsequent conferences in Moscow for 'guidance' of republican legal experts left little room for regional innovation; most codes were still virtual duplicates of one another.

The Thaw, none the less, freed legal theorists from the silence into which Stalinism had frozen them, during which time little if anything of substance had been written on the subject.[30] Publication in the Spring of 1956 of Lenin's (previously suppressed) criticisms of Stalin's 'autonomizing' and chauvinism opened the dispute to greater analysis. The Institutes of State and Law, General History, and Marxism-Leninism were all internally divided by these changes. Everything from Lenin's federal convictions to the virtues of republican constitutions and 'bills of rights' were subject to debate.[31] Some academics even suggested that the time had come for the 'unification' of soviet republics; the federal structure, having served its purpose, could 'fall away' as Lenin had predicted.[32]

Forswearing Stalin's terroristic methods and dismantling his controlling bureaucracy deprived Khrushchev of the most effective tool of the dictatorship of the proletariat. At the same time, his emphasis on decentralization re-opened ethnic agendas that had first been sparked by Bolshevik agitation, then frozen by central domination. Systems of local patronage grew less dependent on Moscow and, consequently, less obsequious. The more Khrushchev allowed for indirect rule, the more patronage, nepotism, and corruption flourished. Ethnic elites became more outspoken in the pursuit of their own agendas. At its most extreme, such localism resulted in the growth of national 'mafias' within the SSR and ASSR Party and state apparatuses, initially left alone provided that they delivered stability and economic growth. As Ronald Suny observed, 'The perverse result of the end of terror and centralization was the strengthening of already powerful ethno-political machines that ripped off the state economic sector, patronised the "second economy", and satisfied significant parts of the local population who either benefited from the spoils system or enjoyed the usually freer way of life in their homelands'.[33]

Under Khrushchev, many national leaders who overstepped these relatively lenient new policies were purged from their positions.[34] Studies have

[30] Hazard in Allworth, 89–90.
[31] See Grey Hodnett 'The Debate over Soviet Federalism', 18 Soviet Studies, 4 (Apr. 1967), 458–81.
[32] See, e.g., P.G. Semenov, 'Programma KPSS o razvitii sovetskikh natsional'no-gosudarstven-nykh otnoshenii', Sovetskoe gosudarstvo i pravo, No. 12 (1961): 24.
[33] Ronald Suny, 'State, Civil Society and Ethnic Cultural Consolidation . . .', 31.
[34] Philip Roeder believes the removal from office of more than a dozen SSR first secretaries since 1960 can be traced to 'either their own endorsement of primordial agendas or their

shown the strong influence, even at the height of the Thaw, of the practice of positioning an ethnic Russian as second secretary in an ethnic republic as a counterweight to the more prominent first secretary, usually a member of the titular nationality. Areas perceived as particularly prone to nationalist outbreaks often had experienced Russian Party members imposed in both positions.[35] On the other hand, those republican elites who learned to adapt to the new rules of the political game certainly benefited from the patronage networks which grew under Khrushchev's relative leniency, despite these constraints. The behaviour exhibited by post-Soviet republican elites could reasonably be traced to skills learned during and after the Thaw. As will be discussed in later chapters, many republican presidents, parliamentary chairmen and other high-level elites started their nomenklatura careers not long after this time.

3. STAGNATION: BREZHNEV'S CONSTITUTION

Khrushchev proposed constitutional reform in the Supreme Soviet in 1962, creating a constitutional commission with himself as chairman. But from 1964 to 1977 neither the commission nor its sub-units held a single meeting. Most of Khrushchev's remaining reforms were reversed by the time of the Central Committee Plenum in September 1965. Leonid Brezhnev inherited a twin problem from his predecessor: the dependence of ethnic elites on the centre was continuing to decrease at the same time that a scarcity of resources was increasingly felt throughout the Soviet Union. This dependence, freed from the politics of fear inspired by Stalin's methods, focused increasingly on Moscow's ability to meet growing expectations of economic growth and material benefit. Brezhnev's policies (e. g. longer terms of office for ethnic elites, less frequent rotations of bureaucratic personnel, etc.) produced stagnation, worsening the situation as the centre was increasingly unable to meet the demands it had stimulated in the periphery and no longer had the ruthlessness to crush with systematic force. The special privileges given to the titular nationality at universities and institutions in the ethnic republics had created an intelligentsia increasingly difficult to

unwillingness to silence others who articulated such agendas'. *See* Roeder, 206–7. Purges in 1959 (Azerbaijan, Latvia, Uzbekistan), 1961 (Kirghizia), 1962 (Tadzhikistan) and 1963 (Turkmenistan) were centred around issues of localism, autonomy and inter-republic relations, lending credence to the fears of the 'Anti-Party Group' that opposed Khrushchev in part out of concern that his reforms would lead to increased nationalism. *See* Hodnett, 122.

[35] John H. Miller, 'Cadres Policy in Nationality Areas: Recruitment of CPSU First and Second Secretaries in Non-Russian Republics of the USSR', 29 *Soviet Studies*, 1 (1977): 3–36.

mollify. In fact, tensions were greatest in areas of relative prosperity, that is, in places where such preferential policies of affirmative action had been operating the longest and ethnic communities had experienced the most returns in development. Party leaders in the ethnic republics seized upon issues of resource distribution as a means to expand their control over resources and thereby their power base as well. Local political machines became even more entrenched under Brezhnev than under Khrushchev. What autonomy was constitutionally promised but restricted in official practice could nevertheless be partially achieved through the clever manipulation of economic agendas and careful utilization of the 'second economy'.[36]

Brezhnev's solution was a new constitution. Khrushchev's dormant commission was abruptly re-awakened and a draft approved for a union-wide discussion campaign in May 1977. The final text was passed unanimously by the Supreme Soviet on 7 October 1977. The Soviet Union, it was declared, was formed on the basis of the previously unheralded 'principle of socialist federalism' (Art. 70). As with 'socialist legality' (Art. 4) and 'socialist democracy' (Art. 9), socialist federalism found all the explication it required within the confines of Article 6, which declared the extra-legal, non-democratic and unfederal Communist Party to be the essential core of all state and social systems.[37]

Little was changed from Stalin's Constitution regarding the limited rights of 'sovereign' union republics and autonomous republics. Both were still subject to the omnipresence of a capricious central body. The 1936 Constitution had ensured rigid centralization through the exhaustive powers exclusively granted the centre in Article 14. Brezhnev's Constitution simply reserved for the center, in the last clause of an equally exhaustive Article 73, the perpetual right to decide what should be of all-union significance in future. Union law was made superior to all other laws in *every* case of divergence by Article 74. Article 36, expanding upon Article 123 of the previous constitution, announced that all Soviet citizens, regardless of nationality, possessed equal rights, the goal of which were to ensure the equal development and merging of nations. Despite explicit legal penalties for the restriction of rights or creation of privileges based on nationality, such subsidies and privileges continued.

---

[36] *See* Klaus von Beyme, 'Social and Economic Conditions of Ethnic Strife in the Soviet Union', in McAuley, ed. *Soviet Federalism, . . .* , 89–109.

[37] No such provision declaring the omnipotence of the CPSU was included in the 1918 or 1924 constitutions. The 1936 constitution included a slightly softer phrasing of this principle under the provisions for freedom of association (Art. 126). Feldbrugge concludes that Art. 6 had the effect of making the Party Programme a sort of super-constitution. Feldbrugge, 104–5.

The new Constitution, expanded by twenty-eight new articles, devoted more than twice as many articles to individual rights as its predecessor and gave them a prominent position in the text. However, what had changed was not the regime's opinion of human rights but a new importance attached to the formalistic appearances of legality. The fluctuation over time in the approaches to the law, from 'revolutionary legal consciousness' to the ossification of legal superstructures, was both a reflection and partial catalyst of the changing *political* needs of successive regimes. The heady legal nihilism in which the Soviet Union was crafted had, by the end of the Brezhnev regime, been replaced by an addiction to structure and stability. After the first constitution of 1918, each successive document was longer, more detailed and in need of lengthier and more complex drafting procedures. The centralized reality of the formation and operation of the Soviet Union could not have been less reflected in its constitutional description. Yet these descriptions, federal in form and national in content, were all that survived the collapse of the Soviet federal façade. In the political chaos that followed, these hollow forms would take on a new life as they were filled with meaning for the first time.

4

Gorbachev's Federalism Problem

Life punishes those who come late.

Gorbachev, October 1989

The contradictory rhetoric of Soviet 'federalism' confounded reform from the start. The 'nationalities problem' was one of the fundamental hurdles that Gorbachev failed to clear in his attempt at systemic transformation of the Soviet Union.[1] Less understood, and far less studied, is Gorbachev's 'federalism problem.' The institutional weaknesses of Soviet 'federalism' presented serious obstacles to would-be reformers of the political system as well as to opponents of reform. After seventy years of Soviet rhetoric, there was deep confusion over just what terms like 'federal' or 'sovereignty' really meant. Efforts to construct a 'renewed' USSR and a new Russian Federation were deeply constrained by Soviet institutions and concepts.

1. THE NATIONALITIES PROBLEM

The most sacred myth of Leninist nationalities policy was that there was *no* nationalities problem in the Soviet Union. As Gorbachev noted in 1986: 'The Soviet people appear as a qualitatively new social and international community, united in a unity of economic interests, ideologies and political aims'.[2] Ethnic tensions, the Party held, were minor, infrequent, and easily resolved by correcting perceived economic imbalances for different regions and nationalities. This corrective function naturally implied rigid central control. Ethnic identity was expected to wither into harmless historical remnants. These beliefs were sincerely held by Gorbachev and his colleagues.[3] Eduard

---

[1] Archie Brown, *The Gorbachev Factor* (Oxford University Press, 1996), 158. Angus Roxburgh calls this issue Gorbachev's 'Achilles Heel'. Angus Roxburgh *The Second Russian Revolution* (London: BBC Books, 1991), 55.

[2] Mikhail Gorbachev, 25 February 1986 at the 27th Party Congress. M.S. Gorbachev, *Izbrannie rechi i stat'i*, Tom 3 (Moskva: Izdatel'stvo politicheskoi literatury, 1987), 233.

[3] Mikhail Gorbachev, *On My Country and the World* (New York: Columbia University Press, 2000): 83–6. Robert Kaiser, *The Geography of Nationalism in Russia and the USSR* (Princeton University Press, 1994), 152.

Shevardnadze, Gorbachev's adviser on issues well beyond his foreign affairs portfolio, noted 'we believed that the nationalities issue or ethnic issue in the USSR had been resolved. We never expected an upsurge of emotional and ethnic factors. We assumed everything was going to develop in a much smoother fashion'.[4] The obligatory recitation of internationalist clichés and strictly guarded access to relevant demographic and sociological data left the depths of inter-ethnic tensions largely unplumbed.[5]

Ethnic conflicts, though their frequency steadily increased, were considered isolated incidents. Large-scale riots in Alma-Ata in December 1986 followed the unceremonious replacement with an ethnic Russian of the corrupt, but ethnic Kazakh, First Party Secretary. National movements with names like 'Awakening' or 'Rebirth' increasingly sprouted under glasnost, often from environmental movements in different regions. Thousands in the Baltic Republics protested, in summer 1987, against the Molotov-Ribbentrop annexation. The crisis in Nagorno-Karabakh rattled many on the Gorbachev team (often recalled in their memoirs as the first 'real' nationalities crisis). Demonstrations in Stepanakurt, Yerevan, and Sumgait in 1988 left scores dead and many more wounded.[6] By 1989, demonstrations, numbering in the thousands, averaged one every three days and increasingly focused on nationalities issues.[7] In April, sixteen demonstrators were killed in Tblisi. In May and June, ethnic conflicts in the Fergana Valley in Uzbekistan left 100 dead, 1,000 injured, and created thousands of Meskhetian refugees. In mid July, ethnic violence in Abkhazia in Georgia caused a score of deaths and over 100 injuries.

Gorbachev's reforms created contradictions for the old thinking on nationalities issues: modernization and equalization of living conditions required direction by the omniscient centre, while at the same time Gorbachev's economic programme stirred increasingly raucous demands

---

[4] Eduard Shevardnadze, Transcript of interview by Brian Lapping Assoc. for the BBC television series The Second Russian Revolution. British Library of Politics and Economic Science [LSE]. (Hereafter 'SRR transcripts'). See also Pavel Palazchenko, My Years with Gorbachev and Shevardnadze: The Memoir of a Soviet Interpreter (University Park: Pennsylvania State University Press, 1997), 99, 104; Interview with Aleksandr Yakovlev. Stephen F. Cohen & Katrina vanden Heuvel, Voices of Glasnost: Interviews with Gorbachev's Reformers (New York: Norton, 1989), 50; Georgii Shakhnazarov, Tsena svobody: Reformatsiia Gorbacheva glazami ego pomoshchnika (Moskva: Rossika, 1993), 43; Nikolai Ryzhkov, Perestroika: istoriia predatel'stv (Moskva: Novosti, 1992), 198.

[5] Lapidus in Brown, New Thinking, 41. The work of the Siberian Institute under Abel Aganbegyan and Tatyana Zaslavskaya is an exception, though their work focused more on economic than on nationalities issues until later under Gorbachev. Valery Tishkov, Ethnicity, Nationalism and Conflict In and After the Soviet Union: The Mind Aflame (London: Sage, 1997), 1–6.

[6] Ronald G. Suny, 'Nationalities and Nationalism', in Abraham Brumberg, ed. Chronicle of a Revolution: A Western-Soviet Inquiry into Perestroika (New York: Pantheon, 1990), 113.

[7] Paul Goble, 'Ethnic Politics in the USSR', 38 Problems of Communism, 4 (1989): 2.

in the regions for more economic decentralization and less central control.[8] The spirit of *glasnost* encouraged the organization of roundtables on national relations and federal structures, with opinions ranging from the unreconstructed Leninist to relatively free-thinking lawyers and academics.[9] Nationalities issues loomed large at the First Congress of People's Deputies.[10]

A new nationalities policy was published in August 1989 and approved in September.[11] Its stated goals: renewal of Leninist nationalities policies, rejuvenation of the federation and increased rights for national autonomy, human rights, culture and language development. Its focus shifted from the perfection of New Soviet Man, the epitome of internationalism, to the protection of political rights inherent in Soviet citizenship for all nationalities. Democratic centralism was to be transformed from the past deviation of 'excessive centralism' to a 'renewed federation', with 'broader rights' for union republican (SSR) Party branches. Gorbachev bluntly rejected, however, suggestions of federalization of the Communist Party of the Soviet Union.[12] Later, such suggestions would be broadened beyond the scale of union republics to include autonomous republics, whose representatives had become increasingly vocal at the First Congress of People's Deputies.[13] The Twenty-eighth Party Congress afforded the opportunity to restructure the Politburo from its traditional membership top-heavy with USSR ministers to one inclusive of First Secretaries from all union republic Party branches.[14]

One of the most significant changes was tactical. Gorbachev recognized and now sought to block the growing challenge to his own Soviet authority from the largest constituent unit of the Soviet Union, the Russian Soviet Federated Socialist Republic (RSFSR). The Russian republic was the only ethnic republic without titular institutions mirroring those at the union level: there was no Russian KGB, MVD (Ministry of Internal Affairs), Academy of Sciences or branch of the CPSU (Communist Party of the

[8]   Gregory Gleason, 'The Federal Formula and the Collapse of the USSR', 22 *Publius* (1992): 147.

[9]   '"Kruglyi stol' zhurnala "Sovetskoe gosudarstvo i pravo": demokratizatsiia sovetskogo obshchestva i gosudarstvenno-pravovye aspekty natsional'nykh otnoshenii v SSSR', *Sovetskoe gosudarstvo i pravo*, No. 1 (1989), 30–48; No. 2 (1989), 18–33.

[10]   'S"ezd narodnykh deputatov SSSR', *Pravda*, 7 June 1989, 3–5.

[11]   Mikhail Gorbachev, *The Nationalities Policy of the Party in Present Day Conditions. Address and Report of the General Secretary of the CPSU Central Committee at the Plenary Meeting of the Central Committee, September 19, 1989* (Moscow: Novosti Press Agency, 1989), 11–12.

[12]   Gorbachev, *Nationalities Policy*, 9, 46–7.

[13]   See the 1 June morning session, speech of Yu.K. Sharipov, authorized to speak for the 29 delegates from the Bashkir ASSR. 'Vystupleniia na s"ezde narodnykh deputatov SSSR', *Pravda*, 3 June 1989, 3.

[14]   Brown, *Gorbachev Factor*, 274.

Soviet Union). The aim had always been to bind the Russian republic inextricably to USSR structures—Russia was rightly seen as the linchpin of the Soviet Union.[15] Gorbachev worked hard to preserve this connection, but his efforts were too little, too late: roughly eight months later, all of the trappings of a titular republic would be established (including a Russian Communist Party) and sovereignty declared.

This was a real dilemma for Gorbachev's new nationalities policy. The popular fronts which had emerged on the pretext of support for *glasnost* and *perestroika* had taken the initiative away from the originator of these reforms and transformed him into a brake on them. Each successive turnover of control to a republican or regional authority left that institution that much less reason for allegiance to the centre and that much more of an incentive to listen to the voices of a newly empowered local electorate. Gorbachev had staked for himself a middle position, increasingly under pressure from conservatives within the regime and a growing radical opposition outside it. At the Second Congress of People's Deputies in December 1989, accusations of a lack of commitment to September's promises were a leitmotif.[16] The fractious leading role played by the Baltic republics, which on virtually every indicator led the USSR in modernization and standard of living, gave the lie to the assumption that economic equalization and privilege were enough to appease national tensions.[17] The bloodshed in Vilnius and Riga during Gorbachev's 'turn to the right' was viewed far less sympathetically than armed clashes in Baku in January 1990 (the first crisis officially deemed a threat to the integrity of the Soviet state). Gorbachev's nationalities problem was also, increasingly, taking the shape of a federalism problem: 'In a word, admitting the possibility of secession in principle, I . . . hoped that the development of economic and political reform would outstrip procedures of the "separation process". Having experienced the real benefits of a federation, people would cease being possessed with the idea of full independence'.[18]

---

[15] Gorbachev recalls his advice to Yeltsin in 1990: 'Boris Nikolaevich, our country, the USSR, consists of two hoops: the Union and the Russian Federation. If one of them falls apart, then everything will dissolve'. Even a decade after events, Gorbachev had difficulty with the idea that Russia and the USSR could have distinguishable interests: 'Neither then nor now has anyone been able to make convincing arguments as to why Russia needed independence from the USSR. The question is a simple one: From whom was Russia supposed to become independent? From itself?' Mikhail Gorbachev, *On My Country and the World* (New York: Columbia University Press, 2000), 110.

[16] *Vtoroi s"ezd narodnykh deputatov SSSR, 12–24 dekabria 1989 g. Stenograficheskii otchet*, Tom I (Moskva: Izdanie Verkhovnogo Soveta SSSR, 1990), 85–6.

[17] Rein Miullerson 'Vpered v. . . proshloe?' *Pravda*, 22 May 1989, 2.

[18] Mikhail Gorbachev, *Zhizn' i reformy*, Kniga II (Moscow: Novosti, 1995), 500.

2. The Federalism Problem

Gorbachev's early speeches and publications reveal a man of two minds regarding decentralization. Gorbachev actively pushed his economic policies of *uskorenie* (acceleration), *khozraschet* (cost-accounting) and socialist competition on all levels, necessary however 'painful' such a 'transfer of rights' from centre to periphery was. *Perestroika* demanded 'a new concept of centralism'.[19] But at the same time, the Party's leading role remained unquestionable, federalization of the Party unthinkable, and renovation of the constitutional bonds of union off the agenda. Economic considerations prompted one of the most important early changes in thinking about Soviet law, critical to any subsequent discussion of constitutional structures or federalism. In the context of market reforms and cooperatives, then Director of the Institute of State and Law, Vladimir Kudriavtsev, wrote in December 1986: 'Of the two possible principles, "You may do only what is permitted" and "You may do everything which is not forbidden", priority should be given to the latter inasmuch as it unleashes the initiative and activism of people'.[20] Kudriavtsev was a frequent adviser to Gorbachev, who agreed wholeheartedly with the idea and soon reiterated it.[21]

2.1 Conceptual Revolutions

Increasingly, Gorbachev promoted the construction of a *sotsialisticheskoe pravovoe gosudarstvo*, a socialist rule-of-law state.[22] The 'Theses' published prior to the 19th Party Conference (radically restructuring electoral procedures, legislative processes and judicial institutions) referred to the importance of a division of powers in a rule-of-law state and established a constitutional review commission. In October 1988, Gorbachev asserted that this was the key to *perestroika*, political reforms he characterized as 'a legal revolution'.[23] Such proposals contained the seeds for federal reform even before such notions were officially on the agenda. Restricting control by one government over another logically implied greater autonomy for that second body, anathema to previous conceptions of Soviet 'federalism'.

[19] Mikhail Gorbachev, *Perestroika: New Thinking for Our Country and the World* (London: William Collins, 1987), 35, 89–91.

[20] Vladimir Kudriavtsev, 'Pravovaia sistema: puti perestroiki', *Pravda*, 5 Dec. 1986, 3.

[21] Brown, *Gorbachev Factor*, 145–6.

[22] Mikhail Gorbachev, 'O zadachakh partii po korennoi perestroike upravleniia ekonomikoi', Doklad na Plenume TsK KPSS, 25 June 1987, in Mikhail Gorbachev, *Izbrannie rechi i stat'i*, Vol. 5 (Moskva: Izdatel'stvo politicheskoi literatury, 1988), 183. 'Cherez demokratizatsiiu—k novomu obliku sotsializma: Vstrecha v Tsentral'nom Kommitete KPSS', *Pravda*, 11 May 1988, 1–2.

[23] 'Interv'iu M.S. Gorbacheva zhurnalu "Shpigel'"...(FRG)', *Pravda*, 24 Oct. 1988, 1–2.

As any federal restructuring would be done on a legal-constitutional level, the establishment of Kudriavtsev's precedent was fundamental. A first attempt at such a principle was favourably noted at a working group formed by the Presidium of the Supreme Soviet in early 1989 on the demarcation of competencies between the Union and its republics: 'a republic has the right to decide all questions not attributed to the authority of the USSR by the Constitution of the USSR and laws of the USSR'.[24] It is unlikely that federal reform could have progressed very far without the 'legal revolution' that preceded it.

But legal revolutions were still secondary to economic concerns. When it came to reconciling expansion of cost-accounting autonomy in enterprise and republican budgets with the requirements of a centralized economy, the latter routinely prevailed. 'That is why we do not want to weaken the role of the centre, because otherwise we would lose the advantages of the planned economy'.[25] Gorbachev seemed aware that his legal revolution should eventually extend beyond the market, but on a deeper level unaware how these principles would ultimately impact nationalities crises. As Robert Ahdieh argued: 'Gorbachev opened a Pandora's box by singing the praises of the law and the constitution, yet continuing to use them not as arbiters of the process but as tools within it'.[26] In this respect, Gorbachev could not escape his very Soviet legal training.

Among the central and regional political elites, conceptual confusion reigned supreme.[27] In Politiburo discussions, Gorbachev listed alternatives to federation (confederation, associated connections, even imperial precedents in Finland and Poland) but seldom discussed options very deeply.[28] Yegor Ligachev saw no inconsistency in his own interpretation of national-

---

[24] 'Zasedanie deputatskoi gruppy', *Pravda*, 16 Feb. 1989, 3. Its draft noted that the USSR Supreme Soviet should draft a law foreseeing the right of republics to act on their own initiative so long as this did not contradict union legislation. 'Proekt: Obshchie printsipy perestroiki rukovodstva ekonomikoi i sotsial'noi sferoi v soiuznykh respublikakh na osnove rasshireniia ikh suverennykh prav, samoupravleniia i samofinansirovaniia', *Pravda*, 14 Mar. 1989, 2–3.

[25] Gorbachev, *Perestroika*, 89.

[26] Robert B. Ahdieh, *Russia's Constitutional Revolution: Legal Consciousness and the Transition to Democracy, 1985–1996* (University Park, PA: Pennsylvania State University Press, 1997), 20, 36.

[27] Exception should be made for Andrei Sakharov, whose support for constitutionalism was hardly rhetorical; his draft constitution was probably the most-read proposal at the time. His views on federalism, calling for over 50 sovereign nation-states utilizing existing boundaries and ideas of 'horizontal federalism', foreshadowing later alterations in the power balance, were less influential.

[28] A. B. Veber et al., (eds.). *Soiuz mozhno bylo sokhranit* (M.: Aprel–85, 1995), 95. E.g. at a March 1990 Politburo meeting, Gorbachev boldly premised the viability of complex federal relations on past imperial practices in Tsarist Russia: 'It is possible to have a federation with the different republics having different status; consequently different relations will result between the republics and the Centre. After all, even in the Russian empire the status of different parts of the empire varied. There was the Grand Duchy of Finland, the Kingdom of Poland, the Khanate of Bukhara, and so on.' Gorbachev, *On My Country and the World*, 106.

ities policy to allow 'the right of nations to self-determination, the sover-eignty of republics, and a renewed powerful Soviet federative state' leaving the centre free to reinforce republics' 'obligations to the union-state'.[29] Algirdas Brazauskas, leader of the Lithuanian Communist Party when it voted to leave the CPSU in December 1989, infuriated an emergency meeting of the CPSU Central Committee: 'Yes, but what is the word "independent?" It is the same as "sovereignty" ... at any rate, it is in Lithuanian'.[30]

Suverenitet, federalizm, and *pravovoe gosudarstvo* (rule-of-law state) were increasingly popular terms. As early as May 1987 over 150 Soviet legal scholars conferred on 'The Legal System and Perestroika'.[31] However, decades of stagnation had ossified critical legal thinking and left a Soviet stamp on the understanding of these terms.[32] At one extreme, conservative thinkers like Zlatopol'skii reiterated Soviet promises of sovereignty for union republics while opposing the Estonian deputies who sought its actual attainment.[33] Others, such as Ruslan Khasbulatov, future chairman of the Russian Supreme Soviet, demonstrated a more nuanced understanding of sovereignty within federations.[34] At the same time, Soviet distinctions and extreme confederal conceptions strongly influenced his thinking. The draft Union Treaty he advanced in August 1990 excluded ASSRs from the com-position of his new 'Community', granted supremacy to the laws of each member-state over that of the central authority, made participation in the Community's International Court subject to the confirmation of the member-state and accepted a right to secession.[35]

Experts like Yulian Bromlei, Vladimir Sokolov and Oleg Rumiantsev incautiously drafted schemes for rearranging borders, plotting the division of Soviet territory into anywhere between three and fifty units.[36] Gavriil Popov advocated 'democratic de-federalization' whereby, either via referen-dum or a transitional period of central autocracy followed by referendums,

---

[29] Yegor Ligachev, *Inside Gorbachev's Kremlin* (Boulder, CO:Westview, 1996), 197, 375.

[30] Roxburgh, 164.

[31] See the report on the conference 'Perestroika v pravovoi sisteme, iuridicheskoi nauke, praktike', in *Sovetskoe gosudarstvo i pravo*, No. 9 (1987).

[32] V.M. Savitskii, 'Pravosudie i perestroika', in 'Perestroika v pravovoi sisteme, iuridicheskoi nauke, praktike', *Sovetskoe gosudarstvo i pravo*, No. 9 (1987): 33, note 19.

[33] D.L. Zlatopol'skii, 'Natsional'naia gosudarstvennost' soiuznykh respublik: nekotorye aktual'nye problemy', *Sovetskoe gosudarstvo i pravo*, No. 4 (1989): 13, 19.

[34] Ruslan Khasbulatov, *The Struggle for Russia: Power and Change in the Democratic Revolution* (London: Routledge, 1993), 44–5, 247–61.

[35] Khasbulatov, 128–36.

[36] *See* Stephan Kux, 'Soviet Federalism', *Problems of Communism* (Mar.–Apr. 1990); Nicholas J. Lynn & Alexei V. Novikov, 'Refederalizing Russia: Debates on the Idea of Federalism in Russia', 27 *Publius*, 2 (1997).

'. . . three, four or even five dozen independent states would then be formed in the place of the USSR'.[37] Not everyone was a supporter of federal solutions. Vladimir Zhirinovsky declared a short time later: 'How can the nationalities crisis be solved under these conditions? Only through fear. We need fear and a strong patriotic government; political life in the country must be frozen, all political parties forbidden, and all representative organs of power disbanded, except for the president and his authorized local representatives (governors [gubernatory], viceregents [namestniki]—whatever). All the republics must be abolished. There should be an administrative division'.[38]

Federalism was constantly confused with confederalism. The historian Leonid Batkin described a new federation which was in fact a disastrously loose confederation, in which republics possessed their own military units, dual citizenship, independent foreign economic ties, and separate policies for emigration and immigration.[39] The chair of a working group at the Institute of State and Law in late 1989 advanced the 'juridical equality of all republics' as a basic tenet for a new federal treaty, but then proposed the possibility of different republics simultaneously operating under different models of federalism or confederalism in their relations with the Union. A fractiously unfederal rule was promoted: 'the primacy of the republics and the secondariness of the Union'.[40] Another analyst struggled to establish the theoretical legitimacy of 'socialist federalism', in which democratic centralism (conducted somehow through the goodwill of all involved national groups) played an integral role. Excessive unitarism, which even this approach could not countenance, was dismissed as a Stalinist deformation. In a federation, the writer continued, there could be no central authority, only the mutual relations of the component subjects.[41]

Noting such imprecision is important. John Miller understates the case when he suggests that 'we should recall how the Soviet experience had promoted the emotional and symbolic side of politics; the implications of

[37] Gavriil Popov, What is to be Done? (London: The Centre for Research into Communist Economies, 1992), 26–8, 48–9. In general, the Inter-regional Group in the USSR Congress of People's Deputies (in which Popov was a leading figure) and its faction Democratic Russia advocated a loose confederal transformation of the Soviet Union and the dismantling of central institutions. Alexander Rahr, 'Inside the Interregional Group', 2 Report on the USSR, 43 (26 Oct. 1990): 2.

[38] 'Interethnic Contradictions in Russia: The Strategy of Parties and Social Movements (A Roundtable)', 32 Russian Politics and Law, 5 (1994): 11–12. This occurred in Moscow, 9 June 1992.

[39] Leonid M. Batkin, 'At a Fateful Fork in the Road', in Brumberg, 210–11.

[40] I. Sh. Muksinov, 'Sovetskii federalizm i kompleksnoe ekonomicheskoe i sotsial'noe razvitie soiuznoi respubliki', Sovetskoe gosudarstvo i pravo, No. 10 (1989): 8, 7.

[41] G.M. Khachatrian, 'Sotsialisticheskii federalizm kak forma i printsip gosudarstvennogo edinstva narodov', Sovetskoe gosudarstvo i pravo, 2 (1990): 13–20.

"federalism", for instance, . . . seem to have been little understood'.[42] These issues were easily the most charged and divisive of their decade. The abundance of misunderstandings and confusion were fuel on the fire of ill-conceived solutions and brash assertions bandied about in a deeply anti-centre atmosphere. Treating 'federalism' with the same naive reverence democracy received left resolution that much more distant—the façade of Soviet federalism was in danger of falling to the superficiality of neo-federalist debates.

2.2 The Kremlin's Hesitant Legal Reforms

The Politburo seemed paralysed by indecision. At a Politburo meeting on 14 July 1989, Shevardnadze was noted as complaining: 'The question has been raised about the transformation of the Soviet federation. But what is meant by this transformation has not been clarified. If we had simply talked about the necessity of transformation two years ago—this would be interesting. But now this is already banal'.[43] As Stephan Kux observed, there was 'a clear, yet constantly shifting line between orthodoxy and heresy on the issue of federalism'.[44]

When, in March 1989, the Supreme Soviet's working group finally published draft 'General Principles' for republican self-government and self-financing, the 'fundamental principle' of Soviet federalism was declared to be 'a strong centre and strong republics'.[45] This phrase resonated quite differently for Gorbachev than it did for the elite of the republics and popular fronts. For Gorbachev it meant that economic decentralization was the key to Party-controlled *perestroika*, the strengthening of the Soviet economy and the best strategy for safe-guarding his reforms against opposition at the centre. But the regions took this to be an empty slogan. Roughly three months earlier, Estonian sovereignty had been rejected by edict of the same Presidium that advanced these General Principles.[46] The Second Congress had provided a Law on Constitutional Supervision widely suspected as a centrist tool to invalidate republican laws at will. 'Imagine a

---

[42] John Miller, *Mikhail Gorbachev and the End of Soviet Power* (London: St. Martin's Press, 1993), 184–5.

[43] Arkhiv Gorbachev-Fonda. Fond No. 2, opis' No. 3. Zapis' Cherniaeva, *Soiuz*, 62–3.

[44] Kux, 3.

[45] *Pravda*, 14 Mar. 1989, 2.

[46] No. 9836—XI, 26 noiabra 1988, Ukaz Prezidiuma Verkhovnogo Soveta SSSR 'O nesootvetstvii Zakona Estonskoi SSR "O vnesenii izmenenii i dopolnenii v Konstitutsiiu (Osnovnoi Zakon) Estonskii SSR" i Deklaratsii Verkhovnogo Soveta Estonskoi SSR o suverenitete Estonskoi SSR, priniatykh 16 noiabria 1988 goda, Konstitutsii SSSR i zakonam SSSR'. *Vedomosti Verkhovnogo soveta soiuza sovetskikh sotsialisticheskikh respublik*, No. 48 (30 Nov. 1988), item 720, p. 803.

sovereign state', one deputy complained, 'the highest representative organs of which do not have the right to pass laws because at any moment they might be recognized as invalid'.[47]

One did not have to imagine for long. By early 1990, two-fifths of the union republics had declared themselves sovereign and ominous threats were sounding from the Baltics of a new round of declarations of *independence* to follow these assertions of *sovereignty*. In February, Gorbachev announced that it was time to negotiate a new Union Treaty. This was a complete reversal of his support for the original 1922 Treaty and one which came ten days before the Lithuanian Declaration of Independence, itself timed to pre-empt the Third Congress of Deputies meeting in mid March. But this announcement seemed too late. The law on secession, passed 3 April 1990, and the economic blockade Gorbachev placed on Lithuania fifteen days later, were evidence that the centre was beginning to lose *de facto* political control. In January 1990 Gorbachev had promised legislation to explicate the never-used constitutional right to secession (Art. 72). Gorbachev acknowledged the *right* to secede but denounced its *use* as invalid in the absence of approved procedures, a tactic reminiscent of Lenin's disingenuous promises regarding secession. Gorbachev hoped this legislation, hardly in the spirit of the constitutional right 'freely to secede' that it purported to clarify, would give him more time. Had Lithuania followed the law's procedures to the letter, and only once triggered one of the law's mandated repeat referendums (an optimistic hypothetical given the complex political climate), independence could have been expected in the year 2022 at the earliest![48] The law 'On the Legal Regime of an Extraordinary Situation', passed the same day, introduced draconian restrictions (based on the principle of democratic centralism) that could further disrupt the activities

---

[47] *Vtoroi s"ezd narodnykh deputatov SSSR*, 85–6.

[48] Delays were built into every stage. Stage one required a referendum held no earlier than 6 nor later than 9 months following a declaration of intent, with separate referendums for both legally defined autonomous areas as well as for any undefined 'locality' where a non-titular ethnic group was in the majority. Stage two required approval of the referendum in the Supreme Soviet of the union republic, the USSR Supreme Soviet and USSR Congress of People's Deputies, along with the recommendations of 'agencies of state power' at all levels. A transitional period followed (not to exceed 5 years) during which USSR laws retained supremacy. A second referendum at the conclusion of the transition period could be triggered by sufficient popular demand, restarting the entire procedure after a mandated 10-year waiting period. Finally, a second decision by the USSR Congress of People's Deputies was required to conclude the process. The whole affair could, at worst, involve three sets of multiple referendums, last 16 years and still *not* result in 'legal' secession. Law 'On the Procedure for Deciding Questions Connected with the Secession of a Union Republic From the USSR', 3 April 1990, *Vedomosti SND SSSR* (1990), No. 15, item 252. Donald Barry, 'The USSR: A Legitimate Dissolution', 18 *Review of Central and East European Law*, 6 (1992): 528–9.

required for 'legal' secession.[49] It was little wonder that these laws were completely ignored.

Gorbachev simultaneously sought to ameliorate tensions in the Baltic states and other union and autonomous republics. The law 'On the Delimitation of Powers between the USSR and Subjects of the Federation', passed roughly a fortnight later, made sweeping grants of principle on the foundations of the union, declared a basic equivalency of rights for SSRs and ASSRs, and consolidated the transfer of economic rights under exclusive and concurrent jurisdictions. It also granted the right to conclude bilateral treaties within the Union, a very important precedent (as will be discussed in Chapter Six).[50] Following his election to the new Soviet presidency, in March 1990, Gorbachev established a Federation Council composed of the fifteen union republic presidents/chairmen. Like its twin the Presidential Council, this body had no official structures by which to implement any decisions, but created the perception of a power shift away from the Politburo and the Party. A weak sense still lingered that some compromise was possible, as Anatol Lieven explains: 'During these years the words "independence", and still more "sovereignty", acquired a whole spectrum of meaning unknown in the West. Indeed, between the Kremlin, the national movements and the local Communist Parties there was a virtual conspiracy that "independence" did not really *mean* independence, that "sovereignty" meant something less than the full right to self-determination, and that both could somehow be accommodated within the Soviet system. It was a convenient self-deception, since no one wanted a stand-up fight...'.[51]

2.3 Gorbachev versus Yeltsin

Russia presented the most serious problems for Gorbachev. Boris Yeltsin surpassed the new Soviet President in public opinion polls sometime in May or June 1990.[52] At a July Politburo meeting, Gorbachev identified the RSFSR as the 'most difficult question today'.[53] Yeltsin personified that difficulty. The

[49] Article Five, Law 'On the Legal Regime of an Extraordinary Situation', 3 April 1990, *Vedomosti SND SSSR* (1990), No. 15, item 250.

[50] Law 'On the Delimitation of Powers Between the USSR and Subjects of the Federation', 26 April 1990, *Vedomosti SND SSSR* (1990), No. 19, item 329.

[51] Anatol Lieven, *The Baltic Revolution: Estonia, Latvia, Lithuania and the Path to Independence*, 2nd Ed. (New Haven: Yale University Press, 1994), 229.

[52] Brown, *Gorbachev Factor*, 6, 151. Brown notes, 'From this point on [Yeltsin's November 1987 public criticism of the Party leadership], neither man was at his most rational when contemplating the other...', 167–8.

[53] Arkhiv Gorbachev-Fonda. Fond No. 2, opis' No. 3. Zapis' Cherniaeva, *Soiuz*, 69.

March 1990, Russian republican elections returned Yeltsin to Moscow as a deputy in the RSFSR Congress of People's Deputies by a resounding margin; with greater difficulty he became its Chairman in May. A fortnight later, on 12 June 1990 the RSFSR declared sovereignty with a harshly worded declaration. The document was designed not only to strike a blow for Russian sovereignty but also to galvanize the support of other republics within and outside the RSFSR against Gorbachev's centre.[54] With the new Declaration its justification, Yeltsin's Congress ten days later passed a resolution to begin work on a new Union Treaty according to their own guidelines for the division of authority between Union and republican bodies.[55] A flurry of legislation followed—the 'War of Laws'—as Yeltsin by fiat transferred rights and resources from the USSR to the RSFSR. Declarations, resolutions, laws and decrees from virtually every authority blurred into legal confusion. Both Gorbachev and Yeltsin quickly grasped the instrumental use of legislation: a tool to deprive each other of the regional support both required to maintain their leadership positions and the integrity of the states upon which those positions depended. The steady disgorge of bilateral treaties, agreements, and communiqués between union republics, autonomous republics, and the RSFSR bypassed traditional institutions and weakened the centre's once exclusive jurisdiction.[56] The boldest of these included the decree 'On Protection of the Economic Foundation of the Sovereignty of the RSFSR' (asserting sole control over all foreign economic activity, natural and industrial resources, and procedures for privatization), the resolution 'On the Participation of RSFSR Citizens in Resolving Inter-ethnic Conflicts Outside the RSFSR' (commandeering decision-making over RSFSR conscripts, military units and policy), the law 'On the Operation of Acts of Organs of the USSR on the Territory of the RSFSR' (granting the Republic supremacy over Union authority) and the law 'On Guaranteeing the Economic Basis of Sovereignty of the RSFSR' (expanding the decree of that August in light of

---

[54] *Deklaratsiia o Gosudarstvennom Suverenitete Rossiiskoi Sovetskoi Federativnoi Sotsialisticheskoi Respubliki*. Moskva: Priniata pervym S"ezdom narodnykh deputatov RSFSR, 12 iunia 1990 goda. Article Nine (approved after heated debate) affirmed 'the need for a substantial broadening' of the rights of ASSRs and other subjects of the Federation, a plank designed to attract regional delegates. See I.Sh. Muksinov, 'O pravovom polozhenii suverennoi respubliki v sostave Rossiiskoi Federatsii', in N.A. Kataev & V.K. Samigullin, eds. *Problemy konstitutsionnogo razvitiya suverennoi respubliki* (Ufa: Izdanie Verkh. Soveta i Soveta ministrov Respublik Bashkortostan, 1992), 12.

[55] A.N. Adrov & S.M. Shakhrai, eds. *Sbornik zakonodatel'nykh aktov RSFSR o gosudarstvennom suverenitete, soiuznom dogovore i referendume* (Moskva: 'Sovetskaia Rossiia' izdatel'stvo, 1991), 7–9. Principal considerations included: subordination of security services, control of oil and gas enterprises, reorganization of Gosbank SSSR into the RSFSR State Bank.

[56] Anwara Begum, *Inter-Republican Cooperation of the Russian Republic* (Aldershot, UK: Ashgate, 1997), 27–35.

the struggling '500 Days' Plan).[57] In a May speech to the RSFSR Congress Yeltsin raged: 'The centre for Russia today is the cruel exploiter, the miserly benefactor, and the favourite who does not think about the future. We must put an end to the injustice of these relations'.[58] Yeltsin enlisted as many autonomous republics as he could in his struggle against Gorbachev, encouraging them to declare sovereignty and join his opposition to the 'Centre', an increasingly popular epithet. Most notorious of his many speeches, and typical of his bombastic and careless promises, was an August appearance in Kazan' at which Yeltsin declared to a packed auditorium, 'Take as much independence as you can hold on to . . .'.[59]

Gorbachev also increased his outreach to regional elites, motivated by the desire to preserve the Soviet Union and to retain control of his reforms. Gorbachev used his Cabinet to increase the strength of his Union-based presidency while the Federation Council (established in March 1990 and now strengthened) diluted Yeltsin's power among republican leaders. By the end of December, the leaders of twenty autonomous republics (ASSRs) had been given full voting membership on the Council, doubling its size. Yeltsin's supporters feared that Gorbachev would decrease their power by elevating ASSRs (the bulk of which were within the RSFSR) to the status of union republics. The draft Union Treaty published in November 1990 made no distinction between union republics (SSRs) and ASSRs.[60] Gorbachev cleverly co-opted Yeltsin's language, declaring that in expediting work on the Union Treaty, 'We are proceeding from an unshakeable principle: every people has the right to self-determination'.[61] Yeltsin's summer promises made objection impossible and Gorbachev calculated that in negotiating a new Union Treaty it was better to crowd the field with equally empowered

[57] Furtado & Chandler, 336 & 339. Vedomosti S''ezda narodnykh deputatov RSFSR i Verkhovnogo Soveta RSFSR, No. 22 (1 Nov. 1990), (Moskva: Izdanie Verkhovnogo Soveta RSFSR), 305–7. Adrov & Shakhrai, 16–17. These were passed 9 August, 24 September, 24 and 31 October 1990, respectively.

[58] Furtado & Chandler, 323. Shortly after these events, Gorbachev remarked to the assembled Congress of People's Deputies that Yeltsin 'is carrying the question of sovereignty to the point of absurdity'. Gorbachev would later characterize Yeltsin's views on Russian sovereignty as 'irresponsible' and 'illiterate'. Gorbachev, On My Country and the World, 109–10.

[59] Elena Chernobrovkina, 'Reshat' vam samim', Vecherniaia Kazan', 10 Aug. 1990, 1.

[60] This was one of the draft's most controversial provisions, extending the April 1990 law which elevated ASSRs to equivalent status with SSRs. It also made promises of sovereignty both more complicated and more dubious. As Ann Sheehy explains, according to the draft, 'The autonomous republics will thus be sovereign states within sovereign states (Union republics), which are in turn part of a sovereign state (the USSR)'. Ann Sheehy, 'The Draft Union Treaty: A Preliminary Assessment', 2 Report on the USSR, 51 (21 Dec. 1990): 1–6.

[61] Chetvertyi s''ezd narodnykh deputatov SSSR, 17–27 dekabria 1990 g. Stenograficheskii otchet, Tom 1 (Moskva: Izdanie Verkhovnogo Soveta SSSR, 1991): 83. Victor Sergeyev & Nikolai Biryukov, Russia's Road to Democracy: Parliament, Communism and Traditional Culture (Aldershot, UK: Edward Elgar, 1993), 179–80.

republics than to give the RSFSR the power to speak for those lesser units buried within its territory. Gorbachev circumvented Yeltsin with an appeal directly to the Soviet population in a March 1991 referendum: the vaguely worded question of support for 'renewed federation' was approved by over three-quarters of voters (more than 60 per cent of the total electorate, 76 per cent of those voting) despite alternative referendums in different republics.[62]

3. THE NOVO-OGAREVO PROCESS

Gorbachev declared the outcome an official mandate for a new Union Treaty. The country was already flooded with draft proposals.[63] One draft, the product of the USSR Supreme Soviet, was so vague and confederal that it was unclear what unifying role such a treaty could play beyond a common signing ceremony.[64] The real work commenced at a state dacha in Novo-Ogarevo, the sort of cloistered negotiating environment in which Gorbachev thrived.[65] Nine of fifteen union republics accepted the invitation (declined by the Baltic states, Armenia, Georgia, and Moldova), hence the sessions were called the '9 + 1 Talks'.[66] Gorbachev recognized Yeltsin as his primary

[62] The USSR referendum question was: 'Do you consider it necessary to preserve the Union of Soviet Socialist Republics as a renewed federation of equal sovereign republics in which the rights and freedoms of people of all nationalities will be fully guaranteed?'

[63] Rafik Nishanov, Chairman of the Soviet of Nationalities of the USSR Supreme Soviet, noted that draft treaties were received from 7 union republics, 2 drafts from the Institute of State and Law, 3 drafts from a prize jury of the Inter-Regional Group and 1 proposed by a consortium of political parties. *Chetvertyi s"ezd narodnykh deputatov SSSR*, 340–1. Viacheslav Mikhailov & Eduard Tadevosian, 'Soiuznyi dogovor i natsional'naia politika', *Kommunist* 7 (May 1991): 69–70.

[64] 'Proekt: Soiuznyi dogovor', *Izvestiia*, 24 Nov. 1990, 1.

[65] Although Gorbachev did the negotiating, Georgii Shakhnazarov, Grigorii Revenko (Gorbachev's Chief of Staff), Vladimir Kudriavtsev (Vice-President of the Academy of Sciences), and Boris Topornin (Director of the Institute of State and Law) were key advisers. In addition to the republican leaders, USSR Supreme Soviet Chairman Lukianov and Council of Nationalities Chairman Nishanov attended almost all the meetings. Gorbachev notes that he also frequently consulted Prime Minister Pavlov, GosBank Chairman Gerashchenko and Yurii Baturin. Gorbachev, *Zhizn' i reformy*, II, 550–1. Brown, *Gorbachev Factor*, 288. Ahdieh, 44. Vadim Medvedev, at that time a Politburo member and Gorbachev adviser, notes as a 'theoretical-ideological prelude' to the Novo-Ogarevo talks a series of reports and briefs prepared by Otto Latsis (then deputy editor of *Kommunist*), Popov (editor of *Dialog*), Gorshkov (director of the Institute of Marxism-Leninism) as well as conversations on statehood with Tsipko, Stankevich, and Shakhnazarov. Vadim Medvedev, *V komande gorbacheva: Vzgliad iznutri* (Moskva: Bylina, 1994), 181. Not all participants were sympathetic to Gorbachev's aims: among Gorbachev's associates were Anatoly Lukianov, Valery Boldin, and Yurii Baturin. Among Yeltsin's advisers were many members of Democratic Russia and Leonid Batkin, a 'hawk' opposed to an agreement with the centre.

[66] Interestingly, Gorbachev repeatedly refers to the '1 + 9 Talks' in his memoirs, calling this 'popular parlance'—an indication of his *primus inter pares* opinion of his role in the gathering.

adversary and the most important factor for the talks: 'It seemed to me important to bind the Russian leadership by a commitment that would be difficult to break'. After a special day-long meeting with Yeltsin at the dacha, the first meeting of all nine republican leaders occurred on 23 April, at which time Gorbachev urged a different rationale, pressing the group to 'place the interests of our country above all else' and 'defuse the stormy atmosphere'.[67] At major meetings on the 24 May, 3 June, and 23 July, Gorbachev sought to retain as great a concentration of powers for the new Union centre as possible. For much of 1990 Gorbachev had revealed a great deal of flexibility, not immediately ruling out extremely confederal options or even a sort of two-tiered structure to encourage some future, looser Baltic and Georgian alliance with a 'renewed' USSR. But now, owing much to Shakhnazarov's impressions of the situation, Gorbachev abandoned this hope and accepted the probable loss of the Baltic states.[68]

Novo-Ogarevo was one of Gorbachev's cleverest gambles, even more so given the weakness of his position. Entering the process without the explicit consent of the CPSU, Gorbachev forced a reluctant Politburo to support his efforts by threatening resignation at the Central Committee plenary session meeting the day after talks began. Still, several tactical errors are apparent in retrospect. Autonomous republics had been invited to attend the talks, but with greatly reduced rights to participate. This was a mistake, especially considering how successfully Gorbachev had played ASSRs against the RSFSR to decrease Yeltsin's collective bargaining power.[69] Full participation of ASSRs at the talks naturally would have increased the complexity of the proceedings and risked giving Yeltsin a controlling vote if he succeeded in coercing these internal republics into support (a serious concern for other union republics). However, limiting their inclusion not only did not prevent Yeltsin from making such overtures to ASSRs, it deprived Gorbachev of one of the best mechanisms for weakening the RSFSR power base, itself a Soviet-style 'federation' as much at risk as the USSR.[70] Most of Gorbachev's reform-minded and liberal supporters encouraged an alliance between Gorbachev

---

[67] Gorbachev, *Zhizn' i reformy*, II, 529, 534. Yeltsin's recollection differs slightly: Gorbachev, he says, proposed a new Union Treaty with a significantly weakened centre and the prospects for reworking the constitution with new institutions. Boris Yeltsin, *The View from the Kremlin* (London: Harper Collins, 1994), 27–37.

[68] Gorbachev came late to such a view compared to Cherniaev's and Shevardnadze's earlier scepticism. Palazchenko, 149, 201.

[69] In an April 1991 note to Gorbachev, Shakhnazarov advised that the status of ASSRs was the 'sharpest' current question regarding subjects of the new Union, especially as it affected the integrity of the RSFSR. Shakhnazarov, 531.

[70] To some extent, Gorbachev was still able to pressure Yeltsin by including the ASSRs in some discussions. In June, Yeltsin insisted that ASSRs sign the Union Treaty as part of the RSFSR

and Yeltsin, believing that this would strengthen both against rising conservative forces. But Gorbachev rejected Shakhnazarov's counsel to custom-fit a USSR Vice-Presidency for Yeltsin and Yeltsin in turn viewed Gorbachev as the main obstacle to his ambitions for Russia.[71]

Even in its finest hour, the Novo-Ogarevo process exposed the confusion about federalism. A serious problem was the very basis for inclusion in the talks: those who were full participants had 'earned' their right to be there by way of declarations of sovereignty and a flurry of republican laws prioritizing themselves above union legislation. These declarations were made the building blocks of the new federal system. However, the most basic interpretation of a federal system requires a far more complex understanding of sovereignty—never absolute, always partial and parcelled among multiple levels of governments. Starting from declarations that overstated a sovereignty dubiously possessed in the first place, republics made necessary compromises very difficult. Republics and centre both demanded a 'renewed federation' but only the centre wanted strong, independent, *federal* powers. A note to Gorbachev in April 1991 from Shakhnazarov exposes the widespread, sometimes deliberate, amphiboly: 'It would be appropriate "to forget" about these concepts, only using the word "Union" and, where it can't be avoided—federalism, federal principle. In essence we should be talking about a combination of features of federation and confederation'.[72] The republics, and Yeltsin especially, actually fought for a loose *confederal* arrangement, with a centre so dependent on the constituent members as to be virtually powerless. *Their* goal was as much a federal façade as the system they were replacing: a federal treaty of union would be declared but powers of purse and sword would rest almost exclusively in the separate hands of the individual members.

Confederal thinking won the day. The final draft of the Union Treaty, ready to be signed on 20 August, had been agreed at the final meeting of the

delegation. The compromise reached, by which the Federation Council would be disbanded following the signing of the Treaty, was strongly opposed by ASSRs who feared their only direct link with the centre would be lost. Ann Sheehy, 'Russia's Republics: A Threat to its Territorial Integrity?' 2 *RFE/RL Research Report*, 20 (14 May 1993): 37. The result gave an elegant symmetry following Yeltsin's overtures in Kazan'. '... throughout 1990 Yeltsin encouraged the rights of autonomous regions within Russia as part of his struggle with Gorbachev. Later in 1991, during negotiations for the projected All-Union Treaty, he tried to maintain a united front against the centre but Gorbachev in turn now strove to weaken his position by encouraging the autonomous territories.' Denis J.B. Shaw 'Geographic and Historical Observations on the Future of a Federal Russia', 34 *Post-Soviet Geography*, 8 (1993), 533. Shakhnazarov, 235–6.

[71] Brown, *Gorbachev Factor*, 287. Shakhnazarov, 231, whose growing impression of Yeltsin was one of 'ironical aloofness'. 'On his lips almost invariably wandered a half-smile, which was saying that he did not take this procedure too seriously... Russia will survive fine and without the Union.'

[72] Shakhnazarov, 533.

Novo-Ogarevo working group, on 23 July 1991.[73] The preamble established the confederal nature of the new structure: 'The states that have signed this Treaty, proceeding from the declarations of state sovereignty proclaimed by them and recognizing the right of nations to self-determination . . .'.[74] Basic principles embraced by the Treaty included the retention by all republics of the right 'to the independent resolution of all questions of their development' (Sec. I, Art. 2), and the right to secede (Sec. II, Art. 1). Dangerously close to the Calhounian principle of nullification and a serious threat to even loose confederal integrity was the right of all republics 'to suspend a Union law on its territory and protest it if it violates this Treaty or is at variance with the republic's Constitution, or with republic laws adopted within the bounds of the republic's powers'.[75] What exclusive powers were enjoyed by the new federal authority were also virtually restated as joint powers to be shared with the republics in the following section: declarations of war and peace and the management of defence were powers exclusive to the centre, but determinations of military policy, foreign policy, and state security all fell under the rubric of joint jurisdiction. Critically, 'The land and its mineral wealth, waters, other natural resources and plant and animal life belong to the republics and are the inalienable property of their peoples. The rules governing their possession, use and disposal (right of ownership) are established by republic legislation'. What property was granted to Union authority was left ill-defined and subject to the will of the republics (Sec. II, Art. 8). Regarding the contentious issues of finance and taxation, the final draft established the confederal rule that, although the Union held the exclusive right to 'confirm and fulfill' the Union budget, fees, and tax rates required the negotiated assent of all the republics (Sec. II, Art. 9). Yeltsin fought the hardest for this principle, recognizing that such a rule in theory gave him the power to starve a dependent centre.[76]

[73] A revised draft Union Treaty, first publicized in Nov. 1990, was published in *Izvestia*, 9 March 1991, 8 days prior to the referendum. *BBC Summary of World Broadcasts*, SU/1017/C1/1.

[74] 'Dogovor o soiuze suverennykh gosudarstv', *Izvestia*, 15 Aug. 1991, 1–2.

[75] In his 11 July 1991 USSR Supreme Soviet report, Nishanov noted this criticism: 'If we move to a federal state, then we must acknowledge that Union laws adopted within the bounds of the jurisdiction of the USSR Supreme Soviet and following established procedures cannot be called in question at the republic and local levels and must be implemented unswervingly...'. 43 *Current Digest of the Soviet Press*, 28 (14 Aug. 1991): 8.

[76] At the 11 July 1991 session of the USSR Supreme Soviet, Nishanov reported concerns about proposals by the RSFSR and Ukraine delegations 'for the establishment of a single-level system of taxes, under which all collections would go into the republics' treasuries and then money would be allocated to the Union for its needs and for all-Union programmes. The Deputies believe that if this were the case, the Union bodies would be brought to their knees and the Union would become lifeless', 43 *Current Digest of the Soviet Press*, 28 (14 Aug. 1991): 8.

The August Putsch was a reaction to Novo-Ogarevo.[77] Its date was selected to prevent the signing of the Union Treaty.[78] Its planning had extended all the way to wiretapping the last meetings at Novo-Ogarevo, where Gorbachev, Yeltsin, and Kazakhstan President Nursultan Nazerbayev had spent time discussing the post-Treaty dismissal of several of the plotters.[79] The Putsch meant that the new Union Treaty would never be signed and, ultimately, this doomed the Soviet Union to dissolution. Yeltsin quickly capitalized on his hero-status to sabotage efforts to restart the Novo-Ogarevo process. The culmination of his efforts was the Minsk Agreement, signed secretly in Belezhovskaia Forest.

Upon Gorbachev's return, the respected journalist Otto Latsis echoed the words Gorbachev had used to greet the world from the airport tarmac: 'Gorbachev has returned to a different country. Does he understand this?'[80] It was not apparent that he did. The Novo-Ogarevo talks resumed fitfully under the auspices of the new State Council, which Yeltsin had devised to replace the Federation Council, conveniently excluding all autonomous republics from the discussions; only union republics were granted membership.[81] The pre-coup pressures on Yeltsin and the other republican heads to meet with Gorbachev, the looming spectre of arch-conservative forces completely opposed to any reworking of the Treaty, had been removed and with them one of Gorbachev's best bargaining chips. Repeated threats by Gorbachev to resign prolonged the Novo-Ogarevo process, but the original energy had been lost and Yeltsin's interest in compromise was gone. At the State Council meeting on 25 November, when the Union Treaty was at last to be signed, Yeltsin (backed by Belarus President Shushkevich) announced that this was no longer possible. Gorbachev was furious but helpless: 'This little game of yours is not just a postponement. You are rejecting what we agreed on. You are destroying the very foundations of the future document'.[82]

Gorbachev was right. On 25 December in a televised address, Gorbachev resigned as Soviet President. According to some, he had resigned from a

[77]   For an example of putschists' contempt for Novo-Ogarevo, see V.I. Boldin, *Krushenie p'edestala. Shtrikhi k portretu M.S. Gorbacheva* (Moskva: Respublika, 1995), 393–4.

[78]   For comments by key plotters, see David Remnick, *Resurrection: The Struggle for a New Russia* (New York: Random House, 1997), 322; and Miller, 177. Boldin was convinced that the Treaty could lead to civil war. His book is an unreliable factual record, but expresses well the plotters' common motivation to stop the signing of the Treaty. Boldin, 8–9, 16, 393–405.

[79]   *Zhizn' i reformy*, 556–7; Yeltsin, 38–9.

[80]   Otto Latsis, 'Gorbachev vernulsia v druguiu stranu. Ponimaet li on eto?' *Izvestiia*, 23 Aug. 1991, 2.

[81]   Sheehy, 37.

[82]   Andrei S. Grachev, *Final Days: The Inside Story of the Collapse of the Soviet Union* (Boulder, CO: Westview, 1995), 119.

country that had already disappeared from the world: on 8 December, an announcement was issued by Russian President Yeltsin and the presidents of Ukraine and Belarus (Kravchuk and Shushkevich) that the Soviet Union could no longer be said to exist under international law. This was itself dubious in terms of international legality, an outrageous act of unilateralism, and far more extreme than any individual act of secession from the Soviet Union conceivably could have been. On 21 December, in Alma-Ata, eleven former Soviet Republics had signed the founding documents of the Commonwealth of Independent States—a loose-knit, hardly confederal assemblage of fully sovereign states.

5

The Process of Federal Transition

The state, ceasing to be an instrument of force in the hands of a totalitarian regime, is being democratized so that it can ultimately commit the courageous act of self-denial, having transformed itself from a political entity into a legal one.

The Conception of Judicial Reform in the RSFSR, October 1991

In considering this question, then, we must never forget that it is a constitution we are expounding.

John Marshall[1]

Russia's 'renewed federation' developed on several different institutional levels and cut across many political interests. As each republic defended its own interests, collectively held 'rules of the game' were established for the very process of rule-making and institution-building. What was the cumulative impact on emerging federal structures and practices of 'winning' strategies in this game? Russia's federal transition divides well into four overlapping stages: the Parade of Sovereignties, the development of a Federation Treaty, the crisis over a new Constitution, and a 'Parade of Treaties'—the proliferation of bilateral treaties between the federal center and regional units. This chapter explores the first three stages, from the RSFSR Declaration of Sovereignty (12 June 1990) to the referendum on a new Constitution (12 December 1993). Chapter Six is devoted to the fourth stage, bilateral treaties.

1. DECLARATIONS OF SOVEREIGNTY: ESTABLISHING THE VOCABULARY OF THE NEW FEDERALISM

In a span of thirty-two months, forty former units of the Soviet Union declared themselves to be sovereign states, an average of one declaration every twenty-three days. Only sixteen of these republics actually aspired to *independence* beyond *sovereignty*; fifteen seceded without war and relatively

---

[1] *McCulloch v. Maryland*, 17 U.S. 316, 407 (1819).

little bloodshed. The exception, Chechnya, can still hardly be considered either independent or sovereign over its affairs, at the cost of tens of thousands of lives.[2] The following four sub-sections analyse in detail the 'Parade of Sovereignties', making comparisons where they are helpful but, just as often, emphasizing the distinctive features of this turning point in Soviet-Russian history.

1.1 Timing and Sequencing of Declarations

What significance did the sequence of the Parade of Sovereignties have for federal transformations? Evidence of correlations, although far from caus-ation, provides an important start to analysis about the relative importance of different institutional actors and the relative effect of different stimuli.

The RSFSR was the seventh of the fifteen union republics (SSRs) to declare sovereignty. All fifteen ultimately became sovereign, independent states. Not a single autonomous republic (ASSR)—the next tier in the federal hierarchy, primarily within Russia—adopted the same strategy before Russia blazed the trail.[3] In the next six months, fourteen of the then sixteen ASSRs situated within Russia followed suit with declarations of their own. As Table 5.1 suggests, the Parade of Sovereignties was marched to the beat of several drummers. Union republics with past histories of independence led well ahead of their ASSR counterparts lodged within Russia. Geographic as well as temporal clustering of declarations is evident. Such clusters, grouped in periods of days rather than a more even distribution and sometimes in bursts of units contiguous to one another, suggest that republics were not only aware of other declarations, but encouraged by them.

This was a confusing time for the ruling elite, who paid close attention to the declarations occurring around them.[4] In Marii El, the process of

---

[2] Estimates of deaths in the first Chechen War range from 20, 000 (Anatol Lieven), to 80, 000 (General Aleksandr Lebed) to 100, 000 (Grigory Yavlinsky). Anatol Lieven, *Chechnya: Tombstone of Russian Power* (New Haven: Yale University Press, 1998), 108. Lebed' quoted in Archie Brown, 'The Russian Crisis: Beginning of the End or End of the Beginning?' 15 *Post-Soviet Affairs*, 1 (1999): 58. Grigory Yavlinsky, 'An Uncertain Prognosis', 8 *Journal of Democracy*, 1 (1997): 4. Thus far, thousands have died in the second war, launched in Autumn 1999.

[3] Union republics were better placed to declare sovereignty and, ultimately, independence: nominally incorporated into the USSR by treaty, a claim to equal status with the RSFSR was more easily defended. Autonomous republics were established *ex nihilo* by unilateral administrative deci-sions. As noted in Ch. 3, directives of the RSFSR had supremacy over the limited autonomy of ASSRs.

[4] One deputy to the Bashkir ASSR Supreme Soviet announced: 'Comrades! Several days ago the Buriat Republic became sovereign. In the Declaration it's written that it remains a component of Russia and the USSR. The announcer of the Central television, who saw this broadcast, especially emphasized this.' Boris N. Pavlov, *Stenograficheskii otchet, Tret'ia sessia Verkhovnogo Soveta Bashkirskoi SSR (dvenadtsatyi sozyv), 10–13 oktiabria 1990 g., 23–24 oktiabria 1990 g.* (Ufa: Izdanie Verkhovnogo Soveta Bashkirskoi SSR, 1991), 158.

Table 5.1 The 'Parade of Sovereignties'

1988	1989	1990	1990	1991
Estonia 16 Nov.	Lithuania 18 May	RSFSR 12 June	Buriatia 8 Oct.	Kabardino-Balkaria 31 Jan.
	Latvia 29 July	Uzbekistan 20 June	Koryak 9 Oct.	Dagestan 15 May
	Azerbaijan 23 Sept.	Moldova 23 June	Komi-Permiak 11 Oct.	Adygeia 2 July
	Georgia 12 Oct.	Ukraine 16 July	Bashkortostan 11 Oct.	
	Belarus 7 Dec.	N. Ossetia 20 July	Kalmykia 18 Oct.	
		Karelia 9 Aug.	Yamal-Nenets 18 Oct.	
		Khakassia 15 Aug.	Marii El 22 Oct.	
		Turkmenistan 22 Aug.	Chuvashia 24 Oct.	
		Armenia 23 Aug.	Gorno-Altai 25 Oct.	
		Abkhazia 25 Aug.	Kazakhstan 26 Oct.	
		Tadzhikistan 25 Aug.	Kyrgyzstan 28 Oct.	
		Komi 29 Aug.	Tuva 1 Nov.	
		Tatarstan 30 Aug.	Karachai-Cherkessia 17 Nov.	
		Udmurtia 20 Sept.	Checheno-Ingushetia 27 Nov.	
		S. Ossetia 20 Sept.	Mordova[a] 8 Dec.	
		Yakutia 27 Sept.		
		Chukotka 29 Sept.		

[a] The Mordovan SSR Supreme Soviet adopted a Declaration redefining its status, but after heated debate, ultimately omitted the word 'sovereignty' from the final draft. See 42 Current Digest of the Soviet Press, 50 (1990): 27.

sovereignisation 'in the beginning was met suspiciously by the Party-Soviet leadership, the corps of deputies. But then the Party-economic activists, meeting under the screen of the Supreme Soviet of the republic, comprehended what sort of benefits this might promise in opposition to democratic reorganization begun by the new Russian leadership'.[5] Unsure what to do, many habitually looked to Russia; one participant in Bashkortostan's sovereignization recalled: 'It was not clear if Russia left the Union what would be the fate of the ASSRs—if Russia declared *independence*, then what to do?'[6] In the absence of clear signals, most Supreme Soviets chose to watch and wait as declarations in the union republics began in November 1988. A strong influence was the First Russian Congress, where delegations of regional elites actively participated in debates over sovereignty. Particularly contentious was Article 9 of the RSFSR Declaration of Sovereignty, which 'confirmed the need to broaden substantially' the rights of sub-units of the Federation. This was an obvious invitation for republics to assert their own autonomy.[7] These debates are discussed below.

Regional elections provided another incentive to republican elites to sponsor their own sovereignty campaigns (Table 5.2). Elections rang the death knell to the days of democratic centralism. Regional politicians became aware that soon they might be more accountable to local constituencies than to minders in Moscow. Keeping in mind that work often began on a draft declaration several months before it was officially ratified, such documents clearly ranked high on the political agenda of newly elected republican elites. Within seven months of elections, two-thirds of republics declared sovereignty. The laggards were almost all North Caucasian republics (Mordova is an exception, noted above). A majority of these men or their close associates remained presidents of these republics through 1998 (see Chapter Seven). Designing the 'rules of the game' paid high political dividends.

Ethnic composition is not a very explanatory variable for the speed with which republics declared sovereignty. Autonomous republics are largely artificial constructs. In twelve of the then twenty ASSRs, Russians outnumbered the titular nationality. Based on the 1989 census, no discernible pattern relating ethnic composition to the sovereignty timetable is detectable.[8]

[5] S.M. Chervonnaia & M.N. Guboglo, *Probuzhdenie finno-ugorskogo severa: Tom 1. Natsional'nye dvizheniia Marii El* (Moskva: RAN Tsentr po izucheniiu mezhnatsional'nykh otnoshenii, instituta Etnologii i Antropologii, 1996), 51.

[6] Venir K. Samigullin, author's interview, 28 April 1997, Law Faculty, Bashkir State University.

[7] Muksinov, 12.

[8] Census data reprinted in *Argumenty i fakty*, Mar. 1991.

Table 5.2   Electoral Effect on Declarations

Republic	Date of declaration	Chairman of Supreme Soviet	Month of election	Months elapsed
N. Ossetia	20 July 1990	Galazov	Mar. 1990	5
Karelia	9 Aug.	Stepanov	Apr.	5
Khakassia	15 Aug.	Shtygashev	Spring	5
Komi	29 Aug.	Spiridonov	Apr.	5
Tatarstan	30 Aug.	Shaimiev	Apr.	5
Udmurtia	20 Sept.	Tubylov	Apr.	6
Sakha	27 Sept.	Nikolaev	Mar.	7
Buriatia	8 Oct.	Buldaev	Mar.	7
Bashkortostan	11 Oct.	Rakhimov	Apr.	7
Kalmykia	18 Oct.	Basanov	Mar.	7
Marii El	22 Oct.	Zotin	Aug.	2
Chuvashia	24 Oct.	Leont'ev	Apr.	7
Gorno-Altai	25 Oct.	Chaptynov	Mar.	7
Tuva	1 Nov.	Ondar	Apr.	7
Karachai-Cherkessia	17 Nov.	Lesnichenko	Mar.	9
Checheno-Ingushetia	27 Nov.	Zavgaev	Mar.	9
Mordova	8 Dec.	Berezin	Apr.	9
Kabardino-Balkaria	31 Jan. 1991	Kokov	Apr. 1990	10
Dagestan	15 May 1991	Magomedov	Apr. 1990	13
Adygeia	2 July 1991	Dzharimov	Mar. 1990	17

Notes: In the case of the four autonomous *oblasti* that later changed status to republics (Altai, Adygeia, Karachaevo-Cherkessia and Khakassia) the date of election to the *oblast'* soviet is shown.

Sources: *Report on the USSR* (21 December 1990); *Politicheskii al'manakh Rossii* (1997).

Republics with predominantly Russian populations appear at the start (Karelia: 73.6 per cent Russian; Khakassia: 79.5 per cent Russian) and at the end (Adygeia: 68.0 per cent Russian; Mordova: 60.8 per cent Russian) of the Parade of Sovereignties. Similarly, republics with predominantly titular ethnic populations are just as randomly distributed: neighbouring North Ossetia and Kabardino-Balkaria both rank in the top five republics for ethnic homogeneity, while North Ossetia was the first to declare sovereignty and Kabardino-Balkaria among the last.

Time lags are further explained by events that explicitly encouraged autonomous republics to imitate the declarations of union republics. Two obvious candidates are the RSFSR declaration of sovereignty, and Boris Yeltsin's twenty-two day tour of the Russian regions later that summer. ASSRs sent delegations to the First Congress, which drafted Russia's declaration, where they paid close attention to the arguments and actions of union republics. Yeltsin's whirlwind speaking tour, which took him from Primorskii Krai to the heart of European Russia, was Yeltsin's first junket following his election as Chairman of the RSFSR Supreme Soviet. While in Kazan', Yeltsin made one of the most quoted and inflammatory statements of his career: 'Take as much independence as you can hold on to.'[9] Between Russia's declaration and Yeltsin's summer 1990 campaign to encourage regional activism, only one ASSR declared sovereignty. Following Yeltsin's tour, the deluge broke.

As Table 5.3 indicates, after the unequivocal support of Yeltsin, first several of the economically stronger regions and then the rest quickly followed with declarations of their own. With less to offer and more to lose than their union republic colleagues, leaders in autonomous republics needed more encouragement. Stirred by the declarations being made all around them, then prodded by internal elections, regional elites increasingly felt the need for more autonomy. But the catalyst for these declarations came from above and beyond.

1.2 Making the 'Rules of the Game'

The 'rules of the game'—both informal norms and formal procedures for drafting declarations—reveal as much about who made the rules as what they sought to achieve. Regional ruling elite had strong motives to take a vanguard role declaring sovereignty, an activity that appeared to pose little risk but offered the possibility of increased regional control and political legitimacy. The reasoning in Marii El was typical: 'Pseudo-sovereignty was found to be advantageous first and foremost for the party-nomenklatura at the top (who in the new conditions had been transferred to soviet and economic structures), for those who were commanding the enterprises and union ministries in the economy of the republic, the military-industrial complex, to which belonged more than 80 per cent of gross production'.[10] The spring 1990 elections overwhelmingly returned rank-and-file *nomenklatury* to republican and local soviets.[11] In Tatarstan, one analysis indicates 92 per cent of the 'new' ruling elite were former nomenklatura: 'If in Moscow the second and third echelons of the nomenklatura came to power, than in Tatarstan it is wholly predominated by the first

---

[9] *Vecherniaia kazan'* 10 August 1990, 1. Four days later, speaking in Ufa, Bashkortostan, he declared: 'Take that part of power that you will be able to swallow'. Cited in A.N. Arinin, 'Problemy razvitiia rossiiskoi gosudarstvennosti v kontse XX veka'. M.N. Guboglo, A.N. Arinin et al. eds. *Federalizm vlasti i vlast' federalizma* (Moskva: TOO IntelTex, 1997), 31, 103.

[10] Chervonnaia & Guboglo, 52.

[11] Dawn Mann, 'Leadership of Regional Communist Party Committees and Soviets', *Report on the USSR* (21 Dec. 1990): 17–22.

Table 5.3 Event Effect on Declarations, 1990

Time-span between events	60 days prior to RSFSR declaration (14 Apr.–12 June)	55 days between RSFSR declaration & Yeltsin's 'Kazan' Speech (12 June–5 Aug.)	60 days following Yeltsin's speech (5 Aug.–3 Oct.)	Next 60 days (3 Oct.–1 Dec.)	Remaining
Declarations	0	1	7	12	4
		N. Ossetian ASSR	Karelian ASSR	Buriat ASSR	Mordova ASSR (8 Dec. 1990)
			Khakassia AO	Koryak AOk	
				Komi-Permiak AOk	Kabardino-Balkaria ASSR (31 Jan. 1991)
			Komi ASSR	Bashkir ASSR	
				Kalmyk ASSR	
			Tatar ASSR	Yamal-Nenets AOk	
				Marii El ASSR	
			Udmurt ASSR	Chuvash ASSR	Dagestan ASSR (15 May 1991)
				Gorno-Altai AO	
				Tuva ASSR	
			Yakut ASSR	Kara.-Cherkess AO	Adygeia AO (2 July 1991)
				Chechen-Ingush ASSR	
			Chukchi AOk		

Note: AO, autonomous oblast; AOk, autonomous okrug.

echelon'.[12] The same was observed in Siberia, where a 'phoenix-like regen-eration of the nomenklatura' filled what had once been considered second-rate posts in representative institutions.[13] Elections empowered constitu-encies below republican *apparatchiks* while *perestroika* simultaneously weakened links 'from above.' Democratic legitimacy was suddenly con-ferred upon officials who had done little in their careers to earn it; those opting to remain in government had every motivation to bolster their positions in an increasingly uncertain environment.[14]

How? Typically, the Chairman or Presidium of the regional Supreme Soviet appointed a special committee to compose a draft declaration. In Bashkortostan, for example, a core group of three wrote the first draft: Venir Samigullin, Ludmila Dol'nikova, and Vladimir Podelianin. All three had legal backgrounds (Samigullin was a dotsent in law; the other two, candidates in law); in addition, Podelianin chaired the Bashkir KGB.[15] Their draft was shown to a larger commission of approximately fourteen people before publication in the official newspaper as one of three official drafts.[16] In comparison with the final version, the drafts were twice as long (twenty or more articles as compared to ten), and more detailed on the interrelationship of Bashkir and Union structures (e. g. two of the three cite the Union law on the delimitation of powers and one notes that sovereignty 'follows from the status of the republic as a subject of the USSR and Russian Federation . . . '), but with few substantive differences either between drafts or with the final version.[17]

Most republics published official drafts before finally declaring sovereignty by (invariably) an overwhelming majority of their Supreme Soviet.[18] But

---

[12] M.Kh. Farukshin, 'Politicheskaia elita v Tatarstane: Vyzvovy vremeni i trudnosti adaptatsii', *Polis: politicheskie issledovaniia*, No. 6/24 (1994): 70. The author included 96 people as 'ruling elite': president, vice-president, leader of presidential apparatus; from the Supreme Soviet: speaker, deputy speakers and leaders of the secretariat; from the Cabinet: Prime Minister, deputy prime ministers, chairs of state committees, head of the secretariat; and finally, heads of city and raion administrations. *See also* Jean-Robert Raviot, 'Types of Nationalism, Society, and Politics in Tatarstan', 32 *Russian Politics and Law*, 2 (1994): 74–6.

[13] James Hughes, 'Regionalism in Russia: The Rise and Fall of Siberian Agreement', 46 *Europe-Asia Studies*, 7 (1994): 1136.

[14] The clientalist-patron system entrenched in the regions was a formidable obstacle, difficult for emerging and mostly Leningrad and Moscow-based democratic opposition movements to penetrate. Philip Hanson, *Regions, Local Power and Economic Change in Russia* (London: Royal Institute of International Affairs, 1994), 15. McAuley, 40.

[15] *Sovetskaia Bashkiriia*, 18 Oct. 1990, 2. Venir K. Samigullin, author's interview, 30 April 1997, Law Faculty, Bashkir State University.

[16] *Sovetskaia Bashkiriia*, 10 Aug. 1990, 2. The other drafts were by the Soviet of Ministers and Supreme Soviet Presidium.

[17] Art. 1, Council of Ministers draft, *Sovetskaia Bashkiriia*, 10 Aug. 1990, 2.

[18] The vote at the 3rd Session of the Bashkir Supreme Soviet was 245 in favour, 1 against, 4 abstentions, 6 not voting, 19 absent. *Sovetskaia Bashkiriia*, 16 Oct. 1990, 2. In Kalmykia, the 18

multiple drafts did not mean either real debate or popular participation. The Kalmyk Supreme Soviet's final version passed in late October essentially duplicated an early September draft.[19] A concise five-articled 'Alternative variant' offered by one Kalmykian People's Deputy in early October appeared to be more a public relations exercise than a genuine alternative.[20] In Komi, the Party newspaper solicited citizen feedback about its published draft. However, the final version, approved three weeks later, manifested only superficial changes.[21] Non-government drafts seemed designed only to provide the semblance of public participation.[22] The declaration accepted by the Sakha (Yakutia) Republic three weeks after publication of an official draft differed by only one article and one clause. Alternative drafts seemed to have had no impact whatsoever.[23] In Buriatia, the close similarity between drafts called into question any *glasnost* in the process or independence in proposals by different groups.[24]

How did referendums feature in the process? From 1987 to 1993 thirty-three referendums were held in Eastern Europe and the former Soviet Union; twelve of these sought popular approval for sovereignty or independence.[25] Of the fifteen Soviet Socialist Republics that ultimately became independent states, eight held referendums on independence and two held referendums on state sovereignty with high percentages for voter turnout

October vote at an extraordinary session of the Supreme Soviet was unanimous. K.N. Iliumzhinov & K.N. Maksimov, *Kalmykiia na rubezhe vekov* (Moskva: Izdatel'stvo 'ZelO', 1997), 155.

[19] *Sovetskaia Kalmykia* 7 Sept. 1990.

[20] 'Al'ternativnyi variant', *Sovetskaia Kalmykia*, 6 Oct. 1990, 2.

[21] *Krasnoe znamia*, 2 August 1990, 1.

[22] Two drafts appeared 13 July 1990. One, by Gennadii Yushkov, a writer and principal founder of the national movement 'Komi Kotyr', proposed legislative and executive institutions and unification with the Komi-Permiak Autonomous Okrug, none of which appear in the government's final version. A nationalist draft by a republican people's deputy and then co-chaiman of Komi Kotyr, Vitalii Osipov, foresaw a bicameral legislature with one house for Komi (possessing a veto on certain questions) and one house for all other nationalities. *Krasnoe znamia*, 13 July 1990.

[23] *Sotsialisticheskaia Iakutiia*, 2 September 1990, 2. N. Egorov, 'Alternativnyi proekt: Deklaratsiia o suverenitete IaASSR', *Sotsialisticheskaia Iakutiia*, 15 Sept. 1990, 2. Dmitrii Mironov, in his comprehensive account of the state-building process in Sakha, notes in addition to the official draft, a group of republican people's deputies, members of the National Front and the national movements 'Sakha keskile' and 'Sakha omuk' also presented drafts, though their impact is unclear. Dmitrii N. Mironov *Konstitutsionno-pravovoi status respubliki sakha (iakutia) kak sub'ekta Rossiiskoi Federatsii* (Novosibirsk: 'Nauka' sibirskaia izdatel'skaia firma RAN, 1996), 54–5, 58.

[24] For a rough draft by the procuracy see *Pravda Buriatii*, 9 Sept. 1990, 4. For one by the Council of Ministers *see Pravda Buriatii*, 3 Oct. 1990, 3. The composite rough draft developed by the Presidium of the Supreme Soviet is published in *Pravda Buriatii*, 6 Oct. 1990, 1.

[25] Henry E. Brady & Cynthia S. Kaplan, 'Eastern Europe and the Former Soviet Union', in David Butler & Austin Ranney, eds. *Referendums Around the World: The Growing Use of Direct Democracy* (Washington: American Enterprise Institute, 1994), 179–80. Of the remaining 21 referendums, 9 ratified constitutions or new forms of government and 12 dealt with specific policy issues.

and approval.[26] *In the autonomous republics, not a single referendum was held on questions of either sovereignty or independence until December 1991.* Referendums occurred only as tactics for legitimizing secession (Ingushetia from Chechnya) or negotiating bilateral treaties (Tatarstan and Bashkortostan).[27] In any event, these referendums were not employed to legitimate with a popular vote existing declarations. Although every Declaration was made 'in the name of the people', the electorate actually played a very passive role.[28] Drafting committees were typically composed of high-level government elites appointed by the Chairman of the Supreme Soviet. Contrary to the Soviet tradition of proletarian representatives on everything from People's Courts to Supreme Soviet Presidiums, citizens was not invited to sit with experts on drafting commissions. Official newspapers published draft 'proposals' with insufficient time for popular reaction before final votes in republican parliaments. In many ways, these drafting processes were the antithesis of the grassroots national movements that preceded them.

Excursus: The Case of Tatarstan

Tatarstan, a republic in the Volga region, was the acknowledged leader of the republican movement. The sovereignty process there was more complex and deserves special mention. Numerous drafts were published in official papers during August 1990. Alone on one side of the spectrum was the draft of Aleksandr Shtanin, a co-ordinator for the opposition group 'People's Power' (*Narodnaia vlast*'). This draft remarkably limited republican sovereignty within the context of the RSFSR and the Union. It was explicitly multinational and lacked the declamatory clauses commandeering property and resources.[29] On the other extreme was the draft of the nationalist Tatar Public Centre (*TOTs*). Starting from a preamble extolling the glories of Tatar independence from the 11th to the 16th centuries, it expounded an extreme nationalist stance in a rambling thirty-six article declaration. Another draft, by the 'Citizens Committee of Tatariia', also mentioned medieval glories, but

---

[26] Brady & Kaplan, 193–4.

[27] On 1 December 1991, the People's Council of Ingushetia held a referendum on the sovereignty of Ingushetia within the RSFSR and on the return of territory lost during Stalinist purges in 1944. 73.7% participation and a 92.5% approval vote was claimed. Tatarstan and Bashkortostan held referendums on 21 March 1992 & 25 April 1993, respectively.

[28] The First Russian Congress, with nearly 1,000 deputies, could arguably pose as a popular assembly convened for the extraordinary purpose of declaring sovereignty. Supreme Soviets of the autonomous republics were elected with no such implied mandate.

[29] Art. 5 reads: 'The TASSR is united with other republics in a federation and a union on the basis of treaties and respects the sovereign rights of republics, the federation and unions'. See 'Proekt narodnogo deputata TASSR A. Shtanina', *Sovetskaia Tatariia*, 8 Aug. 1990, 2.

limited itself to a terse three article exposition of state sovereignty: Tatar-stan was a subject of international law. The rest was left to later legislation.[30]

These different views might imply genuine public debate. This was only partially true. Shtanin's draft was independently created, but the TOTs draft was not. The Chairman of the Supreme Soviet and future president, Minti-mer Shaimiev, harnessed what nationalist sentiment existed in Tatarstan for his own interests. TOTs was not a spontaneous movement, but an organiza-tion engineered from the top echelons of Tatar power.[31] A key founder and the lead ideologist for the Tatar Public Centre was Rafael Khakimov, a close and long-serving adviser to Shaimiev.[32] As Vladimir Beliaev, a political scientist and member of the democratic opposition explained:

I do not think Shaimiev created an ethno-territorial movement. He just played it up. In his time, he was helping the Tatar national movement, making it easier for them to register, finding places for them to meet, finance, etc. He let them, or even ordered directors of enterprises to bring crowds to the 'Square of Liberty', the central square of Kazan'. Then he could literally refer to the 'will of the people'.[33]

The Centre's fear of Tatar nationalism, in the light of increasing ethnic violence throughout the Soviet Union, was a powerful bargaining chip. As Beliaev says, Shaimiev 'understood when it was time to sit on the Tatar nationalist horse'.[34] An editor from Vecherniaia Kazan', one of the few relatively independent newspapers in the republic, recalls how Shaimiev 'manipulated the nationalists in a very clever way', orchestrating large de-monstrations in Lenin square. 'It was a controlled movement', she recalls, 'and they obediently retreated' when their presence became polit-

---

[30] Both drafts in Sovetskaia Tatariia, 8 Aug. 1990, 2.

[31] Jean-Robert Raviot offers a misleadingly reductionist account of the founding of TOTs as the initiative of 'a few dozen intellectuals from Kazan' University' in February 1989. Raviot acknow-ledges the 'latent support' Shaimiev gave the movement's all-Tatar Congress, the Millimejlis. However, Raviot skirts deeper links with Shaimiev's government, neglecting to mention the key role played by Khakimov. Jean-Robert Raviot, "Types of Nationalism, Society, and Politics in Tartarstan." 32 Russian Politics and Law 2 (1994): 69–79.

[32] Dmitrii Toropov, Spravochnik novykh partii i obshchestvennykh organizatsii Tatarstana (Moskva: Informatsionno-ekspertnaia gruppa 'Panorama', iiun, 1992), 6, 14. Interview with Ildus Sultanov, chairman of the executive committee of the 'Equality and Law' electoral bloc, Kazan', 1 June 1997. Interview with Vladimir Beliaev, chief of the Department of Sociology and Political Science at Kazan' State Technical University and leader of the political group 'Social Democratic Union', Kazan', 2 June 1997. Beliaev notes Shaimiev's administration is 'constantly changing' with members of Tatar national movements.

[33] Beliaev interview. See also Toropov, 6.

[34] David Hoffman, 'Artful Leader Slips Moscow's Grip', Washington Post, 16 June 1997, A1.

ically inexpedient.[35] Valery Tishkov, who interviewed key figures in the drafting process, argues that Shaimiev's team 'had tried to find a creative approach to the text that would allow them to satisfy all major public forces and at the same time exploit ethnonationalism as the major argument to provide bargaining power with the Center'.[36]

Shaimiev not only manipulated the nationalist movement, he carefully controlled the Supreme Soviet he chaired. Stenographic records of sessions on the Declaration reveal how adept Shaimiev was at directing debates and silencing his opposition. Ivan Grachev, chairman of the group 'Equality and Law', was one of the only outspoken opponents. In 1990, Grachev led the opposition against Shaimiev as a deputy to the republic's Supreme Soviet. During one of the last sessions, he interrupted the debate to question the competence and composition of commissions reviewing questions of sovereignty. He insisted on changes to the republic's constitution and guarantees to 'be sure that power in the republic is transmitted to the people'.[37] Shaimiev ignored him, but after several minutes Grachev rose again to complain that deputies were deceived by promises that structural reforms to government would commence after the declaration was accepted. Shaimiev announced that Grachev's microphone would be switched off.[38] At one point, in true Soviet style, the arrival of hundreds of admiring telegrams was announced.[39]

The day *after* declaring sovereignty, excerpts from the Supreme Soviet 'debate' on 29 August were published as 'The Main Question on the Agenda'.[40] The tenor of the times and the choice of excerpts suggest ulterior motives for publication beyond citizen awareness. Having drafted the sharpest worded declaration to date, Shaimiev's team now sought to convince

---

[35] Yelena Chernobrovkina, interview with David Hoffman, Kazan', 2 June 1997. In fact, some members of TOTs are extremely resentful: 'Shaimiev does not fear the nationalist movement because we are weak today. Shaimiev, the KGB and the Russian security forces fragmented us, but we are trying to unite'. Interview with Zaaki Zaimullin, Tatar Public Centre, Kazan', 2 June 1997. 'I am not calm. There are hundreds of thousands like me. Assimilation of Tatar culture is taking place....We want our language and culture back and the only way to guarantee that is through Tatar statehood'. Interview with Farit Urazaev, Tatar Public Centre, 2 June 1997.

[36] Valery Tishkov, *Ethnicity, Nationalism and Conflict in and After the Soviet Union: The Mind Aflame.* (London: Sage, 1997), 56–7.

[37] *Stenograficheskii otchet, Zasedanie pervoe, Vtoraia sessia Verkhovnogo Soveta TASSR,* 27 avgusta 1990, utrenee, 13.

[38] *Stenograficheskii otchet,* 24.

[39] 'Dear comrade deputies! The Secretariat considers it necessary to give several pieces of information for the knowledge of the People's Deputies. To address the ongoing second session of the Supreme Soviet of the TASSR a great deal of correspondence, telegrams, appeals, statements and resolutions are arriving. In 15 hours today 685 such documents have been registered, in that number 328 telegrams, 136 letters, 207 appeals and statements.' 612 were said to be about the question of sovereignty; 50% were said to be from Tatariia while the rest came from throughout the Soviet Union. F. Kh. Mukhametshin, *Stenograficheskii otchet, Zacedanie tret'e, Vtoraia sessia Verkhovnogo Soveta TASSR,* 28 avgusta, 1990, utrenee, 291.

[40] 'Glavnyi vopros povestki dnia', *Sovetskaia Tatariia,* 31 Aug. 1990, 1.

Moscow that alternatives to Shaimiev could be far worse. Their message: reject Shaimiev's moderate approach and risk uncontrollable nationalism. The chairman of the Supreme Soviet commission on nationalities questions, R.A. Iusupov, gave a thinly veiled warning that anything less than full sovereignty for Tatarstan would lead to serious weakening of the friendship between peoples, a prospect Moscow dreaded. Particularly odd was the introduction of an alternative draft declaration proposed by R.R. Sirazeev, far more strident than the official draft scheduled for a vote. It categorically rejected USSR legal authority, established dual citizenship (including separate passports and migration policy), expropriated all Soviet property in Tatarstan, and harshly stated that Tatarstan 'will not answer for the debts of the Union'.[41] There seemed little point to such a virulent new draft, published after the final vote rejecting it, except to produce a special spectacle for Moscow. The irony was probably lost at the time that Sirazeev was chief director of the Tatar state theatre.

1.3 What the Declarations Say

For the future Russian Federation, the most important declaration was the RSFSR Declaration of State Sovereignty. It was accepted on 12 June 1990 by a large majority (907–13, with nine abstentions) at the First Russian Congress of People's Deputies. Far more than preceding declarations by other republics, the sheer enormity and power of Russia raised the stakes of centre-periphery conflict to a new level: without Russia there could be no Soviet Union. Dissolution of the Soviet empire was not a direct objective of the Declaration; but the assertion of self-determination by the USSR's linchpin republic was an unprecedented challenge to the integrity of Soviet authority. Further, the Declaration catalysed drafts in the autonomous republics within the RSFSR. The Russian Declaration directly involved ASSR leaders in the drafting process, essentially offering regional elites a 'dry run' before their own declarations. In Moscow, they acquired a particular vocabulary and set of conceptions to bring to their own republics. The Russian Congress began the process of 'sovereignization' with unfavorable portents for the later process of 'federalization'.

The Declaration's preamble and fifteen articles outlined its framers' perception of sovereignty as historically based in a multi-ethnic people (Arts. 1 and 3), as a natural and necessary condition for modern statehood (Art. 2), and a bulwark for rights and freedoms (Art. 4). In fact, as *Pravda* reported, 'during the debate it became clear that many of them

---

[41] 'Glavnyi vopros povestki dnia', *Soveteskaia Tatariia*, 31 Aug. 1990, 1.

had different understandings of the very word sovereignty'.[42] Yeltsin defined sovereignty 'from the ground up', by which he literally meant a pyramid flow of authority from the smallest villages to the Supreme Soviet.[43] Other deputies were more radical, equating sovereignty with independence and secession. Still others debated interpretations as focused on autonomy *from institutions* (the USSR, the Party, etc.) as on autonomy *to action* (cultural development, budget formation, etc.). Complained one conservative analyst: 'So, they talk about economic sovereignty, financial, legislative, political, national, regional, religious and so on. Even about sovereignty of the person. Thereby from this idea they form an image of some fabled many-headed monster, of which the deprivation of one or several heads does not effect its functional characteristics'.[44] That few areas of agreement existed perfectly suited the Congress: 'Because sovereignty was an acceptable, long-sanctioned word, yet one whose meaning was not agreed, a dialogue could be maintained, despite deep disagreements, and resolutions could be adopted which allowed for different interpretations. . . . But clarification was not really in anyone's interest. It would have opened the lid to a Pandora's box of problems whereas ambiguity allowed agreement to be reached on paper'.[45]

As with any document that unilaterally challenges existing authority, the RSFSR Declaration was of minor legal-constitutional significance—but great political significance—within the pre-existing Soviet system. A crucial precedent was established in leaving existing borders untouched.[46] But asserted rights of separate citizenship (Arts. 8, 10, 11), exclusive ownership and authority over all 'natural riches' (Art. 5, §3) and the primacy of RSFSR law over Soviet Union law (Art. 5, §2) would later haunt Russian authorities in dealing with the demands former ASSRs would place on them as the new

---

[42] Quoted in Robert V. Daniels, ed. *A Documentary History of Communism in Russia: From Lenin to Gorbachev* (Hanover, NH: University Press of New England, 1993), 375.

[43] Gail W. Lapidus & Edward W. Walker, 'Nationalism, Regionalism, and Federalism: Center-Periphery Relations in Post-Communist Russia', Gail Lapidus, ed. *The New Russia: Troubled Transformation* (Boulder, CO: Westview, 1995), 82.

[44] N.A. Kataev, 'Problemy pravovoi reglamentatsii statusa respublik Rossiiskoi Federatsii', in Kataev, N.A. & V.K. Samigullin, eds. *Problemy konstitutsionnogo razvitiya suverennoi respubliki* (Ufa: Izdanie Verkh. Soveta i Soveta ministrov Respubliki Bashkortostan, 1992), 40. Kataev was head of the Urals MVD higher school and *dotsent*, candidate of law. He continues, hinting at the difficulties this view of sovereignty created for federalism: 'An approach of this kind is a failure in theory as it is in practice. Thanks to it the illusion is created that an isolated solution to questions of sovereignty is possible, acquisition of it by parts'.

[45] Mary McAuley, *Russia's Politics of Uncertainty* (Cambridge, University Press, 1997), 32, 33.

[46] Caution about redrawing borders was one of the few examples of political wisdom in the development of the new Russian federalism. See, for example, Zakon RF, 'Ob ustanovlenii perekhodnogo perioda po gosudarstvenno-territorial'nomu razgranicheniiu v Rossiiskoi Federatsii', 3 July 1992 *Vedomosti S"ezda narodnykh deputatov RF i Verkhovnogo Soveta RF*, No. 32 (13 August 1992), item 1868, 2397–8.

'Centre', following the dissolution of Soviet power. No legal basis was given for such assertions because there was none: explicit alongside the fiat of these rights was the nullification of any contradicting Soviet law.[47] The only legal principles this newly proclaimed 'rule-of-law state' (Art. 13) asserted were 'universally recognized principles of international law' (Art. 14).

Still less prudent precedents were also created. Article 4 announced the inalienable right of every people to self-determination. In this nominally federal state, physically divided according to ethnic groups, the most recent (1989) census indicated that 'every people' potentially included over sixty nationalities! Article 7 provided for a right to secession. Article 9, accepted only after heated debate, affirmed 'the need for a substantial broadening' of the existing rights of autonomous republics and other subjects of the Federation. The increasingly pitched battles for supremacy between Russian and Union authorities (personified in Yeltsin and Gorbachev), the struggle for control over resources and industry and a Congress dominated by a large ethnic Russian majority left most delegates blind to the politically volatile precedent they were establishing. As Mary McAuley chronicles, most delegates were left convinced that 'the idea of Russia itself breaking up was simply too far-fetched'.[48]

With few exceptions, the ASSR final drafts are remarkably similar to the preceding Russian version. Attempts to explain this fact must rely largely on circumstantial evidence. The similar backgrounds drafters shared, and their common reference to an increasing number of declarations are two strong factors.[49] While declarations varied in length from six articles (Tatarstan) to

---

[47]   The RSFSR Supreme Soviet quickly passed numerous laws and resolutions to strengthen the Declaration's assertions within a new *Russian* legal framework. On 9 August the resolution, 'On the Defence of the Economic Basis of Sovereignty of the RSFSR', asserted control over the sale of everything from gold to grain. A.I. Doronchenkov, ed. *K Soiuzu suverennykh narodov: Sbornik dokumentov KPSS, zakonodatel'nykh actov, deklaratsii, obrashchenii i presidentskikh ukazov, posviashchennykh problema natsional'no-gosudarstvennogo suvereniteta* (Moskva: Institut teorii i istorii sotsializma TsK KPSS, 1991), 456–7. An even more exacting law, defining and asserting control over Russia's 'natural riches', was signed in late October. No mention was made of the rights of ownership accorded sub-union level territories. Zakon, 'Ob obespechenii ekonomicheskoi osnovy suvereniteta RSFSR', *Vedomosti S''ezda narodnykh deputatov RSFSR v Verkhovnogo Soveta RSFSR*, No. 22 (1 Nov. 1990), Arts. 260, 305. Art. 5 of the Declaration, on the supremacy of law, was also further developed in late October with the law, 'On the functioning of acts of organs of the USSR on the territory of the RSFSR'. A.N. Adrov & S.M. Shakhrai, eds. *Sbornik zakonodatel'nykh aktov RSFSR o gosudarstvennom suverenitete, soiuznom dogovore i referendume* (Moskva: Sovetskaia Rossiia izdatel'stvo, 1991), 16–17.

[48]   Mary McAuley, *Russia's Politics of Uncertainty* (Cambridge University Press, 1997), 27–34.

[49]   In explanatory notes to published drafts, the RSFSR and Ukrainian declarations are cited most often as points of reference. In Bashkortostan, the RSFSR, Ukrainian and Tatar declarations were all influential, while Samigullin emphasized the 'ideological stamp on the head' of drafters subjected to efforts to create 'a new Soviet people'. Samigullin strongly emphasized the influence of the U.S. Declaration of Independence on the members of the Bashkir drafting committee, though close readings of the final draft offer no textual similarities. Interviews with V.K. Samigullin, 28 and 30 April 1997, Ufa.

eighteen (Adygeia and Marii El), most contained a core of virtually identically phrased articles outlining change in status (from autonomous republic to union republic), the supremacy of republican law, citizenship and its attendant political rights, and republican possession of most everything of value on the republic's territory. Even the ordering of articles was often the same.

The declarations themselves, as well as analytical works published subsequently by many of the men and women involved in the Parade of Sovereignties, all point to similar stimuli. According to a monograph co-authored by the current president of Kalmykia, the legal basis for declaring sovereignty was the 10 April 1990 USSR law 'On the Fundamentals of Economic relations of the USSR, Union and Autonomous Republics', the 26 April law 'On the Demarcation of Authority...', Art. 9 of the RSFSR Declaration, and speeches by Yeltsin in the RSFSR Congress of People's Deputies. Thus, the autonomous republics, 'had the legislative basis, the moral and legal support of the first Congress of People's Deputies of the RSFSR'.[50] Boris Zheleznov, key drafter of the Tatar declaration argued that the RSFSR Declaration naturally led to other declarations of self-determination.[51] Irek Muksinov, member of the USSR Committee of Constitutional Supervision and an active member of the Bashkir Constitutional Commission identified three linked stimuli for the Parade of Sovereignties: new conditions created by *glasnost* and democratization, which freed republican leaders to react directly against the false autonomy proclaimed in Soviet law; union republic declarations, especially the RSFSR; and USSR legislation of 1990–1 elevating the status of autonomous republics.[52]

Most republics skirted the issue of *who* possessed the right to self-determination that all employed to justify sovereignty. Many were reluctant to press exclusively national bases for claims since titular nationalities were majorities in less than a third of republics; in no republic did the titular nationality account for more than three-quarters of the population and in half of the republics ethnic Russians accounted for 50 per cent or more of the population.[53] In Sakha, for example, Supreme Soviet Chairman Nikolaev's

---

[50] Iliumzhinov & Maksimov, 152–5.

[51] Boris Zheleznov & Vasilii Likhachev, *Pravovoi status respubliki Tatarstan* (Kazan': Tatarskoe knizhnoe izdatel'stvo, 1996): 7, 10–11.

[52] Muksinov, 11–12.

[53] Denis J.B. Shaw, 'Geographic and Historical Observations on the Future of a Federal Russia', 34 *Post-Soviet Geography*, 8 (1993): 532. Only in Tyva, North Ossetia, Kabardino-Balkaria and Checheno-Ingushetia did the titular elite comprise a majority in 1989, in the latter two cases only because of the existence of two titular ethnic groups.

drafting commission specifically ignored efforts by one popular movement ('Sakha omuk') to link the territory of the republic with traditional native settlements.[54] Still, few could resist references in the preamble or first few articles to the special position of the titular ethnic group, their particular inalienable rights singled out above the rights of all others. Preambles universally vaunted the 'historic responsibility' of republics for their multi-national populations, begging the question of exactly *whose* right to self-determination was being exercised. Most declarations demanded protection for titular languages and cultures; some asserted a right to protect ethnic diasporas beyond the republic's borders. Most also sought to assuage the anxieties of Russian populations by preserving Russian as an official lan-guage and providing equal protection for political and human rights regard-less of nationality. Hedged or vague phrasing was not accidental, but an exercise in political manipulation.

Not all declarations were confrontational. The Declaration of the North Caucasian republic of Kalmykia was comparatively hesitant and comprom-ising. The preamble acknowledges the republic's continued status as a subject of both the RSFSR and the USSR and the importance of pursuing economic and social interests in concert with them. Where other republics declared lofty 'responsibilities', Kalmykia held its right to 'socioeconomic progress' and a 'rise in the standard of living' equal to self-determination. Other articles noted the continued applicability of Union laws (e. g. Art. 5). Kalmykia's status as one of the poorest republics in the RSFSR partially explains this approach. The counsel for the republic's Permanent Mission in Moscow accentuated Kalmykia's dependence on federal largesse: character-izing all federal units as either 'blood-donors' or 'blood-recipients', he unabashedly described Kalmykia as the latter: there was no interest in pursuing activities that might jeopardize much needed subsidies. The pur-pose of the declaration was greater control over aid and greater respect for linguistic and cultural rights.[55] Kalmykia's tail-end position in the parade of sovereignties further supports the impression of a republic eager not to miss a window of opportunity, but hesitant to jeopardize relations with Moscow.[56]

[54] Mironov, *Konstitutsionno-pravovoi status . . .* , 58.

[55] Batyshin Marat, author's interview, 7 July 1995, Permanent Mission of the Republic of Kalmykia, Moscow.

[56] Interestingly, in an effort to curry favour with Yeltsin following the October 1993 Events, Kalmykia's President Kirsan Ilumzhinov would offer to renounce his republic's declaration of sovereignty. This strange situation is discussed later in this chapter.

Republican elites were strongly affected by Yeltsin's stimulus to grab what sovereignty they could. The result was like the mirror house in a carnival: the RSFSR declaration could be seen reflected in republican versions, distorted to fit particular circumstance but seldom to the point of losing the original image. Richer republics advanced stronger claims to resources while poorer republics tried to defend their federal subsidies. Republics fearing an exodus of well-trained Russians emphasized inter-ethnic harmony more than republics less dependent on such populations. But the core demands remained virtually untouched: sovereignty (whatever that meant) to replace subordination; supremacy of local laws over federal laws; autonomy to control economic decision-making and natural resources; respect for local languages and customs.

1.4 Effects on Federal Development

The aftermath of the Russian Declaration exposed the general confusion about what sovereignty really meant for a 'renewed' federation. Political manipulation was not only inevitable, it had been intentional. Yeltsin's contest with Gorbachev required allies and resources, both of which his legally vacuous declaration provided at little immediately perceived cost. Declared control of resources, territory and state institutions also accumulated more political capital, if not these stated objectives. A large Congress implied popular legitimacy. Awkward procedural questions were left to be resolved in a future Union Treaty, thus developing a strong bargaining position more than six months before the Novo-Ogarevo process began. Yeltsin's junkets to the republics and exhortations to take as much sovereignty as could be swallowed were part of a strategy to constrain Gorbachev's centre. Little concern was given to the possibility that if this centre ever shifted from Gorbachev to Yeltsin, these grand promises would be very difficult to keep. Gorbachev had legalized a complicated secession procedure convinced that a renewed and successful Union would dispel any desire to exercise such a right. Now Yeltsin seemed to believe that a 'real' federation would devolve enough sovereignty to satiate the regions, while Moscow retained strong, central leadership.

This was a clever gambit. Even Boris Zheleznov, one of the principal drafters of Tatarstan's declaration and its new constitution, understood Yeltsin's strategy. But he also recognized the dangers Yeltsin and Gorbachev courted, comparing misuse of the new vocabulary of federalism with the Soviet doublespeak Bulgakov captured in *The Master and Margarita*:

Yeltsin in all politics is a pragmatist and he was not able *not* to understand that he was going to need the support of the republics.... Gorbachev also launched an attempt to bring to his side the republics. And in particular in April 1990 another Union law was passed according to which republics were declared subjects of the USSR, as if subjects of a second sort, preserving autonomy different than the fifteen union republics.... Of course, this was juridical nonsense because one republic, one state cannot at the same time be a subject of two federations. But many republics accepted this as fact, and their declarations noted that they considered themselves to be union republics, that is subjects of the Union, at the same time they remained in the Russian Federation. We have a joke about a sturgeon of the 'second freshness'— one of the second freshness, that's not a sturgeon![57]

Yeltsin was unconcerned with the effects of his 'War of Laws' against Gorbachev; his aim was solely short-term allegiance from the republics. It was, according to Zheleznov, not a mistake but simply 'a pragmatic move of politics'. The 'Parade of Sovereignties' established a strong negotiating position for Yeltsin at Novo-Ogarevo. But building a federation on the vagaries of the sort of 'feel-good' sovereignty Yeltsin propounded was a much more difficult proposition.[58] Such politics rattled the foundations of a renewed USSR, let alone a renewed Russian Federation. '[Yeltsin] was encouraging the crowd to take freedom and self-determination and he was much loved for it', explained Venir Samigullin, a drafter of declarations and constitutions in Bashkortostan. 'If Gorbachev wanted to reform the USSR so that the union and autonomous republics would be equivalent, as Sakharov proposed, than Yeltsin's attracting them to his side *was* a mistake. But it was *not* a mistake in the sense that this move gave Russia maximum strength in its argument for independence and freedom which in the end is what it received.'[59] How much Yeltsin's promises to the republics helped him to secure Russian independence is debatable. But from the point of view of establishing a solid federal approach to new centre-periphery relations,

[57]   Boris L. Zheleznov, author's interview, 6 June 1997, Law Faculty, Kazan' State University. *See* Mikhail Bulgakov, *The Master and Margarita*, ch. 18.

[58]   Yeltsin's assurances seemed unambiguous while in Tatarstan: 'Naturally, they asked Boris Nikolaevich a great many questions about the status of Tatarstan . . . : will Tatarstan be a union republic, will it leave Russia, what portion of power can it delegate the RSFSR, and who in the event of a declaration of sovereignty will be in charge of the oil? . . . And so forth and so forth. It seems, Yeltsin even grew tired of repeating one and the same thing: These are your questions, these you yourselves should decide, your Supreme Soviet, why do you again want that there should be some kind of instruction from above . . . '. Elena Chernobrovkina, 'Reshat' vam samim,' *Vecherniaia Kazan'*, 10 Aug. 1990, 1. But back in Moscow, Yeltsin promised: 'It [Tatarstan] remains part of Russia, delegating certain functions to it, and through it participating in the solution of all-Union questions'. *Sovetskaia Rossiia*, 2 Sept. 1990, 2.

[59]   Venir K. Samigullin, author's interview, 30 April 1997, Law Faculty, Bashkir State University.

Yeltsin's gambit did little but foment antagonism towards *any* central involvement in regional affairs. Rather than encourage compromise in the renegotiation of autonomy, Yeltsin instigated an all-or-nothing mindset that for the time strengthened him against Union authorities but left him vulnerable to his own promises when he became the embodiment of a new centre.

Autonomous republics followed union republics in declaring sovereignty, but with very different motivations. The most striking of these is the final result each type of republic desired. Union republics, buttressed by declarations of independence, and often referendums on independence and international support, became independent nation-states, members of the international community. This goal, from the first round of declarations, often had considerable historical precedent behind it. Autonomous republics, for the most part, sought only what their names implied: autonomy. Considerable concern existed amongst ASSR elites that their declarations might be misconstrued. 'I suggest', worried one member of the Bashkir Supreme Soviet, 'it is necessary to more precisely define in our Bashkir Declaration, in order to remove false interpretations, here comrades continue to say that if you become a sovereign republic, they claim that you automatically leave Russia. We are receiving wider rights, we are becoming a republic of a new type. But for many this is not entirely understood.'[60]

The Parade of Sovereignties made construction of a 'renewed federation', an ambition most republics ostensibly shared, more difficult. There is a parallel here with analysis by political scientists of the 'sequencing of elections'. In transitions from authoritarian rule, both theoretical and comparative empirical studies suggest advantages to conducting all-Union elections prior to regional elections.[61] This sequence encourages more unifying agendas and broad-based constituencies, improving the chances of constructing all-Union institutions. In Russia, declarations of sovereignty, by their very nature, elevated provincial interests above federal interests. This fact slowly dawned on Yeltsin and his advisers as they found themselves the new occupants of Gorbachev's despised centre. Andranik Migranyan complained: 'The bomb planted under the USSR by the declaration of Russian sovereignty is, it seems to me, facilitating not only the destruction of the USSR but also—to an even greater extent—the destruction of Russia

---

[60] Boris Pavlov, *Stenograficheskii otchet, Tret'ia sessia Verkhovnogo Soveta Bashkirskoi SSR (dvenadt-satyi sozyv), 10–13 oktiabria 1990 g., 23–24 oktiabria 1990 g* (Ufa: Izdanie Verkhovnogo Soveta Bashkirskoi SSR, 1991), 158.

[61] Juan Linz & Alfred Stepan, 'Political Identities and Electoral Sequences: Spain, the Soviet Union, and Yugoslavia', 121 *Daedalus*, 2 (Spring 1992): 123–39.

itself'.[62] Ramazan Abdulatipov, then Chairman of the RSFSR Supreme
Soviet's Council of Nationalities echoed this concern: the ASSRs did not
realize the full meaning of their actions.[63] On the contrary, regional leaders
seem to have understood all too well. The Parade of Sovereignties offered a
special window of opportunity to construct new bases of support while old
nomenklatura foundations weakened. As one regional analyst summarized
the result:

On this track, overcoming the stereotypes of a unitary conception of the federal
construction of the state was essential. The Declaration of state sovereignty of the
Russian Federation gave this process a general background and stimulus. By its own
political content it was directed to the affirmation of the independence of Russia in
the composition of the USSR. But objectively the Declaration pushed the republics,
krais, oblasts and national okrugs towards the search for variants of their own
independence in the composition of the Russian Federation.[64]

These variants utilized a provocative vocabulary not conducive to the
compromise and 'marbleization' of sovereignty that is the basis for federation. Sovereignty, autonomy, self-determination: these terms emphasized
separateness, individuality, freedom from some indeterminate suppressor of
rights. The choice of terms directed the course of the debate, establishing
the 'rules of the game' almost before the players themselves realized the
implications of their actions. Virtually every declaration contained a clause
stipulating the document itself—though patently alegal (if not illegal) in the
Soviet institutional setting—as the basis for *all* future negotiation of federal
relations. The focus of debate about the fate of the Union shifted to one
encumbered with local grievances. An approach that emphasized common
objectives for restructuring the federation could have altered, or at least
delayed, this focus. Before the Parade of Sovereignties, the central issue was
simply the loosening of Soviet centralized power; Yeltsin led regional elites
to question the role of *any* central authority, Soviet or Russian. The 'sequencing of declarations of sovereignty' fostered the creation of local agendas
and constituencies rather than more unifying or broadly federal ones. By
definition, these declarations focused attention on parochial republican

[62] Gail W. Lapidus & Edward W. Walker, 'Nationalism, Regionalism, and Federalism: Center-
Periphery Relations in Post-Communist Russia', in Gail W. Lapidus, ed. *The New Russia: Troubled
Transformation* (Boulder, CO: Westview, 1995), 85.
[63] Ann Sheehy, 'Fact Sheet on Declarations of Sovereignty', *Report on the USSR* (9 Nov.
1990): 25.
[64] A.I. Sukharev, 'Konstitutsionnaia reforma i novaia regional'naia politika rossiiskoi federatsii',
in A.I. Sukharev, ed. *Regional'naia politika Rossiiskoi Federatsii* (Saransk: NII regionologii, 1993), 4.
Sukharev directed the scientific research institute of regional studies at Mordova State University,
Saransk.

interests over (and often at the expense of) the interests of a 'renewed federation'.

2. THE FEDERATION TREATY: TRANSITION TO THE NEW FEDER-ALISM, PART ONE

All autonomous republic (ASSR) declarations shared at least one common clause: these documents were the basis for participation in the conclusion of the Union Treaty of a renewed USSR and for negotiation of a new Federation Treaty within the RSFSR. This was not empty rhetoric, as the exercise of such a right provided *de facto* acknowledgement of the elevated status of the ASSRs in a larger union. It also provided the first opportunity for direct involvement in establishing federal 'rules of the game.' Initial attempts to renegotiate the Union Treaty had excluded ASSRs from all but occasional consultation about a centre-dominated draft.[65] Although the USSR Supreme Soviet approved the draft in early December 1990, a raucous Congress of People's Deputies rejected it later that month. On 12 May 1991, Gorbachev, Yeltsin and the leaders of fourteen ASSRs discussed the Union Treaty at the Kremlin. ASSRs would sign the Treaty as members of the USSR *and* the RSFSR, an awkward compromise implying simultaneous membership in two federations.[66] Only Tatarstan refused: 'Our attitude toward the procedure for signing the [Union] treaty logically follows from the Declaration of State Sovereignty', explained Mintimer Shaimiev, '... our republic will sign this historic document independently and directly; ... as a co-constituent of the USSR...'.[67]

[65] The working group consisted only of representatives from union republics, not autonomous republics. It was established on 12 June 1990—the same day as the RSFSR Declaration of Sovereignty—by decision of the USSR Council of Federation. Ann Sheehy, 'Moves to Draw up New Union Treaty', *Report on the USSR*, No. 27 (6 July 1990): 14. Yeltsin noted at a press conference in early September 1990 that there were already 13 draft union treaties—12 proffered by union republics as well as the centre's version—each so different that combining them seemed impossible. *Sovetskaia Rossiia*, 2 Sept. 1990, 2.

[66] *Izvestia*, 13 May 1991, 1. Participating were Gorbachev, Yeltsin, Rakhimov (Bashkortostan), Buldayev (Buryatia), Kokov (Kabardino-Balkaria), Basanov (Kalmykia), Spiridonov (Komi), Zotin (Marii El), Biryukov (Mordova), Galazov (N. Ossetia), Shaimiev (Tatarstan), Ondar (Tuva), Tubylov (Udmurtia), Zavgayev (Chechnya-Ingushetia), Leontyev (Chuvashia), and Nikolaev (Yakutia). Of these men, Kokov, Zotin and Galazov were still leaders of their republics six years later, at the end of 1996. Yeltsin would remain in office until December 1999. Rakhimov, Spiridonov, Shaimiev and Nikolaev, at the time of writing (November 2001), were still presidents of their respective republics.

[67] N. Morozov, 'Positsiia Tatarstana', *Pravda*, 18 May 1991, 2. True to his strategy of self-portrayal as a moderating influence in an unruly republic, Shaimiev notes in the interview his hopes at preserving stability, even in the face of rumours and high emotion.

With the crumbling of the Union Treaty (discussed in Chapter 4), cracks in Yeltsin's federal policy widened. Yeltsin's advocacy of self-determination and sovereignty rested on being the self-appointed spokesman for complaints against the centre. When union structures collapsed, Yeltsin became the sole occupant of the only centre that remained and therefore the target of the same attacks he had fomented against Gorbachev. Fourteen months after his dissembling and fractious speech in Kazan, Yeltsin was confronted with its echo. Fauzia Bairamova, a people's deputy from Tatarstan and leader of the ultra-nationalist *Ittifak* party demanded all the sovereignty she could swallow in the form of a declaration of independence, 'the last attempt to obtain statehood through peaceful means...':

We will fight until the last drop of blood ... Half of Russia's territory is Tatar lands ... The time has come to raise the question of annexing to Tatarstan the lands that belonged to the Tatars of old, lands where they now dwell—the lands of Simbirsk, Saratov, Samara, Astrakhan and Orenburg, the expanses of the Ufa plateau and all of the Urals' western slope ... In Genghis Khan's army, one Tatar warrior was worth one hundred men. We Tatars should always remember this.[68]

2.1 Centre-Republican Negotiation of the Federation Treaty

Simultaneous with work on a new Union Treaty, preparations began in the Russian Federation on a new federal treaty. In July 1990, Yeltsin signed a resolution (*postanovlenie*) 'On the Federation Treaty', which 'recognizing the necessity of a deep transformation of the whole federation', created a Council of Federation to co-ordinate the work of a new treaty. A first draft of the Treaty was completed in time for the Third (Extraordinary) Congress of People's Deputies in March 1991.[69] The Council included the chairmen of the Supreme Soviets of most of the constituent units of the Federation and recommended a gradual development of basic principles, discussion and conclusion of a treaty.[70] Among the key federal officials directly involved

[68] A. Putko, 'Kak tataram predlagaiut osvobodit'sia ot "russkogo iga"', *Izvestia*, 25 November 1991, 4. Putko is citing a translation of the Tatar language paper 'Shakhri kazan' which appeared in 'Kazanskie vedomosti'.

[69] R.G. Abdulatipov & L.F. Boltenkova, eds. *Federativnyi dogovor: Dokumenty. Kommentarii* (Moskva: Izdatel'stvo 'Respublika', 1992), 5.

[70] Postanovlenie presidiuma Verkhovnogo Soveta RSFSR, 'O Federativnom Dogovore' 17 July 1990, in Doronchenkov, 454–5. 63 members constituted the Federation Council: the chairman of the RSFSR Supreme Soviet, chairmen of the Supreme Soviets of the ASSRs, chairmen of the Soviets of People's Deputies of the autonomous okrugs and oblasts and 31 representatives of the remaining krais, oblasts and selected cities. The resolution recommended inclusion in the final document of basic principles of construction, treaties of constituent subjects with the federal center, bi-and multi-lateral treaties between subjects and treaties about the restoration, transformation, and creation of different types of national and regional formations.

were Ramazan Abdulatipov and Sergei Shakhrai; Russian Supreme Soviet Chairman Russian Khasbulatov and Yeltsin participated directly in the final stages. They envisioned the construction of a federation qualitatively new in Russia's history. Acquiescence to republican assertions of soverei-gnty, self-determination and even secession were tolerated as short-term 'transitional devices' to maintain territorial integrity as the system de-veloped.[71]

Regional delegations of top-level republican elites had different expect-ations. The Bashkir delegation, for example, formally included Rakhimov (then Chairman of the Supreme Soviet), Mirgaziamov (Chairman of the Council of Ministers), Aiupov (Vice-Premier), Bugera (Supreme Soviet Committee Chairman on socioeconomic development), Magazov (People's Deputy and industrial director), and Kataev (member of the Supreme Soviet Presidium and head of the local MVD higher school).[72] Informally, Zufar Yenikeev, a top legal scholar, member of the Bashkir Supreme Soviet and the chief editor in the republic's constitutional committee, occasionally substi-tuted for Rakhimov in Moscow.[73] The objectives of the Bashkir delegation were representative of many republics: the treaty was viewed as a document that would entrench their claims to sovereign status in the new federation. It would establish new centre-periphery relations that could not be summarily abrogated by the *diktat* of the centre. Quick to defend their own interests, ethnic republics wasted little time promoting heightened powers or elevated status for the secondary and tertiary units of the Russian Federation's hierarchy of federal subjects, the mostly Russian oblasts and the autono-mous okrugs and krais.

---

[71] Nicholas J. Lynn & Alexei V. Novikov, 'Refederalizing Russia: Debates on the Idea of Federalism in Russia', 27 *Publius*, 2 (1997): 191–2. Robert Sharlet, 'The Prospects for Federalism in Russian Constitutional Politics', 24 *Publius*, (1994): 119.

[72] Postanovlenie Verkhovnogo Soveta Respubliki Bashkortostan, 'Ob obrazovanii polnomoch-noi delegatsii Respubliki Bashkortostan dlia uchastiia v razrabotke i zakliuchenii Federativnogo Dogovora i Dogovora ob osnovakh mezhgosudarstvennykh otnoshenii mezhdu Respublikoi Bashkortostan i Rossiiskoi Federatsiei', 28 March 1992. Aiupov, 110. Mirgaziamov notes in addition the Vice-Premier for economics Zhamiliadinov and Z.I. Yenikeev. Interview with M.P. Mirgazia-mov, 7 May 1997, AO 'Uzemik', Ufa. This delegation replaced an earlier 13-member delegation charged with representing the republic in concluding the Union Treaty and a treaty with the RSFSR. Many of the same names appear in both delegations. Postanovlenie Verkhovnogo Soveta Respubliki Bashkortostan, 'Ob obrazovanii polnomochnoi delegatsii Bashkirskoi SSR dlia uchastiia v razrabotke i zakliuchenii Soiuznogo Dogovora i Dogovora s RSFSR', 13 Oct. 1990. Aiupov, 80–1.

[73] Z.I. Yenikeev, author's interview, 6 May 1997, Kuraltai (State Assembly), Ufa. Yenikeev was, at the time of this interview a member of the republican parliament and Chairman of the Committee on Local Power Issues, National Questions and Social and Religious Communities.

Regional elites held different impressions of the drafting process. L.V. Batmanova, a consultant of the Department for Questions of Legislation and Law and Order for the Secretariat of the Komi Supreme Soviet, complained that although in September 1990 the Komi Supreme Soviet authorized an official delegation to participate in the drafting of the Federation Treaty, 'no one invited our delegation anywhere, although from unofficial sources we knew that such work was being carried out in smoke-filled rooms...'.[74] Distribution of the committee's agenda was often left until immediately before meetings, leaving no time for preparation or consultation among members. One member used informal methods to circumvent this practice: 'I came an hour early, gave the girls [secretaries] chocolate, and I received the documents'.[75]

The republics were particularly sensitive to the perceived arrogance of centralized authority. 'Acquaintance with the draft Federation treaty creates the impression that the authors strove to create a centralized, unitary state under the pretext of the Russian Federation', Yenikeev complained; sovereign republics would be reduced to 'not more than the former *guberniia* of tsarist Russia'.[76] On the initiative of the Komi republic, representatives of eleven other republics developed an alternative draft of the Federation Treaty, complete with explanatory notes. A large portion of this draft would ultimately enter into a variant federal treaty in December 1991.[77]

2.2 The Federation Treaty

Despite rumblings of discontent, nineteen republican representatives participated in an initialling ceremony for the Federation Treaty at the Kremlin on 14 March 1992.[78] Only Tatarstan and Chechnya refused to sign. A formal signing ceremony was held 31 March and the Treaty was overwhelmingly voted into the text of the (still RSFSR) Constitution by the Sixth Congress of People's Deputies on 10 April, by a margin of 848 to 10.[79] The Federation Treaty was actually three separate treaties and two protocols: one treaty for national-state formations (i.e. ethnic republics), one for administrative-territorial formations (the six krais, forty-nine oblasts and two cities of

---

[74] L.V. Batmanova, 'Federativnyi dogovor i ego znachenie dlia respublik v sostave RF', in Kataev & Samigullin, 38.

[75] Z.I. Yenikeev, author's interview, 6 May 1997, Kuraltai (State Assembly), Ufa.

[76] Zufar Yenikeev, 'Proekt dogovora nas ne ustraivaet', *Leninets*, No. 138 (7644), 24 Nov. 1990, 2.

[77] Batmanova, 38.

[78] Denis J.B. Shaw, 'Russian Federation Treaty Signed', 33 *Post-Soviet Geography*, 6 (June 1992): 414.

[79] Abdulatipov & Boltenkova, 3.

Moscow and St. Petersburg—termed 'cities of federal significance') and one for national-territorial formations (the Jewish Autonomous Oblast and ten autonomous okrugs) of the Russian Federation. These treaties formalized this triple-tiered hierarchy for 'subjects of the Federation' and accepted the ethnic administration of territory buried in the Soviet Union under the centralized command system of the party-state.[80]

The republics that signed the Federation Treaty considered it the keystone of the new federal order, a point collectively underscored by their insistence upon references to it as an integral component of the new Constitution still being drafted.[81] Other major concessions were official acknowledgement of republican sovereignty, the right to self-determination and the 'fullness of state power' on republic territory (Preamble; Art. III, §1–2), explicit participation of republican organs in the implementation of federal authority (Art. I, §2), and express prohibitions against federal intrusion in regional affairs (Art. III, §4; Art. VI). The republics also won extraordinary representation at the federal level. Enough republics remained unsatisfied with the Treaty that a Protocol was accepted between the initialling ceremony and final acceptance. The Protocol promised 50 per cent of the seats in one chamber of the federal parliament to representatives of ethnically defined subjects of the Federation (i.e. the republics, autonomous okrugs and the Jewish autonomous oblast).[82] Had the Protocol been implemented (the October 1993 crisis completely reshaped the Parliament) one-third of the subjects of the Federation would have controlled one-half the seats!

Despite these concessions, republics rightly retained reservations about the Treaty. Exclusive federal powers and concurrent powers shared between republican and federal organs were the subject of long lists in Articles I and II. But there was no list of exclusively republican powers in Article III: four short clauses promised the 'fullness of state power' but without details found in the preceding sections.[83] What powers were accorded were tightly

---

[80] Abdulatipov & Boltenkova, 6.

[81] Art. VII prohibited unilateral alteration of the Treaty. Art. VIII declared that the Treaty would become an independent section of the RF Constitution, changes and additions to which section could only be introduced with the agreement of the Treaty's signatory republics.

[82] 'Protokol k Federativnomu dogovoru', reprinted in B.A. Strashun, *Federal'noe konstitutsionnoe pravo Rossii: Osnovnye istochniki po sostoianiiu na 15 sentiabria 1996 goda* (Moskva: Izdatel'stvo NORMA, 1996), 198–9. A Protocol was also negotiated by signers of the treaty for oblasts, krais, and federal cities, that attempted to reduce the disparity between powers negotiated in that treaty and those won by the republics in their treaty. Sarah J. Reynolds, 'First Steps: Voluntary Union, Constitutional Equality, and the Nature of the Federation', 33 *Statutes and Decisions: The Laws of the USSR and Its Successor States*, 6 (Nov.–Dec. 1997), 9–10.

[83] Denis Shaw calls this 'a mere sop to the concept of republican sovereignty', and notes 'one is reminded of the old Soviet legal formulation describing the virtually powerless local soviets as the "supreme organs of state power" within their respective territories'. Shaw, 1992, 415.

circumscribed by the exclusive federal powers in Article I. Exclusive federal control over most significant economic levers (although not entirely unreasonable) further mitigated any 'fullness' accorded republican state power. Article II, §2 subjected all concurrent powers to federal 'Fundamentals of Legislation', guidelines to which republics were expected to adapt their own republic-specific statutes. This rendered the distinction between Article I and Article II types of legislation a rather deceptive division of authority.

There was broad overlap between exclusive federal powers and shared powers. Eight of the twelve concurrent powers listed in the first section of Article II were closely paralleled by clauses in Article I granting nearly identical powers exclusively to the federal government. Control over the judicial system was named both an exclusive federal power and a power held concurrently with republics; the procuracy was listed as under federal control while control over advocates, notaries, and 'cadres of law enforcement organs' was a concurrent competence of both organs of state power. The concurrent power to establish general principles of taxation (Art. II, §1, 'h') matched exclusive federal authority over federal taxes and collections (Art. I, §1, 'h'). What procedures would resolve inevitable conflicts of authorities? According to Article VI, §1, federal laws automatically applied if republics overstepped their jurisdictional boundaries. With regard to federal intrusion into exclusive republican authority, there was *no* reciprocal statement giving priority to republican laws; the clause merely forbade such activity. The second clause of the article noted that relations are constructed 'on the basis of the RF Constitution, republican constitutions, mutual respect and mutual responsibility'. It is difficult to see what constructive role republican constitutions could play, however, based on the strict decision-rule favouring federal authority, established in the preceding clause. According to the Treaty, disputes on the matter of joint management were referred to the RF Constitutional Court (Art. VI, §2).

Particularly unsettling in a document which purported to establish the ground rules for a federal Russia was Article VIII. Each republic reserved the right *simultaneously* to sign the Treaty and 'to regulate its relations...in accordance with the RF Constitution and the Constitution of that republic'. The final sentence of the document seemed to imply that the Treaty could be signed and at the same time business could be conducted as usual, without reference to the Treaty at all. Did this mean that republics had a choice of documents to which they could appeal according to their interests, for one conflict turning to the Treaty, for another relying on their own or the federal constitutions? What was meant is unclear, evidence of the ambiguity built into the document itself.

2.3 Problems of Implementation of the Federation Treaty

The ink was not yet dry on the final draft of the Federation Treaty before it was under attack. Days before the signing ceremony, the new president of Bashkortostan, Murtaza Rakhimov, vilified his federal adversaries: 'A united and indivisible Russia has become the trump card for those who want to preserve the administrative-command system of relations "centre-republics", who want to hold on to power at the price of robbery of the republics'. 'Innuendoes and tricks', he added, led republics to forfeit too much to federal control.[84] Rakhimov wanted special privileges for Bashkortostan beyond the 'fullness of state power' promised in the Treaty. At the eleventh hour, his representatives to the Treaty talks announced that Bashkortostan would not sign.[85] Three days before the signing ceremony, Rakhimov's Supreme Soviet passed a resolution declaring that the Federation Treaty 'ignored the principles of the Declaration of State Sovereignty of the Republic of Bashkortostan', and the new constitution, laws, and resolutions constructed on its foundation. Rakhimov demanded a bilateral treaty 'on the bases of inter-state relations' between the republic and the Federation.[86] Rakhimov and the Bashkir delegation cleverly played on the pressures confronting federal authorities: with Tatarstan and Chechnya boycotting the Treaty negotiations, Bashkortostan's departure could have collapsed the entire Treaty framework.[87] Even if other republics signed the treaty, a gaping hole would be opened across the important military-industrial Volga region of the Russian Federation, from Kazan' to the edge of Asia.

[84] M.G. Rakhimov, 'Suverennoi respublike—sovremennuiu konstitutsiiu', in Kataev & Samigullin, 5, 7.

[85] Interview with Z.I. Yenikeev, Kuraltai (State Assembly), Ufa, 6 May 1997. Interview with M.P. Mirgaziamov, Ufa, 7 May 1997. Both men were members of the Bashkir delegation.

[86] 'Postanovlenie Verkhovnogo Soveta Respubliki Bashkortostan O Proekte Federativnogo Dogovora', 28 March 1992. Reproduced in Aiupov, 107–9. The resolution emphasized proprietary rights over natural resources and the 'economic and scientific-technical potential' of the republic, direct control over all payments (taxes, fees, etc.) on subjects within its territory, ecological security, its judicial and legislative systems, and foreign relations. Resolutions on 25 and 27 February 1992 hinted at Bashkir concerns over the Treaty, the latter resolution ordering the creation of a group of experts to begin work on different aspects of a bi-lateral treaty. See the resolutions 'O merakh po ukrepleniiu gosudarstvennogo suvereniteta Respubliki Bashkortostan', and 'O peregovorakh po zakliucheniiu Dogovora ob osnovakh mezhgosudarstvennykh otnoshenii mezhdu Rossiiskoi Federatsiei i Respublikoi Bashkortostan', Aiupov et al. 99–103.

[87] Whether the Bashkir delegation would have left the talks is unclear. Several former members of the delegation told the author that Bashkortostan would not have signed without the appendix. Interview with M.P. Mirgaziamov, op. cit. Yuri Afanasiev, adviser in the presidential administration, claims that the Bashkir government from the start was unhappy with the draft treaty but had chosen negotiation rather than defiance, Tatarstan's strategy. Yuri Sil'vestrovich Afanasiev, author's interview, White House, Ufa, 5 May 1997.

The result was an Appendix (*prilozhenie*) to the Federation Treaty exclusively for Bashkortostan. Its preamble referred explicitly to the Bashkir resolution passed earlier; to anyone familiar with the resolution, its close correspondence to the Appendix was obvious. The Bashkir delegation seemed to have achieved its stated objectives: legislative and judicial systems were declared independent and property (with some exceptions) placed under republican control. Independent statehood and the right to attendant foreign relations were acknowledged. The only demand clearly not met was direct control over taxation; the right *independently* to determine general principles, a step above the concurrently held power the Treaty granted, was the compromise. Arguably, these special dispensations were nominal at worst, conditional at best, and often merely a few shades different than what the Treaty already provided. The more lasting effect of the Appendix was the powerful precedent it established from the start of the 'renewed' Russian Federation. To any subject with the moxie to lock horns with the centre it signalled that nothing was above parochial, bilateral renegotiation.

Bashkortostan was the only republic to receive a special appendix to the Federation Treaty, but not the only republic to receive special treatment days before the Treaty was signed. In early 1992, the president of Sakha (Yakutia), Mikhail Nikolaev, advocated secession from Russia and business relations established with international treaties. But on 23 March 1992, the republic almost completely responsible for the Federation's lucrative diamond output signed an accord with federal authorities granting exclusive republican control over 32 per cent of all diamond profits and 20 per cent of all gem-quality diamonds, plus significant percentages of gold and hard currency receipts.[88] Unsurprisingly, Nikolaev signed the Federation Treaty a week later.

Pandora's box had been wrenched opened. While the republics praised the Federation Treaty, few accorded it the gravitas of a founding document. Four days after agreeing to the Federation Treaty in Moscow, Sakha (Yakutia) accepted a new constitution that blatantly contradicted the Treaty, asserting the primacy of republican laws and exclusive control over all natural resources.[89] According to the head of the federal government's

[88] Marjorie Mandelstam Balzer & Uliana Alekseevna Vinokurova, 'Nationalism, Interethnic Relations & Federalism: The Case of the Sakha Republic (Yakutia)', 48 *Europe-Asia Studies*, 1 (1996): 102, 107. This agreement also established the joint-stock company Almaz-Rossiia Sakha, which became a powerful force run under the direction of the republic's vice-president. *See also Vladimir Sobell, The New Russia: A Political Risk Analysis* (London: The Economist Intelligence Unit, 1994), 48. Sobell adds that the republic also gained the right to sign a contract with the South African diamond giant DeBeers to market US$5 billion over the course of five years, a complete reversal of previous, exclusive dealings with Soviet central authorities.

[89] *Konstitutsiia (Osnovnoi zakon) Respubliki Sakha (Iakutia)* (Yakutsk: Natsional'naia izdatel'sko-poligraficheskaia kompaniia 'Sakapoligrafizdat', 1995). The Constitution was accepted 4 April 1992. The conflicting citations are Arts. 41 and 5.

working centre for economic reforms, local Siberian elites pre-emptively seized for themselves federal functions, with or without accompanying legislation.[90] In December 1992, Yeltsin signed a special *ukaz*, 'On Measures for the Realization of the Federation Treaty in the Republic of Komi', establishing a variety of dispensations, including special development funds, an investment bank and tax considerations for the republic.[91] In August 1992, Bashkortostan, Tatarstan, and Sakha (Yakutia), economically the three most powerful republics, issued a joint warning to the federal government not to ignore republican laws and legal rights; all three republics refused to pay taxes to the Centre. This had itself been prompted by the adoption of a federal law permitting sanctions against republics withholding their federal budget contributions.[92] Citing his Appendix, Rakhimov fumed against the 'blockade' imposed on Bashkortostan and threatened to close oil pipelines and 'completely isolate ourselves'. 'For seventy-five years they pumped blood out of us', he raged, 'and left us impoverished and face-to-face with environmental problems, and now they want us to go back to living the old way? That won't play anymore!'[93]

Events in Tatarstan in April 1992 showed the nadir to which federal-republic relations had plummeted. Tatarstan had boycotted the entire Treaty process and had stopped paying federal taxes. Seeking legitimacy for its self-proclaimed status and draft constitution, the republic scheduled a refer-endum on the compound question, 'Do you agree that the republic of Tatarstan is a sovereign state, a subject of international law that builds its relations with the Russian Federation and with other republics and states on the basis of a treaty under which all parties are equal?'[94] The Russian Federation Constitutional Court declared both the republic's referendum and Declaration of Sovereignty unconstitutional, prompting Tatar officials to declare that the Court lacked jurisdiction over Tatarstan! On the eve of the referendum there were threats of arrest by the RF procuracy and rumors

[90] Examples cited include: spurious regulation, licensing or quarantining procedures for inter-state commerce; price regulation; regulation of money circulation by controlling volume via selective payments and money surrogates; declaration of exclusive control of federal properties; attempts to establish one-channel tax systems, etc. Sergei Pavlenko, 'Tsentr—Regiony: kto kogo?' *Mezhdunarodnaia zhizn'*, No. 4 (Apr. 1993): 90–91.

[91] Ukaz Prezidenta RF No. 1622, 'O merakh po realizatsii Federativnogo dogovora v Respublike Komi' (23 Dec. 1992). *Vedomosti S"ezda narodnykh deputatov RF i Verkhovnogo Soveta RF*, 52 (31 December 1992), item 3139, p. 3847–49.

[92] Vera Tolz, 'Regionalism in Russia: The Case of Siberia', 2 *RFE/RL Research Report*, 9 (26 Feb. 1993): 7.

[93] 44 *Current Digest of the Post-Soviet Press*, 33 (16 Sept. 1992): 24.

[94] 44 *Current Digest of the Post-Soviet Press*, 8 (25 Mar. 1992): 5.

of troops mobilizing on Tatarstan's borders.[95] The referendum proceeded, without arrests or invasions; 61.3 per cent of participants affirmed the question.[96] But the results of the referendum, for all they implied, were not half as damaging to federal structures or centre-periphery relations as the tragi-comedy that had preceded it. The rulings of the fledgling Constitutional Court had been ignored, its chairman forced to plead in vain for enforcement of an order the federal government had sought in the first place. Federal authority, not one month old, had been seriously challenged.

3. THE FEDERAL CONSTITUTION: TRANSITION TO THE NEW FEDERALISM, PART TWO

Throughout this process, the Russian Federation was still operating under the heavily amended 1978 RSFSR (Russian Soviet Federated Socialist Republic) constitution. As discussed in Chapter Three, the union republic constitutions of the Soviet-era were little more than duplicates of the central government's Soviet Constitution, which left virtually nothing within the province of the Union's components.[97] As Gorbachev's legal *perestroika* replaced Brezhnevite legal formalism, the RSFSR Constitution was increasingly amended, becoming a mélange of old Soviet dogmatism and hastily drafted reforms.[98] Yeltsin's new presidency clashed with the basic parliamentary structure of Soviet power, eventually provoking violent conflict. The 'Parade of Sovereignties', and all the new republican laws it inspired, confused all previous understandings of Soviet federalism.

A new constitution was required. From the point of view of federal transition, it was fortunate that most major political players converged on what Robert Sharlet dubbed 'the constitutional referent point' as a tacit rule of the game: 'legitimate political action must depart from, operate within, or

---

[95] Edward W. Walker, 'The Dog that didn't Bark: Tatarstan and Asymmetrical Federalism in Russia', unpublished paper (27 Nov. 1996), 9.

[96] 82% of the electorate participated. 'Rezul'taty referenduma Respubliki Tatarstan 21 marta 1992 goda. Protokol Tsentral'noi komissii referenduma Respubliki Tatarstan', in Rafael Khakimov, *Belaia kniga Tatarstana. Put' k suverenitetu (Sbornik ofitsial'nykh dokumentov) 1990–1995* (Kazan': 'Tatpoligraf', 1996), 20–1.

[97] Henn-Jüri Uibopuu, 'Soviet Federalism under the New Soviet Constitution', 5 *Review of Socialist Law*, 2 (1979): 176. F.J.M. Feldbrugge, ed. *The Constitutions of the USSR and the Union Republics: Analysis, Texts, Reports* (Alphen aan den Rijn, The Netherlands: Sijthoff & Noordhoff, 1979), 261.

[98] The RSFSR Constitution was amended by laws of the RSFSR on 27 October 1989, 31 May; 16 June and 15 December 1990; 24 May and 1 November 1991; and amended by laws of the RF on 21 April, 9 and 10 December 1992. William E. Butler *Collected Legislation of Russia* (New York: Oceana, May 1993), 1.

Table 5.4   Official Drafts of Russian Constitutions

Drafting body	Date of draft publication	Disposition
USSR Supreme Soviet Constitutional Commission	May 1977	Adopted 7 Oct. 1977. Amended over 300 times.
RSFSR I Congress Constitutional Commission (Oleg Rumiantsev, Exec. Sec.)	Nov. 1990 'First draft'	Supported by Yeltsin. Communist opposition postpones debate.
RSFSR V Congress Constitutional Commission (Rumiantsev)	Oct. 1991 'Second draft'	Congress refuses to debate; orders third draft.
RF VI Congress Constitutional Commission (Rumiantsev)	Mar. 1992 'Third draft'	Congress approves 'Basic Principles,' 18 Apr. 1992
Executive Branch (Shakhrai et al.)	Apr. 1992 'President's draft'	VI Congress refuses to debate draft.
Constitutional Commission (Rumiantsev)	Nov. 1992	
Executive Branch (Shakhrai)	Apr. 1993 'President's draft'	
Constitutional Conference 'Constitutional Arbitration Commission' (Vladimir Kudriavtsev, Director)	July 1993	Supreme Soviet refuses to ratify draft.
Legislative Branch (Khasbulatov)	July 1993 'Parliament's draft'	Reaction to Constitutional Conference draft.
Constitutional Working Group (Nikolai Riabov)	Convened 8 Sept. 1993	
Executive Branch	Nov. 1993 'Yeltsin's draft'	Ratified by referendum, 12 Dec. 1993; enters into force on publication, 24 Dec. 1993.

refer back to the Constitution'.[99] Such a mindset was tremendously important in the construction of a rule-of-law federal state.[100] Unfortunately, from
the point of view of federal issues, the debates of successive constitutional
commissions and panels were increasingly drawn into the conflict between

[99] Robert Sharlet, 'The Prospects for Federalism in Russian Constitutional Politics', 24 *Publius*,
2 (1994): 117. Even the plotters of the August 1991 putsch felt obliged to couch their illegal attempt in
constitutional terms. Yeltsin surrounded his anti-constitutional decrees of September–October 1993
with constitutional invocations.
[100] There is debate about whether this 'mindset' constituted an advance in the political culture
of Russian institution-builders. See Alexander Lukin, *The Political Culture of the Russian 'Democrats'*
(Oxford University Press, 2000).

Yeltsin's presidency and Khasbulatov's parliament.[101] As Table 5.4 shows, there were plenty of draft constitutions to debate.

Generally, federal officials were reluctant to entrench even the minimal decentralization of the Federation Treaty in a new constitution, though this had been promised. Oleg Rumiantsev, executive secretary of the Constitutional Commission established in 1990 by the first Russian parliament, was philosophically opposed to the 'tribalism' he saw emanating from the ethnic republics.[102] A 'Conception of Judicial Reform in the RSFSR' in October 1991 expressed the executive branch view of the role of a federal judiciary. Republics could establish court systems that were 'most convenient for them' so long as the supremacy of federal jurisdiction was recognized, a bitter pill for republican conceptions of sovereignty.[103] Parliamentarians complained that republics would be disproportionately represented in the new upper house of parliament; Yeltsin's proposals would destroy the Federation 'with the slogan of federalism'.[104] A special four-question referendum, held 25 April 1993, revealed Yeltsin's weakening personal support in the republics and regions. Twenty-six of eighty-seven fully participating units (Chechnya and Tatarstan again held out) could not muster majorities to express confidence in Yeltsin; eighteen returned majorities against him.[105]

Immediately following the referendum, Yeltsin published another draft constitution that was compared to the parliament's reworked November 1992 draft. Both branches left vague the electoral and structural details of the chamber of the legislature reserved for regional representation.[106] With one

---

[101] For comparision of the debates on 5 drafts of the constitution, see Sergei Beliaev, 'The Evolution in Constitutional Debates in Russian in 1992–1993: A Comparative Review', 20 *Review of Central and East European Law*, 3 (1994): 305–19. For a more philosophical and thematic treatment of issues affecting constitutionalism, *see* Erik P. Hoffmann, 'Challenges to Viable Constitutionalism in Post-Soviet Russia', 7 *The Harriman Review*, 10–12 (1994): 19–56.

[102] Sharlet, 119.

[103] B.A. Zolotukhin *et al.* 'The Conception of Judicial Reform in the RSFSR', 30 *Statutes and Decisions: The Laws of the USSR and its Successor States*, 2 (Mar.–April 1994): 45.

[104] Vera Tolz, 'Drafting the New Russian Constitution', 2 *RFE/RL Research Report*, 29 (16 July 1993): 6.

[105] The question (the first of four on the ballot) was: 'Do you have confidence in the President of the Russian Federation, B. N. Yeltsin?' Stephen White, Richard Rose, & Ian McAllister. *How Russia Votes* (Chatham, NJ: Chatham House, 1997), 83. Yeltsin's support exceeded 50% in only 10 of the 20 participating ethnic republics, varying from a high of 69% in Komi to a dismal 2.4% in Ingushetia. Shaw, 1993, 535.

[106] Rita Moore, 'The Path to the New Russian Constitution: A Comparison of Executive-Legislative Relations in the Major Drafts', *Demokratizatsiya*, 48. The presidential, post-referendum draft set a minimum of two deputies from each federal component before adding the possibility of more deputies coming from republics, autonomous oblasts, and autonomous okrugs (Art. 85). The parliamentary draft (also Art. 85) at that time offered two variants: two deputies from each constituent federal unit, or, a maximum of 200 deputies in the chamber, elected according to federal laws which ensured that 50% of seats went to representatives of republics, autonomous oblasts and autonomous okrugs.

exception, the parliamentary draft left all powers jointly held between the two houses.[107] The presidential draft gave the upper chamber the power to affirm changes in boundaries and status of constituent units (Art. 93), approve the Government and control votes of no confidence (Art. 94), ratify appointments to the high courts and Security Council (Art. 95) and ratify treaties, questions of war and peace, and declarations of extraordinary and military situations (Art. 96). The lower chamber's primary exclusive power was control over taxation and monetary policy (Art. 99).[108] But this relatively stronger upper chamber did not satisfy republics, resentful of their exclusion from the drafting process and increasingly skeptical of promises from either President or Parliament.

Yeltsin's Constitutional Convention (a decidedly pro-president assembly) completed a draft in July 1993 that included the Federation Treaty. Simultaneously, it proclaimed the legal equality of all federal subjects, contradicting the Treaty's hierarchy of units. The compromise pleased neither the republics, which insisted on their special status, nor the regions, as fervently opposed to any favouritism.[109] Statements about republican 'sovereignty' and the option of dual citizenship were revoked. The compromise document curtailed many of the advantages the upper federal chamber had held over the Duma in previous drafts. The Federation Council lost the right to review and vote on the presidential candidate for premier. Its range of exclusive legislative oversight also decreased while the Duma retained the power to override its veto by a two-thirds vote. In August 1993, Yeltsin met regional leaders in Petrozavodsk, hoping to win their support with a proposal that they constitute the upper house *ex officio*. It was a weak gesture from the point of view of republican leaders, who disliked the inference of equality for all subjects, especially as they would be outnumbered on a scale of more than four to one by the mostly Russian regions.[110]

When his presidential draft had essentially been scuttled by both the federal and regional parliaments, Yeltsin resorted to his infamous Decree No. 1400, initiating a constitutional *coup d'état* culminating in violence in

---

[107] See Arts. 86–89 of the parliamentary draft. All powers are listed simply as belonging to the Supreme Soviet, without distinguishing between its two chambers, except for Art. 89, §3 (draft legislation is begun in the lower house and then sent to the upper house). *Proekty Konstitutsii Rossiiskoi Federatsii i analiticheskie materialy (v dvukh chastiakh)*. Chast' 1. (Moskva: Izdanie Verkhovnogo Soveta Rossiiskoi Federatsii, undated), 23–5.

[108] *Proekty...*, 49–50.

[109] Only 8 out of 21 republics supported this draft. Steven L. Solnick, 'The Political Economy of Russian Federalism: A Framework for Analysis', 43 *Problems of Post-Communism*, 6 (1996): 15.

[110] Solnick, 15.

early October 1993. Interestingly, the decree blamed Parliament for violating the 'fundamentals of the constitutional structure of the Russian Federation: sovereignty of the people (*narodovlastiia*), the division of powers, and federalism'.[111] With the final assistance of armoured tank divisions in early October, Yeltsin now ruled by decree, virtually uninhibited. Yeltsin and his advisers were far less inclined to consult regional elites as they had occasionally done in the past on important alterations to the draft. His reconvened pro-president Constitutional Convention no longer included a special working group on federalism. The resulting document was far more centralized than anything seen before. While Article 5, §3 retained the phrase 'self-determination', Yeltsin made clear in a speech given the month of publication that, contrary to the explicit declarations of most of the republics, the principle 'excludes the right to secession from Russia'.[112] Article 4, §3 states that the Russian Federation 'guarantees the integrity and inviolability of its territory', which some scholars took as a clear rejection of the right to secede.[113] Most issues of federal concern were outlined in Chapter Three of the Constitution. Article 71 outlined the extensive exclusive jurisdiction of the federal authorities and Article 72 added areas of joint jurisdiction with constituent federal units. However, Article 76, which outlines how areas of jurisdiction are to be governed, states that jointly held responsibilities are governed by federal laws with normative legal acts of republics and regions *adopted only in accordance with the federal initiative.* As Erik Hoffmann notes, this specious conception of joint authority 'virtually ensure[s] that bilateral political and economic bargaining rather than uniform constitutional and other federal law will be decisive in exercising "joint" powers'.[114] While Articles 71 and 72 of the Constitution were nearly exact duplications of Articles I and II of the Federation Treaty, establishing exclusive federal and joint jurisdictions, the weak promise to republics made in Article III— granting them the 'fullness of state power'—was further diluted in the new Constitution. The rather more confederal presumption it had implied, that the republics were the font of all state powers from which certain

---

[111] Ukaz, No. 1400, 21 September 1993, 'O poetapnoi konstitutsionnoi reforme v Rossiiskoi Federatsii', *Sobranie Aktov Prezidenta i Pravitel'stva Rossiiskoi Federatsii*, No. 39, 27 Sept. 1993, item 3597, p. 3912.

[112] S. Beliaev, 307–8, 316. Both Rumiantsev's draft and the July 1993 draft of the Convention explicitly granted the right to republican citizenship. Beliaev deduces from the final wording of Arts. 1 and 3 that 'This suggests that the drafters were inclined to articulate the doctrine of "indivisible sovereignty" which is implicitly attributed to "the multinational people" and to the Russian Federation', a strange doctrine for a self-professed federal state. *See also* Sharlet, 122–3.

[113] Graham Smith, 'Russia, Multiculturalism and Federal Justice', 50 *Europe-Asia Studies*, 8 (1998): 1395.

[114] Hoffmann, 43.

powers were subsequently granted the Federation, was subtly changed. Now constituent units seemed to be the ones who travelled to a *federal* well of power, permitted to take for themselves only what little power remained outside the limits of federal jurisdiction.

The composition of the Federation Council was strictly limited by Article 95, §2 to heads of the executive and legislative branches of each constituent unit, a more rigid demarcation than previous drafts. This made members part-time parliamentarians. Granting two seats to every subject of the Federation, the Constitution broke the promise made in the Protocol to the Federation Treaty that half of the upper chamber's composition would be reserved for republics and ethnic autonomous okrugs. Its powers were also constrained. Bills on taxes, loans, and other financial matters were excepted from the chamber's permitted legislative initiative: now the Government's pre-assent was required (Art. 104, §3). The chamber's enumerated powers were limited to the confirmation of presidential edicts (on martial law, states of emergency, external military activity) and the appointment of presidential nominees (high court judges, the Procurator-General, the deputy chair of the Central Bank). Its powers to affect legislation were also limited: as in other drafts, the upper chamber's objections to proposed laws could be overruled by a two-thirds vote of the lower chamber (Art. 105, §5).

Acknowledgement of republican sovereignty and citizenship were excised from the draft. All federation subjects were explicitly declared juridically equal in status. Article 78 gave federal authorities (principally the president and government) the power to create unspecified 'territorial organs' and install 'appropriate officials' to enforce federal authority. In combination with the preceding Article 77, which established a 'unified system of executive power' in the Federation, the effect on Russian federalism was severe. The President, if he so chooses, may use unspecified 'conciliation procedures' to resolve disputes between federal and regional authorities, only referring the issue to courts if his procedures are ineffective. In the interim, he is empowered simply to suspend the disputed acts of executive power in the regions. As Graham Smith observed, this 'contravenes a basic given that central authorities may not unilaterally redefine the powers of its constituent units'.[115] With special reference to Articles 77 and 78, the American Bar Association observed that the Constitution 'establishes an essentially unitary system having elements of regional representation in the national legislative branch and decentralized governance for what appears to be local housekeeping functions'.[116] It is to these articles that Putin turned to justify the

---

[115] Graham Smith, 1395.   [116] Hoffmann, 44.

expansion of his executive powers in his sweeping federal reforms of the summer of 2000.

By far of gravest concern to the republics was that the November 1993 draft (which soon would be submitted to a popular referendum on 12 December for ratification) completely omitted the hard-fought Federation Treaty and its Protocol. Lest doubt remained, the concluding provisions of Section Two, Article 1 of the Constitution subordinated the Treaty to the Constitution in cases of conflict. For all intents and purposes, this meant the unilateral repeal of the Federation Treaty! Offending clauses were supplanted by the president's constitution, although the Federation Treaty prohibited its unilateral amendment. The three to one predominance of Russian regions over ethnic republics in the Federal Assembly meant that republics had no special protection against amendment of those sections of the Constitution pertaining to their specific rights and privileges.[117] In June, after heated debate, the Federation Treaty had been included in the Conference draft in an attempt to procure republican support. Its sudden omission six months later 'undoubtedly was targeted against the republican leaders who had used the conflict in Moscow quite effectively to carve out a substantial degree of independence'.[118] Table 5.5 provides a summary of the more major contradictions between the Federation Treaty and Yeltsin's new Constitution.

Many regional elites initially took a wait-and-see approach to the battle raging between Yeltsin and Khasbulatov, but when Yeltsin disbanded the federal parliament a general split appeared in the republics. In general, executives sided with Yeltsin while legislative bodies stood with the federal parliament. Roughly two-thirds of the republican Supreme Soviets issued resolutions denouncing Decree No. 1400 as either unconstitutional, unlawful, or otherwise unacceptable. Tatarstan's elites collectively, and publicly, shrugged their shoulders, announcing that the potato harvest was of more importance to the republic than events in Moscow.[119] The presidents of Chechnya and Ingushetia supported Yeltsin, while North Ossetia's leadership was more cautious, considering Yeltsin's actions unconstitutional but leaving it to 'the people' to decide their merits. Those with the misfortune to have supported the losing side, however, as well as those who played

---

[117] Reynolds, 11.

[118] Moore, 54.

[119] Elizabeth Teague, 'North-South Divide: Yel'tsin and Russia's Provincial Leaders', 2 *RFE/RL Research Report*, 47 (26 Nov. 1993): 16. Neither President Shaimiev nor the Chairman of the Supreme Soviet, Farid Mukhametshin, were reported to have returned from their summer vacations. The Prime Minister, Mukhammat Sabirov dismissively noted: 'Frankly speaking, we have other business to attend to'.

Table 5.5   Major Contradictions between the Federation Treaty and the Constitution

Federation Treaty (31 March 1992)	Russian Federation Constitution (24 December 1993)	Discrepancies
Preamble: 'We, ... the sovereign republics...' Hard-fought description of republics as sovereign entitites		'Sovereignty' appears six times in the Constitution, but only in reference to the unified statehood of the Federation.
	Art. 5, §1: '... republics, territories, provinces, ... are equal components ...'	Tripartite nature of Treaty implies different status in Federation.
Art. III, §1: 'Republics (states) possess all fullness of state (legislative, executive, judicial) power on their territory, besides those powers which are handed over (referred) to the jurisdiction of federal organs of state power in accordance with the present treaty.'	Art. 73: 'Outside the limits of the Russian Federation jurisdiction ... and joint jurisdiction ... the components of the Russian Federation shall enjoy state power in its entirety.'	Constitution clause reverses jurisdictional presumption from that which is given by components to that which is not taken by the Federation.
Art. III, §2: 'Republics are independent participants of international and foreign economic relations, ...' Co-ordinated jointly with federal organs.	Art. 72, (n): 'the co-ordination of the international and foreign economic relations of components ...' is subject to joint jurisdiction.	Constitution omits mention of republics as independent participants, instead emphasizing fulfilment of Russian Federation international treaties.
Art. III, §3: 'The land and its wealth, water, animal and vegetable life is the property (possession) of the people inhabiting the territory of the republic.' Questions of ownership and status of federal natural resources determined by mutual agreement/legislation.	Art. 72, (c): 'Issues relating to the ownership, use and disposal of land, mineral resources, water, and other natural resources', fall within joint jurisdiction of components and federal authorities.	Treaty placed presumption under republican powers; Constitution changes to joint powers. Constitutional article in addition to Treaty Art. II, which was otherwise inserted verbatim into Constitution.

president against parliament to maximize returns found themselves in a dire position. Two days following the shelling of the White House, the soviets of the lowest tier of the federal hierarchy were 'invited' to dissolve themselves. Regional and republican soviets were permitted to remain in existence, though presidential orders the following week limited the budgetary and other powers of oblast and krai legislatures. A 22 October decree ordered new elections in all second-and third-tier federal units and 'recommended' republics the same course of action.[120] Sakha (Yakutia), where executive and legislature had both endorsed Yeltsin, reaped the benefits of its support following Yeltsin's victory: while most of the other republics grudgingly were forced to accept the presence of federal presidential representatives in their 'sovereign' republics, Sakha (Yakutia) received special permission to retain all federal taxes within the republic.[121]

Perhaps the most extreme realignment of federal relations took place in Kalmykia. The president of this extremely poor North Caucasian republic, Kirsan Ilumzhinov, had embroiled himself in the centre of the October Events. Together with the president of Ingushetia, Ruslan Aushev, he personally visited the blockaded White House. According to varying reports, Ilumzhinov told the isolated parliamentarians they had the support of the majority of Russian regions in their struggle; immediately after his visit, Alexander Rutskoi (Yeltsin's former vice-president, who sided with the parliamentarians) gave his supporters the order to attack Ostankino and the Moscow mayor's office, with dismal results.[122] Though Ilumzhinov denies any connection, it is a strange coincidence that in early 1994 he offered to renounce his own republic's Declaration of Sovereignty and in April replaced the republic's constitution with a 'Steppe Code' extremely favourable to central authorities. 'This was a transitional period', Ilumzhinov stressed, 'I proposed to Yeltsin that for Russia there should be a single vertical power'. Pressed repeatedly on the timing of these changes, he replied quietly, 'I had a debt'.[123]

---

[120] Teague, 10–11. The head of the government drafting commission for these decrees was then Vice-Premier Sergei Shakhrai who had been one of the key federal officials involved in negotiating the Federation Treaty. In comparison to the other units of the Federation, republics were let off easy with these recommendations, many of which were rarely interpreted in the manner the federal authorities had imagined. According to one analyst, Shakhrai urged this softer approach so as 'to avoid the appearance of issuing binding instructions and to allow republics greater flexibility to meet local needs'. Darrell Slider, 'Elections to Russia's Regional Assemblies', 12 *Post-Soviet Affairs*, No. 3 (1996): 250.

[121] Teague, 23.

[122] Benbia Khylkhachiev, Deputy to RF Duma 1993–5 and a founding member of the People's Party of Kalmykia, says Ilumzhinov boldly told Rutskoi that 80% of the leaders of the subjects of the Federation supported the parliamentarians. Author's interview, Hotel Moskva, Moscow, 26 June 1997. Yulii Oglaev, Chairman of the Social Committee for the Defence of the Constitution and Human Rights of Kalmykia and a *dotsent* of history at the Kalmyk State University Law Faculty, asserts that Rutskoi had promised to make Ilumzhinov Vice-President or Prime Minister after his victory. Author's interview, Hotel Elista, Elista, 28 June 1997. Ilumzhinov himself says that, in the halls of the RF Constitutional Court on 30 September 1993, he was elected chairman of the Council of Leaders of the group Regions of Russia, by 69 of 89 regions. He denies Rutskoi made any offer of future leadership. Author's interview, President's Office, Elista, 1 July 1997.

[123] Author's interview, 1 July 1997. Ilumzhinov insists that he never quarrelled with Yeltsin and that their relations did not change after the October Events. See also Teague, 15–16.

The Constitution of the Russian Federation was officially approved by Federation-wide referendum on 12 December 1993. Whether that vote (which, under a cloud of suspicion, narrowly passed the required margin of participation) endowed the document with democratic legitimacy is a controversial question. Republics certainly questioned its legitimacy. Chechnya refused to conduct the referendum at all, while in Tatarstan, which allowed but did not officially support voting on its territory, only 13.9 per cent of voters participated. In roughly half a dozen other republics voting levels were too low to validate the result. In eight republics where voting levels passed the 50 per cent mark, the majority was *against* the new constitution (in Dagestan, 79.1 per cent opposed).[124] Many of these republics had also expressed their lack of confidence in Yeltsin in the April 1993 referendum. The statement of Yeltsin's chief legal adviser at the time, Sergei Shakhrai, revealed the Centre's curious interpretation of federalism, in which the disapproval of so many *constituent units* meant so little: 'The constitution has been approved by citizens, not by the component units. As citizens have approved the Constitution, it is now in force in all component parts of the Russian Federation'.[125]

The 'Parade of Sovereignties' had developed a vocabulary and a mindset of self-determination, autonomy and provincial control *'snizu-verkh'* ('from the bottom up', as republican elites grew fond of saying) well before attempts were made to develop sound federation-wide organizing principles. Negotiations for the Federation Treaty quickly fell hostage to that mindset as republics realized that they could ignore the centre (e.g. Chechnya and Tatarstan) or make last-minute ultimatums (e. g. Bashkortostan and Sakha) with some degree of impunity. Republican elites spoke in terms of 'treaty-constitution' based federalism, meaning their prerogative to act as subjects of international law and independent republics in arranging their relations, while central federal elites insisted on 'constitution-treaty' based federalism, by which was meant the strong central power that had always before dominated centre-periphery relations in Russian and Soviet history. A vocabulary of federalism built on an interest in multi-lateral, transparent and equal relations, was not being used. Bilateralism, special dispensations, unique cases, hierarchies, and raw power politics were the emerging norms of Russian federal politics, the subject of the next chapter.

---

[124] Only 54.8% of Russian Federation citizens, by official counts, participated in the referendum; of that number 58.4% voted to approve the new constitution, meaning that only 31% of the electorate actively voted in favour of the Second Republic's founding document. White *et al.* 99.

[125] Graham Smith, 1396.

6

Inter-governmental Relations Under Yeltsin's New Federalism

I have not renounced my formula: 'Take as much sovereignty as you can swallow'.

Boris Yeltsin, 30 May 1994[1]

Previous chapters have emphasized the power of the past over the new Russian federalism: the triple problem of Soviet institutions, personnel, and ideas. This chapter examines the institutional asymmetry that is the legacy of Yeltsin's presidency. First, federal asymmetry is placed on the theoretical continuum developed in Chapter Two. Second, conceptions of federalism held by regional elites in the Russian Federation are scrutinized. The bilateral treaties signed between federal executive authorities and forty-seven regional executives are at the heart of this asymmetry. Theoretically and empirically, this 'Parade of Treaties' exacerbated Russia's existing institutional asymmetry, presenting considerable hurdles for a 'democratic, federal, rule-of-law state'.

1. Problems of Asymmetry in Federal States

1.1 Asymmetry in Comparative Perspective

Asymmetry can mean almost anything: differences in territorial size, the distribution of resources, socioeconomic development, demographic variety in the workforce, ethnic groups, cultural or linguistic divisions. Asymmetry may connote political differences in representation, the power to collect taxes or expend revenue. It would be virtually impossible, and probably undesirable, to construct a state composed of sub-units symmetrical in all respects.

The concept of asymmetry is fundamental to federal theory. Asymmetries like those above exist in any polity. Such factors may even encourage federal approaches. Because federations rely on written constitutions and courts to regulate and arbitrate a complex conception of sovereignty,

[1] *Segodnia*, 31 May 1994, 1.

another type of asymmetry—*institutional* asymmetry—is of much greater concern in federal systems. Asymmetry in the powers and institutions of constituent units in a federation exacerbate other forms of asymmetry. Steven Solnick, emphasizing the development of federations, divides institutional asymmetry into two sub-categories: '[T]here is an important distinction between asymmetries that emerge from the federal government's discretion over distributing benefits and allocating costs, and asymmetries agreed to as constitutional norms by a majority (or constitution-producing supermajority) of constituent regions'. The first type of asymmetry he calls *ad hoc* asymmetry, the latter form he calls constitutional asymmetry.[2]

Table 6.1 presents continuums for three issues important to any federal system. On the far left, one theoretical extreme is depicted, total 'state's rights'. This scenario is characterized by high levels of sovereignty assumed by constituent units of a federation. Highly individualized action by each unit—acting according to its conception of itself as sovereign—predictably will result in high institutional asymmetry. Some units will win, assume or claim more sovereign powers than others. On the far right, the opposite extreme is depicted, a hypothetical system that hardly seems federal at all. The central government overwhelms any autonomous authority of constituent units. The 'balancing options' shown suggest how the space between these extremes may be mediated. The problems of institutional asymmetry may be dramatized even in this realm of compromise if these options are applied selectively to, or sporadically ignored by, a fraction of the total number of units in the federation.

Of special pertinence to Russia is the range of possibilities for creating extra-constitutional agreements between the federal government and select regional executive authorities. Such agreements, as Solnick suggests, can provide special *ad hoc* privileges (e.g. subsidies, retention of revenue, etc.) or deeper constitutional exceptions (e.g. creation of unique institutions, exempted or added jurisdictions, etc.). Here, however, Solnick's terminology may cause some confusion. The phrase 'constitutional asymmetry' fails to convey the fundamental point that these privileges may be *extra*-constitutional—by definition, exceptions to what has been agreed by all units in the federation.[3] Institutional asymmetry may be agreed in transparent, all-union negotiations. Alternatively it might be the result of secret processes that conjure mistrust between units and weaken a sense of federal identity. Agreements may be ratified by federal and/or regional parliaments

---

[2] Steven L. Solnick, 'Statebuilding, Asymmetries and Federal Stability in Russia'. Workshop on Democracy, Nationalism, and Federalism. Oxford University, 6–7 June 1997, 9–10.

[3] Some may take issue with my characterization of these privileges as '*extra*-constitutional', pointing, as did regional elites, to Art. 11, § 3 of the Federal Constitution, which states that

Table 6.1   Theoretical Examples of Federal Continuums

	High levels of state sovereignty		Low levels of state sovereignty
	⟵―――――――――――――――――――――――――⟶		
	Extreme 'state's rights'	Balancing options	Extreme centralization
Supremacy of law	State law *de jure* or *de facto* supreme over federal law; Nullification or interposition of laws;	Judicial review by independent courts over enumerated division of powers;	Federal law *de jure* or *de facto* supreme over state law (e.g. emergency powers to dismiss state authorities);
	Right of unilateral secession;	Secession strongly discouraged but multilateral, multi-stage process in place;	No right to secession;
	Separate state citizenship with attendant rights.	Single citizenship but limited privileges linked to residency.	Single federal citizenship.
Law-making	Regional vetoes in federal legislature (i.e. unanimity rule);	Use of simple or super-majorities determined by subject, but no regional veto;	Simple majority rule in federal legislature on all subjects;
	Federal legislature composed *ex officio* of state governors.	No restrictions on candidacy for federal legislature, but membership not simply *ex officio*.	Federal legislators prohibited from holding state offices.
Finance	Exclusive source of taxation;	State and federal sources of taxation;	Federal control over taxation;
	State banks with emission powers over state currencies;	State banks with no emission powers;	No state government banks;
	State customs and excise authority.	Single federal currency.	Single currency.

jurisdictional divisions are delineated by the Constitution, the Federation Treaty 'and other treaties'. From a purely textual point of view, then, 'other treaties' are not outside the range of possibilities imagined to be outside the constitutional sphere because allowance has been made for them within the constitution. My point is that, text aside, the role of a constitution as a foundational document of the utmost importance to a federal, democratic, rule-of-law state, requires a stricter view, especially

or referendums. Or, they may be the exclusive province of executive authorities that exclude other branches of government on both federal and regional levels.

These are crucial choices for political elites to make, choices which will shape the development of the federation from the start of the process of federalization. Assent by the other members of a federation to an otherwise bilateral agreement between the federal government and a constituent unit, most often in the form of approval by the federal legislature, is in keeping with the federal philosophy of a compact, binding separate units into a new entity of blended sovereignties.[4] By definition, inclusion in a process of accession promotes transparency and multiple levels of participation. In assessing the choices made in Russia, a fruitful comparison is with the successfully negotiated transition from authoritarian rule to federal democracy that occurred in Spain. As noted in Chapter Two, the Spanish constitution set out a multi-step process for the creation of an autonomous community that foresaw multiple referendums, negotiations at both the provincial and all-Spain levels, and ratification by regional legislatures and also the *Cortes Generales*.[5] The procedures were constitutionalized and the ratification of the final statute open, transparent and multi-lateral. There are now seventeen autonomous communities spanning fifty Spanish provinces.[6]

This process integrates the notion that, as nationals inhabiting a national homeland, self-determination of their government is a basic right, while at the same time acknowledging the obvious impact of such a change to neighbouring citizens. From its inception, the process of autonomization was carefully circumscribed by Spanish laws which constantly reinforced the link between autonomy statutes and the constitution from which they were derived.[7] Even if closed-door negotiations were probably necessary to reach

for a new and struggling federal system like Russia. The constitution's provisions establishing the separation and division of powers between the federal centre and constituent units are among the most carefully negotiated. And rightly so, given the federal principles of pooled sovereignty and multilateral, transparent inter-governmental relations. Reading this clause to permit bilateral re-negotiation of these foundations, especially without the input of other members of the federation, amounts to an end-run around these principles. Such a clause, at its core, promotes *extraconstitutional* manoeuvres, regardless of the clause's location within the constitution.

[4] Robert Agranoff and Juan Antonio Ramos Gallarin, 'Toward Federal Democracy in Spain: An Examination of Inter-governmental Relations', 27 *Publius*, 4 (1997): 4, 5.

[5] *See* Art. 143 and 151. Albert P. Blaustein & Gisbert H. Flanz, eds. *Constitutions of the Countries of the World: Spain* (Dobbs Ferry, NY: Oceana, 1997), 78.

[6] Robert Agranoff, 'Federal Evolution in Spain', 17 *International Political Science Review*, 4 (1996): 387.

[7] Juan J. Linz, 'Spanish Democracy and the Estado de las Autonomías', in R.A. Goldman, A. Kaufman, & W.A. Shambra, eds. *Forging Unity Out of Diversity: The Approaches of Eight Nations* (Washington, D.C.: American Enterprise Institute, 1989): 261, 269–74, 283.

accord between political elites, *approval* of the final product was a very public process. As explored below, the Russian variant labours under problems of transparency, inclusion, and ratification on both the federal-republican and inter-republican levels. In terms of the process of regionalization, stability of the federation (in terms of federal identity, legal authority and fiscal cooperation) and the transition to democracy and the rule of law, Russia compares unfavourably with Spain in each area.

1.2 Russian Conceptions of Asymmetrical Federalism

How do Russian political elites conceive the effects of such crucial choices? Scholars agree that a consensus on the inherent value of the federal project is very important for its success. In Chapter Two, attention was drawn to the variable Ivo Duchacek labelled 'federal political culture', which Juan Linz also emphasized as the important, though difficult to quantify feeling of federal allegiance: 'the soul of a working federalism'.[8] For Russia's regional and federal elites before, during and now reaching the end of first attempts at institutional engineering, such a consensus has been crucially lacking. Disagreement over just what the 'soul' of Russian federalism entails is a fundamental problem.

Chapter Four examined the weak conceptual foundations of Soviet elites labouring to resolve the surge of federal issues which overran the 'new thinking' on Soviet nationalities policy. Their instrumental view of legal reform reflected unchallenged assumptions about the centralizing role of federal authority. Regional elites who spearheaded regional campaigns against Yeltsin's centre also held notions of federalism strongly influenced by Soviet experience but the very opposite of Moscow's centrist conclusions. These preconceptions were first encouraged by Yeltsin's exhortations for the loosest of confederal relations, then enflamed by Yeltsin's omission of the Federation Treaty from his new Constitution.

The adoption of the tripartite Federation Treaty in March 1992 signalled not basic agreement over federal theory and practice but a poorly designed cover to hide unresolved conflicts under the rubric of 'joint jurisdiction'. The Treaty was both symptom and catalyst for growing interest in federalism. Less than two months after the Treaty's signing, the First All-Russian Congress of Finno-Ugric Peoples drafted a resolution 'On Relations toward the Federation Treaty', which denounced a document 'thrust from above and signed by the leaders of the national republics behind the back of [their] peoples' and declared that republican legislatures had no right to ratify it.[9]

---

[8] Juan J. Linz, 'Democracy, Multinationalism & Federalism'. Paper presented at the International Political Science Association Meeting in Seoul, Korea, August 1997.

[9] Proekt rezoliutsiia 'Ob otnoshenii k Federativnomu Dogovoru', Chervonnaia and Guboglo, Vol. 1, 243.

Conferences on federalism and self-determination proliferated. In September 1993, the Republic of Tatarstan organized an international conference attended by specialists from the USA, Europe, India, China, and throughout the CIS.[10] A few months later the Russian Federation and the Council of Europe jointly sponsored an international conference on federalism.[11] Both conferences (and there were many others) were well attended by regional and federal officials; Sergei Shakhrai, then Minister for Nationalities Affairs and Regional Policy, attended both. Topics ranged across federal and multi-national issues in the former Soviet Union, China, India, Canada, Sri Lanka, and elsewhere. In interviews with the author, numerous republican officials and academics repeatedly referred to the federal experiments of Germany, Switzerland, Canada, and the United States.

With such apparently high awareness of federal issues, what views influenced republican elites? One pervasive belief was that lasting federal solutions could only be constructed *snizu vverkh*, 'from the bottom up'. The resolution drafted at the Finno-Ugric Congress insisted that regional powers remain unabridged and superior to those of the federal government:

2. The Congress does not hold to the position of unconditional negation of the Federation Treaty with Russia, but at the same time notes that:
– entry into the Russian Federation is not the sole and without alternative means to interstate integration and realization of state interests of the national republics of the Finno-Ugric peoples!
– voluntary entry into one or another federation (or confederation) should mean the right to unimpeded recall of transferred authorities, right up to exit from the federation (confederation). Only this may guarantee the observance of all other proclaimed rights.[12]

The resolution conveys its drafters' strongly confederal view of republics as sovereign states not subject to Russian jurisdiction prior to the Federation Treaty. It emphasizes their conviction that a federation is no more than the sum of its parts, lacking any sovereignty of its own, and at risk of dissolution with every controversial decision. It is hard to find an example of a confederal state with fewer powers than these regional activists ascribed to the Russian Federation.

The principle of *snizu vverkh* was broadly shared by republican elites. Rashit Vagizov, Chairman of the Committee on Questions of Legislation,

[10] Zilia R. Valeeva, *Mezhdunarodnaia nauchno-prakticheskaia konferentsiia 'Federalizm—global'nye i rossiiskie izmereniia'* (Kazan': Tipografiia Tatarskogo gazetno-zhurnal'nogo izdatel'stva, 1993).

[11] Sovet Evropy, *Konferentsiia po federalizmu: federativnoe ustroistvo Rossiiskoi Federatsii i realizatsiia printsipov pliuralisticheskoi demokratii, pravovogo gosudarstva i prav cheloveka.* Moskva, 15–18 fevralia 1994 g. Protokoly zasedanii. The conference coincided with the signing of the first bilateral treaty between Russia and Tatarstan.

[12] Chervonnaia & Guboglo, Vol. 1, 243.

Legality, Law and Order, and Deputies' Ethics in the Tatarstan Parliament insisted that the voluntary delegation of power 'from the bottom up' is a core principle of federalism.[13] Yeltsin's summer 1990 advice to elites to take all the sovereignty they could swallow planted some of the seeds for this thinking. In Bashkortostan, the Chairman of the Supreme Soviet parroted Yeltsin as he and his fellow deputies shrugged off the guiding hand of federal authorities: '. . . we appealed to Boris Nikolaevich Yeltsin during his visit in Bashkiria: how does he see the future structure in the Soviets on different levels? He answered: "As the [republican] Supreme Soviet takes a solution, so it will be, because we can't dictate our own conditions of the Center. In the Kuban one [solution] should be, in Bashkiria—one, in Tatarstan—another. Therefore, please, consider it at your own Supreme Soviet" '.[14]

Tatarstan's leaders produced the dominant lexicon for future federal debates in Russia, translating this principle into action. Its most eloquent proponent is Rafael Khakimov, a personal adviser to the Tatar President: 'There are two basic approaches to the federalization of Russia: one is constitutional-treaty, the other is treaty-constitutional'.[15] The constitutional-treaty approach was the straw man, 'traditional of the official structures of Russia' (a euphemism for Russian authoritarianism) that Khakimov promised would lead to a dominant centre and ever-weaker republics. In contrast, the treaty-constitutional approach demanded 'establishing relations with the central government "from below upwards", i.e. through the voluntary transfer of their authority by means of bilateral treaties. In this case, sovereignty becomes a necessary legal basis for the self-determination of the subjects of the Federation'. Khakimov calls this sort of government 'concordant federation'.[16] The phrase 'treaty-constitutional' quickly proliferated in official documents, a sign that this was more than an academic catchphrase.[17]

---

[13]   Rashit G. Vagizov, author's interview, 10 June 1997, Tatarstan State Soviet, Kazan'.

[14]   Vneocherednaia Vtoraia Sessiia Verkhovnogo Soveta Bashkirskoi ASSR Dvenadtsatogo Sozyva Zasedanie Pervoe (3 September 1990, morning session), Stenograficheskii otchet Izdanie Verkhovnogo Soveta Bashkirskoi ASSR (Ufa, 1990), 15.

[15]   Raphael S. Khakimov, 'Prospects of Federalism in Russia: A View from Tatarstan', 27 Security Dialogue, 1 (1996): 70. R.S. Khakimov, 'Podkhody k federalizmu: variant Tatarstana', D.M. Iskhakov, ed. Sovremennyi natsional'nye protsessy v respublike Tatarstan. (Kazan': Akademiia nauk Tatarstana, Institut iazyka, literatury, i istorii im. G. Ibralimova, 1994), 58–65.

[16]   Khakimov, 70.

[17]   The law 'On the order introducing into action the Constitution of the Republic of Tatarstan', passed approximately three weeks after acceptance of that constitution, appeals to the Russian Federal Supreme Soviet to construct 'treaty-constitutional relations' between the republic and the Federation. An official letter to Yeltsin sent roughly five months later by Shaimiev and the Chairman of the Supreme Soviet of Tatarstan, Farid Mukhametshin, restates this special relationship. Rafael' Khakimov, ed. Belaia kniga Tatarstana: put' k suverenitetu, 1990–1995 (Kazan': Tsentr

Whether articulated as principle ('from the bottom up') or system ('treaty-constitutional relations'), republican elites signaled their rejection of the more accepted federal principle that federation entails a pooling and reduction of the individual sovereignties of constituent units into a new, fully sovereign entity. In the eyes of republican leaders, their newly declared sovereignty was neither divisible nor diminishable by a new Russian Federation. While economic and security considerations (at the very least) made secession a moot point for all but Chechnya, republican elites were reluctant to part with a right to secede *in principle*.[18] Declarations of sovereignty and republican constitutions drew from these principles the view that republican laws (by virtue of state sovereignty) retained supremacy over federal legislation. A hierarchy implicit in the treaty-constitutional approach raised republics above the federal government in all matters save those explicitly transferred by the republics, which reserved the right to redeem such powers as need be. From the point of view of the republics, in contrast to accepted federal theory, the Russian Federation was *not* greater than the sum of its parts.

To summarize, for regional political elites a 'treaty-constitutional' approach meant not federation but a loose confederation of sovereign states. Regional elites pointed to Article 11, §3 of the federal constitution, which establishes that the division of powers is determined 'by the present constitution and the Federation Treaty and other treaties'. Federal elites held (and still hold) the reverse view: the Federation is a free-standing sovereign entity that neither required nor sought nor took its justification from its member-units.[19] They pointed to Article 15, §1 of the federal constitution, which establishes the 'supreme legal force and direct effect' of the constitution above any other law or legal act. In an interview with *Rossiiskie vesti* in 1994,

gumanitarnykh proektov i issledovanii, 1996), 23–4. President Shaimiev himself used both the phrase *snizu vverkh* and *dogovorno-konstitutsionnyi* to describe what 'international experience' shows is the best guarantee of federal stability. M.S. Shaimiev, 'Privetstvie prezidenta respubliki Tatarstan M. Shaimiev', in Valeeva, 7.

[18] A leading member of the Bashkir Constitutional Commission, V.K. Samigullin argued that as Bashkortostan had voluntarily entered into the composition of Russia (in 1557) and the RSFSR (in 1919), in the new Bashkir Constitution '. . . it would be expedient to provide for a right of the Bashkir nation to separation, to exit from the composition of the Russian Federation'. V.K. Samigullin, *Konstitutsiia Respubliki Bashkortostan (voprosy teorii)* (Ufa: Bashkirskii Gosudarstvennyi Universitet, 1993), 17.

[19] Sergei Shakhrai notes, 'One thing may be firmly stated—the contemporary practice of concluding treaties does not mean a transformation of our federation from a constitutional to a constitutional-treaty or to a treaty [-based federation]. The federal Constitution is the legal basis of our federative state and its effective functioning'. S.M. Shakhrai, 'Rol' dogovornykh protsessov v ukreplenii i razvitii rossiiskogo federalizma', in M.N. Guboglo, ed. *Federalizm vlasti i vlast' federalizma* (Moskva: IntelTekh, 1997), 153.

Yeltsin's then chief-of-staff Sergei Filatov summarized aspects of this orientation in both regional and federal elites: 'The most general trends are the aspiration of the republic elites to represent the powers of the Russian Federation as the sum of powers delegated by the components (this is notably characteristic of the constitutions of Bashkortostan, Buryatia, Sakha, Tatarstan, and Tuva). However, the powers of the Russian Federation ensue from its own sovereignty as a single, integral federative state, and they do not depend on the components'.[20]

1.3 The 'Parade of Treaties'

Forty-seven of the eighty-nine units of the Federation negotiated bilateral treaties with the federal government (most recently, the City of Moscow, 16 June 1998). Each 'treaty' is actually a complex package including a general statement of principles (the actual treaty, *dogovor*) and up to a score of detailed agreements (*soglashenie*). How these treaties have been negotiated, what political and institutional parameters have affected their content and what factors have influenced the sequencing or omission of units in the list of signatories are as important to understand as how these treaties interacted with the federal constitution and federal laws to regulated relations in the Yeltsin era.

This section presents a detailed analysis of the negotiation of the first bilateral treaty with Tatarstan, followed by a broader analysis of the remaining republican treaties and their effects on federal relations. A focus on Tatarstan's treaty is worthwhile for several reasons. Being first, it set the standard for bilateral treaties which followed; references continue to be made to 'the Tatarstan model'. Second, as the eighth most populous region in Russia (3.7 million inhabitants) and by most measures one of the richest, resolution of what amounted to a constitutional crisis was an important milestone for the Russian Federation as a whole. As the respected Russian ethnographer (and a participant in the treaty negotiations) Valerii Tishkov observed:

The free development of the Tatar people can be conceived of and realized only within the framework of the Russian Federation, since three-fourths of the Tatars (or even more) live outside Tatarstan. Even if Tatarstan's status as a sovereign state is firmly established and put into effect, when it comes to questions of implementing the rights and interests and effecting the cultural development of the Tatars as the second largest people in Russia, numerically speaking, it will still be impossible to

---

[20] 'Filatov on Centre-Region Constitutional Issues', *FBIS Daily Report: Central Eurasia*. FBIS-SOV-94-171 (2 Sept. 1994): 18.

do without the participation of administrative bodies of the whole Russian Federation.[21]

Excursus: The Tatar-Russian Bilateral Negotiations

The 'Treaty on the Demarcation of Objects of Jurisdiction and the Mutual Delegation of Powers Between the Bodies of State Power of the Russian Federation and the Republic of Tatarstan', was signed on 15 February 1994. Negotiations during the protracted two-and-a-half year period were always controversial and sometimes volatile. Each side exerted extra-legal pressure on the other. The Chairman of the Tatarstan Supreme Soviet, Farid Mukhametshin, candidly acknowledged one such tactic, non-payment of federal taxes: 'Yes, this is a unilateral action, it's wrong, but we were forced to do it'.[22] The Russian authorities engaged in similar methods, closing pipelines of once prosperous oil wells and retaliating against regional industry.[23]

Negotiations officially began a week before the August 1991 putsch against Gorbachev and were based, according to one participant, on two fundamental assumptions: (1) the Republic of Tatarstan was a genuine state with a long history of statehood (and therefore with a right to property), and (2) relations therefore required negotiation on a legal-treaty basis. A protocol including these points was drafted and signed by both sides.[24] From the start, the process was influenced by the 'new thinking' on federalism outlined above. In the first of four rounds of talks, the Tatar delegation set the agenda: the question was not *whether* Tatarstan should be entitled to a special status, but what the extent of that relationship would be.

The opening negotiations were characterized by a treaty-constitutional mindset and Soviet era conceptual influences. Members of the Tatar delegation, top-heavy with academics and legal scholars, demanded strict

---

[21] Dmitrii Mikhailin, 'Russia and Tatarstan—One Old Friend is Better than Two New Ones', 44 *The Current Digest of the Post-Soviet Press*, 37 (1992): 4.

[22] Inna Muravyova, 'Notes to the Point: Test of Responsibility' (*Rossiiskaya gazeta*, 6 March 1992): 1–2; 44 *Current Digest of the Post-Soviet Press*, 8 (1992): 6.

[23] Hafeez Malik, 'Tatarstan's Treaty with Russia: Autonomy or Independence', 18 *Journal of South Asian and Middle Eastern Studies*, 2 (Winter 1994): 1–36.

[24] Marat G. Galeev, Chairman of the Commission on Economic Development and Reforms, author's interview, 14 June 1997, State Council, Kazan'. Galeev participated in the preparation of documents throughout the negotiations, and sometimes directly in the negotiating process. *See* 'Protokol po itogam konsul'tatsii delegatsii Rossiiskoi Sovetskoi Federativnoi Sotsialisticheskoi Respubliki i Respubliki Tatarstan, sostoiavshikhsia 12–15 avgusta 1991 goda v gorode Moskve', in *Belaya kniga . . .*, 31–2.

adherence to the laws of the Soviet federal system.[25] The delegation, as Hafeez Malik describes it, 'invoked the resolutions of the third Russian Congress of the Soviets, which was held in January 1918, saying: (1) that the Russian Federation was based upon the principle of freedom and the equality of Soviet republics; (2) the republics were to join the Federation voluntarily; and (3) it was up to the republics to decide for themselves whether to join or to get out of the Federation'.[26] Gennadii Burbulis, the head of the Russian delegation,[27] accepted these points but considered them to be merely rhetorical and ideological. A clearer example of rebuilding the Russian Federation amidst the rubble of the Soviet regime is harder to find. If federal structures were intended to have any more legitimacy than during Soviet times, the issues raised by the Tatar delegation required resolution.

After six months, the talks had gained sufficient momentum to adopt a fourteen-point agreement (soglashenie) on economic cooperation.[28] Momentum notwithstanding, the agreement had little immediate practical effect. In 1992, the Federal Finance Ministry reported that Tatarstan withheld roughly 43 billion rubles due the federal government.[29] The following year, together with Bashkortostan, Tatarstan withheld approximately 400 billion rubles.[30] From the standpoint of future negotiations, the agreement

---

[25] The Tatarstan delegation was led by Vice-President Likhachev (a professor of law), and included Boris Zhelezrov (professor of law, member of the Tatar Committee of Constitutional Supervision), Indus Tagirov (professor and dean of the History Faculty, Kazan' State University), F.R. Gazizullin (deputy PM and candidate in economics) and Rafael Khakimov, among others. 'Ofitsial'noe pis'mo Prezidenta Respubliki Tatarstan M. Shaimieva Prezidentu Rossiiskoi Federatsii B. El'tsinu', 30 July 1991, Belaia kniga..., 30. President Shaimiev participated in the final stages.

[26] Malik, 14.

[27] The Russian delegation changed over time but initially included Sergei Stankevich (State Adviser on Cooperation with Public Associations), Sergei Shakhrai (State Adviser on Legal Policy), Nikolai Fedorov (Minister of Justice and future president of Chuvashia), Oleg Lobov (First Deputy Premier), and Fedor Shelov-Kovediaev (Chairman of the Subcommittee on Inter-Republic Relations, Supreme Soviet). 'Rasporiazhenie Prezidenta RSFSR o sostave delegatsii RSFSR dlia soglasovaniia s Tatarskoi SSR pozitsii po ekonomicheskim i pravovym voprosam', 9 August 1991, Belaia kniga..., 3–31. At various times it also included Gennadii Burbulis, nationalities experts Valery Tishkov and Ramazan Abdulatipov, Prime Minister Viktor Chernomyrdin and Yeltsin.

[28] Soglashenie Pravitel'stva Rossiiskoi Federatsii s Pravitel'stvom Respubliki Tatarstan ob ekonomicheskom sotrudnichestve. Belaia kniga Tatarstana; and F.M. Mukhametshin & R.T. Izmailov, eds. Suverennyi Tatarstan (Moskva: 'INSAN', 1997), both publications of the Tatar government, date this agreement 22 January 1992 and 6 December 1991, respectively. A signed copy given to the author by Tatiana Vasilieva, Director of the Programme on Russian Legal Education, is dated 22 January 1992

[29] Organization for Economic Co-operation and Development. OECD Economic Surveys: The Russian Federation (Paris: OECD, 1995), 59, 157.

[30] G. Semonov, 'Establishing More Rational Relations Between Federal and Regional Budgets: Ways of Updating the Tax-Budget Mechanism', 36 Russian Social Science Review, 5 (1995): 6. To put this amount into perspective, it was the equivalent that year of half the entire federal budget for Russian higher education.

was a success for Tatarstan, acknowledging Tatar jurisdiction over natural resources (including oil), certain property and enterprises and a widening of influence over the Tatar affliate of the Central Bank. A precedent was established for later agreements which implicitly accepted Tatarstan as a sovereign unit with whom negotiations, not directives, were required. Meanwhile, Tatarstan disregarded its federal responsibilities with apparent impunity.

The idea for the 1992 referendum on Tatar sovereignty (held ten days before the Federation Treaty signing ceremony) not only originated in these negotiations, but came from the Russian side from Burbulis himself. Burbulis evidently expected that sufficient numbers of Russians resident in the republic would answer negatively a question on Tatarstan's sovereignty, international status, and 'treaty-constitutional' approach, giving the lie to the Tatar claim to multinational support. When Russian officials realized they had misjudged public opinion, the referendum was declared a threat, a 'coup d'état' according to Sergei Shakhrai (then vice-premier for nationalities and regional policy).[31] Marat Galeev, a Tatar negotiator, noted his own unease during the referendum, which:

...was connected with a definite risk including direct threats of arrest in the case of a legal referendum. There was a list of several tens of people who were bigger activists and who should have been arrested as enemies of the people. Khasbulatov at that time, if you remember, was chairman of the Supreme Soviet and he was located at the time of the results in Volzhk not very far from here. On the borders of Tatarstan there were large military manoeuvres at that time. And he said frankly that it was necessary to bring the president of Tatarstan back [to Moscow] in an iron cage [most likely, a reference to the fate of the 18th-century rebel leader Pugachev].... When I went on the roads of Tatarstan to prepare for the referendum and on the day of the referendum, there was a huge quantity of troops.[32]

[31] Sergei Chugayev, *Izvestia*, 17 Mar. 1992, 2 [44 *CDPSP*, No. 11 (1992): 21] Shakhrai suggested that prosecutors should warn local election commission officials that their 'unconstitutional' actions could result in criminal charges. On 5 March the RF Supreme Soviet sent an official appeal to Tatarstan in which the referendum was labelled an 'act of disrespect to the multinational people of Tatarstan, [and] to the statehood of the Russian Federation', directed towards the secession of the republic. 'Obrashchenie k narodu, Verkhovnomu Sovetu i Prezidentu Respubliki Tatarstan', *Vedomosti S''ezda narodnykh deputatov Rossiiskoi Federatsii i Verkhovnogo Soveta Rossiiskoi Federatsii*, No. 12 (19 Mar. 1992), item 644, 847.

[32] Galeev, author's interview, 14 June 1997, State Soviet, Kazan'. Rafael Khakimov asserts that army exercises were held along the republic's borders. Raphael S. Khakimov, 'Prospects of Federalism in Russia', 74. Confirming rumours of troop mobilization at a discussion hosted by the Open Media Research Institute, he claimed that 'there was a real danger that [Tatarstan] would suffer the fate that subsequently befell Chechnya in December 1994'. Peter Rutland, 'Tatarstan: A Sovereign Republic Within the Russian Federation', 1 *OMRI Russian Regional Report*, 5 (25 Sept. 1996), Part I.

In any event, the Tatar president remained in his Kazan' Kremlin, more than 61% of voters approved the referendum, and Gennadii Burbulis was replaced by Sergei Shakhrai less than six months later.[33]

This was the nadir of the negotiating process. Russian officials petitioned the Russian Constitutional Court to stop the referendum. A week before the referendum, the Court declared that the referendum, the 1990 Declaration of Sovereignty and amendments to the 1992 Tatar constitution contradicted the federal constitution. Tatarstan, not recognizing the Court's jurisdiction, did not send representatives to its proceedings. Likewise, the Russian delegation did not recognize the results of the referendum. According to one Tatar participant, relations froze and talks ceased for six months. An economic blockade was levied by federal authorities against Tatarstan, a response to the 'illegal' referendum as well as to Tatarstan's refusal to sign the Federation Treaty ten days later. Although the blockade's impact is debatable (some goods were denied Kazan, but Moscow was denied taxes from one of its richest republics), it undeniably revealed the depths to which relations had sunk. When talks resumed in August 1992, a mutual desire to restart negotiations was palpable.

In the course of negotiations, the Tatar delegation employed a changing battery of tactics. During the early stages, when the Federation Treaty and federal constitution were themselves being drafted, Tatarstan sought to establish a coalition of like-minded former autonomous republics to demand a treaty-based emphasis to federal relations and recognition of their sovereign status as republics. Tatarstan, however, demanded its own special relationship outside the Federation Treaty, as *primus inter pares*, in accordance with its constitutional assertion to unique treaty-based 'association' with the Russian Federation.[34] Ratification of this constitution thirteen months *before* adoption by referendum of the federal constitution was itself a major negotiating tool. The ultimatum led to Tatarstan's refusal to participate in the federal constitutional conference and a period of general isolation.

More conciliatory tactics were the norm as negotiations approached their final stages. As Tatarstan's President Shaimiev assessed world opinion on a claim to international status (especially the unlikelihood of UN membership) and the prospects of political and economic alienation, the most

---

[33] The referendum question was 'Do you agree that the Republic of Tatarstan is a sovereign state, a subject of international law, forming its relations with the Russian Federation, other republics and states on the basis of legal agreements?'

[34] Art. 61 of the Tatar Constitution, passed 6 November 1992, asserts 'The Republic of Tatarstan is a sovereign state, a subject of international law, associated with the Russian Federation—Russia—on the basis of a Treaty on the mutual delegation of authority and subjects of jurisdiction'. *Konstitutsiia Respubliki Tatarstan* (Kazan': Tatarskoe knizhnoe izdatel'stvo, 1995), 61.

extreme demands for independence were dropped.[35] Although there remained significant conflicts (e. g. Shaimiev's refusal to support the April 1993 federal referendum; the sobering effect on negotiators of the October 1993 events) in some sense these events also served to expedite the final stages of the process.

Throughout the negotiations, but particularly in their final stages, special agreements (*soglashenii*) were concluded. These helped to establish a protocol for the final treaty. Agreements were issued in the name of the governments of the respective parties, signed by their prime ministers, and were not sent for ratification to either the federal or republican legislature. On 22 January 1992, a fourteen-article agreement 'On Economic Cooperation' was signed by Yegor Gaidar and Tatar Prime Minister Sabirov. On 5 June 1993, a bundle of three agreements was signed between Moscow and Kazan' on cooperation in oil refining and transport, environmental protection, and higher education. On 22 June, another three-agreement bundle produced common positions on property, jurisdiction over local defence industries and customs.

The final treaty (*dogovor*) was signed by the presidents and prime ministers of the Russian Federation and Tatarstan.[36] It was not subject to ratification either by the Federation Council or by the Tatar legislature but entered into force seven days after the signing ceremony.[37] The treaty recognized that Tatarstan was 'united' with Russia, not 'associated' as stated in the Tatar Constitution. Along with the bilateral treaty, both the Russian and Tatar constitutions—but not the Federation Treaty—were recognized to govern the division of powers. The Treaty established exclusive and joint jurisdictions. Tatarstan was accorded the right to create its own budget funded with its own taxes and a variety of financial mechanisms necessary for foreign economic activity, including a national bank. Tatarstan was entitled to 'decide issues of republican citizenship' and to engage in international affairs, provided that these did not contradict federal international obligations. Exclusive federal authority was agreed for the enforcement of federal law, levy of federal taxes, establishment of unified federal policies (e. g. foreign affairs, fiscal and monetary policy), and a unified federal legal and judicial system.

The Treaty had several potential problems. Twenty-three matters of joint jurisdiction were established, ensuring that resolution of any issue the least

[35] Radik Batyrshin, 'Kazan' prorubaet okna', *Nezavisimaia gazeta*, 11 Sept. 1992, 1.

[36] Russian and English translations of the Treaty in Mukhametshin & Izmailov, 40–6.

[37] It is a revealing contradiction that Tatarstan should consider its bilateral treaty with Russia a treaty between sovereign states while at the same time not submitting the document to ratification by the Tatar State Council in conformity with Art. 89, §29 of the Tatar Constitution, which grants the State Council jurisdiction over 'ratification and denunciation of international treaties of the Republic of Tatarstan'.

bit contentious was postponed for later negotiation. Many of these over-
lapped subjects simultaneously set aside for exclusive jurisdiction in the
same treaty, such as vague references to a 'common policy in the social
sphere' or 'personnel for justice and police enforcement'. Distinctions such
as the federal power to 'regulate and defend' civil and human rights versus
Tatar authority only to 'guarantee' their defence were confusingly ambiguous. Matters of fiscal authority and control over property were equally
unclear, and seemed more descriptions of present conditions than determinations of future authority. No specific procedures or venues were
agreed for the resolution of conflicts.

These discrepancies produced real conflicts. Under whose jurisdiction is
citizenship? Legal authority belongs jointly to Russia and Tatarstan on
common questions of citizenship, exclusively to Tatarstan on republican
citizenship and exclusively to Russia for federal citizenship. Tatar legislators
passed a first reading of a law on citizenship in April 1998 permitting the
right to Tatar citizenship independent of possession of Russian federal
citizenship.[38] Such a law has serious ramifications for the large Tatar
diaspora living outside of the republic. It also implied that citizens of
Tatarstan could enjoy the benefits provided by Kazan without the obligations demanded by Moscow. Not before Vladimir Putin's assent to the
Russian presidency, and the sweeping federal reforms that were the hall-
mark of his first year in office, was some accord reached on citizenship.

Another constitutional problem was the precedent that the Tatar negotiators sought to establish. As mentioned above, negotiations began with a
jointly signed protocol acknowledging that Tatarstan and the Russian Federation would build their relations on 'a new basis' using a 'treaty form'. To
the Tatar side, this clearly meant a 'treaty-constitutional' relationship established between two sovereign states, not between one constituent of a
federation and its federal government. This was reflected in the compromise 'united' status expressed in the preamble of the treaty. As one respected
Tatarstan legal scholar assessed the result, 'Tatarstan devised new forms of
mutual relations and thereby proved that the integrity of the federation is
to be achieved via the independence of its subjects'.[39] Shakhrai would later
declare this position anathema to Russia's federal construction: '[T]here
may not be a treaty between the Russian Federation as a whole and a

[38] Shamil' Idiatullin, 'Grazhdanin Tatarii—eshchë ne znachit grazhdanin Rossii', *Kommersant''-
daily*, 17 Apr. 1998, 2. Dmitrii Mikhailin, 'Odin pasport—dva gosudarstva?' *Rossiiskaia gazeta*, 21 Feb.
1998, 5.

[39] Gennadii Kurdiukov, 'Treaty-Based Relations of the Subjects of the Russian Federation', in
Katlijn Malfliet & Liliana Nasyrova, eds. *Federalism: Choices in Law, Institutions and Policy. A
Comparative Approach with Focus on the Russian Federation* (Leuven, Belgium: Garant, 1998), 204.

subject of the federation as equal rights states. The RF Constitution secures
the equal rights of subjects of the federation between themselves, and not
their equal rights with the federal state in which they are a part'.[40] This
issue presents a potential future conflict which leaves the very question of
Russia's federal structure unresolved.

Perhaps the most serious issue was not wrapped in the details of the
Treaty itself, but in the brinkmanship inherent in the negotiating process. As
Laurence Hanauer observed, the treaty was realized 'only by taking drastic
actions that would plunge Russia into chaos' if all 89 units engaged the same
approach. In addition to the usual path of a declaration of sovereignty
followed by a new constitution, Tatarstan refused to pay its taxes throughout the process, rejected the Federation Treaty in March 1992, did not
officially participate in the April 1993 federal referendum, withdrew from
the Russian Constitutional Assembly in June 1993 and essentially boycotted
federal elections (including the referendum on the Constitution) in December 1993. Republican elites praised the Tatarstan model as a glorious success
for the regions, building a Federation *snizu verkh*. 'The question', remarked
Hanauer, 'is whether, over the long term, the Federation can survive such
resounding successes'.[41]

•   §   •   §   •

Yeltsin's treaty launched a parade of similar treaties throughout Russia, just
as his speech in that republic's capital three and a half years earlier began a
parade of sovereignties. Emil Pain, head of the Presidential Council's Group
on Nationalities Policy, confirmed the agreement as 'the first harbinger of
these treaty-based relations'. Sergei Shakhrai continued:

It is legally and economically possible to conclude treaties similar to the one with
Tataria with each subject of the Russian Federation. And this is not Shakhrai's
opinion. This is the eleventh article of the Russian Federation Constitution, point
three of which says that the demarcation of subjects of jurisdiction 'is established by
this Constitution, the Federal Treaty and other treaties'.[42]

At the end of May 1994 Yeltsin declared: 'I have not renounced my formula:
"Take as much sovereignty as you can swallow" '.[43]

[40] Shakhrai, in Guboglo *et al.* 156.
[41] Laurence S. Hanauer, 'Tatarstan and the Prospects for Federalism in Russia: A Commentary',
27 *Security Dialogue*, 1 (Mar. 1996), 85.
[42] Tamara Zamiatina, 'Federalizm ili dezintegratssiia—tret'ego ne dano', *Segodnia*, 25 Feb. 1994, 9.
[43] Elena Tregubova, 'Boris El'tsin v Tatarii', *Segodnia*, 31 May 1994, 1.

In July 1994 a bilateral treaty was signed with the Republic of Kabardino-Balkaria; that August, Bashkortostan received the next bilateral treaty. The following year, four more republics—and only republics—signed treaties with the centre. Of the first fifteen bilateral treaties signed, nine were with republics. By the end of 1998, eleven republics (52 per cent) had successfully negotiated bilateral treaties (See Table 6.2).[44]

It is difficult to discount the republican dimension in assessing the first years of the 'Parade of Treaties': two years elapsed and seven treaties were signed with ethnic republics before an administrative oblast or krai received similar treatment. Republics were endowed with numerically more, and more deeply entrenched institutions than other federal units. In keeping with this Soviet legacy, treaties initially followed the Tatarstan model—they were signed between heads of state of 'sovereign republics'.[45] In each case, republics had installed a constitution and, in all but one case, an elected president prior to signing a treaty.[46] As James Hughes noted, it was only in September 1995, coinciding with the move towards elected heads of regions

Table 6.2   Bilateral Treaties between the Russian Federation and its Republics

1994	1995	1996	1997	1998
Tatarstan (15 Feb.)	N. Ossetia (Alania) (23 Mar.)	Komi (20 Mar.)	Chechnya (12 May)	Marii El (20 May)
Kabardino-Balkaria (1 July)	Sakha (29 June)	Chuvashia (27 May)		
Bashkortostan (3 Aug.)	Buriatia (11 July)			
	Udmurtia (17 Oct.)			

Note: Republics without treaties: Adygeia, Altai, Dagestan, Ingushetia, Kalmykia, Karelia, Khakassia, Mordova, Karachaevo-Cherkessia, Tyva.

[44]   The treaty signed with Chechnya in May 1997, essentially an armistice agreement, bore little resemblance to any other bilateral treaty. *See* Otto Latsis, 'Dogovor s Chechnei: kto pobedil, kto proigral', *Izvestiia*, 14 May 1997, 1.

[45]   Boris Zheleznov, participant on the Tatar side in the preparation of the bilateral treaty, strongly emphasized that the treaty should *not* be understood as an agreement signed between organs of the Russian Federation, but an inter-governmental treaty signed between two states. Author's interview, 6 June 1997, Law Faculty, Kazan' State University.

[46]   The exception is Udmurtia, which maintained a parliamentary system, and hence lacked an elected president; the treaty was jointly signed by the Chairman of the State Council, acting as head of state, and the Chairman of the Government. Non-republican units of the Federation were not permitted to draft constitutions, only charters (*ustavy*) of government. From August 1991 to the Spring of 1993 their chief executives were appointed by Yeltsin. Following the October 1993 Events, Yeltsin again decreed for himself the power to appoint all non-republican chief executives. With few exceptions, gubernatorial elections were not permitted until December 1995 (and then only in selected regions).

(rather than presidential appointees) that Yeltsin and Prime Minister Chernomyrdin publicly discussed the possibility of including oblasts and krais in the treaty process.[47] The total number of treaties—the last was signed 16 June 1998—is shown in Table 6.3.

Republican elites naturally preferred that treaties remain an exclusively republican prerogative. In early 1995 three of the most powerful republics, Tatarstan, Bashkortostan, and Sakha— all of which had received or would soon conclude treaties themselves—jointly signed a declaration cautioning the centre that treaties should reflect the differences of status in the hierarchy of federal units.[48] Employing his theory of iterated federal bargaining, Steven Solnick emphasizes that purely ethnic factors, apart from the institutional factors distinguishing republics, explain very few of the variations in the substance or order of treaties in comparisons *between* republics. The ethnic difference republics shared could, however, be seen to 'serve as a co-ordinating mechanism across different ethnic republics, distinguishing them from the Russian regions. Any proposal to eliminate the distinction between regions and republics, in other words, can be recognized immediately by each of the republics as a direct threat to its own interests'.[49]

Only two republics, Komi and Chuvashia, signed treaties in 1996, suggesting that earlier rules limiting treaties to republics had changed. The first non-republics to receive treaties that year were the oblasts of Kaliningrad, Sverdlovsk, Orenburg, and Omsk, and two krais: Krasnodar and Khabarovsk. Solnick notes that these regions were home constituencies for Vladimir Shumeiko (Kaliningrad), Boris Yeltsin (Sverdlovsk), Viktor Chernomyrdin (Orenburg) and Leonid Polezhaev (Omsk), the head of the then influential regional organization *Siberskoe soglashenie*.[50] Kaliningrad's governor, Yurii Matochkin,

Table 6.3   Results of the Bilateral Treaty Process for All Federal Units

Federation subject	Total No. of units	No. with treaties	Per cent
Republics	21	11	52
Oblasts	49	26	53
Krais & autonomous oblasts	17	8	47
Federal cities	2	2	100

[47] James Hughes, 'Institutional Design and Political Stability: Asymmetric Federalism in Russia's State of Transition', Paper prepared for the ESRC Research Seminar on Regional Transformations in Russia (London School of Economics, 21 Oct. 1998), 17.

[48] James Hughes, 'Moscow's Bilateral Treaties Add to Confusion', 2 *Transition*, 19 (20 Sept. 1996): 41.

[49] Steven L. Solnick, 'The Political Economy of Russian Federalism: A Framework for Analysis', *Problems of Post-Communism* (Nov./Dec. 1996), 21.

[50] Solnick, 'Statebuilding, Asymmetries...', 23.

was at the time also personally close to Yeltsin. Nikolai Yegorov, who replaced Shakhrai as Minister for Nationality Affairs and Regional Policy in May 1994, had been governor of Krasnodar krai before being called to Moscow.[51]

1.4 Explaining the 'Parade of Treaties'

Why didn't the 'Parade of Treaties' include all the republics? Geography, nationalism, economics, and, of course, elections and politics are all potential explanations.

An initial observation is that treaty activity was geographically clustered. With the exception of Mordova (the central Volga republic that had the distinction of declaring sovereignty while studiously avoiding use of the term), all republics without treaties are situated on the periphery: Karelia on the Finnish border; Khakassia, Altai and Tyva at the Mongolian border; and the five republics of the North Caucasus (Adygeia, Dagestan, Ingushetia, Kalmykia, and Karachaevo-Cherkessia). Although the treaty-recipient republics of North Ossetia-Alania, Kabardino-Balkaria, and Buriatia are border republics, the majority of treaties have been signed with republics locked within the Russian Federation (Sakha's Arctic coastline exhibits few of the vital characteristics of an external border).

Nationalism and ethnic composition are poor explanations for treaty acquisition. Chapter Four explored how Tatarstan's President Shaimiev manipulated nationalist sentiment as a tactic against the federal centre. But after its initial use in the Parade of Sovereignties, Shaimiev earned the hatred of Tatar nationalists by crushing their formerly state-sponsored movements in preparation for final treaty negotiations with Moscow. No other republican leadership is known subsequently to have manipulated national movements in a similar fashion. On the contrary, republican presidents, such as Komi's Yurii Spiridonov, who is Russian, and Sakha's Mikhail Nikolaev, who is ethnic Sakha, emphasized ethnic harmony in their bids to prevent an exodus of well-trained Russians from their northern republics. This suggests that popular support for what some have called 'political nationalism' was less important than the realpolitik of regional political elites.[52] Both republics received

---

[51]   Hughes, 'Moscow's Bilateral Treaties . . . ',43.

[52]   Dmitry Gorenburg argues, based on data from late 1993, that political elites joined a 'push for nationalism' to increase their political power. The survey research on which he relies, however, shows stark differences in such political nationalism. In Sakha, 87% of respondents completely or partially supported declarations of sovereignty, while only 33% felt similarly in Komi. While 20% of Komi supported a right to secession, over 60% of Sakha did. Regardless of these jarring differences in popular opinion, both the Komi and Sakha presidents pursued similar policies aimed to convince much-needed skilled Russians to remain in their republics. Dmitry Gorenburg, 'Nationalism for the Masses: Popular Support for Nationalism in Russia's Ethnic Republics', 53 Europe-Asia Studies, 1 (Jan. 2001): 84, 85, 102. Explanations for the pursuit of greater political autonomy must lie elsewhere.

bilateral treaties. According to the last official census, of the ten republics to sign treaties, only four of them have had titular ethnic populations which outnumbered ethnic Russians in the republic.[53] Almost as many republics without treaties are predominantly inhabited by titular ethnic groups (Dagestan, Kalmykia, and Tyva).

A stronger explanation for treaty distribution is economic. Richer regions have on the whole received treaties earlier, and with greater privileges, than poorer regions. Economic factors support Steven Solnick's account of an iterated bargaining game: those republics with the most to bargain stood the best chance of treaty success. Poorer republics, dependent on federal subsidies, were poorly placed to demand a bilateral treaty decreasing federal control: Karachaevo-Cherkessia, Dagestan, Altai, Tyva, and Ingushetia— none with treaties—received some of the highest levels of federal budget contributions at the peak of the parade of treaties.[54] Using data assessing federal support for regions in 1995, Aleksei Lavrov determines that nine out of ten republics without treaties were substantially subsidized by the federal government—four republics receiving between 64 and 78 per cent of their budget revenue from federal sources, three more receiving between 33 and 45 per cent from Moscow.[55] Those republics most dependent on federal largesse could safely be ignored. With the exception of Karelia, the republics which do not have bilateral treaties are among the poorest regions in Russia. Tyva, which declared a right to secession in violation of the federal constitution, had nowhere to secede save a worse fate squeezed between Russia and Mongolia. However, an excessive focus on economic 'bargaining chips' does not explain why some rich regions either do not receive treaties or receive them only after poorer neighbours. Nor does it explain why some poor republics, such as Marii El, should receive treaties while others, such as neighbouring Mordova, do not; seven republics with treaties received comparable federal support with five non-treaty republics.[56] Only the extremes are explained by a rich-poor gap, a variable which may be a proxy for other overlapping effects.

[53] North Ossetia (Alania) and Chuvashia have an absolute majority of the titular ethnic group over ethnic Russians. Kabardino-Balkaria and Tatarstan have a plurality of the titular ethnic group but not an absolute majority. Data from the 1989 census reprinted in *Argumenty i fakty*, 13 (Mar. 1991): 1.

[54] Solnick, 'Statebuilding, Asymmetries...', 34.

[55] Data (which omits Ingushetia) from Aleksei Lavrov, a budget specialist from the Presidential Administration, reprinted in Alastair McAuley, 'The Determinants of Russian Federal-Regional Fiscal Relations: Equity or Political Influence?' 49 *Europe-Asia Studies*, 3 (1997), 431–44.

[56] Lavrov in McAuley, 442–3.

The order of treaties signed in 1996, an election year for the federal presidency, suggests political explanations. Anticipating elections that June, Yeltsin signed ten more treaties with non-republics.[57] It has been widely speculated that treaties were an important tactic in Yeltsin's re-election campaign, in which capacity they were an excellent tool. Regional recipients of election season treaties were acutely aware that, as treaties were exclusively executive controlled, Yeltsin's re-election was the best assurance that negotiated promises would indeed be honoured.[58] The geography of treaties signed in 1996 tends to support this hypothesis: regions in the 'Red-Brown' belt of southern Russia (where Yeltsin's support was weakest) were largely avoided as were northern areas (such as Karelia) with openly anti-Yeltsin leaders. Treaty distribution in the months immediately before and after the elections concentrated on supporters and fence-sitters.[59] To be plausible, an explanation proposing that bilateral treaties were used by Yeltsin's election campaign as a means to secure republican support would imply the federal executive's belief that republican executives could actually deliver votes in exchange for treaty promises. Firm evidence for such a proposition is extremely difficult to obtain, although surprising vote swings between rounds occurred in republics.[60] Although the difference in votes was too large to have been fabricated, Michael McFaul does acknowledge that structural fraud, intimidation and even ballot stuffing played a role in several republics, notably Tatarstan, Dagestan, and Kalmykia.[61]

The list of treaty recipients does suggest a related explanation: republics perceived to be under the control of strong executives were, *ceteris paribus*, more likely to obtain treaties. Powerful republican executives were more likely than weak leaders to be able to marshal control sufficient enough over their republic's resources to negotiate successfully. As Daniel Treisman has observed in his analysis of fiscal federalism, by preying on federal anxieties

[57] Daniel Treisman documents that regions visited by Yeltsin between January and June 1996 (i.e. during an increasingly hot campaign season), 'received more than 400, 000 rubles per capita more in net transfers that year... Previous visits by high officials had not been associated with discernible outpourings of cash—but evidently presidential election years are somewhat different'. Daniel S. Treisman, *After the Deluge: Regional Crises and Political Consolidation in Russia* (Ann Arbor: University of Michigan Press, 1999), 74.

[58] Rafael Khakimov publicly stated Tatarstan's anxieties that regime change in Moscow might upset executive-driven agreements unratified by parliament. Anna Paretskaya, 'Party Building Heats Up in Tatarstan', 1 *OMRI Russian Regional Report*, 12 (13 Nov. 1996).

[59] Hughes, 'Moscow's Bilateral Treaties ... ', 43; Hughes, 'Institutional Design ... ', 18.

[60] Treisman calculates that 'the signing bonus appeared to amount to more than two additional points of the vote'. Tresiman, *After the Deluge*, 98, 100. If results are analysed by republic, rather than in the aggregate, the pay-off is even more pronounced.

[61] Michael McFaul, *Russia's 1996 Presidential Election: The End of Polarized Politics* (Stanford, CA: Hoover Institution Press, 1997), 72–4.

about the integrity of the state and the potential 'bandwagon effect' of protests and opposition, regional executives could essentially blackmail federal executives into providing various forms of fiscal appeasement.[62] But whereas Treisman perceives in Moscow's fiscal appeasement a strategy to decrease threatened regional instability, Russia's regions may well have perceived this strategy not as a means but as an end in itself. Republics, especially, played a risky game of nationalist bluffs and grandiose assertions of sovereign power. These seem less designed toward the goal (pursued by Chechnya) of genuine independence, but toward realization of the ambition of greater autonomy and increased economic benefits. Federal fiscal appeasement did not persuade regions to give up their threats so much as it played into regional strategies to win exactly what they were offered. Rather than demobilizing regional leaders from pursuing still more dangerous secessionism by 'buying off their constituencies', as Treisman concludes, Moscow may simply have acceded to demands beyond which regional leaders were themselves unwilling to go, bluffs to the contrary notwithstanding.

The Tatar strategy of baiting and threatening federal authorities demonstrates that negotiations could be protracted and complex affairs. Sergei Shakhrai, a key federal negotiator, emphasized the necessity of 'political reason and will towards constructive dialogue' on the part of republican leaders to negotiate a successful compact.[63] Republics riven with internal dissent would seem less likely to be able to organize a successful drive against central federal authority. Republics such as Adygeia, Altai, Khakassia, and Mordova—all without treaties—would seem to fit this category.

Conversely, bilateral treaties were not as crucial in republics in which the executive exercised tight control *and* where that executive already had strong federal ties. That Dagestan and Kalmykia lacked treaties but drew fire for electoral fraud on behalf of Yeltsin appears less incongruous in this light. Both republics were dependent on federal largesse and run by presidents loyal to Yeltsin. This is one strong explanation for the lack of a bilateral treaty with Ingushetia, where Ruslan Aushev rose from his November 1992 post in charge of the federal state of emergency in the republic to twice uncontested election as president. Karachaevo-Cherkessia, where the president Vladimir Khubiev was first appointed to the post by Yeltsin's *ukaz* in April 1995, also fits this explanation.

As a general rule, republics fared best that were able to balance economic resources desired by the federal centre with enough political pressure (but

[62] Daniel S. Treisman, *After the Deluge.*

[63] Shakhrai, in Guboglo, 151. Treisman's conclusions have a similar ring: 'The most effective regional strategy, where it could be sustained, combined credible challenges with a readiness to negotiate'. Treisman, *After the Deluge*, 134.

not too much) to show that compromises were possible. Many of the republics which appear as outliers are less exceptional when viewed as individual cases. The situation of Mordova, the only republic in the Volga region without a treaty, is clarified when attention is paid to the numerous internal conflicts that left the republic without a united front capable of negotiations for most of the period of the parade of treaties—in April 1993 the legislature voted to eliminate the post of president, a post which was not fully restored until a September 1995 meeting of a Constitutional Assembly.[64] Kabardino-Balkaria and North Ossetia (Alania), the only Caucasian republics to receive treaties, on the other hand may be partially explained by the solid control their executives displayed over their republics.

The treaty process favoured republics whose executives had visible control over their republics but who were also astute enough to articulate demands that left room for negotiation and compromise. Republics that possessed substantial natural or industrial resources were more likely to have their appeals heard by the centre than those which were dependent on federal aid. Republics destabilized by internal leadership struggles or whose leaders misjudged the prevailing political winds in making their demands were also less successful. The problem with a strategy of appeasement is ascertaining who should (or can) be appeased. Republics that successfully balanced menace with moderation in their signals to the federal centre fared best.

1.5 Comparative Analysis of Treaty Provisions

A comparative analysis of the content of republican treaties with Moscow reveals important substantive differences among them. The selectivity with which republics received treaties might also be explained by the diminishing powers offered in successive treaties. As more and more treaties were signed, the range and depth of powers ceded by the federal government decreased. One example of this trend is the very description of the republic, usually found in the preamble or first article of the treaty. Tatarstan was described in the preamble of its treaty as 'a state united with the Russian Federation', a step down from the 'associated' status claimed in the republic's constitution but still a remarkable statement of autonomy. The next five treaties, how-

---

[64] Factors that contributed to this weak position were an unpopular first president whose parliamentary conflicts led to a period of two simultaneous governments in the republic, infighting between rival nomenklatura factions, and late ratification of a new constitution (September 1995— the third latest republic). Michael McFaul & Nikolai Petrov, eds. *Politicheskii al'manakh Rossii 1997*, 2 Vols. (Moskva: Moskovskii Tsentr Karnegi, 1998), 207–13.

ever, returned to the formulaic expression 'a state within the composition of the Russian Federation', found in the federal constitution and Federation Treaty. This formula varies only slightly: Bashkortostan is described as a 'sovereign state' in that composition, though that sovereignty is modified by a preceding phrase, 'a full rights subject of the Russian Federation'. Similar trade-offs occur in descriptions of North Ossetia (Alania), Sakha, and Buriatia. No description was made of signatory Udmurtia, the seventh treaty signed, while successive treaties described Komi merely as 'one of the northern regions of the Russian Federation' and Chuvashia as a 'subject of the Russian Federation'.

As descriptions of republics as distinctive states weakened, references to articles in the federal constitution increased. In the first four treaties, no references are made to individual articles, emphasizing the strong 'treaty-constitutional' form promoted by republics. The division of powers is explicitly enumerated with only general references to either republican or federal constitutions and laws. Beginning with Sakha, references are repeatedly made in treaties to two articles of the federal constitution. The first reference is to Article 72, enumerating areas of joint jurisdiction between federal and regional authorities (a slightly expanded version of Article Two of the Federation Treaty), is included in the treaties of Sakha, Buriatia, Udmurtia, Komi, and Chuvashia. For Sakha, the first clause of its Article Two is an exact duplicate of Article 72; a second clause lists other areas of co-ordinated activity, especially special funds and programs for northern territories. Article Six of the treaty refers again to Article 72 for purposes of treaty 'realization'.

There is a substantive shift between the content of the first four treaties and the remaining six. The documents concerning Tatarstan, Kabardino-Balkaria, Bashkortostan, and (to a lesser extent) North Ossetia (Alania) have a style and content which clearly distinguishes them from those under the exclusive remit of the federal constitution and Federation Treaty. Treaties for these republics establish principles for inter-governmental relations, Solnick's *constitutional* asymmetries (though, as mentioned before, this terminology disguises the fact that these privileges are *extra*-constitutional bilateral amendments to federal constitutional provisions). Beginning with Sakha, style and content shifts from a recognition of distinctiveness to agreement to conformity with established rules and jurisdictions. In descriptions of the republics not only is a return made to the formula of previous documents but a new formula describing the republic as, 'a plenipotentiary subject', (*polnopravnyi sub"ekt*) reconfirms the subordinate status of republics. Later treaties were used not to establish the center-republic relationship anew—the 'Tatarstan Model'—but to confirm compliance with existing documents, especially the federal constitution. In exchange, special allowances, not always unreasonable, were agreed. The treaty with Buriatia promises special programmes for the peculiar environmental needs of contiguous Lake Baikal and agrees to joint jurisdiction over the regionally important Baikal-Amur branch line. The treaty with Chuvashia adds such particulars as reparations for flood damage from a local reservoir and the clean-up of by-products of the chemical weapons industry to the joint jurisdiction listed in the federal constitution.

For Sakha, Udmurtia, and Chuvashia, a second federal constitutional article is also mentioned. Article 78 of the federal constitution grants federal and regional executives the power to transfer to one another different authorities. This power, which previous treaties had stipulated without reference to the federal constitution, explicitly stated the right to negotiate agreements (*soglashenie*) between the centre and regions. Whereas treaties outlined general principles for future relations (exceptions noted above notwithstanding), it was left to agreements to work out the pressing details of current relations. As can be seen in Table 6.4, agreements often preceded the final signing ceremony by several months as stepping stones towards the final document. In general, agreements are precise statements ranging from tax obligations to privatization to export quotas, especially of natural resources like oil or precious minerals. These are what Solnick has termed *ad hoc* asymmetries.

The changing role of treaties is also reflected in the timing of agreements. With Tatarstan and Bashkortostan, specific agreements preceded principle-focused treaties by months or even years. In later treaties, which dispensed more specific privileges in exchange for acceptance of existing federal relations, agreements do not precede treaties by more than a few days. These treaties shed their treaty-constitutional roles as *dogovory* increasingly resembled oversized *soglashenii*.

The diminishing powers accorded republics by each treaty might suggest that 'thin end of the wedge' predictions are flawed. Do these iterated 'bargaining games' tend to reduce asymmetry over the long run, by 'levelling up' regional demands? As each successive republic or region observes the spoils of its predecessor, incentives build amongst remaining units to equalize powers. There are several reasons why institutional symmetry did not result, necessitating the sweeping reforms of Vladimir Putin (discussed in Chapter Eight).

Although successive treaties did tend to be less ground-breaking, treaties never ceased to append special prerogatives and areas of authority beyond norms established for all regions. This is despite numerous assurances by federal authorities that treaties only elaborate upon—but never change or

Table 6.4   Agreements (*Soglashenie*) with Selected Republics

Republics (bilateral treaty)	Jurisdiction agreements	Agreements on existing industrial infrastructure	Economic agreements
Tatarstan (15 Feb. 1994)	5 June 1993: Environment; Education; Customs (22.VI.93)	5 June 1993: Oil industry	Economic co-operation (22.I.92)
	15 Feb. 1994: Law enforcement; Budget relations; Banking, credit & currency; Military sphere	22 June 1993: Defence industry	5 June 1993: Property

15 Feb. 1994: Foreign economic connections |
| Bashkortostan (3 Aug. 1994) | 25 May 1994: Environment; Law enforcement & social security; Customs; Education
3 Aug. 1994: Budget Relations | 25 May 1994: State property; Fuel & energy complex; Defence industry; Agro-industry complex | 25 May 1994: Economic co-operation; Foreign economic connections |
| North Ossetia (Alania) (23 Mar. 1995) | 23 March 1995: Environment | 23 Mar. 1995: Property; Defence industry; Tourism/sanitoriums; Ownership of land/resources | 23 Mar. 1995: Foreign economic relations |
| Sakha (29 June 1995) | 28 June 1995: Management of sea routes; Environment; Customs; Education; Migration & employment; Implementation of federal programmes; Budget relations | Economic questions; (31.III.92)

28 June 1995: Agro-industry complex; Fuel & energy complex; Travel-transport complex; Mining industry | 28 June 1995: Connections in economic sphere; Foreign economic connections |
| Udmurtia (17 Oct. 1995) | 17 Oct. 1995: Environment; Law enforcement & social security; Customs; Budget relations | 17 Oct. 1995: State property; Defence complex; Forest resources; Oil resources; Agro-industrial complex | |
| Komi (20 Mar. 1996) | 20 Mar. 1996: Migration & employment; Education; Environment; Budget relations | 20 Mar. 1996: Fuel & energy complex; Agro-industry complex | 20 Mar. 1996: Socioeconomic development; Foreign economic connections |

abrogate—subjects of jurisdiction established in the federal constitution.[65] On the contrary, one distinguished constitutional scholar, B.A. Strashun, has argued:

... clauses of corresponding treaties have a higher juridical force than those referred to in articles of the Constitution, not to mention clauses of the Federation Treaty. Such a conclusion flows from Article 11 §3 in Chapter 1 which presents itself as if a constitution in the Constitution, for its jurisdictional force is higher than that of the remaining parts of the Constitution. Consequently, deviations in the treaties from the norms of Articles 71–73 of the Constitution cannot be regarded as violations of it.[66]

Treaties replaced universal constitutional provisions with their special exceptions. Such additions frequently created new space for conflict with federal authority without the establishment of effective arbitration (see footnote 3, *supra*).

1.6 More Asymmetry, Not Less

One theory suggests that *ad hoc* asymmetry 'gets washed out of the system' as regions without privileges, eager for a reduction of the relative privileges of stronger regions, are forced to underbid for their own benefits (since the centre requires their support less and less). As the federal centre gains the support of these regions at lower 'cost', regions which previously negotiated extensive benefits (at higher cost to the centre) may be expected to lose their leverage against 'a new coalition of the centre and the weak', a process of systemic evolution tending to decrease asymmetry.[67] This was roughly true of the bargaining process in transition Spain.

This scenario does not seem to fit Russia's asymmetry. It clearly does not describe the Russian Federation's Parade of Treaties, roughly 1994–8. While relative latecomers might have engaged in 'underbidding', the centre did not become noticeably less dependent on the strongest republics, Tatarstan,

---

[65] Sergei Shakhrai, who chaired the presidential commission that drafted treaties and was the President's representative to the RF Constitutional Court, maintains that 'no new treaties may change or cancel constitutional statutes on the demarcation of subjects of jurisdiction and authority' for either the federal government or its constituent governments. This echoes presidential *ukaz*, No. 370 (12 March 1996). Guboglo, 155, 157.

[66] B.A. Strashun, *Federal'noe konstitutsionnoe pravo Rossii* (Moskva: Izdatel'stvo NORMA, 1996), ix. Strashun drew the attention of Western political scientists for his unconventional views on contested elections and studies in comparative socialism long before *glasnost* and *perestroika*. See Ronald J. Hill, *Soviet Politics, Political Science and Reform* (White Plains, NY: M.E. Sharpe, 1980). Art. 11, §3 states that the division of subjects of jurisdiction is determined by the Constitution, the Federation Treaty and 'other treaties on the demarcation of subjects of jurisdiction and authority'.

[67] Solnick, 'Statebuilding, Asymmetries, . . . ', 13–14.

Bashkortostan, Sakha. Under Yeltsin, strong republics maintained their privileges, successfully fending off attempts either to revamp the treaty process as a whole or to renegotiate existing treaties. As the first agreements signed with Tatarstan reached their five-year limits in 1998, the federal government failed in its bid to renegotiate the documents to its greater advantage.[68] Disparities in *ad hoc* privileges have not shown indications of evening out; in fact, the 'Parade of Agreements' that accompanied the signing of treaties arguably represents an increase in *ad hoc* asymmetry. Little support can be found for the argument that, whatever was signed, political and economic weakness meant little was actually put into force. The accumulation of *de facto* powers seized by republics *without* attendant agreements in the face of federal weakness skyrocketed. Protectionist measures taken by republics to restrict imports from competitors in other regions has torn at the seams of Russia's unified market.[69] Regional reaction to the 17 August 1998 financial crisis was compelling evidence of how little respect existed for established constitutional norms.[70] Sakha President Mikhail Nikolaev signed a decree prohibiting sale to federal authorities of gold mined in the republic. The head of the Republic of Khakassia, Aleksei Lebed', declared economic independence, and refused to meet his federal obligations. Needless to say, the extra-constitutional institutional asymmetry established in the first treaties with relatively strong republics did not decrease following iterated bargaining by others.

Even the strongest republics, possessing the 'best' treaties, remained unsatisfied with the asymmetrical advantages (*ad hoc* and *constitutional*) that were negotiated. Interviews in Tatarstan in 1997 and 1998 found that republican elites were unsatiated by their acquired privileges. The treaty was viewed as one step in a perpetual process of acquiring more sovereignty. The same mentality lay behind its Declaration of Sovereignty: it was a stepping stone to the next concession, as it turned out, a bilateral treaty. According to one high-ranking committee chairman in the legislature, the 1994 treaty was

[68] James Hughes, 'Institutional Design, . . .', 18.

[69] Restrictions on vodka imports, for example, were ubiquitous. Robert Orttung, 'Russia Becoming a Series of Closed Markets', 2 *OMRI Russia Regional Report*, 12 (26 Mar. 1997). Midkhat Faroukshine, 'Tatarstan Intensifies Protectionist Policies', 3 *IEWS Russian Regional Report*, 35 (1 Sept. 1998).

[70] 'Anti-Crisis Programs' introduced by regions throughout Russia included price controls (Tatarstan, Chuvashia, N. Ossetia, Sakha), seizure of federal taxes (Kalmykia), formation of hard currency reserves (Sakha) and other measures. In contradiction to the federal Constitution, Buriatia declared a state of emergency in the republic. Paul Goble, 'Tatarstan Introduces Anti-Crisis Programme', 2 *Radio Free Europe/Radio Liberty Newsline*, 176, Part I (11 Sept. 1998). Julie A. Corwin, 'Buryatia, Kaliningrad Declare State of Emergency', 2 *Radio Free Europe/Radio Liberty Newsline*, 173, Part I (8 Sept. 1998). Julie A. Corwin, 'Regions Aim for Self-Sufficiency', 2 Radio Free Europe/Radio Liberty Newsline, 175, Part I (10 Sept. 1998).

'only the first treaty' in a gradual, ongoing process to steadily 'broaden and deepen' Tatarstan's authority.[71] Every region, encouraged an adviser to the Tatar president, should take what powers it chooses to exercise and delegate the rest to the federal centre.[72] How closely this sentiment seems to echo Yeltsin's words uttered in the region back in 1990!

Such a position exemplifies the weak level of *Bundestreue* in Russia, which Juan Linz termed the soul of a working federalism. One of the strongest expressions of this federal loyalty is the entrenched authority given to written compacts, typically constitutions, in federal states. The Russian 'treaty-constitutional' approach diminished this federal public virtue in two ways. First, the importance of the federal constitution diminished with its repeated asymmetric abridgement by treaties. As the phrase implies, individual treaties were more important to republics than the federal constitution. Second, although no time limit was established for treaties (nor special procedures for bilateral amendment), agreements typically required renegotiation after five years. Elevating treaties and agreements to the level of constitutional importance, but subjecting them to perpetual renegotiation alongside an already unclear relationship to the federal constitution, decreases the stability an entrenched and difficult to amend set of rules provides a federation. It also seems likely to reinforce regional identities over federal ones.

A civic identity that places federal and regional allegiances on a par with one another is an asset a federation squanders at its peril. Survey research conducted in Russia in November–December 1993 by a respected team of American and Russian political scientists revealed that with few exceptions Russian and titular ethnic group respondents to the question 'Of what polity do you consider yourself a representative?' predominantly answered 'Equally my republic and Russia'. This response outstripped 'Only my republic' and 'More my republic than Russia' in many regions by more than two to one, though there were considerable differences between Russian and titular ethnic levels of support. Only in Chechnya and Tyva did republican identity supplant federal identity in the responses.[73] This is a great advantage for a federation struggling with federal-regional conflicts, but one which bilateral

---

[71]   Rashit Vagizov, author's interview, 10 June 1997, State Soviet, Kazan'. Vagizov listed several areas slated for future autonomy (the court system, procuracy, and internationally recognized passports) which the 1994 bilateral treaty assigns to federal jurisdiction.

[72]   Timor Akulov, Director, Department of Foreign Affairs, State Adviser to the President on International Affairs. Author's interview, 13 June 1997, Presidential Administration, Kremlin, Kazan'.

[73]   Survey organized by Colton, Hough, Lehmann and Guboglo. Reprinted in Valery Tishkov, *Ethnicity, Nationalism and Conflict in and after the Soviet Union: The Mind Aflame* (London: Sage, 1997), 262.

treaties and other forms of asymmetry could conceivably undermine, especially given the weakness of other unifying forces such as all-union political
parties. At least one survey conducted from March–August 1994, showed
that when the same question was asked again in Tatarstan (*after* the treaty
had been published) a markedly larger percentage of both Tatar and ethnic
Russian respondents answered that they felt 'More republican than Russian'
(i.e. civic, not ethnic identity) than before. Similar results in North Ossetia
(Alania), Sakha, and Tyva, suggested that identification with a larger federal
polity was at least in danger of weakening.[74] A survey Leokadia Drobizheva
conducted in 1998 regarding secessionist feeling in Tatarstan, North Ossetia
(Alania) and Sakha showed 54, 44.5 and 60.4 per cent support, respectively, in
favour of a right to secession, which may be taken as another indirect
indication of decreased federal loyalty.[75]

By comparison with the non-transparent and bilateral Russian model, the
Spanish approach to ratifying charters for *autonomías* is transparent and
multilateral. Surveys in the Spanish *autonomías*, in contrast to Russian
republican data, show that this federal loyalty remained undamaged and
may even have been reinforced in the years following the cautious five-step
approach of the *Cortes Generales*.[76] In Russia, where both the federal and
republican legislative branches—and therefore interest representation for
the rest of the Federation—are excluded from bilateral negotiations, concern
for the effect on the overarching federal identity of citizens of Russia is
warranted.

All treaties and agreements thus far concluded have been exclusively
executive-driven legal documents. No treaties or agreements required ratification by republican or federal legislatures to enter into force. Treaties
remain highly dependent on cooperation between the federal president
and his regional counterparts. This was the implicit warning Yeltsin's flurry
of treaties sent to regions prior to the 1996 presidential elections.
Yeltsin's victory over Gennadii Zyuganov (considered an opponent of the
treaty process) meant that the strength of treaties after their executive

[74] This survey was organized by Leokadia Drobizheva. Reprinted in Tishkov, 263. For a more
positive view of this phenomenon see Graham Smith, 'Russia, Multiculturalism and Federal
Justice', 50 *Europe-Asia Studies*, 8 (1998): 1407.

[75] Unpublished manuscript quoted in Gail W. Lapidus, 'Asymmetrical Federalism and State
Breakdown in Russia', 15 *Post-Soviet Affairs*, 1 (1999), 76.

[76] Linz and Stepan, citing a survey by Juan Linz conducted in 1982, found respondents were
twice as likely to feel 'Equally Catalan and Spanish' than 'More Catalan than Spanish' and more
than four times as likely to feel equal loyalties than feel simply Catalan. Linz & Stepan, 102. Citing
a 1996 survey, Juan Linz found that in four Spanish *autonomías* (including Catalonia), respondents
felt high levels of pride in their 'Spanish' identity. Linz, 'Democracy, Multinationalism & Federalism', 75.

signatories left office remained untested. The personalized nature of the treaty process, combined with the conception of these treaties as impermanent, left basic questions of federal-regional relations in flux.

Institutional asymmetry was aggravated by suspicion that the bilateral treaty process was not transparent. This mistrust was fed by the executive-personal nature of the process and felt within republics by excluded legislators as well as across competing republics. Sakha's bilateral negotiations were boosted by a secret Yeltsin *ukaz* worth US$10 million that 'helped sweeten the overall bilateral negotiations'.[77] In Tatarstan, the Chairman for the regional bloc of the all-Russian party *Vybor Rossii* complained that deputies felt forced into the treaty: 'Deputies could not get the treaty to read or even the Agreements until 1995. . . . [I]t was a closed subject'.[78] Secrecy in treaties establishing fundamental relations runs contrary to basic democratic principles of accountability. It is also contrary to one of the most fundamental of legal principles: a law that is not published is not a law. A key component of the constitutional structure of the federation is removed from constitutional review by the legislature, courts and electorate at the same time that its importance relative to the Constitution increases.[79] The *suspicion* of secrecy and non-transparency in many ways can be worse than the reality of the situation. In addition to stimulating the impression that the treaty process represents a zero-sum game for republics, the credibility of the federal government may become so tarnished that assurances of transparency become unbelievable. The federal government is left the impossible task of proving a negative—that it is not engaging in secret deals.

Almost six years after the adoption of Russia's new federal constitution, the federal law 'On the Principles and Manner of Demarcation of Subjects of Jurisdiction and Authority Between Organs of State Power of the Russian Federation and Organs of State Power of Subjects of the Federation', entered into effect. This law permitted the legislative branch of the region in question and the Federation Council of the Russian Federation to examine treaties and agreements. It did *not* require ratification through these bodies, leaving them impotent, if now at least aware. The law further ordered that

[77] Marjorie Mandelstam Balzer & Uliana Alekseevna Vinokurova, 'Nationalism, Interethnic Relations and Federalism: The Case of the Sakha Republic (Yakutia)', 48 *Europe-Asia Studies*, 1 (1996): 108, 119.

[78] Aleksandr V. Shtanin, interview with the author and David Hoffman, 3 June 1997, Kazan'. In numerous interviews with the author, executive branch officials repeatedly denied the existence of 'secret' or unpublished agreements.

[79] 'Because some of these treaties—especially amendments to the treaties—are kept secret to avoid inter-regional rivalries, they totally escape constitutional review'. Constitution Watch, 5 *East European Constitutional Review*, 1 (1996), 25.

treaties and agreements already agreed be brought into conformity with federal law and the federal Constitution within a three year transition period. A detailed examination of this paper tiger is left to Chapter Eight. In any event, the law was never utilized and no new treaties were signed for the rest of Yeltsin's term in office.

2. Centre-Republican Relations in a Treaty-Constitutional Federal Environment, 1994–2000

Analysis of bilateral treaties exposes the conceptual and practical confusion in the development of Russian federalism. Federal and republican elites divided as to whether the Russian Federation was a 'constitutional-treaty' or a 'treaty-constitutional' entity. The multiplicity of treaties and agreements did little to clarify issues of immediate jurisdiction or to establish principles for the resolution of future centre-periphery conflicts. Despite the proliferation of treaties, the RF Ministry of Justice announced in late 1996 that 19 of 21 republican constitutions violated the federal Constitution.[80] Federal legislation aimed to resolve conflicting redivisions of power have only aggravated the contradictions inherent in these 'founding' documents. According to one assessment:

There are about 150 laws on different subjects of joint jurisdiction of the Russian Federation and its subjects. Article 72 of the Constitution of Russia foresees 35 subjects of joint jurisdiction which demand a demarcation of authority. Thus, on average for each of these there are approximately 5 laws. But this figure does not say anything, that is, it is highly relative. In fact, many subjects of joint jurisdiction either in general don't have legislative provision or, if there is one, it is quite fragmentary.[81]

The so-called 'War of Laws,' coincident with the parade of treaties, produced thousands of republican laws in contradiction with the federal constitution, federal law and sometimes even the very treaties negotiated.[82]

---

[80] Irina Nagornykh, 'Regiony staviat na konfrontatsiiu', *Segodnia*. 22 November 1996, 2.

[81] Tat'iana Sukhomlinova, 'Sto piat'desiat zakonov odnogo ne zameniat', *Rossiiskie vesti*, 22 Aug. 1996, 7. This estimate is corroborated by Vladimir Lysenko, Chairman of the Duma Committee on Federation Affairs and Regional Policy. Guboglo *et al.* 167–8.

[82] According to one report, approximately 22, 000 regional laws and executive orders contradicted the federal constitution. Dmitrii Dokuchaev, 'Tsentr ob''iavil voinu ekonomicheskomu separatizmu regionov', *Izvestia*, 4 Nov. 1997, 1. In January 1998 the RF Procurator-General Yurii Skuratov stated that in a 24–month period 2, 000 regional laws had been ordered annulled as violations of the federal constitution. Lapidus, 78.

The most problematic contradictions concern the foundation of a unified legal space, a benefit, if not basic requirement, of federations. In the Russian lexicon, this is a problem of the 'supremacy of laws'. Virtually all republics declare the supremacy of republican law to some degree, often incorporating the Federation Treaty or bilateral treaties as limitations on that power in select areas. Most republics utilize the language of *snizu vverkh* or 'treaty-constitutional relations', noting that federal authority extends only so far as those powers delegated by republics. Some statements are starkly unilateral, such as Ingushetia's declaration that federal legislation is 'lawful' only in so far as it does not impinge the 'sovereign rights' of the republic. The Republic of Sakha is another example. Federal legislation must pass a vote in the lower chamber of its bicameral parliament to be accepted in its jurisdiction! Several republics, such as Adygeia and Dagestan, reserve the right to suspend federal legislation, either pending appeal to an agreed body of arbitration or simply upon the decision of the republican authorities. Examples of these variations are found in Table 6.5.

These are extraordinary claims with serious implications for a federation: At least through the final year of the Yeltsin administration, these republics did not recognize a unified legal space for the federation which was beyond appeal to their sovereign idiosyncracies. According to Yeltsin's adviser on legal questions, Mikhail Krasnov, Tatarstan and Bashkortostan simply 'do not take in Russia's judicial system'.[83] This view undergirds statements such as that of Aleksandr Kim, the president of the Sakha Republic's Association of Banks:

As you know, in Russia shortly will be accepted new laws on banking activity, which materially strengthens and widens the rights and resources of banks. The board of directors is now conducting work on the parallel preparation of new laws of the Republic of Sakha on banking activity, in so far as acceptance of new Russian [federal] laws still does not mean that they will work on the territory of the republic if they will not be in conformity with our new laws.[84]

This conception demands that federal laws be locally approved prior to implementation, or in some way correspond to the varying levels of authority republics are willing to offer for federal jurisdiction, as through the use of bilateral treaties. Laws which fail this test may be suspended or simply 'lose force' on their territories. This is nothing less than the doctrine of nullification discussed in Chapter Two. Such a doctrine is anathema to the most

---

[83]   Konstantin Katanian, 'Chto deliat Moskva i Kazan'?' *Nezavisimaia gazeta*, 12 Feb. 1998, 3.

[84]   Aleksandr N. Kim, 'Problemy razvitiia bankovskoi sfery', speech to the general meeting of the Association of Banks of the Sakha Republic, 10 May 1994. Reprinted in A.N. Kim, *Pravovye aspekty perekhodnogo perioda v respublike Sakha (Iakutiia)* (Yakutsk: Sakhapoligrafizdat, 1996), 3.

Table 6.5   Supremacy Clauses in Selected Republican Constitutions

Adygeia Article 56 10.III.1995	1. Laws of the Republic of Adygeia possess supremacy on its territory on questions related to its jurisdiction. 2. RA has the right to suspend the activity on its territory of laws and other normative acts of the RF pending decision of the RF Constitutional Court if they are issued outside the boundaries of the jurisdiction of the RF or its joint jurisdiction with the RA and contradict the RA constitution, RF constitution, violate the Federation Treaty.
Bashkortostan Article 128 24.XII.1993	Laws of the Republic of Bashkortostan possess supremacy on all of the territory of the RB. Laws of the RF which are accepted on questions which have been transferred by the RB by Treaty to the jursidiction of the RF are obligatory on the territory of the RB.
Dagestan Articles 1 & 65 26.VII.1994	Art. 1: Republic of Dagestan passes its own Constitution and republican laws, which have supremacy on all of its territory. Art. 65: (1) RF Constitution and federal laws accepted according to the subjects of jurisdiction of the Russian Federation have direct activity on the territory of RD. (2) According to subjects of joint authority of the RF and RD, RF promulgates the fundamentals of legislation and RD passes laws and other normative legal acts. (3) Outside the limits of jurisdiction of the RF and of joint jurisdiction with the RF the jurisdiction of the RD realizes its own legal regulation, including accepting laws and other normative legal acts. (4) Laws and other normative legal acts of the RD may not contradict federal laws, accepted in conformity with the first and second parts of the present article. (5) In the case of contradiction between federal law and normative legal acts RD, which are promulgated in conformity with part three of the present article, the normative legal act RD is active. (6) Activity of federal laws and other legal acts of the RF, which are in contradiction to the sovereign rights and interests of RD, may be suspended by the RD on its territory. These acts may be protested in the established legal manner.
Ingushetia Article 7, §2 27.II.1994	... Laws and other normative-legal acts of organs of state power and management of the Russian Federation are lawful on the territory of the Republic of Ingushetia if they do not contradict the sovereign rights of the Republic of Ingushetia ...
Sakha Article 41 20.IV.1994	Republic of Sakha laws possess supremacy on its territory on all questions with the exception of those which have been delegated by it to the jurisdiction of the federal organs of state power of the Russian Federation. RF laws accepted on questions of joint authority enter into force on the territory of the RS after their ratification by the House of Representatives of the State Assembly... The RS has the right to suspend the action on its territory of laws & other acts of the RF or protest them in the manner established by treaty if they violate the Federation Treaty, contradict the constitution or laws of the RS.

Table 6.5   (*contd.*)

Tatarstan Article 59 6.XI.1992	Republic of Tatarstan independently determines its state-legal status, decides questions of political, economic, sociocultural construction. RT Laws possess supremacy on all of its territory, if they do not contradict international obligations of the RT.
Tyva Article 11 21.X.1993	...RT Constitution possesses supremacy on its territory, determines and establishes the fundamental principles and provisions of state and social construction... The RT possesses all fullness of state power on its territory besides those authorities which have been transferred to the jurisdiction of federal organs of state power... and other subjects of international relations on the basis of corresponding treaties.
Udmurtia Article 7, §4 7.XII.1994	The RF constitutional and federal laws on subjects of jurisdiction of the RF are directly active on its territory... Questions of joint jurisdiction... are regulated by federal laws and on their basis by legislation of the RU. Disputes on questions of acceptance of legislation on subjects of joint jurisdiction are resolved in the form of constitutional legal proceedings.

basic understanding of a federation and has empirically been a significant factor in the collapse of confederations based on such an extreme form of autonomy. It is in stark contrast to the more successful regionalization process which occurred in Spain. Statutes of the autonomies were integrated into general Spanish law both by the process of their creation and the manner of their enforcement, an approach reinforced by the respect all sides showed the Constitutional Court.[85] Russia's approach, intended or not, has been just the opposite: exclusivist, executive-driven negotiations disconnected treaties from a hierarchy of law, exposing and increasing federal weakness with each successive conflict.

An anarchic legal-political environment is a serious problem for any state, especially one in supposed transition to democracy. In a federation, which by definition encourages a certain level of decentralization and protected spheres of autonomy, the problems presented by such a war of laws are much more difficult to resolve. Analysis of the institutions designed to arbitrate such situations and the problems inherent in both success and failure to enforce conformity with a legal hierarchy follows below.

2.1 Problems in the Development of a Unified Legal Space

As discussed in Chapter Two, the judicial branch of government plays a critical role in federal systems. Notwithstanding Alexander Hamilton's de-

---

[85] Opposing exclusive use of statutes in interpreting powers, the Court emphasized the 'principle of supremacy of the constitution over the remainder of the legal order'. Linz, 'Spanish

scription of the judiciary as the least dangerous branch of government, its power is understated as that of 'merely judgement'. The most persuasive justification for such a federal arbiter also belongs to Hamilton:

... there ought always to be constitutional method of giving efficacy to consti-tutional provisions. . . . This power must either be a direct negative on the State laws, or an authority in the federal courts to overrule such as might be in manifest contravention of the articles of Union . . . The mere necessity of uniformity in the interpretation of the national laws decides the question. Thirteen independent courts of final jurisdiction over the same causes, arising upon the same laws, is a hydra in government, from which nothing but contradiction and confusion can proceed. . . . the peace of the WHOLE ought not to be left at the disposal of a PART.[86]

Most federal systems, influenced by the American conception of judicial review, grant a judicial system the substantial power to resolve disputes between different levels of government. A constitutional court that deter-mines the conformity of legislative acts of all law-making bodies in the federation to the federal constitution is an important institution used by most federal systems to promote their long-term stability and durability.

The Russian Federation is no exception: the supremacy of the Consti-tution over ordinary law is established (Art. 15, §1) and exclusive jurisdiction is accorded to the federal government to establish a unified judicial system (Art. 71 'a,' 'd,' 'n'; Art. 118, §3). The RF President has the power to appoint all federal judges throughout the federation (Art. 83, 'f'). A Constitutional Court is created to 'resolve cases relating to the conformity with the consti-tution of the Russian Federation' of federal laws and normative acts; repub-lican constitutions (and charters of other units), laws and normative acts; and treaties between organs of state power (Art. 125, §2). The Court is given jurisdiction to resolve disputes within the federal government, between federal organs and regional organs, and between the highest state organs of different constituent units (Art. 125, §3). A federal constitutional law 'On the Constitutional Court of the Russian Federation' was signed into law in July 1994, defining more precisely the general constitutional principles.[87] This law ended Yeltsin's suspension of the first Constitutional Court for its opposition to his October 1993 *ukazy* (decrees) against Parliament.

Democracy . . . ', 284–5. Agranoff (1997), 12–18. Agranoff (1996), 388, 390–1, 395: 'most of the more sensitive struggles have been ultimately resolved by the Constitutional Tribunal, which has treaded a fine line between self-government and national interests'.

[86] See *The Federalist*, Nos. 78 and 80.

[87] 'Federal'nyi konstitutsionnyi zakon o Konstitutsionnom Syde Rossiiskoi Federatsii', ot 21 iiulia 1994 g. Reprinted in *Rossiiskie zakony. Sbornik tekstov* (Moskva: Izdatel'stvo BEK, 1996), 1–44 (ZoKS 655).

Despite the Court's renewal, no dearth of cases, and the avowed goal of at least one of its nineteen justices to consolidate federal relations, the Court has been an ineffective and infrequent arbiter in federal disputes.[88] An attempt by sixteen republican executives to argue key provisions of a law on the judicial system in the RF Constitutional Court was rebuffed by the Court, which refused to examine the question.[89] With one exception, bilateral treaties do not mention the Court or the federal judiciary in general as venues for settling conflicts.[90] But as one group of Russian experts observed comparing this with the treaties of Tatarstan, Bashkortostan, and Sakha, 'such a provision is contained only in the treaty with the republic least of all prepared to dispatch a challenge to federal powers'.[91]

Executive bodies have taken upon themselves the task of resolving conflicts they themselves judge to exist between laws, blurring the authority between the federal executive and the Constitutional Court. Contradictory legislation between Russia and Tatarstan is resolved by a special executive-driven commission on power sharing.[92] The pronouncements of the RF Ministry of Justice on the unconstitutionality of republican legal acts are not based on court rulings. Similar declarations are made by the Procuracy. Although this department is charged with supervision over the execution of laws, it has no authority to inveigh against their constitutionality.[93] At the same time, the vast majority of these apparent violations (and few analysts would disagree that there is a high degree of nonconformity) are not brought to the courts for resolution. Some of the most prolific and extreme violations occur in the republics. Kalmykia, which has lost almost every vestige of a rule-of-law state, drew neither judicial, ministerial or even procuratorial reactions during Yeltsin's presidency. Cases there and in other republics are examined more closely in Chapter Seven.

Even when its opinions are directly sought, the Constitutional Court is often reluctant to take a stand. This exacerbated the establishment of a

[88] Justice Boris Ebzeev: 'The Court's docket is full and we sometimes choke on the number of requests.... In my opinion, the Court today has three major goals. The first is to complete the legal framework for Russian statehood. I am thinking especially of the relationship between the federal centre and the regions'. Interview conducted by Leonid Nikitinsky, 6 *East European Constitutional Review*, 1 (1997): 86–7.

[89] Konstantin Katanian, 'Chto deliat Moskva i Kazan'?' *Nezavisimaia gazeta*, 12 Feb. 1998, 3.

[90] The North Ossetia (Alania) treaty permits appeals to the Court regarding the conformity of all laws to the treaty (Art. 8).

[91] L.M. Drobizheva, A.R. Aklaev, V.V. Koroteeva, & G.U. Soldatova, *Demokratizatsiia i obrazy natsionalizma v Rossiiskoi Federatsii 90-kh godov* (Moskva: Mysl', 1996), 225.

[92] Oleg Soskovets and Vladimir Potanin, both former First Deputy Prime Ministers, have served as previous chairmen. Laura Belin, 'Potanin Appointed Head of Russian-Tatar Commission on Power Sharing', 2 *OMRI Russian Regional Report*, 6 (12 Feb. 1997).

[93] 'Federal'nyi konstitutsionnyi zakon o prokurature Rossiiskoi Federatsii', 17 November 1995. Reprinted in *Rossiiskie zakony*, 1–30 (ZP 670).

coherent legal environment and respect for the Court. During the 1998 Bashkir presidential election campaign, the RF Constitutional Court was asked to decide the constitutionality of language requirements for candidates. This was an issue with broad application: knowledge of both Russian and the titular language was at the time required of candidates in nine republics. On 9 April 1997 the RF Duma made an official inquiry to the Court, which finally decided on 27 November simply to postpone its judgment indefinitely.[94] Forced into action by the Bashkir election, the Court ruled on 27 April 1998 that the language provisions of the Bashkir constitution and election law should not be utilized in that June's elections. The Court did *not* rule that the provisions were unconstitutional, merely that, no Bashkir legislation having been passed stipulating the required level of proficiency, they were too vague.[95] It is unsurprising that other republics did not rush to amend their election laws.

Just as damaging as ambivalent court decisions is non-compliance with explicit rulings. In some cases, the Court's authority has been disputed by one of the parties. Such was the case with the Court's sweeping decision (*postanovlenie*) of 13 March 1992 on the constitutionality of the Republic of Tatarstan's declaration of sovereignty, selected amendments to the republican constitution, republican law on referendums and decision of the Tatar Supreme Soviet to schedule a referendum.[96] The Court decided that select provisions of each document were unconstitutional.[97] Tatarstan did not recognize the authority of the Court over its internal affairs (precisely the issue) and refused to send any representation to the Court. The Court's ruling was ignored by the republic's leadership, which proceeded with its referendum. Presented with this *fait accompli*, the federal government made no subsequent appeals to the Court on any of these unresolved issues.

[94] The Bashkir State Assembly accused the RF Duma of ignoring the provisions of the Russian-Bashkir bilateral treaty, though neither legislature had been allowed to ratify it. The Bashkir parliament subsequently passed a decree attacking the RF Duma for 'open contempt' of the constitution and laws of Bashkortostan. Vladimir Bugaev, 'Kto razzhigaet etnicheskie strasti?' *Rossiiskie vesti*, 13 Jan. 1998, 2.

[95] RIA News Agency, Moscow, in *BBC Worldwide Monitoring*, 27 Apr. 1998. Laurie Belin, 'Court Strikes Down Electoral Rules in Bashkortostan', 2 *RFE/RL Newsline*, 83, Part I, 30 Apr. 1998.

[96] Relevant excerpts of the decision in M.S. Salikov, *Konstitutsionnoe pravo Rossiiskoi Federatsii: Sbornik sudebnykh reshenii* (Sankt-Peterburg: Paritet, 1997), 67–77.

[97] Interestingly, the Court did *not* nullify the republic's right to hold a referendum on issues within its jurisdiction, arguing instead that it was the question itself which was at fault. The Court emphasized in its decision the importance the case held for the Federation as an entity in transition, and for that reason specific attention was directed to the questions of supremacy of law, the relationship of federal subjects to international law, and the distinction between treaty-based vs. constitution-based federal relations. Decree of the Constitutional Court of the RSFSR, 13 March 1992, in 30 *Statutes and Decisions: The Laws of the USSR and its Successor States*, 3 (May–June 1994), 32–48.

Such an approach did not abate with the 'Parade of Treaties'. A more recent example is that of the Komi republic. In a 15 January 1998 decision, the RF Constitutional Court struck down sections of the republic's constitution and law on organs of executive power.[98] The offending republican legislation had subordinated heads of local administrations (i.e. local self-government) to the head of the republic (president), who appointed them virtually at will. Republican law allowed for popular election of local councils which then elected mayors nominated by the president. Yurii Spiridonov, Komi's president, declared that the Constitutional Court had not considered the fact that centre-republican relations were regulated by the Federation Treaty, which preceded the RF Constitution, and which gave jurisdiction over this matter exclusively to republics. Only the republic's own legislature, Spiridonov declared, could decide these matters.[99] The Court did not mention Komi's bilateral treaty with the federal government, which contradictorily granted the republic exclusive jurisdiction to establish principles of local self-government (in accordance with federal legislation) but also re-established joint jurisdiction over all subjects enumerated in Article 72 of the RF Constitution, which included the establishment of general principles of local self-government. Elections in Komi went ahead as scheduled and without regard for the Court-ordered changes. All of Spiridonov's nominations successfully became mayors.[100]

Another form of non-compliance involves decisions affecting republics which do recognize the authority of the Constitutional Court, but nevertheless refuse to comply with unfavorable rulings. The case of Udmurtia, which also involved local self-government, is a good example. In order to put local self-government under the direct control of the legislature, the Udmurt parliament redefined all entities larger than villages as 'municipalities of republican subordination', dissolved their representative councils, and transferred those powers to parliamentary deputies. As Alexander Blankenagel explains, 'The ruse by the Udmurtian legislature led to the erosion not only of local autonomy itself, but also to the erosion of federal authority to regulate this matter. By treating the problem as a territorial reorganization issue, the organization of state administration fell to the exclusive jurisdic-

---

[98] 'Postanovlenie Konstitutsionnogo Suda Rossiiskoi Federatsii po delu o proverke konstitutsionnosti statei 80, 92, 93 i 94 Konstitutsii Respubliki Komi i stat'i 31 Zakona Respubliki Komi ot 31 oktiabria 1994 goda "Ob organakh ispolnitel'noi vlasti v Respublike Komi"'. *Rossiiskaia gazeta*, 31 Jan. 1998, 4.

[99] Dmitrii Kamyshev & Maksim Zhukov, 'Glava Komi otkazalsia podchiniat'sia Konstitutsionnomu sudu', *Kommersant-daily*, 3 Feb. 1998, 4.

[100] Yurii Shabaev, 'Komi Local Governments Remain Subordinate to Republican Executive', 4 *EWI Russian Regional Report*, 10 (18 Mar. 1999).

tion of the Udmurtian republic as a subject of the federation'.[101] The Court
held the republican law to be in part unconstitutional on its face and also
unconstitutional as applied in Udmurtia. Freely elected local councils could
not be dissolved before the end of their terms.[102] The republican legislature,
bizarrely, interpreted this to be a favourable ruling. The Chairman of the
Parliament, Aleksandr Volkov, continued to oversee the implementation of
the law, persuading officials to resign prematurely. This prompted a clarification to be issued by the Court. This the republic ignored.[103] An *ukaz* from
Yeltsin ordering compliance followed a month later.[104] Claiming Yeltsin had
been misinformed and that the Court had held the law to be sound in
principle, Volkov disregarded the decree.[105] Yeltsin was forced to issue a
second decree in early March accompanied by instructions to the federal
procuracy. It was the combined pressure of two presidential *ukazy*, not the
repeated decisions of the Court, that finally led to the Udmurt State Council's
compliance.[106]

Perhaps the starkest case in this category occurred in Ingushetia. In early
1998, Ingush President Ruslan Aushev announced plans to subordinate all
judicial officials in the republic (including federal judges and prosecutors) to
personal appointment, to be confirmed by a referendum held simultaneously
with presidential elections. A February 1998 decision by the RF Supreme
Court that such a referendum could not be held was denounced by Aushev.
Yeltsin established a special conciliation commission to draft a bilateral
agreement on the question in exchange for Aushev's promise to postpone
the referendum.[107] A year later, Aushev's continued threats of a referendum
were only pacified by an agreement which increased his influence over the

[101] Alexander Blankenagel, 'Local Self-Government vs. State Administration: The Udmurtiia
Decision', 6 *East European Constitutional Review*, 1 (1997): 51.
[102] 'Postanovlenie Konstitutsionnogo Suda Rossiiskoi Federatsii po delu o proverke konstitutsionnosti Zakona Udmurtskoi Respubliki ot 17 aprelia 1996 goda "O sisteme organov gosudarstvennoi vlasti v Udmurtskoi Respublike"', 24 January 1997, *Vestnik Konstitutsionnogo Suda Rossiiskoi
Federatsii*, 1 (1997): 2. The decision resulted in two sharply dissenting opinions from Justices
Gadzhiev and Vitruk (in Salikov, 539–7), which pointed out that the Court had avoided decision
of the larger issues of self-government to deal only with certain particulars of the Udmurt
case. Blankenagel provides an excellent discussion of these issues and the weakness of the
decision.
[103] Anna Paretskaya, 'Udmurt Authorities Continue to Ignore Constitutional Court Decision', 2
OMRI Russian Regional Report, 6 (12 Feb. 1997).
[104] Anna Paretskaya, 'Yeltsin Orders Udmurtiya to Observe Court Ruling', 2 *OMRI Russian
Regional Report*, 8 (27 Feb. 1997).
[105] Anna Paretskaya, 'Udmurt Leader Continues to Defy Yeltsin Decree', 2 *OMRI Russian
Regional Report*, 9 (6 Mar. 1997).
[106] Anna Paretskaya, 'Udmurtiya Restores Local Self-Government', 2 *OMRI Daily Digest*, 50, Part
I (12 Mar. 1997).
[107] 'Constitution Watch', 7 *East European Constitutional Review*, 1 (1998): 33.

appointment of federal judicial officials in the region and granted him the power to pardon certain federal crimes.[108]

Even when the authority of the courts is undisputed, there are serious problems of enforcement. Although the Constitution and constitutional laws grant the RF President the power to appoint federal judges and nominate the Procurator-General (who in turn appoints republican and regional procurators) the ability of the federal centre to retain influence over these officials is very weak. Salaries—when they come at all—come from Moscow, but housing, health care, education, and virtually every other service required by federal officials and their families in the republics comes from those republics. The potential for co-optation is enormous.

The 'War of Laws' was the express result of a doctrine of nullification.[109] Such a doctrine is anathema to a working federation. It asserts the right of constituent units of a federation to select for themselves which federal laws are applicable on the territory of their constituent governments. This was precisely the practice of Russia's republics, tacitly acknowledged by federal efforts to mitigate the damage with bilateral treaties. In fact, these treaties only further muddied dark waters. Constitutional discrepancies, federal laws, and court rulings have simply been ignored.

2.2 Problems of Fiscal Federalism

Looking beyond attempts to create a unified legal environment, one of the most significant issues is the budgetary and tax relationship between the centre and the republics. As Leonid Smirnyagin, the respected political geographer, noted: '...the essence of the [constitutional] disputes comes down, not to the testaments of Montesquieu or Madison, but to the distribution of federal funds among regions'.[110] Emerging from a Soviet environment in the late 1980s in which upwards of 90 per cent of regional taxes were sent directly to the centre, republican elites feverishly seized as much

[108] Liz Fuller, 'Ingush President Backs Down Over Referendum', 3 *Radio Free Europe/Radio Liberty Newsline*, 35, Part I (19 Feb. 1999).

[109] The war of laws has not abated under Vladimir Putin. The Constitutional Court continued to hear cases on these subjects in the first year of his administration. In November 2000, the Court again held unconstitutional—as it had in the Udmurtia and Komi decisions—laws and constitutional clauses of the republic of Kabardino-Balkaria permitting the republic's president to appoint and dismiss heads of local administration (e. g. municipal and other forms of local self-government). Opredelenie Konstitutsionnogo Suda Rossiiskoi Federatsii po zaprosu Verkhovnogo Suda Kabardino-Balkarskoi Respubliki o proverke konstitutsionnosti punkta 'e' stat'i 81 Konstitutsii Kabardino-Balkarskoi Respubliki, stat'i 2 i punkta 3 stat'i 17 Zakona Kabardino-Balkarskoi Respubliki 'O mestnom samoupravlenii v Kabardino-Balkarskoi Respublike, 2 November 2000, *Vestnik Konstitutsionnogo Suda Rossiiskoi Federatsii*, No. 2 (2001): 20.

[110] *OECD Economic Surveys: The Russian Federation* (Paris: OECD, 1995), note 102, p. 157.

control as they could over taxation, enterprise privatization and natural resources.[111] This is reflected in the treaties and agreements negotiated with the centre. Fiscal federalism is an enormously complicated subject which has become its own mini-specialization in analysis of Russian federalism, involving statistics which are notoriously unreliable and invariably incomplete. The federal government's fiscal relations with the republics are Byzantine in their complexity.[112] Taxes, transfers, subsidies, and scores of other aid programmes flow between governments according to a multitude of formulas for their division in an environment of distrust. Some mechanisms are considered budgetary components while others, such as pension funds, types of bank credits, and other exemptions are 'off-budget', and therefore even harder to track. Closed-door deals with the RF Finance Ministry are still the best means to acquire funds from the centre.[113]

There is no doubt that greater fiscal autonomy and resource control were primary goals of the bilateral treaty process. Indeed, budgetary arrangements are invariably part of the package of *soglashenie* (agreements) negotiated as part of a bilateral treaty. But who gets what? Daniel Treisman detected a 'powerful logic of appeasement' in the transfers and budgets he analysed: 'Rather than rewarding the politically loyal regions, Moscow seemed to be buying off the regions that threatened the federal status quo'.[114] Treisman's statistical regressions demonstrate that 'if a region's leaders had been among those who declared sovereignty in the first outburst of demands in late 1990, their province received nearly 20,000 rubles per inhabitant more in additional transfers and tax breaks in 1992'.[115] Steven Solnick developed a complex theory of bargaining which divides regions into 'essential, alienated, pivotal and irrelevant'.[116]

Between 1992 and 1994, the OECD estimates that more than seventy presidential decrees and resolutions gave special federal dispensations and exemptions to fourteen republics and three oblasts in the form of export quotas, licences and special resource rights.[117] As these agreements came

---

[111] Darrell Slider, 'Federalism, Discord and Accommodation: Inter-governmental Relations in Post-Soviet Russia', in Theodore H. Friedgut, & Jeffrey W. Hahn, eds. *Local Power and Post-Soviet Politics* (Armonk, NY: M.E. Sharpe, 1994), 249.

[112] For an excellent summary of its major features, see Daniel Treisman, 'Moscow's Struggle to Control Regions Through Taxation', 2 *Transition*, 19 (20 Sept. 1996): 45–9.

[113] Treisman, 'Moscow's Struggle . . .', 45–6.

[114] Treisman, 'Moscow's Struggle . . .', 48. *See also* Daniel Treisman, 'Deciphering Russia's Federal Finance: Fiscal Appeasement in 1995 and 1996', 50 *Europe-Asia Studies*, 5 (1998): 893–906; and Daniel S. Treisman, *After the Deluge: Regional Crises and Political Consolidation in Russia* (Ann Arbor: University of Michigan Press, 1999).

[115] Treisman, *After the Deluge*, 65.

[116] Solnick, 'Statebuilding, Asymmetries, . . .', *passim*.

[117] OECD, 50.

under fire, bilateral treaties were used by most republics to secure a greater share of funds from the centre and to retain as much republic-generated revenue as possible. While general principles were established in the treaty (*dogovor*) itself, specifics were left to special agreements (*soglashenie*). For example, the agreement on budgetary relations signed with Tatarstan specified Tatar payments to the Russian Federation of 13 per cent of a profits tax, 1 per cent of income tax and an unspecified percentage of VAT to be determined annually by the finance ministries of Tatarstan and Russia. Tatarstan was authorized to retain for its own budget excise duties on spirits, vodka and similar products, oil, gas, land fees, income from privatization and other special taxes.[118] Bashkortostan, Sakha, Udmurtia, and Komi each signed agreements with the centre outlining budget cooperation ranging from explicit percentages of tax transfers to vague statements of jurisdiction.

Republics rich in natural resources sought to wrench control of resources and industries from federal ministries. The most well-known example is Sakha, responsible for virtually all of Russia's vast diamond resources.[119] The price of Sakha's signature on the Federation Treaty was a special agreement 'On Economic Questions', which set specific shares of diamond extraction and profits controlled exclusively by Sakha, created a republican hard currency fund and a National Bank and established principles and time-scales for future negotiations.[120] In November 1992, Yeltsin issued an *ukaz* creating 'Almazy Rossii-Sakha' (Alrosa), a joint-stock company involved in the division of diamond profits between Russia and Sakha. The company was given a twenty-five year lease on diamond deposits conditioned on the right for all sides to re-examine terms every five years.[121] Other agreements followed that year and culminated with the 1995 bilateral treaty, all of which carefully divided the spoils expected from sales to the DeBeers diamond cartel.

It is unclear how closely these agreements mirror reality. Closed-door, backroom lobbying in ministries and departments is not new to Russia and it is reasonable to expect that the old habits of former Soviet apparatchiks

---

[118] 'Soglashenie mezhdu Pravitel'stvami Rossiiskoi Federatsii i Respubliki Tatarstan o biudzhetnykh vzaimootnosheniiakh mezhdu Rossiiskoi Federatsiei i Respublikoi Tatarstan', 15 February 1994. Mukhametshin, 175; Guboglo, 434.

[119] For a fuller treatment of economic relations between the federal government and the Republic of Sakha, see the excellent M.Phil. thesis by Tanya Argunova, *Federal Relations between Yakutsk and Moscow.* Scott Polar Research Institute, University of Cambridge, June 1995.

[120] 'Soglashenie o vzaimootnosheniiakh mezhdu Pravitel'stvami Rossiiskoi Federatsii i Respubliki Sakha (Iakutiia) po ekonomicheskym voprosam', signed 31 March 1992. Reprinted in Guboglo, 484–7.

[121] Drobizheva *et al.* 181. For an excellent summary of the Moscow-Yakutsk-DeBeers relationship by the key players in the negotiations, see 'Press Conference with Alrosa Company and DeBeers Corporation Officials', *Federal News Service*, 21 Oct. 1997.

now in charge of republican governments have continued.[122] Even when formal agreements are signed, there is suspicion among most analysts that the 'real' settlements remain informal and secret.[123] It is not entirely clear if even the federal government has a comprehensive understanding of its republican accounts. Steven Solnick quotes a budget specialist from the Presidential Administration, Aleksei Lavrov, who complained that agreements like these were not carefully incorporated into the federal budget, nor was there a clearing house for the tangle of special deals between republics and federal ministries.[124] Real or imagined, such a lack of transparency combined with more apparent resource asymmetries damages republican relations with the centre and with other regions in the Federation.

The republics also managed to obtain institutional mechanisms that further weakened the centre's attempts to collect and disburse tax and other resources. Although the State Tax Service (STS) is a federal body the republican branches of which are financed and supervised by the centre, tax collectors are often co-opted by republican governments.[125] A World Bank economist summarized the approach: 'the regions can control regional STS offices because the social infrastructure facilities of federal agencies are provided for by the regions. In order to guarantee access to municipal housing, schools, good health service, sanatoria, etc., the managerial staffs of regional STS departments have to comply with the desires of the regional governments. To strengthen this link, some regions (for instance, Tataria) even try to add funds to the STS departments' coffers from their own regional funds'.[126]

Regional co-optation of federal officials does not stop with the tax man. Darrell Slider has carefully documented how regional elites managed to infiltrate local branches of the federal committee controlling privatization, *Goskomimushchestvo*, and create 'property funds', to a large extent controlling regional privatization in 1992 and 1993.[127] Numerous republics later negotiated agreements from 1994 through 1998 to establish control over the remaining state properties. The bilateral treaty with Chuvashia, signed 27

---

[122] 'To sit in a regional governor's office this past summer was to overhear phone calls in which the governor advised aides in Moscow on how best to "beat out" money from the federal administration'. Treisman, 'Moscow's Struggle...', 46. For an analysis of regional elites' bargaining strategies in the late Soviet era, see Donna Bahry, *Outside Moscow: Power, Politics, and Budgetary Policy in the Soviet Republics* (New York: Columbia University Press, 1987).

[123] Alexander Morozov, 'Tax Administration in Russia', 5 *East European Constitutional Review,* 2–3 (1996): 41. Treisman, 'Moscow's Struggle, ...', 45.

[124] Solnick, 'The Political Economy of Russian Federalism, ...', 24, notes 21, 23.

[125] OECD, 33. Daniel S. Treisman, *After the Deluge,* 48.

[126] Morozov, 42.

[127] Darrell Slider, 'Privatisation in Russia's Regions', 10 *Post-Soviet Affairs,* 4 (1994): 367–96. Solnick, 'Federal Bargaining in Russia', 4 *East European Constitutional Review,* 4 (1995): 56.

May 1996, even extended joint control over the appointment and dismissal of federal representatives to the boards of directors of joint stock companies in the republic in which the federal government had a share of stocks.[128] An agreement with North Ossetia (Alania) on property identified the right to hold 'Golden Shares', that is, special shares by which the government could retain control of specified powers over an enterprise or industry without holding a majority of normal shares.[129] This practice was also used in Bashkortostan to retain state control over key industries.[130]

While these practices operated sporadically in the republics, a 'prize' of the Parade of Treaties was the recognition of a National Bank for a republic. Tatarstan, Bashkortostan, Sakha, Chechnya (and possibly others) were granted the right to establish National Banks as filials of the Central Bank of Russia. As the practice of naming 'authorized banks' is an integral part of the machinery of tax collection, control of *both* the local tax office and the bank through which revenues flow to the centre is a powerful tool. *De facto* control of such banks even before republican control was officially acknowledged by *soglashenie* may be part of the explanation for the relative ease with which Tatarstan, Bashkortostan and Sakha withheld tax revenue from the centre from 1992 through 1994.

All of these aspects of Russia's fiscal federalism present serious problems for the development of federal relations. One of the fundamental advantages offered by federal systems is the formation of an economic space free from barriers to trade, and protected from external incursions and internal decay by the financial contributions of its constituents. This positive feature has been seriously damaged by the non-payment of federal taxes by republics and other regions. At the height of the 'tax wars', roughly 1992–3, republics justified non-payments with statements that, rather than send funds to Moscow to be redistributed later, those federal programmes benefiting the republic would be financed directly by the republic itself. Bypassing Moscow was seen as a method of curtailing federal discretionary powers while at the same time paying for the federal services which operated within the republics.[131] Of course, this did little to disguise the fact that republics were not contributing to the general infrastructure and defence of the federation as a whole. Selective federal payments, which is what such a scheme amounted to, were the fiscal equivalent of the selective implementation of federal laws. It was another expression of the doctrine of nullification that emerged from the philosophy of a 'treaty-constitutional' federation.

[128] Art. 12. The treaty is reprinted in Guboglo, 287–92.
[129] Art. 3. The agreement is reprinted in Guboglo, 470–2.
[130] Yurii Afanas'ev, Chief Expert, Department for Foreign and Ethnic Issues, Administration of the President, author's interview, 14 May 1997, White House, Ufa.   [131] Drobizheva, 215.

Another concern is the degradation of a unified legal environment and confidence in the strength of legal agreements. Bilateral treaties, agreements, presidential *ukazy*, and ministerial pronouncements are all products of the executive branch. They have remained highly personalized, enforcement of negotiated settlements a function almost exclusively of the strength of elite relations. The courts are not used to seek redress for broken agreements any more than they are used to arbitrate conflicting interpretations of power-sharing bilateral treaties. As agreements terminate or come due for renewal, political shake-ups and brinkmanship reveal that economic conflicts are rarely resolved, only postponed. This was the lesson learned by Sakha's President Nikolaev as Alrosa approached the latest round of negotiations over its lease on diamond sales. Despite previous claims that agreements were signed between 'two equal republics', Nikolaev was reduced to pleading for meetings with federal ministers as the term limits of agreements ap-proached.[132] Attempts to discuss the panoply of agreements guaranteeing rights to lease diamond fields and exploit profits evoked a chuckle from the chief executive of one of several Sakha government 'funds' used to invest diamond profits. Asked in 1998 how much weight to ascribe to diamond leases and other agreements, he cited Russian law, the civil code and inter-national standards before concluding: 'Therefore on a juridical foundation there will be twenty-five years. But *politically*, anything may happen. In Russia, you understand, there might be a putsch tomorrow, they shoot people at the White House'.[133]

3. CONCLUSIONS: THE NEW FEDERALISM AND THE TRANSITION TO DEMOCRACY

The 'parade' of bilateral treaties affected political identities, nascent legal foundations and basic federal norms and structures. Dmitrii Mironov, Chair-man of the Sakha Constitutional Court, drew a line between the rule of law and practical politics:

When you say they are moving away from law, away from legality but [rather] consolidate a personification of relations between leaders . . . , I think that this is secondary to legality and constitutionality. But, this does not mean that in *practical*

---

[132] Interview with Mikhail Nikolaev, *Nezavisimaia gazeta*, 14 Apr. 1992. John Helmer, 'Yakut diamond leaders face purge by Moscow', *The Moscow Tribune*, 20 June 1997, 8. The lease period in question expired 31 December 1997, according to the then CEO of Alrosa, Viacheslav Shtyrov, *Federal News Service*, 21 Oct. 1997.

[133] Fedot Semyonovich Tumusov, President, SAPI Corporation, author's interview, 8 June 1998, SAPI Headquarters, Yakutsk.

life one's own signing of such a treaty does not put influence to the test, or the political state of affairs determined by the situation.[134]

As Juan Linz observed with reference to the Spanish transition: 'decisions made during the transition period by a government that is either weak or not fully institutionalized become irreversible at a later stage'.[135] In stark contrast to Spain, Russia's leaders engaged in a process of treaty negotiation that did little to reinforce the federal constitution that had only just been ratified. Treaties were negotiated with entities that had been encouraged to write their own constitutions, in some cases ratified before the federal constitution. Treaties were never subjected to prior public or parliamentary debate, referendum, or ratification.[136] With each ignored court order, nullified law, withheld tax and subsequent back-room agreement, the unresolved and unaddressed effect of *snizu vverkh*, from-the-bottom-up 'treaty-constitutional' approaches grew. The negative effect this had on the individual transitions in the republics was substantial.

Contrary to theories predicting that asymmetry would diminish with the signing of ever more treaties, both *ad hoc* and constitutional asymmetry increased in the Russian Federation during Yeltsin's presidency. Secretive, bilateral executive-driven negotiations had the effect of eroding conceptions of a federal civic identity, a unified legal space, and fiscal burden-sharing. The Spanish *autonomías* offer a more positive example of a process leading to more successful manageability of asymmetric multinational relations. Spain has avoided such conflicts by more fully incorporating later agreements into the constitutional fabric of the federation. This is both a cause and an effect of commonly held conceptions of federal civic identity and of what constitutes the legitimate basis of federal power. The process of regionalization has not created symmetry among the seventeen autonomous communities. But the transparent, multilateral negotiations involving both executive and legislative branches on regional and central levels has managed to avoid the pitfalls of 'treaty-constitutionalism'. The Constitutional Court is utilized to resolve conflicts according to a hierarchy of laws crowned by the Spanish Constitution. Inter-governmental fiscal transfers have steadily grown and branches of all-Spanish parties have developed regionally.[137]

While the different starting points of the Spanish and Russian transitions cannot be understated, Russia's experience with asymmetric federalism contrasts unfavourably in every respect.

---

[134] Dmitrii N. Mironov, author's interview, 4 June 1998, Il Tumen, Yakutsk.
[135] Linz, 'Spanish Democracy...', 273.
[136] Stepan, 'Russia's Federalism in Comparative Perspective...', 27–31.
[137] Agranoff, 388–9.

7

Federal Effects on Transitions in Russia's Republics

> It is not usual for political scientists to construct analytical models defined initially by constitutions. However, no one would dream of watching a game of football or of bridge without taking into account the rules of the game. They constitute a fundamental aspect of the players' strategy and tactics, the framework of which they define.
>
> *Maurice Duverger*

If, contrary to Riker, democracy is so important to (if not a precondition for) federalism, then democracy in the regional units of ostensibly federal systems is important to the integrity of the federation as a whole. Regional governments affect the daily lives of citizens far more than federal governments. Local institutions mediate citizen participation in both regional and federal politics. Regional government shapes the political identity of citizens, their sense of allegiance to different authorities, and their conceptions of the value of inclusion in a federal system. If efforts are made to make regional boundaries congruent with ethnic boundaries, the potential for political mobilization along more and deeper political cleavages is even greater.

After Yeltsin abandoned attempts to influence the course of republican transitions, few republics persevered along clearly democratic paths. This chapter examines the course those transition paths followed, with particular attention paid to the republican constitutions and electoral activity that characterized the Yeltsin era.[1] Constitutions 'matter' because they provide

[1] Following the sweeping reforms initiated by Vladimir Putin in Spring 2000, many republics began to introduce substantial amendments to—or even rewrite anew—their constitutions. This period of flux makes analysis of these fundamental documents difficult. In this chapter, constitutions are examined as they functioned during the Yeltsin presidency, June 1991–December 2000. The following 20 constitutions (excluding Chechnya) were utilized in this analysis (dates of ratification appear in parenthesis): Adygeia (10 March 1995); Altai (23 January 1997); Bashkortostan (24 December 1993); Buriatia (22 February 1994); Dagestan (26 July 1994); Ingushetia (27 February 1994); Kabardino-Balkaria (26 May 1976; latest amendments 4 August 1994); Kalmykia (1994); Karachaevo-Cherkessia (5 March 1996); Karelia (30 May 1978; latest amendments 20 January 1994); Komi (17 February 1994); Marii El (24 June 1995); Mordova (21 September 1995); North Ossetia (12 November 1994); Tatarstan (6 November 1992); Tyva (12 December 1993); Udmurtia (7 December 1994); Khakassia (May 1995); Chuvashia (1978); Sakha (4 April 1992).

the formal rules of the political game. Observed or ignored, they influence the players of this game, the stakes at issue, and the strategies used to win political power. Furthermore, these are founding documents to which republican leaders themselves devoted considerable time and effort. Virtually every republican constitution proclaims a 'sovereign democratic rule-of-law' state.[2] Impressive lists of civic, political, and economic freedoms follow: the division of powers; the supremacy of law; the invalidity of secret laws; open, free, and fair multi-party elections; basic freedoms of speech, assembly and conscience, the defence of all forms of property rights, etc. Nevertheless, their institutional design frequently falls short of basic democratic standards. These documents embed special rights and privileges for select sub-groups of citizens. Specific rights regarding language, culture, and ethnic identity present serious citizenship issues and sources of potential conflict for these multinational republics, further complicated by membership in a multi-national federation. Such enumeration, by republics insistent on their democratic credentials, allows for analysis on their own terms and in the wider context of democratic theory. This methodology was not possible under Soviet legal conceptions, which explicitly subordinated the rule of law to the vanguard role of the Communist Party.

This chapter examines these problems of constitutional engineering, in particular issues of citizenship and representation in republican legislatures. The strong presidentialism found in virtually all of the republics is a recurring theme. Next, ten years of presidential and parliamentary elections are examined to discern the effect of these institutional choices. Throughout the chapter, examples are drawn from all of the republics in the Russian Federation. Concluding this chapter, a case study of the Republic of Kalmykia presents a picture of all of these problems at work in one republic.

1. PROBLEMS IN THE CONSTITUTIONAL CONSTRUCTION OF THE STATE

1.1 Citizenship

Democratic states crave legitimacy, usually sought in the sovereign will of citizens and expressed through representative institutions. In search of this legitimacy, republics in the Russian Federation struggled to reconcile their

---

[2] Out of 18 constitutions analysed for this question, only 2 did not contain the phrase *demokraticheskoe pravovoe gosudarstvo*: Tyva expresses adherence to 'generally recognized international principles of the development of a democratic society'; Karelia intermittently states adherence to most of the same principles expressed in the first chapters of other republican constitutions.

ethnic origins with their new political aspirations. Many elites sought to distinguish their republics by renewing claims to self-determination in declarations of sovereignty and new constitutions. Constitutional commissions, however, soon realized the awkward difficulty of expressing self-determination in the name of one nationality: only four republics had populations even half composed of the ethnic group for which they were named. Republican elites were also extremely reluctant to open the Pandora's box of nationalism that they had watched the Soviet leadership struggle, and ultimately fail, to control.

In whose name could the 'inviolable right to self-determination' be claimed? The preambles of most new republican constitutions begin with variations on the phrase 'We, the multi-national people of . . .', but conclude, either in the preamble or in the first articles on the construction of the state, with the assertion of the right to self-determination of a *particular* national group. Republican institutions were founded on the above-mentioned right to self-determination and the primordial heritage of the titular nationality, alleged to permeate the very soil of the republic, but also, simultaneously, on behalf of *every* nationality. Thus, Article 69 of Bashkortostan's constitution declared that the republic 'was formed as a result of the realization of the right of the Bashkir nation to self-determination and to defend the interests of all of the multinational people of the republic'. Bashkir heritage aside, the 1989 Soviet census determined that the population of Bashkortostan was only 21.9 per cent ethnic Bashkir.[3] In Adygeia, where ethnic Adygei are 22.1 per cent of the population, the constitution declares that the republic was formed 'as a result of the realization of the right to self-determination of the Adygei people and the historically formed community of people who live on its territory'.[4] Similar statements are found in other constitutions, as shown in Table 7.1.

These are ambivalent and fascinating claims. What special right to national self-determination could be possessed by a 'multi-national people?' Was the Bashkir nation really obliged 'to defend the interests' of non-Bashkir residents who did *not* possess an equal right to self-determination? What greater basis was there for self-determination in multi-national republics than in any other oblast, okrug, or autonomous region—a higher status nevertheless claimed by *every* republic? After all, the borders of republics were the artificial creation of Bolshevik strategists and claims to ethnic representation were based on demographic patterns eighty years old. Self-determination for multi-national peoples was a peculiar approach for republics originally conceived to favour a particular nationality above all others.

[3] The 1989 census (the last official Soviet census) is used. *Argumenty i fakty,* No. 13 (Mar. 1991): 1.
[4] Art. 51, *Konstitutsiia respubliki Adygeia.*

Table 7.1   The Right to Self-determination in Republican Constitutions

N = 18 republics	Reference in Constitution to multi-nationalism	Reference in Constitution to Self-determination	Additional references to titular nationality (except state languages)
No. of republics	17	12	9
Republics	Adygeia, Bashkortostan, Buriatia, Dagestan, Ingushetia, Kabardino-Balkaria, Kalmykia, Karachaevo-Cherkessia, Komi, Marii El, Mordova, N. Ossetia, Sakha, Tyva, Tatarstan, Udmurtia, Khakassia	Adygeia, Bashkortostan, Buriatia, Dagestan, Ingushetia, Kabardino-Balkaria, Marii El, Karachayevo-Cherkessia, N. Ossetia, Sakha, Tyva, Udmurtia	Adygeia, Bashkortostan, Buriatia, Dagestan, Kalmykia, Karelia, Komi, N. Ossetia, Sakha

Note: Altai, Chechnya and Chuvashia are omitted.

Such phrases had real and sometimes undemocratic consequences, despite the theoretical prediction that decentralization decreases protections accorded minorities by 'group rights'. This reflected an underlying tension in the Soviet-era organization of republics as homelands for non-Russian ethnic groups, even though minorities in their 'own' republics. To paraphrase Will Kymlicka, selected national minorities in Russia were granted specific territories in which external protections for their culture and language could guard against assimilation by the surrounding Russian majority. Certain group-specific rights and privileges were also provided. However, the post-Soviet practices that developed are the opposite of those about which Kymlicka expressed concern. In Soviet times, non-titular minorities and the (often majority) Russian populations in these republics counted on the centralized, predominantly Russian state to protect their interests. The collapse of the Soviet Union removed these protections, but the traditions and institutions of group-specific rights remained. National minorities were left to regulate—and often expand—their own external protections in an environment of increasing self-government, taking 'as much sovereignty as they could swallow'. Kymlicka expressed concern that, unless linked to self-government, decentralization 'may actually work to the disadvantage of minority groups' who might find more protection from central authorities than regional ones.[5] The emerging situation in Russia revealed the opposite danger: leaders of titular national minorities actually expanded institutionalized group-rights as earlier Soviet controls were lost. In some republics these

[5] Will Kymlicka, *Multicultural Citizenship: A Liberal Theory of Minority Rights* (Oxford: Clarendon Press, 1995), 70–1.

privileges remained at the level of reasonable external protections for national minorities. In too many republics, Russians and other non-titular minorities found themselves partially disenfranchised.

In many republics, provisions were made for heightened awareness and protection of indigenous languages and cultures. For the most part these were reasonable external protections for national minorities, unlikely to infringe the rights of other groups. These promises seem to have been made in a spirit of goodwill or to allay anxieties of national movements. Even provisions that granted more civil and political rights to titular ethnic citizens were not necessarily designed to disenfranchise competing national groups. The total level of democratic participation may even have increased. For example, in Karelia the constitution established a special district to represent the sparsely populated Vepsskii national unit, the sole exception to the proportional electoral districts of its legislature's upper house.[6] In Sakha, where dozens of nomadic 'Small Peoples of the North' live in harsh Siberian conditions, constitutional provisions aimed to include these often forgotten minorities in the affairs of state. These provided for alternative forms of tribal justice and established nomadic soviets instead of fixed territorial-administrative boundaries for the purposes of their representation in the republican parliament.

Other privileges were more sinister: restrictions of franchise and restrictions based on the adoption of official languages. Buriatia and Komi provide two examples of ethnic restrictions on the franchise.

In Buriatia, the 'authorized representatives of the multi-national people' declared their recognition for the right of all peoples to self-determination. Specifically, they noted the historical legacy of Russians, Buriats, and Evenks in the republic. Article 60 established that Buriatia was 'formed as a result of the realization of the rights of the Buriat nation to self-determination', although ethnic Buriats comprise only 24 per cent of the population. Having established distinctions among citizens, the constitution next established privileges. The constitution stipulated that alterations of the 'state-legal status' of the republic require a special referendum. One-half of the total number of citizens must vote in favour of the referendum question for its passage, but the vote would be valid *only* if 50 per cent of the ethnic Buriats choosing to vote also support the motion.[7] The provision implies that a voter's ethnicity must be identified on his/her ballot paper and creates

---

[6] Art. 47, §3, *Konstitutsiia (Osnovnoi zakon) Respubliki Kareliia.*

[7] 'Change to the state-legal status of the republic and also to its territory is realized by way of a referendum, with this decision considered accepted if more than half the citizens of the republic votes for it, in that number more than half the citizens of Buriat nationality, who have participated in the vote'. Art. 60, §4, *Konstitutsiia Respubliki Buriatiia.*

the potential for extremely undemocratic scenarios. If, for example, the entire non-ethnic Buriat population (75 per cent of the total population) were to support such a referendum question, and half of the ethnic Buriat population participated in the referendum (for a total participation of 75 per cent + 12 per cent = 87 per cent of the electorate), a minimum blocking win-set could be achieved by 6.01 per cent of the total population (just over half of participating ethnic Buriats). The votes of ethnic Buriat citizens are, for purposes of such referendums, more important than other citizens, a difficult proposition in a democratic, rule-of-law, multi-national republic.

Privileged franchise for the titular ethnic group was still more pervasive in the Komi republic. Nationalists and state officials took seriously the opening words of their Declaration of Sovereignty: Komi was a 'national state' (although ethnic Komi themselves comprise only 23 per cent of the population).[8] Drafting these documents, the Komi Supreme Soviet worked under increasing pressure from Komi national movements seeking to institutional- ize privileges based on this special status. A self-designated nationalist Congress of the Komi People and its executive organ, 'The Committee for the Rebirth of the Komi People', proclaimed itself to be the highest repre- sentative organ of the indigenous people. It convinced the Supreme Soviet to bestow that title by law, and to provide state financing for congresses once every two years.[9] In the stormy debates over the constitution which followed, national movements kept up the pressure.[10] The 'Committee' as well as the movement 'Komi kotyr' (Komi Comradeship) promoted draft

---

[8] E.V. Shishkin, State-Legal Directorate of the Administration of the Head of the Republic: 'This Declaration should be considered not only as a political statement, but as an important legal document, which determined the fundamental principles of the organization of the state—the Republic of Komi, as a basis for preparation of a new Constitution of the Republic, the improvement of republican legislation'. E.V. Shishkin, 'O Nekotorykh osobennostiakh konstitut- sionnogo razvitiia Respubliki Komi', in O. Yu. Kuzivanova, ed. Aktual'nye problemy politiko- pravovogo, sotsial'no-ekonomicheskogo i kul'turnogo razvitiia evropeiskogo sevara Rossiiskoi Federatsii (istoriia i sovremennost') (Syktyvkar: Ministerstvo po delam natsional'nostei Respubliki Komi, 1995), 8.

[9] 2nd Extraordinary Congress, declaration of November 1991. In February 1992 the Presidium of the Komi Supreme Soviet passed a resolution 'On the Decisions of the 2nd Congress of the Komi People'. The 'Law on the Status of the Congress of the Komi People' was passed by the Supreme Soviet in May 1992. Yu. P. Shabaev 'Vstupitel'nyi ocherk. K izucheniiu teorii i ideologii komi natsional'nogo dvizheniia', in Yu. O. Shabaev & M.N. Guboglo, eds. Shtrikhi etnopoliticheskogo razvitiia Respubliki Komi: Ocherki, dokumenty, materialy, Tom 1 (Moskva: RAN Tsentr po izucheniiu mezhnatsional'nykh otnoshenii instituta etnologii i Antropologii im. N.N. Miklukho-Maklaia, 1994), 25, 186. The text of the Law 'On the Status of the Congress of Komi People' is reprinted on pp. 128–9.

[10] Michael McFaul & Nikolai Petrov, eds. Politicheskii al'manakh Rossii 1997, 2 Vols. (Moskva: Moskovskii Tsentr Karnegi, 1998), Vol. 2, Book 1, 185. The former Chairman of the Republican Council of Ministers, V. Khudiaev, at the time a strong rival of the current head of the republic,

constitutions that established a bicameral legislature, one chamber of which was set aside exclusively for the representation of Komi interests, its work done exclusively by ethnic Komi legislators. One failed variant envisaged ethnic Komi receiving two ballots at elections, non-Komi citizens receiving just one.[11] The final result was a compromise. Article 3 of the Constitution, passed in February 1994, established that 'the Komi people are the source of statehood'. On this premise, Article 76 granted both the Congress of Komi People and its 'executive organ' the right to legislative initiative in a reconstituted unicameral republican parliament that was to be elected without rules for its ethnic composition.[12] The composition of a new State Committee on Nationalities, however, was strongly influenced by the nationalist Committee for the Rebirth of the Komi People. This right for ethnic Komi was very different than those special rights extended to the 'small peoples' of Sakha. Whereas rights given in Sakha expanded inclusion in state affairs, the Komi clauses were by nature exclusive.

Language issues were the most prolific and potentially most undemocratic issue. As Will Kymlicka observed, the choice of an official language is 'one of the most important determinants of whether a culture survives'. The argument in favour of 'benign neglect', advocated by those who view universal citizenship rights as sufficient to protect minority cultures, overlooks the unavoidability of the need to choose a language for schools, courts, and all other state-citizen interactions, inevitably privileging some and disadvantaging others.[13] Almost all the republics declared Russian and the titular language to be the exclusive official languages of the republic. Some republics privileged particular dialects for development (e.g. North Ossetia (Alania), Art. 15); in most, the indigenous language was declared the basis of national self-consciousness and its expansion a 'prioritized aim of the organs of power' (e.g. Kalmykia, Art. 18). In Tyva, *only* Tyvan was established as the state language; Russian, mandated for equal use in all state capacities, was relegated the status of 'general federal state language' (Art. 33). Tatarstan's Supreme Soviet adopted a 'programme' to develop the languages 'of the peoples of the Tatarstan Republic' but which in reality focused essentially on just the Tatar language, recommending a list of professions for

supported this proposal. One analyst, Yu. P. Shabaev, notes: ' "The Committee" had at its disposal appreciable financial means and successfully lobbying in the government turned into a sufficiently exclusive ethnocratic organization closely connected with the ruling elite, especially in the Soviet of Ministers of the Republic'. Shabaev & Guboglo, 26.

[11] Shabaev & Guboglo, 30, 129–45. The Committee participated in the drafting of the law on state languages and, in 1993, submitted a draft 'Law on Citizenship'.

[12] Art. 1, §1; Art. 76, §1, *Konstitutsiia Respublika Komi*.

[13] Kymlicka, 108, 111.

which Tatar should be required and providing for salary bonuses to reward bilingualism.[14]

Ten republics required candidates for select offices to know both Russian and the titular language. Republican elites justified such rules as efforts to represent the entire republic. In fact, large sections of the polis were excluded from participation at the highest level of political life. In Sakha, where Russians and ethnic Sakha respectively comprise 50.3 per cent and 33.4 per cent of the population, knowledge of both languages is required for candidates for president and chairman of either house of the parliament. But as a respected Sakha academic and member of its parliament conceded, 'The fact is, only 2 per cent of Russians here know how to speak Sakha. At the same time, only 5 per cent of ethnic Sakha use their native language in school; in VUZy [higher education institutions] there is neither study nor instruction in Sakha'.[15] The Bashkir requirement of bilingualism for presidential candidates neglected the languages of the Tatar, Chuvash, Marii, and other nationalities that comprise 36 per cent of the population.[16] In Buriatia, Article 71 of the constitution requires bilingualism for presidential candidates; Article 118, however, delays implementation of this requirement until elections for the *second* president. By no coincidence, the first president of the republic, Leonid Potapov, was Russian. Such exceptions give the lie to republican arguments that mandatory bilingualism promotes inter-ethnic harmony. Rules that privilege speakers of one language—almost always a proxy for members of that ethnic group—work as filters for the entire executive branch, as presidents extend the logic of these requirements to subordinate posts. In Bashkortostan, informed sources identify between half and two-thirds of ministers as Bashkirs, a deliberate policy of the president.[17] A comparison of republics that mandate bilingualism for the highest posts reveals significant disenfranchisement (see Table 7.2).

The highly politicized route towards a 'renewed' Russian Federation actively encouraged republics to strengthen and expand political institutions based on privileges for the titular ethnic group. Most republics ratified their

---

[14] Dmitry Gorenburg, 'Regional Separatism in Russia: Ethnic Mobilisation or Power Grab?' 51 *Europe-Asia Studies*, 2 (1999): 261.

[15] Uliana A. Vinokurova MP, author's interview, 1 June 1998, Yakutsk. According to a 1989 study, 15 per cent of urbanized ethnic Sakha could not speak the Sakha language. According to Vinokurova, language training has increased but is not mandatory. *See* Marjorie Mandelstam Balzer & Uliana Alekseevna Vinokurova, 'Nationalism, Interethnic Relations and Federalism: The Case of the Sakha Republic (Yakutia)', 48 *Europe-Asia Studies*, 1 (1996): 104, 117.

[16] Vladimir Bugaev, 'Kto razzhigaet etnicheskie strasti?', *Rossiiskie vesti*, 13 Jan. 1998, 2. McFaul & Petrov, 82.

[17] Gorenburg, 264, 273. Gorenburg cites sources within the presidential administration and in the political opposition for these figures.

Table 7.2 Constitutionally Required Language Ability for Candidates

Republic	Bilingual requirement	% ethnic composition		% with knowledge of titular language	
Bashkortostan	President (Art. 92)	Bashkir	22	Bashkir	76
		Russian	39	Russian	0.3
		Tatar	28	Tatar	0.7
		Chuvash	3	Chuvash	0.8
		Marii	3	Marii	0.2
Buriatia	President (Art. 71)	Buriat	24	Buriat	91
		Russian	70	Russian	0.3
Sakha	President (Art. 66); Chairmen of both legislative chambers (Art. 55)	Sakha	33	Sakha	96
		Russian	50	Russian	2.0
		Ukrainian	7	Ukrainian	0.3
		Tatar	2	Tatar	1
Tatarstan	President (Art. 108)	Tatar	49	Tatar	97
		Russian	43	Russian	1
		Chuvash	4	Chuvash	4
Tyva	President (Art. 69)	Tyvan	64	Tyvan	99
		Russian	32	Russian	0.6
Marii El	President (Art. 76)	Marii	43	Marii	90
		Russian	48	Russian	1
		Tatar	6	Tatar	1

Note: Adygeia, Altai, Ingushetia and North Ossetia (Alania) have been omitted due to incomplete data.

Source: Valerii Tishkov (1997), 93–5. The data for Sakha is contested by Vinokurova, above.

own constitutions in advance of the charters passed by oblasts and other federal subjects, which as a rule operated with less initiative and under tighter control by federal authorities. The Federation Treaty further marked the growing divide. The issues discussed above are a result of the unequal federal development of the Russian transition. In many republics, the illiberal privileging of group-rights in republican institutions has often contributed to extreme over-representation of titular ethnic minorities and the under-representation of far more numerous Russian and non-titular populations.

1.2 Republican Legislatures

Although virtually all of the republics emerged from one system of Soviet power with identical legislative organs, the new environment of Russian federalism produced a wide variety of institutional approaches. A minority of republics (four) mimicked the federal centre by creating bicameral legislatures. Most republics (sixteen) settled on unicameral parliaments, although there was considerable variation within that model. In all four bicameral systems and in six of the unicameral systems, representatives (universally called 'deputies') are elected from two different types of electoral districts: territorial districts and administrative-territorial districts. 'Territorial districts' are districts based on proportional representation, created for this electoral purpose. 'Administrative-territorial districts' are districts that trace the boundaries of existing, Soviet-era administrative units; both their physical size and population vary considerably. Table 7.3 illustrates this classification of republics.

The institutional structure of almost three-quarters of these legislatures leads to three serious distortions of the democratic process. First, the distinction between types of electoral districts affects the status of deputies elected from them. Some deputies are considered 'professional' parliamentarians, while others are considered to serve on only a 'part-time' basis. These distinctions permit a minority of the members of the parliament to engage in an array of legislative activity, including law-making. Second, the creation of 'part-time' deputies, who are usually from administrative-territorial districts, erases crucial divisions between the executive and legislative branches of government. The most serious breach of the division of powers occurs when the president possesses the power to appoint local officials ('heads of local administration'), who then become these part-time deputies. Unsurprisingly, such deputies are easily controlled by their patron-president. Third, the effect of these and other mechanisms in all types of legislatures leads to serious problems of over-representation of titular national groups.

Preliminary classifications reveal that unicameral versus bicameral distinctions are of little analytical value. Bashkortostan, Kabardino-Balkaria, Karelia, and Sakha operate bicameral systems, but have little else in

Table 7.3 Classifications of Republics by Legislative Structure

Bicameral legislatures	Unicameral legislatures (Deputies chosen from 2 types of districts)	Unicameral legislatures (Deputies chosen from the same type of district)	Other legislative systems
4	6	6	4
Baskortostan	Adygeia	Altai	Dagestan
Kabardino-Balkaria	Buriatia, Komi	Karachaevo-	Ingushetia
Karelia	Marii El, Tatarstan	Cherkessia	Kalmykia
Sakha	Chuvashia	Mordova, N. Ossetia (Alania), Udmurtia Khakassia	Tyva

common. The republics are located in different corners of Russia and have very different histories and economies. The legislatures themselves range in size from 188 deputies in Bashkortostan to 61 in Karelia. Bashkortostan's House of Representatives is more than three times the size of its Legislative House; the other republics maintain houses of similar size. Bicameralism has traditionally been employed to balance competing or contrasting forces in parliaments: to prevent 'tyrannies' of both majorities and minorities, to reduce the power of 'agenda setters' and the instability of Condorcet's paradoxical vote cycling.[18] In federal systems, territorial units may be accounted equal representation in one house while popular representation is provided via equal-sized electoral districts. These four republican bicameral legislatures exhibit few of these salient differences or traditional objectives. There is little consistency among republics regarding the relative importance between houses of parliament. There is also little reason to believe that representatives from administrative-territorial districts which compose these upper chambers have any characteristics to justify their role as 'senators' in a bicameral system.

Although analysis of these bicameral systems *as bicameral systems* reveals little, it does point towards a feature shared by half of republican legislative structures. I call this feature 'intra-bicameralism'. It is observed in all four bicameral republics and six republics with unicameral legislatures. 'Intra-bicameralism' exists when deputies in a single legislative chamber (or in a unicameral parliament) are: (1) elected from two different types of electoral districts and, (2) by virtue of that distinction, are accorded different rights and responsibilities. As if operating in different houses of parliament, legislators function under different rules and possess different privileges. Deputies elected from territorial districts (based on proportional representation) are usually given the status of 'full-time' deputies, while those elected from 'administrative-territorial' districts (that overlap existing administrative boundaries) are given the status of 'part-time' deputies. In the majority of cases of intra-bicameralism (though not all) another condition attaches: 'part-time' deputies are simultaneously the heads of the local administrations who control local government in administrative-territorial districts. In many republics, this office is appointed by the president. This appointment almost invariably results in election to the legislature (or dismissal from the administrative post if unsuccessful). There they are the president's men.

Intra-bicameralism is distinguishable from a combined system of plurality (i. e. 'first-past-the-post') and proportional 'party list' representation, which

---

[18] See George Tsebelis and Jeannette Money, *Bicameralism* (Cambridge University Press, 1997), 35–43.

occurs in many bicameral and unicameral legislatures. The lower house of Russia's bicameral legislature, the Duma, has members elected from single-member electoral districts as well as party lists; in Belgium, legislators may be elected from territorial and linguistic-cultural districts. Arend Lijphart, in his comprehensive study of elections in twenty-seven post-war democracies, isolates ten countries that utilize two 'tiers' of districts in various electoral systems.[19] In all of these countries, however, all legislators possess complete equality of status in parliament, regardless of the manner of their election. In an intra-bicameral system, equality of privileges does not exist.[20] Part-time deputies may be excluded from competition to leadership posts in the legislature, presidiums, or permanent committees. Intra-bicameral systems use two types of districts not to increase proportionality in party representation (as will be shown, most republics run plurality elections and have grossly underdeveloped party systems), but to differentiate between types of deputies. None of the electoral systems in the democracies that Lijphart describes permit the intrusion of the executive branch into the composition and activities of the legislature. In intra-bicameral systems, this violation of the division of powers is part of their design. Intra-bicameralism is a form of gerrymandering, except instead of altering the *boundaries* of electoral districts, it is the *type* of district that is manipulated to achieve a desired *type* of deputy. The closer one examines these 'unicameral' legislatures, the clearer becomes the image of a house divided.

Why does intra-bicameralism pose concerns for democratic governance? First, such a system may create situations in which a minority of deputies is empowered to pass a majority of laws, excluding from participation the corps of 'part-time' deputies. As explained below, this is the case in Tatarstan. Second, the *de jure* existence of part-time legislators can result in the *de facto* creation of part-time legislatures, or Soviet-style institutions such as plenary sessions in which 'amateur' parliamentarians are infrequently con-

---

[19]   Such systems might use an upper tier 'at-large' national district and lower tier single-member districts to combine 'the advantage of close representative-voter contact in low-magnitude districts with the greater proportionality of high-magnitude districts'. Arend Lijphart, *Electoral Systems and Party Systems: A Study of Twenty-Seven Democracies, 1945–1990* (New York: Oxford University Press, 1994; reprinted, 1998), 30–46, 145–8.

[20]   Intra-bicameralism is clearly a matter of degree. Representatives from the District of Columbia and Puerto Rico do not have equal rights with other Congressmen in the U.S. House of Representatives. But this is not sufficient to label this chamber an example of intra-bicameralism. The distinction between life peers and hereditary peers sitting in the House of Lords does not provide the basis for discriminating between their activities in that chamber. The French practice of permitting members of the National Assembly to serve simultaneously as mayors in their respective districts is also not a form of intra-bicameralism. A deputy's double mandate does not accord him additional privileges as a member of parliament, nor does it place him under the control of the executive branch.

vened to rubber stamp the work of the 'professionals'.[21] Third, electoral districts that coincide with existing administrative units to return 'part-time' deputies frequently result in election of deputies who are at the same time executive heads of these administrations. This result blurs the distinction between executive and legislative branches of power. In those cases where the president appoints or otherwise influences heads of administration the executive branch gains a powerful lever in the legislature. Where heads of administration are prohibited from becoming part-time deputies, a similar rule can privilege a different group (e. g. industrial managers, state farm directors, etc.) with equally strong links to the executive. Fourth, while territorial districts are supposed to be designed to encompass constituencies of equal population, administrative-territorial districts are drawn to Soviet-era boundaries without regard to equal representation. This situation invariably favours rural over urban constituencies. In Komi, for example, the 200, 000 residents of the town of Vorkuta and the 13, 000 residents of Kortkerosskiy *raion* (district) each have one deputy.[22] Distinctions between deputies may also be used as a mechanism to expand the representation of minority ethnic groups well beyond realistic demographic expectations.

The most brazen example of intra-bicameralism reveals its possible abuses. Tatarstan's unicameral parliament, the State Council, is composed of 130 deputies. Sixty-nine deputies are elected from territorial districts designed to approximate equal representation. Sixty-one deputies are elected from administrative-territorial districts that overlap pre-existing administrative boundaries and vary considerably in size.[23] Territorial district deputies work on a 'permanent basis', while their counterparts function 'as a rule not breaking off with production or service activity'.[24] The constitution uses this distinction to formulate the difference between 'sessions' of the State Council and 'plenary sessions':

---

[21] In the bicameral system of Bashkortostan, meetings of the House of Representatives (composed of part-time legislators) 'are conducted as necessary, but not less than four times a year' (Art. 85). As a rule, hidden bicameral systems do not overtly make this distinction in their constitutions but do establish plenary sessions and presidiums which may lead to the same result.

[22] Yurii Shabaev, 'Komi Republic Fights Over Electoral System', 3 *IEWS Russian Regional Report*, 12 (26 Mar. 1998).

[23] The 1936 Constitution of the Tatar ASSR stipulated election to the Supreme Soviet solely on the basis of territorial electoral districts: 1 deputy per 15, 000 citizens. The amended 1978 Constitution, following the declaration of a Tatar SSR in 1990, maintained this system to elect the 250 members of the Supreme Soviet. Boris L. Zheleznov, *Pravovoi status Respubliki Tatarstan* (Kazan': Tatarskoe knizhnoe izdatel'stvo, 1996), 100–1. The system described above is based on the Tatar Constitution passed on 6 November 1992.

[24] *Konstitutsiia Respubliki Tatarstan*, Art. 84, §1–2.

Article 91: Sessions of the State Council are convened in the composition of deputies, who work in parliament on a permanent basis.
For examination of more important questions plenary sessions of the State Council are convened composed of elected deputies...

Article 95:... A law is considered to be passed if at a session more than half the deputies working on a permanent basis, vote in favour of it or if at a plenary session more than half of the established composition of the State Council votes in favour of it....

The State Council has twenty-nine broad areas of jurisdiction, seventeen of which require approval in plenary session for passage into law (Art. 89). The remaining twelve subject-areas are within the purview of mere 'sessions' of the State Council. As Article 95 makes clear, decisions on these questions are passed into law by the vote of thirty-five 'permanent' deputies, that is, *just over one-quarter of the total composition of the State Council.*[25] This minority wields substantial powers. It can legislate (passing any law that does not involve confirmation of the budget or involve non-budgetary state funds), establish new taxes and sources of revenue, and call elections (also confirming the Central Election Commission). It can make interpretations of republican laws, annul decisions of raion and city soviets, and examine questions about the guarantee of constitutional rights, language and national culture in the republic. This minority is sufficient to conduct the management of state property, regulate private property relations, and create or liquidate state banks. Thus, this intra-bicameral division of deputies has very real implications.

Unfortunately, the remedy for this undemocratic outcome, greater inclusion of the remaining 'part-time' deputies, is in many ways even worse. This is the second half of the problem presented by most (but not all) intra-bicameral legislatures. In Tatarstan, the president essentially controls the sixty-one 'part-time' deputies chosen from administrative-territorial districts. Article 111, §3 of the Tatar constitution grants the president the sole power to nominate candidates for the post of 'head of administration' (subject to confirmation by the local council or election) and the unilateral power to dismiss those officials. Parliamentary elections in 1995 resulted in the election of forty-two heads of administration and seventeen directors of industry or agriculture. Empirically, the president has met no resistance to his choices, who by virtue of their local power find election to the State

---

[25] This feature has been noted by one of Tatarstan's distinguished legal scholars: '... the fundamental mass of ordinary laws may be definitively passed by a session composed of less than a third of the deputies of the Republic of Tatarstan'. Zheleznov, 107.

Council virtually unimpeded: 40 per cent of heads of administration ran unopposed for the legislature in 1995.[26] Dismissal is just as easy. In late March 1999, by-elections were held for fifteen seats in the State Council, thirteen of whom were heads of administration appointed and then dismissed by the president. The results of the by-election: twelve seats were won by heads of administration newly appointed by the president, one seat by the head of the president's administration and the remaining two by directors of enterprises with close ties to the executive.[27] The effect on the division of powers and the level of democracy in Tatarstan cannot be overstated. As Professor Faroukshine summarized, 'Therein lie the roots of servile obedience, hypocrisy, and flattery that the appointed officials abundantly exhibit for the person of President Shaimiev and for the Kazan Kremlin's policies'.[28] Intra-bicameralism is found in ten republican legislatures, nine of which are described in Table 7.4.[29]

In the preponderance of cases (though not all), the executive has direct control over officials who frequently serve simultaneously in the legislative branch. In other cases, although elections formally take place, the outcome is predictable—the full weight of the executive branch is brought to bear on a local administration, usually freezing out (by a variety of methods) any competition. The breakdown is summarized in Table 7.5.

At least ten of the twenty republics surveyed here operate intra-bicameral systems. What of the remaining ten? These republics maintain unicameral legislatures in which all deputies are elected from territorial electoral districts. However, only six of these (Altai, Karachaevo-Cherkessia, Mordova, North Ossetia (Alania), Udmurtia, and Khakassia) elect deputies solely according to single seat, first-past-the-post electoral districts based on equal populations of voters. In Ingushetia, Kalmykia, Tyva, and Dagestan unicameral legislatures exist, but each with an unusual twist.[30]

---

[26] McFaul & Petrov, 247–8. Other sources place this number even higher. One professor of political science at Kazan' State University, states that 51 heads of local administration won election in 1995, with only 3 losing contested races. Including directors of state schools, doctors in state hospitals, and directors of state-owned enterprises, 78 members of the parliament are also state officials in another capacity. Midkhat Faroukshine, 'Regional Authoritarianism Flourishes in Tatarstan', 2 *IEWS Russian Regional Report*, 38 (6 Nov. 1997).

[27] 'Tatarstan Deputies Resign', 4 *East West Institute Russian Regional Report*, 11 (25 Mar. 1999). 'Shaimiev Supporters Fill Out Tatarstan Legislature', 4 *East West Institute Russian Regional Report*, 12 (1 Apr. 1999).

[28] Midkhat Faroukshine, *IEWS* ..., (6 Nov. 1997).

[29] The Republic of Buriatia might be considered a tenth case. Article 80, §2 states: 'The People's Khural consists of 65 deputies, elected from territorial and national representations', but does not elaborate any further about this distinction.

[30] Udmurtia and Dagestan may warrant classification somewhere between intra-bicameralism and genuine unicameralism. The Udmurt Constitution permits some deputies to be elected on a

Table 7.4   Intra-bicameralism in Republican Legislatures

Republic	Territorial districts		Administrative-territorial districts	
No. of deputies in unicameral parliament	No. of districts (deputies/district)	Status of deputies	No. of districts (deputies/district)	Status of deputies
Adygeia (45)	27 (1)	Unspecified[a]	9 (2)	Unspecified[a]
Bashkortostan (188)[c]	40 (1)	Full-time	74 (2)	Part-time
Kabardino-Balkaria (72)[c]	36 (1)	Full-time	12 (3)	Part-time
Karelia (61)[c]	25 (1)	Full-time	18 (2)	Part-time
Komi (50)	30 (1)	Unspecified[b]	20 (1)	Unspecified[b]
Marii El (67)	50 (1)	Unspecified[b]	17 (1)	Unspecified[b]
Tatarstan (130)	69 (1)	Full-time	61 (1)	Part-time
Chuvashia (47)	19 (1)	Full-time	28 (1)	Part-time
Sakha (70)[c]	35 (1)	Full-time	35 (1)	Part-time

[a] Art. 64, §5 of the Constitution of Adygeia states: 'Deputies of the State Soviet–Khase of the Republic of Adygeia, working on a permanent paid basis compose not more than one-third of the established number of deputies'. The Constitution does not specify whether this rule applies to all deputies or just those elected from territorial districts.

[b] The Constitutions of Komi and Marii El distinguish between deputies elected from different districts, but leave ambiguous which deputies are full-time 'permanent' deputies. It is reasonable to assume, based on patterns in other republics, that the deputies from districts designed for proportional representation are the permanent members.

[c] These four republics maintain bicameral systems. The numbers in parentheses indicates the total membership in both houses. The breakdown by districts corresponds to the composition of each house.

Ingushetia operates the simplest of these systems: all parliamentary elections are conducted within a single twenty-seven seat electoral district. In other words, every voter is given a ballot to choose the entire legislature. According to Michael McFaul and Nikolai Petrov this system is: 'uncommonly bad from the point of view of democratic norms: in the first place, because of the complete suppression of the opinion of the minority, in the second place, because of the defenselessness from falsification: voters almost certainly don't mark on a ballot 27 candidates (in the best case, 15–20), and the electoral commission has the possibility to add onto incomplete

'permanent paid basis' while others, presumably, are neither paid nor permanent. It seems reasonable to speculate that permanent paid deputies are more likely to serve on permanent commissions, and win election to special posts than their part-time colleagues. The Dagestan Constitution notes: 'Part of the deputies, elected to the composition of each of the committees, work in the People's Assembly on a permanent professional basis'. The rest of the parliament meets at least once a month. It is a matter of interpretation whether these clauses indicate the general weakness of the parliament *vis-à-vis* the executive branch or a subtler form of intra-bicameralism. Examination of republican electoral laws, in addition to analysis of constitutions, is crucial to define these divisions more precisely.

Table 7.5 Executive Control over Heads of Administration

Head of local administration	Elected or appointed?	May be elected to parliament?	May be dismissed by president?
Adygeia	Elected (Art. 95)	No (Art. 65, §3)	Yes (Art. 78, '1')
Bashkortostan	Appointed (Art. 95, §14)	Yes: House of Reps only (Art. 85)	Yes (Art. 95, §14)
Buriatia	'subordinated to the president' (Art. 96)	Yes	Yes (Art. 96)
Kabardino-Balkaria	Elected (Art. 128)	Yes (Art. 96)	Nothing in Constitution
Karelia	Unclear	Yes: House of Reps only (Art. 50)	Nothing in Constitution
Komi	President nominates candidate (republican law)	Yes (republican law)	Unclear (Art. 94)[a]
Marii El	Elected (Art. 105, §4)	Yes (Art. 67)	Nothing in Constitution
Tatarstan	President nominates candidate (Art. 111, §3)	Yes (Art. 84)	Yes (Art. 111, §3)
Sakha	Elected, but may be 'under the control of the Government' (Arts. 91 & 97)	Yes (Arts. 52 & 57)	Unclear (Art. 97)[a]

Notes: Chuvashia is omitted due to lack of data. In Karelia, the executive appoints 'heads of republican organs' (Art. 68) but organs of local self-government 'do not enter into the system of organs of state power' aside from 'transferred authorities... under the control of the state' (Arts. 80, 81).

[a] Art. 94 of the Komi Constitution describes a local administration as 'an organ of executive power' that is part of 'the system of executive power in the Republic of Komi'. Art. 97 of the Sakha Constitution states 'Control of the Government of the Republic of Sakha (Yakutia) over organs of local administration is permitted within the limits determined by legislation'.

ballots marks for those candidates in need'.[31] The constitution grants the president exclusive jurisdiction over the appointment and dismissal of district heads of administration. These officials, along with directors of state enterprises and farms (also under the control of the president) won 40 per cent of the seats in the parliament.

In Kalmykia, two-thirds of the twenty-seven member People's Khural is elected according to single seat, first-past-the-post electoral districts. The remaining third, nine deputies, are chosen from a list of candidates nominated solely by the president. They require only 15 per cent of the vote (valid with only 35 per cent participation) to win their seats.[32] This is a strikingly

[31] McFaul & Petrov, 135.
[32] Darrell Slider, 'Elections to Russia's Regional Assemblies', 12 Post-Soviet Affairs, 3 (1996): 254. McFaul & Petrov, 152.

direct executive incursion into the affairs of the legislative branch. The so-called presidential list deputies are equal in all respects to the remaining nineteen deputies. In Tyva, twenty-seven of the thirty-two seats in parliament are filled via elections from single seat districts. The remaining five seats are chosen through a single, all-republic, five-mandate district.

The most complex system operates in Dagestan. There, 121 single-seat electoral districts are established according to equal shares of the population. Candidacy in these districts is not open to all. Article 72 of the constitution charges the People's Assembly to guarantee the representation of all peoples, but leaves the manner of providing that representation to the discretion of the legislature. The Law on Elections passed 21 October 1994 established a quota system in Dagestan: selected seats in the parliament are reserved for particular nationalities, a certain number for women, and a certain number for deputies with 'professional status' in the parliament. In some districts, voters may be constrained to vote for a deputy that fits all three classifications (e.g. a female Avar with 'full-time' status). Only 48 of 121 seats (39.67 per cent) are free from any quota limitations.[33] Needless to say, the fact that different nationalities are interspersed throughout the republic makes it difficult to assign quotas that accurately reflect the composition of districts. Deputies elected by nationality quotas are constitutionally empowered to demand a two-third super-majority for approval of any proposal to alter the 'administrative-territorial organization, and also demographic, linguistic, social-economic and cultural environment' that they represent.[34]

The remaining republics do not distinguish between types of electoral districts. Altai, Karachaevo-Cherkessia, Mordova, North Ossetia (Alania), Udmurtia, and Khakassia all have unicameral systems in which all deputies are elected from single-seat electoral districts which approximate similar shares of voters. Although districts remain equivalent, the corps of deputies is still divided. As electoral results for these republics show, the rules of the game have been written to privilege certain types of candidate over others. In these republics, deputies are elected either on a 'professional' or 'non-professional' basis. Those professional deputies, who are paid a salary, are prohibited from membership in most state posts. However, posts that may be occupied simultaneously with non-professional membership in the legislature include directors of state farms (*kolkhozy* and *sovkhozy*), state enterprises and state institutions. These positions may rival heads of local administrations in terms of local authority, influencing the lives of thousands of voters, and operate very close to the boundaries of executive

---

[33] McFaul & Petrov, Carnegie, 111–27.
[34] Art. 81, §2, *Konstitutsiia Respubliki Dagestan*.

power. Unlike the system of intra-bicameralism, under which the number of part-time deputies must be fixed according to districts, there are rarely any constitutionally established restrictions on the number of part-time deputies in these republics.

Following the 1993 October Events, eighteen republican constitutions were either adopted anew or severely amended. Since January 1997, only one republic has retained a parliamentary form of government: Udmurtia. The rest display characteristics of strong presidentialism. The existence of the 'part-time' deputies described above, who simultaneously serve as local executives in their administrative districts, is an expression of the strong executive focus of these republics and one of the most serious violations of the principle of separation of powers. A common phrase in constitutions describes administration of local government as part of a 'unified system of executive power'. In both intra-bicameral and some unicameral systems, the vast majority of deputies from such districts are, if not the heads of local administrations, then their subordinates, heads of state enterprises or other executive branch officials. In Buriatia, for example, the president as prime minister 'unites and directs' organs of local administration, which are 'subordinated to the President' (Art. 96). Executives in Tatarstan and Mordova have the power to appoint heads of local administration with the approval of local soviets. In Tyva, heads are popularly elected but the president, with approval of parliament, has power to dismiss 'heads of organs of local self-government'. In Komi, republican law grants the head of the republic the power to nominate candidates for head of city and *raion* (district) councils, who are then elected by council members. It would not be unreasonable to speculate about the high level of loyalty such deputies might provide their president.

There are many possible explanations for the emergence of intra-bicameralism in half of the republics. This intra-bicameralism may have been a result of compromises following attempts to create explicitly bicameral systems.[35] A draft resolution 'On Self-Determination' formulated at the First All-Russian Congress of Finno-Ugric Peoples (held in Izhevsk, Udmurtia, in May 1992) made some extraordinary demands for legislatures in republics named for members of these titular ethnic groups:

... in the future organs of state power of the republics—of professional parliaments and local organs of power—representation of peoples should be guaranteed:

---

[35] In Adygeia, Karachaevo-Cherkessia, Komi, and Marii El, attempts at ethnic gerrymandering and formal bicameralism preceded, with varying degrees of intensity, the establishment of hidden bicameral legislatures.

(a) by quotas for deputies' places, in harmony with the portion of the people [*narod*, in this context, ethnic group] numbering in the population;

(b) by means of a bicameral parliament for republics, which consist of a House of the Republic and house of the native people.[36]

In Komi, several of the strongest national movements promoted draft constitutions reserving one chamber of a bicameral system *exclusively* for ethnic Komi![37] In Adygeia, national movements pressed the Chairman of the Supreme Soviet to increase the number of Adygei represented in the Khase (parliament) by establishing equal representation of Russians and Adygei (Russians outnumber Adygei by more than three to one). In October 1991, the Supreme Soviet bowed to pressure from a recently convened Congress of the Adyge People, and 'in the aim of guaranteeing international and civic accord' reserved half of the parliament for Adyge nationals; perhaps not coincidentally, on the same day the Supreme Soviet established the post of republican president (still held by the above-mentioned chairman, for whom it was designed). Only the unexpected repercussions of the October 1993 Events led to the restructuring of the Supreme Soviet into the current Khase, reducing the deputy corps by more than half, eliminating overt quotas, but preserving a system which still over-represents Adyge and other categories of deputies with allegiance to the president.[38] In Tatarstan, one of the leading drafters of the constitution promoted intra-bicameralism for the opposite reason, as a means to protect new democratic institutions from extreme nationalists: 'For now we should recognize that there is a place for some deviation from the principle of division of powers . . . of course its clear that here the executive power shows a very large influence on the legislative power. In current temporary conditions it is sometimes necessary to hold onto power; if we engaged democracy completely, nationalist forces could send us back to an unstable environment'.[39]

---

[36] Proekt rezoliutsiia, 'O samoupravlenii', Dokumenty pervogo vserossiiskogo s''ezda finno-ugorskikh narodov (Izhevsk, 16 maia 1992 g.), in S.M. Chervonnaia & M.N. Guboglo, eds. *Probuzhdeniie finno-ugorskogo severa: Tom 1. Natsional'nye dvizheniia Marii El* (Moskva: RAN, 1996), 246–7.

[37] One of the most outspoken nationalists was then Prime Minister V. Khudiaev, who in 1989 published a short article called 'In the Soviets—only Komi', in which he demanded all deputies to the USSR and Komi ASSR Soviets be Komi nationals, and deputies to local soviets 'principally Komi nationals'. Heads of local administrations, enterprises, institutions, and organizations in the republic should all be Komi as well. Reprinted in Shabaev & Guboglo, 113–14.

[38] McFaul & Petrov, 66–74.

[39] Boris Zheleznov, Doctor of Law, Member RAN and Honoured Scientist of the Republic of Tatarstan, author's interview, 6 June 1997, Law Faculty, Kazan' State University. Zheleznov was a member of the Tatarstan Constitutional Commission. He later worked on the Commission for Constitutional Surpervision.

In Bashkortostan, the October Events also seem to have played a role in system change. The current bicameral parliament was a last minute creation. A Constitutional Commission was formed by resolution of the Supreme Soviet (chaired by the current president, Murtaza Rakhimov) one week after the republic declared sovereignty in October 1990, and was unsurprisingly top-heavy with nomenklatura.[40] Nominally chaired by Rakhimov, the editor-author (*otvetstvennyi redaktor*) was actually Zufar Yenikeev, who completed four preliminary drafts (dated 1991, 30 March 1992, 1 June 1992, and 1 November 1993) before acceptance of the final version on 24 December 1993.[41] These preliminary drafts foresaw the maintenance of a unicameral parliament composed of deputies elected by single-seat territorial (i.e. not administrative-territorial) districts; the second, third, and fourth drafts stipulated that all deputies worked on a permanent basis (by the fourth draft specifically ruling out any other state service).[42] All of this changed with the October Events. After three years of work and fifty-four days after a meeting to discuss the draft composed *prior* to the October Events, a rewritten draft established not only a bicameral legislature but also created two types of electoral districts (territorial districts with one deputy each, and administrative-territorial districts with two deputies each), the latter with a 'non-professional' corps of deputies. Perhaps not coincidentally, on 4 November 1993 (three days after its Constitutional Commission reconvened to scrap the previous four draft constitutions) the Bashkir Supreme Soviet repealed a year-long moratorium on all republican elections and decided to conduct presidential elections, suspended since November 1991.[43] Via these elections, on 12 December 1993, Murtaza Rakhimov changed his position from Chairman of the Supreme Soviet to President

[40] 'Postanovlenie Verkhovnogo Soveta Bashkirskoi SSR: Ob obrazovanii Konstitutsionnoi Komissii Bashkirskoi SSR', *Sovetskaia Bashkiriia*, 18 Oct. 1990, No. 237, p. 2. There were 63 members of the commission: 26 People's Deputies, 16 members of the Supreme Soviet, 5 members of the Council of Ministers, 2 Supreme Court justices, Procurator, Chief State Arbitrator, Chairman of the Committee for State Security (KGB), member of the Committee for Constitutional Supervision, the chair of the presidium of the College of Advocates and 14 academics (7 of these held law degrees or were members of the BGU Law Faculty).

[41] F.M. Raianov, professor & former dean, Law Faculty BGU, member of Constitutional Commission, author's interview, 30 April 1997, Law Faculty BGU, Ufa. V.K. Samigullin, former legal adviser to the Supreme Soviet, member of Constitutional Commission, *dotsent*, Law Faculty BGU, author's interview, 30 April 1997, Law Faculty BGU, Ufa. Zufar Yenikeev, Chairman of the Committee on Local Power Issues, National Questions, Social and Religious Communities, doctor of law, author's interview, 6 and 8 May 1997, Kuraltai, Ufa.

[42] Copies of these drafts, provided to the author by Zufar Yenikeev, show editorial comments, crossed out clauses and numerous hand-written additions and corrections. For an official history, written when a unicameral legislature was still expected to prevail, *see* V. K. Samigullin *Konstitutsiia Respubliki Bashkortostan (voprosy teorii)* (Ufa: Bashkirskii Gosudarstvennyi Universitet, 1993).

[43] McFaul & Petrov, Carnegie, 82–98.

of the Republic. Twelve days later, led by its Chairman-turned-President, Bashkortostan changed from a parliamentary system to a strongly presidential system.

2. REPUBLICAN ELECTIONS

2.1 Presidential Elections

Between 1991 and 1999, the nineteen presidential republics examined here have held twenty-eight successful direct presidential elections.[44] In five republics, seven uncontested elections have been held, ensuring victory for the incumbent every time.[45] In seven elections (not entirely overlapping these uncontested races), the victor won with more than 85 per cent of the votes. In fourteen elections, half of the total number of elections, the winner's share was more than 70 per cent of the votes cast. In eleven out of nineteen republics, the current president occupied the leading Party and/ or top government post in 1990.[46] Even republics that previously rejected *nomenklatura* incumbents in contested elections can still produce surprising results. In 1991, the hold of the Party apparat was broken in Mordova when, after two rounds of elections contested by eight candidates, the presidency was won by a non-incumbent. Mordova held its second presidential election in February 1998. Despite temperatures dipping to −30°C. on election day, the republic's Central Election Commission certified Nikolai Merkushkin (a former *obkom* Second Secretary, i.e. a high-ranking Communist Party official in the region) the winner: voter participation was recorded at 75

[44] Successful meaning sufficient voter turnout resulting in a majority vote for one candidate. In several cases, either participation thresholds were not met, no candidate received more than 50 per cent of the vote, or an indirect election took place (a parliament or constitutional assembly choosing the executive). In addition to the Chechen Republic of Ichkeria, excluded from this study, the Republic of Udmurtia is also not counted, as it has a parliamentary system.

[45] Tatarstan (1991, 1996), Ingushetia (1993, 1994), Karelia (1994), Kalmykia (1995), Kabardino-Balkaria (1997).

[46] It should be emphasized that this number reflects presidents who were *directly* elected by the *general electorate* of the republic. If *indirectly* elected presidents are included (i.e. elected by the legislature), then the list of republics grows to 13: the last two indirectly elected leaders of the Altai republic were Vladilen Volkov (former 2nd *obkom* secretary and deputy chairman of the Supreme Soviet) and his predecessor Valerii Chaptynov (Chairman from 1992 to his death in 1997); Vladimir Khubiev of Karachevo-Cherkessia was appointed by Yeltsin in April 1995 and then approved by the People's Assembly of the Republic. He has held executive power (as Chairman of the Soviet executive committee, head of the administration and Chairman of the Assembly) continuously since 1979; Magomedali Magomedov, Chairman of the State (née Supreme) Soviet of Dagestan, was uncontestedly elected head of the republic's 14-member presidency by a special Constitutional Assembly in 1990 and 1994.

per cent, with 96 per cent of the vote for Merkushkin. His nearest competitor received 4 per cent of the vote. Few believed the result an accurate barometer of either candidate's support.[47] Merkushkin, who between these two popular elections had won the presidency in 1995 via an uncontested indirect vote by the republic's Constitutional Assembly, had utilized all of the powers of his brief incumbency to secure his re-election. As Table 7.6 shows, Merkushkin was not unique in his high electoral results or his incumbency.

In the fifteen republics that held first-time presidential elections between 1991 and 1994, twelve elections produced victories for the Soviet incumbent, that is, the then Chairman of the Supreme Soviet or Council of Ministers.[48] If exceptions are made for Kalmykia and Ingushetia, where incumbents did not run for the office, in only two cases did non-incumbents win elections (Mordova and Chuvashia). Table 7.7 presents these results.

In other words, 85 per cent of the time the men who chaired the bodies responsible for creating the post of president became its first office-holder.

Table 7.6   Overview of Presidential Election Results in Selected Republics

Over 85% of the vote			Over 70% of the vote			
Republic/year	Winner	Vote (%)	Republic/Year		Winner	Vote (%)
Ingushetia 1993	**R. Aushev**	**99.9**	Tyva	1992	Sh. Oorzhak	83.2
Tatarstan 1996	**M. Shaimiev**[a]	**97.1**	Sakha	1991	M. Nikolaev	76.7
Mordova 1998	N. Merkushkin	96.6	Buriatia	1996	L. Potopov	71.7
Ingushetia 1994	**R. Aushev**	**94.2**	Buriatia	1994	L. Potopov	71.1
Kabadino-Balkaria 1997	**V. Kokov**	**93.0**	Tyva	1997	Sh. Oorzhak	70.6
Kabardino-Balkaria 1992	V. Kokov	88.9	**Tatarstan 1991**		**M. Shaimiev**[a]	70.6
Kalmykia 1995	**K. Ilumzhinov**	**88.3**	Bash-kortostan 1998		M. Rakhimov	70.2

Note: Entries in **bold** indicate an uncontested election.

[a] Tatarstan's Mintimer Shaimiev won a third term as president on 25 March 2001. The official result was 79.52% for Shaimiev. His nearest competitor received 5.78% of the vote. Elena Tregubova, 'Mintimer Shaimiev poshel na chetvertyi srok', *Kommersant''-daily,* 27 March 2001, 2.

[47] Natal'ia Gorodetskaia, 'Glava Mordovii b'et rekordy', *Segodnia,* 17 Feb. 1998, 3.
[48] The case of the Altai republic is peculiar, in that it retained a parliamentary system until 1997. However, its head of state, V.I. Chaptynov, is included in this list as he won elections to the Supreme Soviet (where he was repeatedly elected chairman and therefore head of state) and election to the Federal Assembly in 1993. He died in office in August 1997 shortly after the post of president had been introduced in a new constitution. Thus, he certainly qualifies as both a Soviet-era incumbent and a successful candidate in elections the rules of which he helped to establish.

Table 7.7   Soviet-era Incumbents

Republic	Incumbent	Previous position
Adygeia	A. Dzharimov	*Obkom* 1st Secretary, Chairman Oblast Soviet
Altai	V.I. Chaptynov*	*Obkom* 1st Secretary, Chairman of Supreme Soviet
Bashkortostan	M. Rakhimov	Chairman of Supreme Soviet
Buriatia	L. Potopov	*Obkom* 1st Secretary, Chairman of Supreme Soviet
Dagestan	M. Magomedov	Chairman of Supreme Soviet *Obkom* 1st Secretary
Kabardino-Balkaria	V. Kokov	Chairman of Supreme Soviet
Karelia	V. Stepanov	Chairman of Supreme Soviet
Komi	Yu. Spirodonov	*Obkom* 1st Secretary, Chairman of Supreme Soviet
N. Ossetia (Alania)	A. Galazov	*Obkom* 1st Secretary, Chairman of Supreme Soviet
Sakha	M. Nikolaev	Chairman of Supreme Soviet
Tatarstan	M. Shaimiev	Chair of Council of Ministers, Chairman of Supreme Soviet
Tyva	Sh. Oorzhak	Chair of Council of Ministers

*Died in office (see note 48).

These data suggest that many republican electoral systems were designed to produce precisely such results. What evidence supports such a hypothesis of *systemic* or *structural manipulation* of the electoral process? If constitutions are viewed as the formal 'rules of the game' played by political elites, then election procedures are among their most crucial components, providing new players with entrance into the political arena and incumbents with mechanisms, in the worst case, to close those entrances. As Richard Rose notes in his analysis of electoral options, 'the selection of a particular system is much influenced by what it is instrumentally expected to produce. . . . Elections may decide who governs, but constitutions decide what the government is'.[49] Design of the 'rules of the game' provides a significant advantage to political elites. Election rules regulate party formation and campaign activity prior to an election, voting and counting procedures on election day, and post-election procedures for accusations of fraud and recounts. The effect of election rules invariably extends far beyond any particular election, not only in terms of

[49] Richard Rose, 'Elections and electoral systems: choices and alternatives', in *Democracy and Elections: Electoral systems and their political consequences*, Vernon Bogdanor & David Butler eds. (Cambridge University Press, 1983), 20.

the policies of the victor but also in terms of democratic legitimacy. As Linz and Stepan have argued, 'Repeated surveys in democracies show that at the apex of a hierarchy of democratic legitimacy are the overall democratic processes (e.g. elections, multiple parties, and free speech)'.[50]

An election authority, the Central Election Commission (CEC), is often established in republican constitutions.[51] By federal law, this body is jointly responsible with the federal CEC for the guarantee of electoral rights; in recent practice, however, CECs in different republics operate with almost complete autonomy from the centre.[52] Central Election Commissions establish the boundaries of electoral districts, compose electoral registers, vet and register potential candidates, adjudicate disputes during campaigns, ensure the free and fair operation of polling stations on election day, count the final ballot and announce the results.

With regard to presidential elections, the candidate's first hurdle is registration. Although procedures vary, a universal aspect of registration is the provision of signature lists in support of candidacy: a minimum threshold number of signatures is required. Federal law does not set a standard threshold, leaving this to the republics to decide. In addition, 'protocols' of support from the candidate's electoral bloc or association and a certain number of assemblies of voters are required. In Sakha, for example, signatures from 5 per cent of the population must be gathered from at least seven of the thirty-three districts (there called *ulusses*) of the republic. In Bashkortostan, 2 per cent of the population must sign for a candidate, with no more than 3 per cent of the signatures coming from any one district.

As discussed earlier in this chapter, several republics require potential candidates to prove ability in the titular language as a condition of registration. Although such a condition is inherently discriminatory, it is often advanced as a means to ensure inter-ethnic harmony and equal representation. This rule has been repeatedly contested in different republics by mono-lingual candidates and has been ruled unconstitutionally vague by the RF Constitutional Court

---

[50] Linz & Stepan, 438.

[51] 13 of 18 constitutions examined with regard to elections and electioneering (excluding Altai, Chechnya and Chuvashia) note nomination or confirmation of the CEC as a power of the executive and/or the legislature. In Adygeia and Dagestan the legislature is given exclusive power to appoint the CEC. In Tatarstan, half its composition is chosen by the president (including the CEC chairman) and half by the chairman of the State Council. In other republics, the constitution vaguely grants the legislature the power to confirm the CEC (Bashkortostan, Buriatia, Ingushetia, Mordova, N. Ossetia [Alania], Sakha) without specifying who is responsible for its nomination. Federal law requires no less than 1/2 of the composition of regional CECs to be determined by the legislative branch of the respective federal unit (Art. 13, §2) *See* below, note 52.

[52] Art. 12, §5 & 6. No. 56-FZ, 6 December 1994, 'Ob osnovnykh garantiiakh izbiratel'nykh prav grazhdan Rossiiskoi Federatsii', *Sobranie zakonodatel'stva Rossiiskoi Federatsii*, No. 32, item 3406, p. 4855. A revision of this law has since been made. For its analysis, see Joseph Middleton, 'The New Russian Law on Electoral Rights', 7 *East European Constitutional Review*, 3 (1998): 59–63.

(see Chapter Six). In some republics, minimum and maximum age limits have been set and proof of a minimum number of years resident in the republic required. In Sakha, the republic with the strictest requirements, only native-born citizens may compete to become president.[53] Other requirements regard sources and reporting of election funds, use of the mass media and 'pre-election agitation' (i.e. campaigning). As might be expected, all of these requirements follow a strict timetable for compliance.

Requirements are defended as protections for the electorate against frivolous candidates and campaign trickery. Everything from signature lists to campaign funds must be disclosed to ensure that only serious candidates compete, that they compete fairly, and that they are not the puppets of wealthy vested interests. In fact, registration requirements have provided excuses for incumbents to disqualify candidates widely regarded as legitimate candidates and, more importantly, serious threats to the incumbent office-holder. The very rules which are purported to prevent campaign fraud have been utilized to steer election campaigns to the advantage of incumbents. Even if a candidate is registered and allowed to run, the delays and problems caused his campaign may be all but insurmountable. An unregistered candidate, even while appealing the decision of the CEC, is forbidden to campaign, spend campaign funds or utilize the state-controlled mass media. Delays may continue so far into the campaign that success in court is an illusory victory at best; even if time remains to print the candidate's name on ballot papers, there may no longer be enough time to campaign adequately. If electoral rules and commissions can be manipulated with sufficient mastery, election day may be conducted with the utmost decorum and integrity, free from crude frauds like ballot stuffing. Through structural fraud, an election can be won long before election day. The Bashkortostan presidential election of 1998 may serve as an example. Another example of such practices—and of the authoritarian regime that is both a cause and effect of them—is found in Kalmykia, discussed at the end of this chapter.

Excursus: The June 1998 Bashkir Presidential Elections

Presidential elections were held in Bashkortostan on 14 June 1998. The incumbent president, Murtaza Rakhimov, an ethnic Bashkir, had been Chairman of the Bashkir Supreme Soviet from 1990 to 1993, after which

---

[53] Art. 66, *Konstitutsiia (osnovnoi zakon) Respubliki Sakha*. In addition, candidates must be bilingual in Russian and Sakha, have lived without interruption in the republic not less than 15 years and be between the ages of 40 and 60.

he was elected president in a direct contested election.[54] The June date was six months earlier than expected, Rakhimov's term not officially over until December. The election date proved to be among the first issues in the campaign: Rakhimov's critics charged (and unsuccessfully pursued in the courts) that Rakhimov had deliberately accelerated the election cycle. Had the vote been held in December he would have been ineligible to run due to age. The RF Central Election Commission's (CEC) ruling that early elections were unlawful was ignored by the Bashkir State Assembly and republican CEC.[55] When the campaign season officially began that spring, three serious opponents emerged: Aleksandr Arinin, an ethnic Russian and a RF Duma deputy with democratic credentials; former candidate and banker Rafis Kadyrov, Bashkir; and Marat Mirgaziamov, Bashkir, the former prime minister and at that time director of a plastics factory in Ufa. In addition, Rif Kazakkulov, Rakhimov's own Minister of Forestry, later declared his candidacy, for reasons to be explored below.

The rules for the election were outlined in the Constitution and, in greater detail, in a Code on Elections. The right to become a candidate was limited to citizens of the republic between the age of thirty-five and sixty-five who had lived in the republic for not less than one year and who spoke the Bashkir and Russian languages. To be registered as a candidate, one was required to collect signatures from not less than 2 per cent of the total republican electorate, with no more than 3 per cent of these signatures acquired from any particular city or district. The prospective candidate was required to declare all revenue and property held in the last two years and form an election fund.[56] Election would require an absolute majority of the votes cast by at least 50 per cent of the electorate, with a run-off between the top two contenders if necessary. To be valid, there had to be at least two candidates. The Bashkir CEC was given the authority to register candidates, adjudicate on violations of the electoral rules, oversee the campaign and election and to

---

[54] The first election was held 12 December 1993. With voter turnout of 70.5 per cent, Rakhimov soundly defeated Rafis Kadyrov, a local banker, 64 per cent to 28 per cent. A short time after the elections, Kadyrov was fined by a local court for publicly insulting an official (Rakhimov) during the course of the campaign. McFaul & Petrov, 94. More than one Bashkir citizen has told the author that, following the election, banking in Bashkortostan suddenly became extremely difficult for Kadyrov and that pressure exerted by the government ultimately convinced him to leave for Moscow.

[55] Viktor Banev, 'Bashkirskii variant presidentskoi izbiratel'noi kampanii', *Nezavisimaia gazeta*, 17 June 1998, 4. Laura Belin, 'Bashkortostan Court Validates Presidential Election', 2 *RFE/RL Newsline*, 136, Part I, 17 July 1998. Laurie Belin, 'Supreme Court Overturns Bashkortostan Court on Presidential Election', 2 *RFE/RL Newsline*. 140, Part I, 23 July 1998.

[56] Arts. 39, 81, 82, 83. *Kodeks Respubliki Bashkortostan o vyborakh*, 1 September 1997 (Ufa: Redaktsionno-izdatel'skii otdel Sekretariata Gosudarstvennogo Sobraniia Respubliki Bashkortostan, 1997), 37, 81–4. The Code was also reprinted in full in *Izvestiia Bashkortostana*, 25 Mar. 1998, 1–4.

count the ballots. It was composed of fourteen members, seven chosen by the president and seven by the State Assembly.[57]

The first significant conflict in the race was resolved not by the CEC but by the Russian Federation Constitutional Court. In an attempt to remove Arinin from competition, even before he had registered as an official candidate, Rakhimov demanded that all candidates take a test in the Bashkir language, in keeping with the Constitution and election law of the republic. The Court ruled that Arinin could not be disqualified on the basis of language skills, *not* because such a requirement was deemed unconstitutional, but because no legislation had been passed to set a standard of proficiency for the vague wording of the rule. This would be the first of four attempts to remove Arinin, Rakhimov's most serious opponent, from the race.

Over March and April the candidates gathered signatures. Their supporters fanned out across the republic with official CEC forms (which required the name, address and passport number of the voter alongside a dated signature in order to be valid) to begin the time-consuming process of proving sufficient popular support to warrant candidacy. This was not made any easier by heads of district administrations, all of whom were appointed by President Rakhimov. 'In Chekmagush *raion* [district] there was an incident', recalled Sergei Fufaev, one of Arinin's advisers:

A group of five people searching for signatures, a woman and some young people, went to present themselves to the raion administration and were told that it was prohibited to collect signatures because the raion soviet had passed a resolution that the entire raion supported Rakhimov and therefore gathering signatures here [for other candidates] is forbidden.[58]

Such examples were supported by independent journalists, who noted that local populations were easily intimidated with threats to their families and jobs.[59] 'Rakhimov's has turned out to be a very big presidential vertical line',

[57]   Baryi Kinzyagulov, Chairman of the Bashkir Central Election Commission, interview by Jeff Kahn & Tomila Lankina, 14 June 1998, Kurultai, Ufa. President Rakhimov had extensive indirect powers over the composition of the State Assembly; it is safe to assume he influenced the selection of more than just his 7 members.

[58]   Sergei Fufaev, interview by Jeff Kahn & Tomila Lankina, 14 June 1998, Arinin Campaign Headquarters, Ufa. In an article a few weeks later, Fufaev extended the charge to include many other districts: '... the police were engaged in a real hunt for activists of groups of supporters of Aleksandr Arinin and Marat Mirgaziamov.... They intimidated signature collectors with punishments, threw them out of the districts, seizing beforehand the signature lists. Their activities the police ingenuously explained are because local powers gave instructions to support only the candidacy of Rakhimov and to sign for all the rest is forbidden'. Sergei Fufaev, 'Glavnym "izbiratelem" v bashkirii stal militsioner: Mestnoe MVD khorosho porabotalo na Rakhimova', *Nezavisimaia gazeta*, 27 June 1998, 4.

[59]   One student volunteer, Gulnaz Ahmetzianova, reported: 'I had been collecting signatures against Rakhimov in my home village. Then, one night, about twenty policemen drove up in five

said one, confirming Fufaev's story almost verbatim.[60] By the end of April, Arinin, Mirgaziamov and Kadyrov were ready to register. In Arinin's case, another procedural delay had to be overcome before his application could come under scrutiny. Arinin was registered on the 29 April. The following morning, however, his headquarters received an order to come to the CEC at noon. Fufaev: 'Our people went at the appointed hour, waited two hours, waited still two more hours and finally at five in the evening on 30 April we received a decree about the cancellation of the decision to certify'. The reason? On 29 April the CEC had lacked a quorum of members, and was therefore incapable of registering anybody.[61]

Subsequently re-registered, Arinin's signature lists were carefully scrutinized, along with those offered by Mirgaziamov and Kadyrov. According to the chairman of the CEC, 56,500 signatures were required (2 per cent of the population) for registration. Kadyrov, offering his lists to the CEC on 4 May, was denied registration four days later after 3,724 of the 58,352 signatures deposited were deemed 'not authentic' or in violation of the recording procedure, leaving him 4.3 per cent shy of the necessary total.[62] Arinin, whose lists of more than 60, 000 signatures were deposited 29 April, was declared on 4 May to have been 7.2 per cent short of valid signatures, despite having more signatures than required.[63] Mirgaziamov was likewise dispatched, along with Kadyrov on 8 May, leaving only the president and his Minister of Forestry, Rif Kazakkulov—just enough registered candidates to continue with plans for the election, 41 days away.[64] All of the opposition candidates accused Rakhimov of using the powers of his office to intimidate voters into removing their names from petitions.

cars. They went from house to house demanding to know whom everyone had signed for and why'. Ahmetzianova says her father, a collective farm worker, was threatened with loss of his job and loss of his daughter's place at university. Mark Franchetti, 'Yeltsin's pet dictator puts the revolution on hold', *The Sunday Times*, 7 June 1998, 22.

[60] Independent journalist (name withheld by the author), interview by Jeff Kahn & Tomila Lankina, 13 June 1998, Ufa.

[61] Interview with Sergei Fufaev, 14 June 1998. Alexandra Utkina, 'Alexander Arinin Calls Glaring Violation of Democratic Election Procedure the Decision by Bashkiria's Central Election Commission on Cancelling his Registration as Presidential Nominee', *RIA Novosti*, 6 May 1998, Issue 081.

[62] 'Vybory. Postanovlenie tsentral'noi izbiratel'noi komissii respubliki bashkortostan ob otkaze v registratsii kandidata na dolzhnost' prezidenta respubliki bashkortostan R.F. Kadyrova', Bashinform, Ufa, 14 May 1998.

[63] Aleksandra Poryvaeva, Irina Nagornykh, Maksim Zhukov, 'Deputata Dymy lishili prava ballotirovat'sia v prezidenty', *Kommersant''-daily*, 7 May 1998, 5. 'Vybory: V isbiratel'noi kampanii Aleksandra Arinina okazalos' slishkom mnogo prokolov', *Bashinform*, Ufa, 15 May 1998.

[64] Aleksandra Poryvaeva, 'Rakhimov izbavliaetsia ot poslednikh konkurentov', *Kommersant''-daily*, 12 May 1998, 5.

Police from the MVD and OMON were alleged to be calling on voters late at night, pressuring them to retract their signatures from petitions.[65]

All three candidates appealed to the Bashkir Supreme Court, which rejected their complaints. Undeterred, the candidates separately petitioned the Federal Supreme Court which, with only eleven days left to the campaign, declared that Arinin had been illegally de-registered and must be allowed to compete.[66] The other candidates continued to wait. But even if they were ultimately returned to the ballot, their chances had been drastically diminished. 'Who has the right to campaign? That right both according to federal law and according to our [Election] code in synonymous language is *only* for registered candidates. Before the moment of registration the candidate does not have the right to print in the mass media of the republic for free, on the TV or radio.'[67] In the meantime, Rakhimov had used his position to barnstorm the republic, doling out gifts and patronage. Only Rakhimov's campaign posters appeared on city streets, only his face and voice on television and radio. On airline flights from Moscow, stewardesses distributed his campaign brochures.[68]

Attempts to influence voters using private funds was extremely difficult. There is virtually no mass media not controlled by the state. Articles alleging official corruption were enough to close down the paper *Vechernaya Neftekamsk* in April.[69] An independent journalist who works on several of these newspapers summarized the situation in the capital on the eve of the election:

There was a newspaper *Ekonomika i my* under Kadyrov and this they finished off. There was a Tatar national newspaper *Idi Ural* and now it is published as a hand-written manuscript. The newspaper *Vmeste* was closed three times in 1991, three times it closed. The last reason was that we were subpoenaed because we didn't have our information [publisher, address, etc.] in the proper place in the newspaper.... There is the newspaper *Otechestvo*. It is published outside the republic. There are lots of examples with this newspaper thanks to the police. When they [the police] said that

[65] Interview with Sergei Fufaev, 14 June 1998. Such an accusation is extremely difficult to confirm and was denied by the authorities. However, this author was told by numerous citizens in Bashkortostan of their own experiences. On more than one occasion, such information was volunteered, not solicited in interview, with virtually identical scenarios described.

[66] Chloe Arnold, 'Court Orders Arinin Put Back On Ballot', *The Moscow Times*, 5 June 1998.

[67] Interview with Baryi I. Kinzyagulov, Chairman, Bashkir CEC, 14 June 1998.

[68] Chloe Arnold, 'Bashkortostan Chief Set To Sweep Election', *The Moscow Times*, 11 June 1998. Franchetti, 'Yeltsin's Pet Dictator', 22. Franchetti includes a picture of the aerial campaign phenomenon.

[69] David McHugh, 'Bashkiria Leader Accused of Blocking Election Bid', *The Moscow Times*, 8 May 1998.

they had gotten a call that there was a bomb at our editorial office, they came, they expelled everyone, 'We will search for the bomb', and they confiscated our whole circulation and they left.... Viktor Shmakov began to print [Otechestvo] in Chelyabinsk oblast. Rakhimov personally went there, came to an agreement with the local administration and they banned it.[70]

Nor was radio an option. Altaf Galeev, the owner of Radio Titan, the only independent radio station in Ufa, perhaps thought that his links to 'Voice of America' would allow him freedom to interview the opposition on the air. In the middle of an interview in May the power to the station was cut. Galeev was arrested and jailed until his trial, scheduled for February 1999.[71] Televised interviews with Arinin from Moscow were replaced with local programmes.[72] Only Rakhimov appeared routinely.

On 3 June, the RF Supreme Court ordered Arinin's registration reinstated and, following orders, the Bashkir CEC re-registered him on 5 June. On 6 June, Arinin was de-registered a third time for failure to declare an election fund. When the author asked Arinin if it was true that he did not have an election fund, he agreed, laughing: 'My election fund is absent because there was not a need to stipulate [one], for I didn't begin the campaign. I didn't turn out even one poster, not one leaflet, because there was no need, for they didn't register me'.[73] Arinin was disqualified eight days before the election for failure to declare funds his previous de-registrations had prevented him from using. The Bashkir CEC, rather than disqualify Arinin once for numerous alleged violations had cleverly chosen to space the accusations over the course of the campaign season. Even had Arinin been allowed to remain registered, there was another problem: according to the chairman of the Bashkir CEC, *at no time during the campaign had ballots ever been printed with names other than those of Rakhimov or Kazakkulov.*[74]

Though members of the federal CEC had come to Bashkortostan for three days during the campaign, none were in the republic on election day. There were no election monitors from other Russian or international sources and Duma deputies that Arinin had asked to observe the elections declined the

---

[70] Interview with independent journalist (name withheld by the author), Ufa, 13 June 1998.

[71] Franchetti, 'Yeltsin's Pet Dictator', 22. 'Old Russian Habits Die Hard', *The Economist*, 23 Jan. 1999, 42. Exactly two months to the day after the elections, journalist and Arinin adviser Sergei Fufaev was attacked and beaten by three assailants whom, he reports, told him to 'get away from Bashkortostan'. Fufaev labelled the attack an act of 'political terrorism'. Paul Goble, 'Journalist Attacked in Bashkortostan', *RFE/RL Newsline*, Vol. 2, No. 157, Part I, 17 Aug. 1998.

[72] Arnold, 'Court Orders', 5 June 1998.

[73] Aleksandr Arinin, RF Duma Deputy and candidate for Bashkir presidency, interview by Jeff Kahn & Tomila Lankina, 14 June 1998, Arinin Campaign Headquarters, Ufa.

[74] Baryi Kinzyagulov, Kurultai, Ufa, 14 June 1998. In an effort to get a truthful answer to this question, I posed a hypothetical case to Kinzyagulov, asking what would happen to an absentee

offer once Arinin was again de-registered. Asked if he found it disturbing that there were no federal observers present, former candidate Marat Mirgazia-mov smiled, 'Why aren't there any [election observers]? Because there were no candidates to see'.[75] At polling station No. 173 in Ufa, Rif Kazakkulov, still serving as Minister of Forestry and sole remaining opposition candidate, cast his ballot on election day morning. Perhaps only half in jest, he asked report-ers, 'But why have you decided that I am voting for myself?'[76]

Thirty-six hours after the polls closed, results had been compiled from every district in the republic (which is roughly the size of France) except from four districts. Each reporting district recorded clear victories for Rakhimov. Strangely, the four districts that had yet to report were city districts in Ufa, where the president's support was weakest and the Russian population high. No explanation was given as to why these particular four, walking distance from the CEC, should have remained unavailable when results from the far corners of the republic had found their way to the CEC. Three other Ufa city districts were tallied, all with favourable results for Rakhimov, but also showing a high protest vote 'Against All Candidates' ranging from 33 to 36 per cent. In Salavat, a large industrial centre with a high Russian population, the unofficial protest vote rose to 38 per cent.[77] Official newspapers reported the preliminary results two days later: with 69.8 per cent partici-pation, Rakhimov had won 70.2 per cent, 'Against All Candidates' had taken 17.1 per cent of the vote and Kazakkulov took third place with 9.0 per cent.[78]

2.2 Parliamentary Elections

Between 1991 and 1999, over twenty-five republican parliamentary elections were held. Some elections have been plagued with low voter turnout. The

---

ballot cast for Arinin and mailed to the CEC 15 days prior to the election (possible under federal law). Without pausing to think, Kinzyagulov quickly replied that that would be impossible, because only Rakhimov's and Kazakkulov's names had ever been printed on ballots. When I said that his answer implied that as much as two weeks before the election the CEC already seemed to know that neither Arinin nor any other candidate would ever be re-registered, Kinzyagulov recounted a long tale of telegrams allegedly sent to polling stations in these final days warning that the elections might have to be suspended for that very reason.

[75] Marat Mirgaziamov, candidate for Bashkir presidency and former Prime Minister Republic of Bashkortostan, interview by Jeff Kahn & Tomila Lankina, 15 June 1998, Factory Complex AO 'Uzemik', Ufa.

[76] Gennadii Bassov, et al. 'Respublika vybrala prezidenta', Izvestiia Bashkortostana, 16 June 1998, 1.

[77] Official preliminary tally sheets were provided by Yurii Afanasiev from the Presidential Administration. The four non-reporting city districts (Demskii, Oktiabr'skii, Ordzhonikidzevskii, and Sovetskii) were areas of higher Russian concentration which had been considered by Arinin's supporters to be favourable for their candidate.

[78] Official preliminary results were reported in Sovetskaia Bashkiriia and Izvestiia Bashkortostana, both 16 June 1998.

Chuvash elections begun in March 1994 were followed by seven rounds of elections over the course of two years in an attempt to fill a forty-seven seat parliament. What profiles emerge of successful candidates? How have elections differed, in their formats and results? And, as alluded above, what is the involvement of the seemingly omnipresent (and omnipotent) executive branch?

Although low voter participation occasionally results in inconclusive elections, the same malaise does not appear to afflict candidates. Almost 400 candidates ran for a seat in the sixty-five member Buriat Parliament in June 1994; 286 candidates registered for the January 1995 election to the fifty member Komi Parliament. Almost 550 candidates sought a place in the 121 member Dagestan parliament in March 1995 and roughly 170 candidates campaigned in the December 1995 elections in Adygeia, a forty-seven seat parliament.[79] If there has been no dearth of elections or candidates, the same cannot be said of political parties. Despite constitutional claims to political pluralism and multiple parties, the number, size, and share in victory of political associations in the republics has been very small. This is true of both federal and republican-based parties. Re-analysing the numbers of candidates in the examples above, well under half (154) of the 398 candidates in Buriatia came out of electoral associations (by which is meant anything from full-fledged all-federal parties to regional or even electoral district action groups). Less than one-fifth of Komi's candidates were sponsored by parties. The number of deputies taking their seats with allegiance to electoral associations is even smaller. In Adygeia, the two largest parties, Communists (thirty-one candidates) and Agrarians (twenty candidates), won only half of their races (fifteen and ten, respectively), a relative success story. In nearby North Ossetia, only ten of the Communist's sixty-four candidates won their seats; the remaining sixty-five seats in the parliament were won by independents. In most republican elections, if there was any significant party activity, the Communists and conservative Agrarian Party of Russia typically fielded the most candidates and won a handful of seats for their troubles. Local parties which emerge are, invariably, the parties of opposition candidates, small and weak.[80] Candidates who either identify themselves or are

---

[79] Data on parliamentary elections is primarily taken from McFaul & Petrov's collection of republican results found primarily in Vol. 2, Book 1 of the *Politicheskii al'manakh Rossii*, 1997, 73, 108, 125, 189.

[80] E. g. Chervonnaia & Guboglo list 12 republican parties in Marii El one month after the parliamentary elections in December 1993. Only three parties have more than 1,000 members, two with more than 300, the rest with less than 50 members. S.M. Chervonnaia & M.N. Guboglo, eds. *Probuzhdenie finno-ugorskogo severa: Tom 2. Natsional'noe dvizhenie Marii El* (Moskva: RAN, 1996), 256–7.

identified with incumbent leaders are implicitly members of the 'party of power', therefore with less need for any party.

Are patterns apparent for other types of classifications? A breakdown of available election results by profession reveals some interesting tendencies across the republics. Many deputies simultaneously occupy another official post in the republic. These posts may be divided into three types: posts within the 'unified system of executive power' (e.g. heads of local administration, deputy ministers, and heads of ministry sub-departments); posts in state-managed industry or agriculture (e.g. collective farms and state enterprises); and, posts in district-level representative assemblies. In 1999, in Bashkortostan, seventy-three of seventy-four heads of administration were also members of the upper house of parliament. In Tatarstan's unicameral State Soviet, forty-two of the forty-three heads of administration were deputies that year. In Kabardino-Balkaria's thirty-six member upper chamber, twelve deputies were heads of administration, nine were heads of state or collective farms, seven were heads of enterprises. Former deputies in Soviet-era legislatures are another recurring category: In Dagestan's 121-seat parliament in 1999, twenty-two deputies were heads of administration, seven were deputy ministers or heads of ministry subsections, thirty were former deputies of the old Supreme Soviet (three of whom are former leaders in the Supreme Soviet), and fifty members were 'economic leaders'.[81] A fuller treatment of this phenomenon is given below.

What sort of ethnic dimension is observed in these election results? Although the disparity between ethnic share of the population and share of seats varies considerably, variance is always in favour of the titular ethnic group (Table 7.8). In the most extreme case, Sakha are disproportionately represented in parliament on a scale of more than two to one, while the ethnic Russians in the republic are represented by a margin of less than one-half to one. The presence of many ethnic groups in Karachaevo-Cherkessia had an unexpected effect. While the larger of the two titular ethnic groups, the Karachai, are over-represented, the smaller Cherkess people are represented on a par with ethnic Russians, although Russians outnumber them by more than four to one.

How does the constitutional design of these institutions encourage or discourage these results? The skewed ethnic composition of these parliaments has several possible explanations. Due to the prevalence of a high percentage of former Soviet *nomenklatura* in the chambers of these parliaments, representation of titular ethnic groups disproportionate to their numbers might be attributed to a holdover effect from the previous regime.

[81] McFaul & Petrov, 95,125, 146, 247.

Table 7.8   Ethnic Composition of Selected Republican Legislatures

Republic	Ethnic Russian		Titular ethnic group		Ratio of seats: population	
Election: No. of seats	Population (%)	Seats in parliament (%)	Population (%)	Seats in parliament (%)	Ethnic Russian	Titular ethnic group
Buriatia (Jun. 1994: 65 seats)	69.9	53.9	24.0	43.1	0.8 : 1	1.8 : 1
North Ossetia (Mar. 1995: 75 seats)	29.9	11.5	53.0	83.6	0.4 : 1	1.6 : 1
Tatarstan (Mar. 1995: 130 seats)	43.3	23.9	48.5	70.0	0.6 : 1	1.4 : 1
Sakha (Dec. 1997: 69 seats)	50.3	20.3	33.4	73.9	0.4 : 1	2.2 : 1
Karachaevo-Cherkessia (Jun. 1995: 73 seats)	42.4	35.6	31.2 (K) 9.7 (C)	38.4 (K) 8.2 (C)	0.8: 1	1.2 : 1 (K) 0.8 : 1 (C)

Note: The number of seats given in the first column reflects seats *won*, not seats *available*, thus the ratios more accurately reflect the actual composition of the parliament.

Source: *Politicheskii al'manakh Rossii, 1997*.

In Soviet times, weak and purely formal structures, such as Supreme Soviets, contained a high number of deputies from the titular ethnic group. Certainly, the parliamentary leadership in many republics is virtually unchanged from its composition in the late 1980s. Another, stronger explanation returns again to the effects of intra-bicameralism: administrative-territorial districts, in contrast to territorial districts, reflect municipal and rural district boundaries, not demographics. This has two effects. First, it results in over-representation of rural districts *vis-à-vis* urban districts. Rural areas tend to have higher concentrations of the titular ethnic group, Russians tending to settle in industrialized urban areas.[82] Over-represented rural areas translates into over-representation of the titular ethnic group. More difficult to quantify is the effect of patronage politics, as ethnic elites are placed in positions of power and authority which may improve their ability to win election to parliament. None of these explanations is mutually exclusive; rather, they are mutually reinforcing.

Only the constitution of Adygeia explicitly excludes heads of administration and other members of the executive branch from service in

[82] E.g. Rural Marii El is 70.1%Marii and 22.7% Russian, while the urban population is 57.5% Russian and 29.2% Marii. Chervonnaia & Guboglo, 250–1. Art. 65 of the Constitution stipulates that one deputy is elected from every district and city of republican significance. There are 14 (rural) districts and 3 such cities in Marii El.

parliament.[83] In the remaining republics with part-time deputies, and even a few which do not distinguish between deputies, few if any restrictions are placed on their full-time profession. In the republics for which data are available on the professional composition of the legislature, only two republics with an executive presence in the legislature do not have parliaments with strong elements of intra-bicameralism. These republics are Kalmykia and Tyva, the peculiarities of whose systems have already been discussed.

Directors of state enterprises and collective farms who seek to become part-time deputies have special advantages. Thanks to their position, they have a strong influence over a captive audience that might range into thousands of citizens. Electoral laws that allow nominations from the workplace obviously work in their favour. These directors, as managers of state property, are responsible to departments within the republican government. These departments invariably fall under the general control of the executive branch. Pressure along this channel may be placed on directors-turned-deputies just as easily as directors may pressure their employees to support their candidacy.

Parliaments with an intra-bicameral element often have an unusually high number of heads of district administration in their composition, made possible by the distinction between part-time and full-time deputies. These heads are considered part of the 'unified system of executive power' to which many republican constitutions refer and, as such, are more often responsible to the president of the republic than to the electorate in their districts. In Adygeia, Bashkortostan, Ingushetia, Mordova, Tatarstan, and Tyva, presidents are granted varying constitutional powers of nomination and dismissal over these officials.[84] Other republics, such as North Ossetia (Alania), while not specifying this power in their constitutions, have subsequently passed laws for the same purpose.[85] It is worth noting that these powers are in addition to the already extensive powers presidents wield over resource distribution and other benefits.

[83] *Konstitutsiia Respubliki Adygeia*, Chapter Four, Art. 65, §3. The President nevertheless has the power to dismiss heads of administration. *See* note 99 below.

[84] Adygeia (Art. 78, §1'), Bashkortostan (Art. 95, §14), Ingushetia (Art. 54, §11), Mordova (Art. 70, §15), Tatarstan (Art. 111, §3; Art. 130). In Adygeia, the president has the power only of dismissal. In Mordova and Tatarstan, the president has the power of nomination of the candidate for confirmation by the local district council. In Bashkortostan and Ingushetia, the president has unbridled powers of appointment and dismissal. In practical terms, these powers have proven more or less equivalent. They have also proven unconstitutional, as is discussed in Ch. 6.

[85] The president of the republic has the power to appoint mayors. 'North Osetiya President Takes Right to Appoint Mayors', 3 *EWI Russian Regional Report Internet Edition*, 46 (19 Nov. 1998). The constitution does not prohibit 'part-time' deputies, stating merely that deputies 'may work in Parliament on a professional permanent basis' (Art. 68, §3). In Kabardino-Balkaria, Article

Table 7.9 shows the growing shares of seats that part-time deputies affiliated with different sections of the executive branch take in republican parliaments. In Bashkortostan, where seventy-three of 188 deputies are heads of administration, a controlling majority of the upper house is controlled by presidential appointees. In Tatarstan, almost a third of deputies are presidentially appointed heads of local administrations (forty-two deputies). Including deputies who may be less directly controlled, but nevertheless part of the 'unified system of executive power', leads presidential influence to skyrocket, the percentages in the final column, reflecting the inclusion of enterprise and collective farm managers in the calculation of influence.[86]

Table 7.9 Shares of Seats of Deputies in Republican Parliaments[a]

Republic & election	No. of deputies	Heads of administration, deputy heads of administration, heads of executive departments (1)	Share of seats (%)	Directors of state enterprises or managers of state farms (2)	Total % share of seats (1) + (2)
Altai (Mar. 1994)	27	15	56	4	70
Bashkortostan (Mar. 1995)	188	104	55	40	77
Buriatia (June 1994)	65	24	37	21	69
Ingushetia (Feb. 1994)	27	5	19	6	41
Kalmykia (Oct. 1994)	27	9	33	6	56
Karelia (Apr. 1994; upper house)	36	6	17	15	58
Komi (Jan. 1995)	50	18	36	15	66
Mordova (Nov. 1994)	75	24	32	20	59
Tatarstan (Mar. 1995)	130	65	50	19	65
Tyva (Dec. 1993)	32	20	63	4	75
Udmurtia (Mar. 1995)	100	31	31	32	63
Chuvashia (Mar. 1994)	47	15	32	11	55

[a] Data from Darrell Slider, 'Elections to Russia's Regional Assemblies', 245–7 (table 1). Some republics have been omitted because of incomplete data or discrepancies with Slider's data.

128 stipulates heads of local administration are elected, not appointed. Article 124 of the Dagestan constitution notes, '... local self-administration enters into a single system of organs of executive power...'. In Komi, Art. 94 suggests a similar interpretation: 'Local administration is the organ of executive power which directly realizes state management... Local administration enters into the system of executive power of the Republic of Komi'.

[86] Data from McFaul & Petrov.

The Russian Federal Constitutional Court has acknowledged the serious-ness of this blurring of the separation of powers.[87] Such high shares of the legislature give the executive a powerful blocking power: super-majorities for constitutional laws and amendments, to override vetoes or to dismiss officials or impeach the president become virtually impossible. Even control of less than a majority of deputies gives the president the power to halt the activity of the legislature by preventing the gathering of a quorum to do business. It may not always be the case that these deputies respond to the executive's orders. The pressure the president is able to exert on recalcitrant deputies will vary according to many factors: the personalities involved, the issues at hand, and the particulars of the relationships between actors. But the conflict of interest for such parliamentarians is strong and unavoidable. It is also much more possible in republics that make the distinction between 'part-time' and 'full-time'.

Heads of local administration, regardless of the degree of presidential control over them, possess important powers with regard to elections: by federal law, heads of local administration are responsible for reports on the number of eligible voters in their districts, to be supplied to the Central Election Commission.[88] In most republics, they are also charged with estab-lishing, together with the local representative council, election commissions for the lowest levels of the electoral system. As seen in the case of the Bashkir presidential elections, their power can extend to closing whole districts to the campaign activists of their opponents. Or, as one observer noted in Tatar-stan:

Political stability in Tatarstan is to a certain extent determined by... heads of district and city administration, who are not elected here but are appointed by President Mintimer Shaimiev. After that they participate in two election procedures—in their local Council and the republic's State Council from their administrative-territorial constituency, that is from the very territorial division they head. Of course, they win both elections, since the local election law does not provide for effective controlling procedures. They immediately become chairmen in local Councils and constitute almost half of the State Council's members. Local Councils and administrations create election commissions and the State Council appoints all the judges. Thus, what comes out is a politically homogenous system, with no place for the opposition.[89]

[87] In May 1998, the Court ordered the end of simultaneous service in the executive and legislative branches in Komi. 'Constitution Watch', 7 *East European Constitutional Review*, 3 (1998): 33.

[88] *Federal'nyi zakon ob osnovnykh garantiiakh izbiratel'nykh prav grazhdan RF*, Chapter Two, Art. 8, §2.

[89] Igor' Kotov, 'Iurist iz Naberezhnykh Chelnov khochet vzorvat' politicheskoe spokoistvie Tatarii', *Segodnya*, 6 June 1997, 2. According to Mary McAuley, a presidential decree issued

3. Assessing Democratization in the Republics: Kalmykia

Republics might be assessed not according to how closely they approximate transitional democracies, but as to how closely they still resemble authoritarian regimes. At this stage, the evidence is considerable that many republics are remotely far from completing a transition to democracy. The 'winner-takes-all' nature of the strong presidentialism exhibited in most of these republics can lead to problems of democratic legitimacy and a polarized political arena. Patronage politics have substituted for republican political parties. Party activity in republican elections is low and weak; presidential 'parties of power' have naturally stunted party activism.[90] More than one student of federalism has remarked on the importance of party systems to the development of different federal governments.[91] Indices of authoritarianism seems to capture the state of these republics far more accurately:

> ... the absence of free elections, the inability of the ruled to hold rulers to account, and the weakness or absence of a rule of law—especially in politically sensitive cases.... Political freedoms are, at best, strictly circumscribed and political opposition is not accorded legitimacy.[92]

An examination of the resemblance of every republic in the Russian Federation to this bleak description is not possible here. But concluding remarks that concentrate on one example is worthwhile, particularly as it displays how many of the problems discussed in this chapter fit together to produce highly undemocratic results.

Students of the regime typology that Linz and Chehabi termed 'sultanism' (classic examples include the Duvaliers' Haiti, Marcos' Philippines, and Ceausescu's Romania) would find much that is familiar in Kalmykia.[93] The republic of Kalmykia, roughly the size of Scotland, is located on the

---

sometime after ratification of the constitution allows heads of local administrations simultaneously to become chairmen of the local soviets (i.e. simultaneously head of the executive and legislative branches of local government). Mary McAuley, *Russia's Politics of Uncertainty* (Cambridge University Press, 1997), 61.

[90] Peter C. Ordeshook, 'Russia's Party System: Is Russian Federalism Viable?' 12 *Post-Soviet Affairs*, 3 (1996): 212.

[91] *See*, in particular, William Riker.

[92] Archie Brown, 'The Study of Totalitarianism and Authoritarianism', in Jack Hayward, Brian Barry & Archie Brown, eds. *The British Study of Politics in the Twentieth Century.* (The British Academy in association with Oxford University Press, 1999), 354.

[93] Juan J. Linz & H.E. Chehabi, 'A Theory of Sultanism: 1. A Type of Non-Democratic Rule', in Juan J. Linz & H.E. Chehabi, eds. *Sultanistic Regimes* (Baltimore: Johns Hopkins, 1998): 3–25. For a briefer description with more emphasis on the contrast with other regime typologies, see Linz & Stepan, 44–5, 51–4.

north-eastern edge of the North Caucasus bordering the Caspian Sea. Almost 320, 000 people live in the republic and they are predominantly Kalmyk (45 per cent) and Russian (37 per cent). Kalmykia is among the poorest of the republics, its steppes turning to desert thanks to a Soviet legacy of overgrazing sheep, which still dominates a stagnating economy.

The President of Kalmykia is Kirsan Nikolaevich Ilumzhinov, at the time of his first election on 11 April 1993 a thirtysomething self-professed multi-dollar millionaire. Ironically, this was the focal point of his campaign; his election slogan was 'A Rich President—Incorruptible Power'.[94] During his campaign, Ilumzhinov promised to make Kalmykia a 'Second Kuwait', every shepherd would receive a mobile phone, and every inhabitant would be given US$100.[95] Ilumzhinov won 65 per cent of the vote, his nearest of two opponents taking 21 per cent. Once in power, he quickly established himself as the centre of power in the republic.

Ilumzhinov oversaw the writing of a new constitution—'the Steppe Code'—promulgated on 5 April 1994 with virtual unanimity (285 out of 287) by a specially convened Constitutional Assembly. Coincidentally, 5 April is Ilumzhinov's birthday—now an official holiday in the republic.[96] Following passage of the Steppe Code and a new law on political parties, independent political activity in the republic for all intents and purposes was placed outside the law. For the registration of a political organization it is necessary to have 3,500 members (1 per cent of the population of the republic). Branches of all-Russian parties do not have the right to present candidates to election to the People's Khural (the republic's legislature), which as a result is virtually party-less.[97] The Steppe Code establishes a twenty-seven-member legislature, one-third of whose deputies are nominated by the President via a special all-republic electoral list, with lower thresholds for voter participation and success than in the eighteen territorial

[94] McFaul & Petrov, 151, 154. In 1993, Ilumzhinov boasted that he was the founder of approximately 50 commercial ventures with annual returns of US$500 million. He is fluent in Japanese and English and is reputed to have made most of his money in import-export ventures through his corporation 'Sun', using his Japanese connections as the Soviet Union crumbled.

[95] Kirsan Ilumzhinov, President of Kalmykia, interview by Jeff Kahn & Andrew Kramer, 30 June 1997, Office of the President, Elista. Ilumzhinov claims he merely suggested that living standards should make Kalmykia a second Kuwait thanks to Caspian Sea oil. Regarding promises of money: 'I said that although the revenue in a month was only 5 or 10 dollars it should be 100 dollars. And I promised that in a month in Kalmykia we will receive up to 100 dollars. That was my programme'. Ilumzhinov noted that journalists would not stop bothering him about this. 'Earth to Kalmykiia, Come in Please', Economist, 20 Dec. 1997, 50.

[96] Interview with Kirsan Ilumzhinov. The President insists that this was a simple coincidence and wholly unintentional.

[97] McFaul & Petrov, 154–5. Ann Sheehy, 'Kalmyk President Renounces Sovereignty of Republic', RFE/RL Research Report, Vol. 3, No. 22 (3 June 1994): 17–18.

districts. The President has sweeping powers of appointment and exclusive powers to create and dissolve any part of the executive branch, including all ministries and departments, and repeal any of its acts. If the legislature three times rejects a bill proposed by the President he may dissolve the legislature.[98]

Two years before the expiration of his first term, and after the Legislative Assembly (now fully under his control) established a new seven-year term for the presidency, Ilumzhinov called for new elections, scheduled for 15 October 1995. The electoral law passed by the Khural on 15 August 1995 established that the elections could be held without alternative candidates, with a participation threshold of 25 per cent of voters. If the candidate were running unopposed, he need only win 15 per cent of the votes. In a quixotic gesture, one opponent, Benbia Khulkhachiev, attempted to run against Ilumzhinov, but at the start his initiative group was refused registration by the republic's Central Election Commission and then by its Supreme Court on the basis that ten of the thirteen protocols of support required from meetings of workers collectives lacked the required stamp, and that in seven cases the meetings had lacked quorums. According to the local election committee, Ilumzhinov nevertheless received 88.3 per cent of the votes with 74.5 per cent attendance. Ballot papers carried his picture, even though he was the only candidate.[99] Although the federal Central Election Committee sharply criticized the law and refused to recognize the elections, no further action was taken. His term now ends in 2002.[100] In a personal interview with the author, the President admitted that he might consider re-election.

According to the Carnegie Center in Moscow: 'The authorities with which the president is endowed do not much differentiate him from a khan. The formation of all branches of power take place with his direct participation, and from there long ago has been banished everyone who displayed even a hint of personal opinion. Chairman of the Government

[98] *Stepnoe ulozhenie (Osnovnoi Zakon) Respubliki Kalmykiia*, Art. 28, §7, 8, 12.
[99] Interview with Kirsan Ilumzhinov. The President said that this was a decision of the republic's Central Election Commission. See also Andrew Kramer, 'Far From Moscow's Reach, Politicians Write Their Own Ticket', *San Francisco Chronicle*, 1997, A10.
[100] McFaul & Petrov, 158. Benbia Khulkhachiev, RF Duma Deputy 1993–5 and opposition candidate to Ilumzhinov, author's interview, 26 June 1997, Hotel Moskva, Moscow. Khulkhachiev says a case was lodged with the RF Constitutional Court, but that action on the case was delayed until after the 1996 RF presidential elections, when the court ruled in his favour, resulting in a change in Kalmykia's election laws. He says that when he asked Sergei Shakrai, then Yeltsin's representative to the RF Constitutional Court, if there would be new elections due to the Court's ruling, Shakrai told him that this was a matter for Kalmykia and its parliament. No new elections were held. See also Aleksei Kirpichnikov, 'Novaia tekhnologiia polnomochnogo predstavitelia: Sergei Mikhailovich Shakhrai protianul Kirsanu Nikolaevichu Iliumzhinonu ruku pomoshchi Borisa Nikolaevicha El'tsina', *Itogi*, 11 Feb. 1997, 18.

Vice-President V. Bogdanov, Chairman of the Khural K. Maksimov, Deputy Chair V. Sergeev to all intents and purposes are representatives of the president in their respective departments'. Ilumzhinov's older brother Vyacheslav is adviser to the president on political questions, his second brother is deputy minister for internal affairs, his brother-in-law Gennadii Aminov is also an adviser to the president.[101] In an interview with the author, the president was asked about his style of rule. Ilumzhinov proceeded to read his day's agenda, which showed meetings with everyone from high cabinet ministers to dispute resolution required by two farms. He took personal credit in convincing his entire cabinet to stop smoking. On 16 February 1998, Ilumzhinov, in a slightly more drastic move, suddenly dissolved his entire government, placing all ministries directly under his supervision.[102] His actions would seem to qualify as unrestrained, arbitrary and an almost wanton personalization of power.

Personalism is found in abundance. In addition to having drafted most of the Steppe Code, Ilumzhinov takes credit for design of the republic's flag. He has published numerous books.[103] His birthday continues to be celebrated as an official state holiday. Alongside the three roads into the capital, Elista, stand enormous billboards, one on each road displaying a large picture of Ilumzhinov alongside the Catholic Pope, the Orthodox Patriarch or the Dalai Lama. In the author's hotel room in Elista a smaller version of the Dalai Lama–Ilumzhinov photograph was pasted to one wall. The President has built a beautiful Buddhist temple (Kalmyks are traditionally Buddhist) on the outskirts of the city and is encouraging a renaissance of Kalmyk culture and traditional religion. Ilumzhinov also has an ideology of his own: 'He subscribes, for example, to a concept called "ethnoplanetary thinking", which was developed for him by Kalmykia's "state secretary for ideology". Schools have been encouraged to adopt a teaching principle called "the enlarging of didactic units", supposedly discovered by a Kalmyk scientist'.[104]

In addition to these efforts, the President has a personal passion for chess, which he has extended to his republic. In November 1995, Ilumzhinov was elected President of the 'Fédération Internationale des Echecs' (FIDE). The FIDE flag flies alongside the Kalmyk and Russian flags at his White House in

---

[101] McFaul & Petrov, 151–2.

[102] Laura Belin, 'Kalmykian President Dissolves Government', *Radio Free Europe/Radio Liberty Newsline*, 2/34, Part I (19 Feb. 1998).

[103] Kirsan N. Ilumzhinov & K.N. Maksimov, *Kalmykia na rybezhe vekov* [*Kalmykia on the Border of Centuries*] (Moskva: Izdatel'stvo 'ZelO', 1997). See also Peter Severtsov, *Kirsan: The Universal President. Kirsan Ilyumzhinov's story in comics* (Moscow: Zarealye, 1996). The cover declares: 'They call him extraordinary, unpredictable, phenomenal. There are many rumours about him. But the truth is much more surprising...'.

[104] *The Economist*, 20 Dec. 1997, 50.

Elista and at the republic's representative office in Moscow. The year before, by presidential decree, chess was made a required subject in Kalmyk secondary schools. On the outskirts of Elista he has ordered the building of a special 'Chess City' in which to host tournaments. These practices seem to fit this characteristic as well: 'The purer a regime's sultanism, the more its ideology is likely to be mere window dressing, elaborated after the onset of the ruler's regime to justify it'.[105]

The Steppe Code utilizes the vocabulary of a constitution to endow the President with virtually unlimited power. His cabinet, the legislature, the judiciary: there are no official positions beyond his reach. In interviews he has allowed himself to be compared to a khan, in reference to the ancient Mongol leaders. 'Consider me the president of Kalmykia Corp.' he has declared.[106] Ilumzhinov seems to maintain, if not a strong social base, then at least a quiescent one.[107]

Opposition to the regime has largely been discredited and political parties, when they operate, do so at a disadvantage that is practically insurmountable. Opposition to Ilumzhinov proved also to be extremely dangerous. The case of Larisa Yudina is the best example.

Larisa Yudina, main editor for the sole opposition newspaper in the republic, *Sovetskaia Kalmykia*, had been an outspoken critic of Ilumzhinov since his first election. In the winter of 1993 she opposed Ilumzhinov, printing his campaign promises alongside harsh criticisms in an effort to reveal the 'emperor's new clothes'. Upon entering office, Ilumzhinov attempted through a variety of channels to strip Yudina of her editorship and the paper.[108] In an interview with the author, Yudina recounted how she learned of a decision to fire her by listening to the radio. Arriving at her office in July 1994, she was confronted by a newly installed editor and plain-clothed

[105]   Linz & Chehabi, 14.
[106]   Interview with Kirsan Ilumzhinov. *See also* David Filipov, 'Regional ruler calls himself "democratic khan"', *The Boston Sunday Globe*, 19 Oct. 1997.
[107]   Interviews with several Kalmyk citizens and members of the opposition brought this point home. Most notably, a collective farm director, who boasted that his *sovkhoz* had a return of 90% for Ilumzhinov at the last election. Just prior to the election, by no coincidence, Ilumzhinov personally had given the director a gift for his farm and its inhabitants, for whom he was responsible: the keys to a new ambulance. Said the director: 'The last winter was *very* hard. Without Ilumzhinov we couldn't have managed. Everyone here knows that it was Ilumzhinov who helped us through the winter—he made sure the roads were clear'. Name of *sovkhoz* director and *sovkhoz* withheld by the author. Interview with Jeff Kahn & Andrew Kramer, 29 June 1997.
[108]   The contest for the newspaper, although extremely revealing of Ilumzhinov's method of rule, is too complicated to retell here. For a sharp commentary and collection of documents relating to the battle, see Aleksei Simonov, *Delo No. 2: Respublika Kalmykiia protiv 'Sovetskoi Kalmykii'* (Moskva: Izdatel'stvo 'Prava cheloveka', 1997). The book was funded by the Glasnost Defence Fund and underwritten by the National Endowment for Democracy.

guards she recognized from the National Bank of Kalmykia. As the battle for the newspaper continued and circulation fell, Ilumzhinov prohibited the paper from being printed in the republic. The newspaper was driven first to Stavropol krai and then to Volgograd, where printing continued sporadically. Yudina: 'He was saying all this time that he wanted to be a khan—this was no joke. He was serious'.[109]

Indeed, things became much more serious. One morning Yudina's family awoke to discover the door to their apartment doused with gasoline and set alight. Threatening phone calls came in the middle of the night. Yudina's husband and a relative suddenly lost their jobs. Repeated letters for help went unanswered from all but a sympathetic, federally appointed procurator, who soon found himself transferred to Moscow. Yudina remembered the moment she realized there was no hope. On a trip to Moscow to appeal to Duma deputies and other officials for help, she happened to see Ilumzhinov on television, playing chess with the federal procurator-general, Yurii Skuratov.

On 8 June 1998, the corpse of Larisa Yudina was found in a wooded area near the Chess City. Almost a dozen stab wounds marked the body. It appeared that she had been lured to a meeting with her assailants by promises of information relevant to a series of articles she was writing on corruption within Ilumzhinov's regime. Her death was immediately denounced as a 'political assassination' by leading Russian democrats, who demanded a federal investigation.[110] Ilumzhinov completely disappeared from view for several days, not appearing as scheduled at a meeting of the Federation Council. By the end of June, four suspects had been arrested for the murder: two convicts, a former assistant to Ilumzhinov and the president's representative in Volgograd oblast. Inexplicably, two of the suspects were released shortly afterwards with the assistance of the Kalmyk presidential administration.[111]

The murder was never solved.

In the early run-up to the 2002 Kalmyk presidential elections, the few remaining opposition figures in the republic have reported receiving death

---

[109] Larisa Yudina, editor 'Sovetskaia Kalmykia', interview with Jeff Kahn & Andrew Kramer, 30 June 1997, Yudina family apartment, Elista.

[110] Stepan Krivosheev, 'Zhurnalistku iz Elisty zarezali v 30 kilometrakh ot doma: Fraktsiia "Iabloko" uzhe nazvala gibel' Larisy Iudinoi politicheskim ubiistvom', *Segodnia*, 10 June 1998, 7. Petr Brantov & Vasilii Gulin, 'V demokraticheskoi Rossii opasno imet' demokraticheskie ubezhdeniia', *Izvestiia*, 11 June 1998, 1. Vladimir Emel'ianenko, 'Olimpiiskii vznos Larisy Iudinoi', *Moskovskie novosti*, 14–21 June 1998, 2–3.

[111] 'In the case of the murder of the journalist Yudina the fourth defendant has been arrested', *Interfax*, 29 June 1998. 'Prosecutor: New Facts Shed Light on Russian Journalist's Murder', *Interfax*, 2 July 1998. *See also* 'Constitution Watch', *East European Constitutional Review*, 7/3 (Summer 1998): 33.

threats that promise them the same fate as Larisa Yudina. Gennadii Yudin, Larisa Yudina's husband and a former editor of *Sovetskaia Kalmykia*, reported in 2001 that Ilumzhinov had succeeded in his takeover of the newspaper. *Sovetskaia Kalmykia*, the former flagship paper of the opposition, now published celebratory photographs of the president in honour of his birthday.[112]

---

[112] Julie A. Corwin, 'Political Opposition Continues to Face Harrassment in Kalmykia', 5 *RFE/RL Newsline*, 37, Part I, 22 Feb. 2001. Julie A. Corwin, 'More Political Oppression Reported in Kalmykia', 5 *RFE/RL Newsline*, 24, Part I, 5 Feb. 2001.

8

The Federal Reforms of Vladimir Putin

> Happy families are all alike; every unhappy family is unhappy in its own way.
>
> *Leo Tolstoy,* Anna Karenina

> No one argues that Russian executive power must be enforced, but what does that have to do with the rights of the regions? It is impossible to form a strong family by force; one can do so only with consent and mutual affection.
>
> *Farit Mukhametshin, Chairman, Tatar State Council,* 3 August 2000[1]

On the eve of the new millenium, Tolstoy's description of the state of affairs at Oblonsky's house seemed an accurate pronouncement on Boris Yeltsin's federal relationships: everything was in confusion.[2] Federal authority was as often openly flaunted as resentfully acknowledged. The eighty-nine presidential envoys Yeltsin dispatched to the regions in 1997 to enforce federal law were easily corrupted by the regional authorities on whom they and their families depended for housing, education, and even their own offices. By 1999, they had been all but forgotten by the federal centre. Yeltsin's regional policy had regressed from one of hesitant negotiation with a few regional powers to incessant deal-making. With each new bilateral deal, Moscow weakened its power to enforce its will, and muddied the constitutional authority to assert its rights. The Federation was held together by two unstable forces: personal agreements between elites (many of whom had been in power since Soviet times), and the economic necessity born of desperate times.

---

[1] Paul Goble, 'Tatarstan Official Says Unitary Approach Undercuts Democracy', 4 *Radio Free Europe/Radio Liberty Newsline,* 151, Part I, 8 Aug. 2000. Mukhametshin was speaking at a conference in Ufa, Bashkortostan, as reported by the RFE/RL Tatar-Bashkir Service.

[2] In an unpublished paper written in Feb. 2000 for working groups in the Duma and Federation Council, Vladimir N. Lysenko, Deputy Chairman of the Duma Committee on Federal and Regional Policy, wrote: 'In the 1990s, there took shape in Russia a super-presidential regime with a mono-subjective power, a weakly federal state (with elements of both unitarism and confederalism), a quasi-multi-party structure, burdened by a nomenklatura-clan type of management, a corrupted ruling class and, to all intents and purposes, the absence of local self-government'. V.N. Lysenko, 'Federatsiia v Rossii v nachale XXI veka: Perspektivy razvitiia', 28 Feb. 2000.

The inauguration of Vladimir Putin led almost immediately to substantial changes for Russian federalism, though no one at the time predicted the reforms that would spring from the colourless *chekist* who replaced Sergei Stepashin as Prime Minister in autumn 1999. Prior to Yeltsin's surprise New Year's Eve resignation, Putin's regional politics extended to the brutal war he had restarted in Chechnya. The first year of Putin's presidency, however, proved to be the most concerted and fundamental shake-up of federal relations in Russia since the 1993 Constitution.

1. Requiem for the Bilateral Treaty Process

Throughout the Yeltsin administration, bilateral treaties (*dogovory*) and agreements (*soglasheniia*), from negotiation to signature, were an exclusively executive branch activity. Federal and regional legislatures were neither required nor invited to participate at any stage of the process. Only the signature of presidents and prime ministers appeared at the bottom of these documents, without any process of legislative ratification. This omission was deliberate. Struggling to control both an obstreperous parliament and feisty regions, Yeltsin's super-presidential powers could only be diminished by adding more players to the negotiation game. For regional executives, many of whom held their parliaments under their thumb, ratification by another branch of government was either superfluous or an unnecessary risk. Past practice in Soviet patron-client relations, in which all of the participants had received their political schooling, further encouraged the personalization—rather than the institutionalization—of federal-regional politics.

Resort to the old patron-client politics, however, placed treaties and agreements in an ambiguous legal position. Certainly, these documents did not have the status of federal constitutional law, or even federal law, having completely circumvented the Federal Assembly.[3] What standing such documents had in regional law was equally unclear given the absence of any legislative approval in regional parliaments. Nor could they be considered the equivalent of federal or regional presidential decrees (*ukazy*), as these acquire legal force through official publication, a requirement never established for bilateral arrangements. Indeed, throughout the 'Parade of Treaties', popular wisdom held that the most sensitive (and lucrative) deals were purposely kept hidden from scrutiny.

---

[3] *See* unpublished paper by S.M. Shakhrai, 'Theses for the seminar "The Improvement of Federal Relations"', 7–3–2000.

Aside from this problem of hierarchy of laws, the highly personalized manner in which treaties and agreements were concluded created political problems. All forty-seven treaties agreed between 1994 and 1998 were signed by Boris Yeltsin. The vast majority of names on the other side of the page were those of regional elites who were still in office in 1999. What would happen to these documents when one or both men (and they were all men) left office? Would they still be accorded the force of law? Or would they be considered personal understandings subject to renegotiation, no stronger than the strength of the personality behind them? Circumstantial evidence suggests that such anxieties were a factor in the decision of regional leaders to support Yeltsin over Zyuganov in the 1996 presidential elections. Regional (especially, republican) elites had good cause for concern that Zyuganov would not honour the alegal arrangements made by his despised predecessor.[4] Wavering support (or even open hostility from the republics) for Yeltsin in his 1991 presidential bid changed into support five years later.

Too late, Yeltsin attempted to reform this system. On 30 July 1999, a new federal law came into force to regulate the bilateral treaty process.[5] *Prima facie*, this law seemed to institutionalize mechanisms for wider participation in the passage of federal laws dividing issues of joint competency between the Federation and the regions. The law re-emphasized the supremacy of federal laws and the RF Constitution in the hierarchy of laws (Art. 3 §1; Art. 4). The principle of *glasnost* in drafting and promulgating treaties was also categorically asserted (Art. 10). Regions were given three years to bring existing treaties and agreements into conformity with federal law (Art. 32 §2). Of course, after years spent disregarding similar passages in the Federation Treaty, Constitution and countless federal pronouncements, these old mantras had a hollow ring. There was no rush to reform.

The empty repetition of fundamental principles belied a more serious lacuna in the law. A fundamental shortcoming of the new law was the absence of a stronger role for the Federal Assembly and regional legislatures in the treaty-making process. The 1999 law did not require the *ratification* of treaties by federal and regional legislatures, only *examination* (*rassmotrenie*)

---

[4] Throughout the campaign, Yeltsin depicted himself as the guarantor of stability. He made 25 visits to regions outside Moscow, signed 6 bilateral treaties, distributed suitcases of rubles and extended dozens of promises. While some analysts convincingly argued that a cause-effect relationship between largesse and votes is quite difficult to prove, the signal was certainly not lost on regional elites that only Yeltsin could promise the status quo. *See* Michael McFaul, *Russia's 1996 Presidential Election* (Stanford: Hoover Institution Press, 1997), 32–5, 59, 63.

[5] Zakon, 'O printsipakh i poriadke razgranicheniia predmetov vedeniia i polnomochii mezhdu organami gosudarstvennoi vlasti Rossiiskoi Federatsii i organami gosudarstvennoi vlasti sub''ektov Rossiiskoi Federatsii', *Sobranie zakonodatel'stva Rossiiskoi Federatsii* [*SZRF*], No. 26, 28 June 1999, item 3176, pp. 5685–92. *See also* Aleksandr Sadchikov, 'Suvereniteta stanet men'she', *Izvestia*, 30 July 1999, 2.

(Art. 23 §§2–4).[6] Results of the examination by the Federation Council, the law stated, were to be 'communicated to the President of the Russian Federation' (Art. 23 §4), first by the 'authorized agent' (invariably appointed by the regional executive) of the subject of the Federation, who then communicated to the Federation Council. All of these results were to be 'taken into consideration' (*uchityvaiutsia*) before signature of the treaty (Art. 23 §4). Lacking any right of refusal, or even redaction, legislatures were children at the negotiating table—best seen, but not heard.[7]

Time showed the change to be a superficial one. Yeltsin, who had signed the previous forty-seven regional treaties, never signed another treaty, and Putin, in the first year of his presidency, radically changed the rules of the federal game with his sweeping package of reforms—a future the benefactors of this personality-driven process had always feared. From June 1998 through November 2001, no new treaties or agreements were signed and no existing ones renewed as deadlines passed.[8] In a speech to the nation in May

[6] A more sympathetic analysis of the law would argue that, by definition, ratification of these documents was unnecessary. Agreements (*soglasheniia*) are defined by the law to be 'the legal form of transfer by federal organs of *executive* power and organs of *executive* power of subjects of the Russian Federation between one another for the realization of part of their authority' (Art. 2, §7). To the extent that treaties (*dogovory*) are made between organs of *state* power (Art. 2 §6), their subject matter is merely the 'concretization, . . . conditions and manner of transfer, . . . [and] forms of co-operation and collaboration . . .', (Art. 17) of jurisdiction and authority already established in the federal constitution, which itself establishes no ratification requirement for such arrangements. However, such a reading leaves unsolved the federal problems the law ostensibly was designed to ameliorate.

[7] Buried in the text of a law passed in October 1999 is a clause asserting the authority of the subject of the Russian Federation with regard to treaties. Art. 5, §2, part 'z' of the federal law 'On general principles of organization of the legislative (representative) and executive organs of state power of the subjects of the Russian Federation' states that 'By law of the subject of the Russian Federation the conclusion and cancellation of treaties of the subject of the Russian Federation are confirmed'. However, what is meant by 'confirm' is far from clear and, although Art. 5 deals with the authority of the legislative branch, it is unclear what role for that branch is implied by the phrase 'by law': the authority to confirm itself, or the authority to make a law regarding confirmation? In any event, this unheralded clause seems to have had even less impact on the bilateral treaty process than Yeltsin's law of late June. See No. 184-FZ, 6 Oct. 1999, 'Ob obshchikh printsipakh organizatsii zakonodatel'nykh (predstavitel'nykh) i ispolnitel'nykh organov gosudarstvennoi vlasti sub"ektov Rossiiskoi Federatsii', *SZRF.* No. 42, 18 Oct. 1999, item 5005, p. 9417.

[8] Of potential interest, however, is the signing in November 2001 of *soglasheniia* with (by some accounts 9) regions in the Far East Federal District. Aleksei Chernyshev, 'Novosti. Dal'nii Vostok privedut v sootvetstvie', *Kommersant"-daily.* 2 Nov. 2001, 2; Paul Goble, 'Justice Ministry Plans Accords with Federation Subjects', 5 *RFE/RL Newsline*, 210, Part I, (5 Nov. 2001). Under the watchful eye of Presidential Envoy Konstantin Pulikovskii, Justice Minister Yuri Chaika signed agreements outlining steps to be taken in the process of bringing regional constitutions and laws into conformity with federal law. However, these *soglasheniia* would appear to be fundamentally different in kind from the bilateral agreements made in the Yeltsin era. Whereas experienced regional negotiators of Yeltsin-era agreements focused primarily on extracting as much *regional* control over natural resources, industry, and other economic issues from the federal centre as possible, these new agreements seem in part a federal response to frustration over inadequate tax

2000, Putin declared, 'I am addressing the law-makers once again. Once again I would like to stress that the period of forced compromises leading to instability is over'.[9] Yeltsin's law on the bilateral treaty process, like the treaties and agreements that were its target, was left to wither on the vine.

2. 'THE DICTATORSHIP OF LAW'

Early in his presidential campaign, Vladimir Putin introduced a strange phrase into the political lexicon: 'the dictatorship of law'. Putin's speeches and writings on democracy and law were at once encouraging and chilling. His use of democratic concepts often left unclear in what manner he thought them best applied:

In a non-law-governed (i.e. weak), state the individual is defenseless and not free. *The stronger the state, the freer the individual.* In a democracy, your and my rights are limited only by the same rights enjoyed by other people. It is on recognizing this simple truth that the law is based, the law that is to be followed by all—from an authority figure to a simple citizen.

But democracy is the dictatorship of the law—not of those placed in an official position to defend that law. . . .

I know there are many now that are afraid of order. But order is nothing more than rules. And let those who are currently engaged in substituting concepts for one another, trying to pass off the absence of order for genuine democracy—let them, I say, stop looking for hidden dirty tricks and trying to scare us with the past. 'Our land is rich, but there is no order in it', they used to say in Russia.

Nobody will ever say such things about us in future.[10]

Such statements sent shock waves through Russia's weak democratic opposition.[11] Did the Russian president mean the 'rule of law', or a more

collection and the perennial goal of conforming regional laws to federal standards. They are, in other words, about establishing greater *federal* control, quite the opposite of earlier regional objectives. Also of interest, are reports that the only region in the Far Eastern District *not* to sign an agreement was the only republic in the District, Sakha-Yakutia.

[9] Russian Public TV, Moscow, in Russian 1700 gmt, 17 May 2000, reported by BBC Monitoring. Reprinted in *Rossiiskaya gazeta*, 19 May 2000, 3.

[10] 'Open Letter to Russian Voters', 25 Feb. 2000. Campaign website: *http://putin2000.ru/07/05.html*. Emphasis in original.

[11] Contrary to the assertion by Peter Rutland that this phrase was a 'throw-away remark that Putin made while talking to journalists', ('Putin's Path to Power', 16 *Post-Soviet Affairs*, 4, 2000: 345) Putin has repeatedly expressed (on national television) his well-known maxim of government. In a televised address to the nation on the eve of his reform package, Putin linked the phrase to his 'strengthening of the vertical of executive power', saying: 'This is what the dictatorship of law means. It would mean we are living in one strong country, one single state called Russia'. Russian

frightening, bureaucratized rule through laws? Was Putin's oxymoronic linkage of dictatorship and law compatible with the tremendous act of self-restraint that is government *under* law?[12] Transition away from authoritarianism, as well as the development of stable federal relations, hinged on that choice.

Vladimir Putin's reforms can be divided into three categories. The first reform, the establishment of federal districts and presidential envoys, reshaped the geographic space of federal politics. The second reform was in fact a reassertion of existing powers: Putin seized on presidential authority, left virtually unused by Yeltsin, to suspend the decrees of five regional executives and place Chechnya under direct presidential control. At the same time—some have suggested operating under political pressure—the Constitutional Court issued two sweeping rulings that restated its deeply pro-centralizing philosophy of federalism and declared the constitutions of seven republics to be riddled with fundamental violations of the federal constitution. Putin commenced a programme, more stick than carrot, of establishing his executive 'power vertical' over the regions, demanding the 'harmonization' of their laws and constitutions with federal law and the federal constitution. His disinterest in revisiting bilateral treaties was palpable. Third, Putin successfully reshaped the Federation Council and strengthened his 'executive vertical' powers with a summer legislative package.

Public TV, Moscow, in Russian 1700 gmt, 17 May 2000, reported by *BBC Monitoring*. The text of the speech was also reprinted in 'Vladimir Putin: Vlast' dolzhna byt' rabotaiushchei!' *Rossiiskaya gazeta*, 19 May 2000, 3. In another televised speech on 8 July 2000 before both houses of the Federal Assembly, Putin managed to give a fundamental concept of civil law—the importance of maintaining a space outside the domain of public law—an ominous tinge: 'That is why we insist on just one dictatorship—the dictatorship of the law, although I know that many people dislike the expression. That is why it is so important to indicate the boundaries of the domain where the state is full and only master, to state precisely where it is final arbiter and to define those spheres where it should not meddle'. One is left to wonder what size such a non-state sphere could have in Putin's Russia. Translated by *BBC Monitoring*. Source: Russia TV, Moscow, in Russian, 0800 gmt, 8 July 2000.

[12] At least two distinguished scholars have noted that Putin purposefully seemed to contrast his dictatorship of law with the Bolshevik slogan 'dictatorship of the proletariat'. *See* Peter Rutland, 'Putin's Path to Power', 16 *Post-Soviet Affairs*, 4 (2000): 345; Robert Sharlet, 'Putin and the Politics of Law in Russia', 17 *Post-Soviet Affairs*, 3 (2001): 204. As Professor Sharlet observes: 'These casual, metaphoric usages seem to have evoked little or no noticeable reaction in a country where the word "dictatorship" had long held a privileged place in official discourse to mean the highest and ultimate authority, as well as its unrestricted dominion over polity and society.' However, that is precisely the reason human rights observers both within and outside of Russia were so concerned: a society too used to dictatorship and too unfamiliar with law, like its president, risked erring on the side of *too much* law. As Bernard Rudden noted, for example, 'there is a precious sphere of non-law' in the development of private civil law and, by extension, civil society. Bernard Rudden, 'Civil Law, Civil Society, and the Russian Constitution', 110 *Law Quarterly Review* (Jan. 1994): 60.

2.1 Presidential Envoys and Federal Districts

The first salvo in Putin's federal reforms was fired less than a week after Putin swore his oath of office. On 13 May 2000, Putin signed a presidential decree (*ukaz*) on 'The Plenipotentiary Representative of the President in a Federal District'.[13] The decree and accompanying regulations (*polozhenie*) divided Russia into seven federal districts. These districts coincided with existing military districts. Yeltsin's eighty-nine presidential representatives—one for each subject of the Federation—were replaced by the heads of these new districts; officially termed 'plenipotentiaries' (*polnomochnye predstaviteli*, or *polpredy* for short), they were more commonly called 'presidential envoys', or less favourably, '*namestniki*', referring to the tsarist 'governors-general' established by Catherine the Great.[14] According to the decree, these *polpredy* were officially part of the Administration of the President (the Main Control Directorate—GKU), and charged with overseeing the President's constitutional authority in the districts. The Russian press quickly adopted the evocative metaphor of 'seven samurai', suggesting great powers, even though the presidential decree and resolution were cryptically vague regarding specific duties, powers, and limitations of this new office (Table 8.1).[15]

District capitals were chosen to deflate the leadership pretensions of the most powerful regions. In the Volga district, which included such power-houses as Tatarstan and Bashkortostan, the seat of power became Nizhnii Novgorod (not Kazan or Ufa, the respective capitals of these republics), the power base of its first plenipotentiary, Sergei Kirienko. In *no* case was a district capital located in a republic. While Moscow, St. Petersburg, and Ekaterinburg seemed inevitable choices, Khabarovsk, Rostov on Don, and Novosibirsk appeared to be chosen to reshape the balance of power.

The decree surprised analysts and regional elites alike.[16] No one expected federal reform to be Putin's first project. Putin asserted that his decree,

---

[13] Ukaz Prezidenta Rossiiskoi Federatsii 'O polnomochnom predstavitele Prezidenta Rossiiskoi Federatsii v federal'nom okruge', No. 849, 13 May 2000; *SZRF*, No. 20, 15 May 2000, item 2112, p. 4318. *See also Rossiiskaia gazeta*, 16 May 2000, 5.

[14] The decree annulled Yeltsin's decree of 9 July 1997, which established the post of presidential plenipotentiary for each of the 89 units of the Federation. Ukaz Prezidenta Rossiiskoi Federatsii, 'O polnomochnom predstavitele Prezidenta Rossiiskoi Federatsii v regione Rossiiskoi Federatsii', No. 696, 9 July 1997; *SZRF*, No. 28, 14 July 1997, item 3421, p. 5549.

[15] Two exceptions to this norm were that: (1) *polpredy* were given extensive control over federal cadre policy in the districts; and (2) *polpredy* were given general rights of access and participation not only in federal organs operating in the district, but also organs of state power of the regions themselves and their organs of local self-government. Even these assertions of authority, however, could be interpreted in both power-generating and power-deflating ways.

[16] According to Michael Wines, 'Mr Putin is said to have sprung the plan on top governors last week in a meeting that ran so long that the president's next appointment—his new prime minister, Mikhail Kasyanov—cooled his heels for more than an hour'. Michael Wines, 'Putin's Move on Governors Would Bolster his Role', *New York Times*, 22 May 2000, A3. *See also* 'Russia's Putin discusses government structure with Premier Kasyanov', ITAR-TASS news agency, Moscow, in English 1526 gmt, 17 May 2000 /BBC Monitoring.

Table 8.1   The Seven Federal Districts

Federal district	Composition	District capital	Population (%)
Central	Republics (0) Oblasts (17): Belgorod, Briansk, Vladimir, Ivanovo, Voronezh, Kaluga, Kostroma, Kursk, Lipetsk, Tver, Moscow, Orlov, Riazan, Smolensk, Tambov, Tula, Yaroslavl Other (1): Moscow	Moscow	25.5
Northwest	Republics (2): Karelia, Komi Oblasts (7): Arkhangelsk, Vologda, Kaliningrad, Leningrad, Murmansk, Novgorod, Pskov Other (2): St. Petersburg, Nenets Aut. Okrug	St. Petersburg	9.8
North Caucasus (Southern)	Republics (8): Adygeia, Dagestan, Ingushetia, Kabardino-Balkaria, Kalmykia, Karachaevo-Cherkessia, North Ossetia, Chechnya Oblasts (3): Astrakhan, Volgograd, Rostov Other (2): Stavropol krai, Krasnodar krai	Rostov on Don	14.4
Volga	Republics (6): Bashkortostan, Marii El, Mordova, Tatarstan, Udmurtia, Chuvashia Oblasts (8): Kirov, Nizhegorod, Orenburg, Penza, Perm, Samara, Saratov, Ulianovsk Other (1): Komi-Permiak Aut. Okrug	Nizhnii Novgorod	22.1
Ural	Republics (0) Oblasts (4): Kurgan, Sverdlovsk, Tiumen, Cheliabinsk Other (2): Khanty-Mansii Aut. Okrug, Yamalo-Nenets Aut. Okrug	Ekaterinburg	8.7
Siberian	Republics (4): Altai, Buriatia, Tyva, Khakasia Oblasts (6): Irkutsk, Kemerovo, Novosibirsk, Omsk, Tomsk, Chita Other (6): Altai krai, Krasnoyarsk krai, Agin-Buriat Aut. Okrug, Taimyr Aut. Okrug, Ust-Ordin Buriat Aut. Okrug, Evenk Aut. Okrug	Novosibirsk	13.4
Far East	Republics (1): Sakha (Yakutia) Oblasts (4): Amur, Kamchatka, Magadan, Sakhalin Other (5): Primorskii krai, Khabarovsk krai, Jewish Aut. Oblast, Koriak Aut. Okrug, Chukotka Aut. Okrug	Khabarovsk	5.0

designed to strengthen state unity, was supported 'by governors, deputies and all citizens of Russia. It is possible to say, that in the country, for the first time, there is no disagreement about the question of principle'.[17] His hyperbole

---

[17] 'Vladimir Putin: Vlast' dolzhna byt' rabotaiushchei!' *Rossiiskaya gazeta*, 19 May 2000, 3. The speech was given on Russian television on 17 May.

could be excused. Few openly challenged the new president, who rode a wave of popularity not possessed by a high federal official since the early 1990s. Governors publicly endorsed the decree, though many no doubt grumbled in private.[18] By announcing the creation of districts without announcing who would be envoys, Putin left governors in a tactical dilemma: wondering whether they themselves or officials they controlled might be appointed (or at least host the district capital), his critics bit their tongues.[19] Pointing to the legal anarchy that had been the method and the misery of Yeltsin's presidency, Putin declared, 'It is seemingly isolated instances like these, drop by drop, that give rise to separatism, which sometimes becomes the springboard for an even more dangerous evil—international terrorism'.[20] Who dared oppose such logic behind the 'dictatorship of law'?

Boris Nemtsov, a former governor and leader of the Union of Right Forces, was among the first to recognize the key to the decrees: '[E]verything namely depends on which figures appear in these posts. It may be that they are just run-of-the-mill bureaucrats, and then the whole new system you will call none other than decorative'.[21] Putin's choices indicated his resolve: five of the seven *polpredy* held the rank of general in the armed forces (Table 8.2).[22]

Central District *polpredy* Poltavchenko successfully gathered a staff of over forty people in Moscow (with additional workers in each of eighteen regions in his district). Who *polpredy* appointed as deputies was almost as telling as the selection by Putin of the *polpredy* themselves. It was, perhaps, predictable that the civilian-politicians would gather different types of deputies than their colleagues plucked from military positions. The entourage of Sergei Kirienko, undoubtedly, was the most professionally trained, including such well-known and respected advisers as Vladimir Zorin.[23]

The first few months under the new system of federal districts led some to suspect that the *polpredy*, like Yeltsin's envoys, were paper tigers. The

---

[18] The day after the decree, television station NTV aired the positive remarks of Samara Governor Konstantin Titov, Voronezh region head Ivan Shabanov, Saratov Governor Dmitri Ayatskov, and others. NTV International, Moscow in Russian 1200 gmt, 14 May 2000, reported by *BBC Monitoring*. Among those few analysts and politicians who made early criticisms of the reforms are Radio Free Europe Editor Paul Goble and Chuvash President Nikolai Fedorov, who became the unofficial opposition spokesman to Putin's reforms.

[19] Liz Fuller has suggested that this is precisely what initially led Tatarstan's Mintimer Shaimiev to endorse the reform. 2 *RFE/RL Russian Federation Report*, 22, 14 June 2000.

[20] *Rossiiskaya gazeta*, 19 May 2000, 3.

[21] *Segodnya*, 16 May 2000, 4.

[22] 'The Bridling of Russia's Regions', *The Economist*, 11 Nov. 2000, 61; 52 *Current Digest of the Post-Soviet Press*, 20 (2000): 2–4; *Rossiiskaia gazeta*, 20 May 2000, 3; *Segodnya*, 31 May 2000, 1–2.

[23] For Kirienko, see http://www.pfo.ru/, the official website. For Latyshev, see http://www.ur-alfo.ru/, the official website. For Drachevskii, see http://www.sfo.nsk.su/, the official website.

Table 8.2   Vladimir Putin's Plenipotentiaries

Federal district	Plenipotentiary	Previous position	Military rank
Central	POLTAVCHENKO Georgii Sergeevich	Career KGB officer; St. Petersburg Chief, Federal Tax Service	General
Northwest	CHERKESOV Viktor Vasil'evich	1st Deputy Director, FSB (dissident-hunter)	Lt. General
North Caucasus (Southern)[a]	KAZANTSEV Viktor Germanovich	Commander, North Caucasus Military District	General
Volga	KIRIENKO Sergei Vladilenovich	Prime Minister (April–Aug 1998)	No military rank
Ural	LATYSHEV Petr Mikhailovich	Deputy Minister, MVD	Col. General
Siberian	DRACHEVSKII Leonid Vadimovich	Career diplomat, Ministry of Foreign Affairs	No military rank
Far East	PULIKOVSKII Konstantin Borisovich	Deputy Commander, 1st Chechen War	Lt. General

[a] Renamed by presidential decree No. 1149, 21 June 2000, *SZRF*, No. 26, 26 June 2000.

combative governor of Sverdlovsk oblast, Eduard Rossel, defiantly went on vacation rather than greet Petr Latyshev, arriving in Ekaterinburg to introduce himself to the governors of his district. Some *polpredy* found it difficult to acquire offices or even living space.[24] Although numerous press conferences and considerable media exposure were given to the seven *polpredy*, work on the ground appeared to be no more substantial than under the previous system. An announcement by the Government that it would establish its own representative offices in the seven federal districts to facilitate the work of its ministries and agencies was quietly retracted five days later.[25] Criticism grew that the reform was in fact illusory: just another layer of federal bureaucracy.

[24] 5 *East West Institute Russian Regional Report*, 29, 26 July 2000. Two months following his appointment, Konstantin Pulikovskii was still living in a hotel in Khabarovsk. In Ekaterinburg, Petr Latyshev found himself the victim of dirty tricks: accepting an offer by *oblast'* authorities to set up offices in an old Pioneers' Palace, Latyshev found himself the centre of scandal, accused of displacing the children who had previously been granted its use. Natalya Mints, 'Latyshev Steps Up Activities in Urals Federal District', 5 *EastWest Institute Russian Regional Report*, No. 35, 27 Sep. 2000.

[25] 4 *RFE/RL Newsline*, 151, Part I, 8 Aug. 2000. 2 *RFE/RL Russian Federation Report*, 29, 16 August 2000. The distinction between the Administration of the President and the Government is an important one. Some theorists have suggested that the establishment of federal districts under the former was an attempt by the Presidential Administration to wrest more authority from the Government, whose prime minister and cabinet are nominated by the President, but whose

By autumn 2000, however, there were increasing indications that the reform might have a bite to match its bark. *Polpredy* were made full members of the Security Council. Julie A. Corwin, analysing reports from several newspapers, noted that *polpredy* topped the pay scale of federal officials, earning more than four times the salary of Putin himself![26] According to Sergei Samoilov, then chief of the Main Territorial Department of the Administration of the President, *polpredy* ranked close to a deputy prime minister in the hierarchy of power.[27] As *polpredy* and their federal inspectors set to the task of creating a 'unified legal space' in the federation, scouring regional constitutions, bilateral treaties and laws for conformity or violation of federal norms, Putin strengthened their political power by tasking them with the creation of a 'single information space' as well. A presidential *ukaz* in late September stripped regional elites of the right to nominate regional directors of Russian state-owned radio and television stations. From now on, his envoys would make the recommendations.[28] In the Southern Federal District, Viktor Kazantsev established what most observers called a 'District Government,' a Territorial Collegium bringing together district representatives of all federal ministries and agencies (excepting the federal procuracy).[29] All districts soon followed such developments with the creation of 'security councils' comprised of the regional executives in each district, mirroring the larger State Council that Putin had decreed at the federal level to win regional acquiescence to his reform of the Federation Council. Circumstantial proof of the increasing anxiety of governors about the strengthening of *polpredy* was the proposal of Yegor Stroev, Speaker in the Federation Council and Governor of Orenburg Oblast, for a law that would delimit the role and powers of *polpredy*.[30] Conflicts between the Main Territorial Department and the *polpredy* led Putin to trim the powers of both sides in late December (the former appeared to lose considerable power over regional staff and access to the president), subordinate *polpredy* to the control of Aleksandr Voloshin, Chief of the Presidential Administration, with an *ukaz* at the end of January 2001, and dismiss Samoilov in

---

institutional agenda may on occasion be at odds with the Presidential Administration because of its special connection to both the executive and legislative branches.

[26] Julie A. Corwin, 'Least Seniority, Highest Pay?' 5 *RFE/RL Newsline*, 8, Part I, 12 Jan. 2001.

[27] Quoted in Peter Rutland, 'Putin's Path to Power', 16 *Post-Soviet Affairs*, No. 4 (2000): 348.

[28] *Nezavisimaya gazeta*, 27 Oct. 2000, translated by *BBC Monitoring*. The decree met with only moderate success, as some regions reorganized media holdings to circumvent federal control.

[29] Andrei Miroshnichenko, 'Kazantsev Creates "District Government" in Southern Federal District', 5 *EastWest Institute Russian Regional Report*, 32, 7 Sep. 2000.

[30] 'Federation Council Head Calls for Law on Presidential Representatives,' 2 *RFE/RL Russian Federation Report*, 40, 1 Nov. 2000.

February.[31] Eight months later, in October, the Ministry for Federation Affairs, Nationality, and Migration Policy was abolished and its head, Aleksandr Blokhin, dismissed. Analysts speculated as to why the reshuffle, which further consolidated power under the presidential administration, had occurred. Did it signal the successful reassertion of federal authority, or yet another bout of Kremlin infighting? In any event, few doubted that Putin had accomplished what Yeltsin could not: for the first time since the 'War of Laws' had begun, the federal government had the clear upper hand.

2.2 The Quasi-judicial Power of Presidential Decrees

Although the federal districts signaled the *ground-breaking* stage of Putin's efforts at federal reform, it was not the *first* stage. 'Above everything else, the state is the law', Putin exclaimed in his address to the nation introducing his reforms. Putin claimed that more than 20 percent of regional legislation was unconstitutional—and swore to combat it.[32]

Eight days prior to naming his *polpredy*, Putin, by his own decree, suspended the legal force of a decree made by the president of Ingushetia, Ruslan Aushev, and a resolution by the Ingush government.[33] The Ingush president's decree, nearly two and a half years old, improved collection of gas and electric payments in the republic; the government resolution,

---

[31] 'Putin Clarifies Powers of Presidential Representatives', 6 *EastWest Institute Russian Regional Report* 1, 10 Jan. 2001. *Ukaz*, No. 97, 30 Jan. 2001, 'O vnesenii dopolneniia i izmeneniia v Polozheniie o polnomochnom predstavitele Prezidenta Rossiiskoi Federatsii v federal'nom okruge, utverzhdennoe Ukazom Prezidenta Rossiiskoi Federatsii ot 13 maia 2000 g., No. 849,' *SZRF*, No. 6 (5 Feb. 2001), item 551, p. 1624. Samoilov was not left to wait out in the cold for long. By September 2001, he had been appointed secretary of a federal presidential commission for the demarcation of authority between the centre and the regions.

[32] 'Above everything else, the state is the law. It stands for constitutional law and order and discipline. If these tools are weak, the state is also weak or simply nonexistent. . . . It is outrageous that—think about this figure—one-fifth of the legal regulations adopted by the regions contradict the country's fundamental law, ...' Russian Public TV, Moscow, in Russian 1700 gmt, 17 May 2000, reported by *BBC Monitoring*. The text of the speech was also reprinted in 'Vladimir Putin: Vlast' dolzhna byt' rabotaiushchei!' *Rossiiskaya gazeta*, 19 May 2000, 3.

[33] No. 790, 5 May 2000, 'O postanovlenii Pravitel'stva Respubliki Ingushetiia ot 3 avgusta 1998 g., No. 204 "O merakh po ispolneniiu Ukaza No. 72 ot 28 fevralia 1997 g. Prezidenta Respubliki Ingushetiia, Postanovleniia Soveta Bezopastnosti Respubliki Ingushetiia No. 4 ot 27 maia 1998 g." ', *SZRF*, No. 19, 8 May 2000, item 2060, p. 4208.

No. 791, 5 May 2000, 'Ob Ukaze Prezidenta Respubliki Ingushetiia ot 16 sentiabria 1997 g. No. 229 "O merakh po uluchsheniiu sbora platezhei za potreblennye gaz i elektroenergiiu" ', *SZRF*, No. 19, 8 May 2000, item 2061, p. 4209. Two more Ingush decrees were later suspended by President Putin. *See* Ukaz, No. 132, 7 Feb. 2001, 'O priostanovlenii deistviia Ukaza Prezidenta Respubliki Ingushetiia ot 22 Aprelia 2000 g. No. 76 "Ob uprazdnenii Gosudarstvennogo komiteta Respubliki Ingushetiia po sviazi" i postanovleniia Pravitel'stva Respubliki Ingushetiia ot 20 maia 2000 g. No. 192 'Ob uchrezhdenii gosudarstvennogo unitarnogo predpriatiia "Upravlenie elektricheskoi sviazi Respubliki Ingushetia" ', *SZRF*, No. 7, 12 Feb. 2001, item 627, p. 1812.

executing a nearly three-year-old decree of the Ingush president, involved licenses to foreign workers. These regional acts, Putin's decree asserted, violated the Constitution, federal law, and the federal tax code. That same day, Putin issued another decree suspending a nearly year-old resolution by the governor of Amur Oblast that permitted Russian citizens access to a bordering Chinese trading complex.[34] ITAR-TASS reported that an additional fifteen such decrees were expected soon, on advice from the Procurator-General.[35] Two days after his decree on the new federal districts, Putin decreed the suspension of a two-year-old resolution made by the governor of Smolensk Oblast that established levies for transport-related environmental contamination.[36] According to Putin's decree, this contradicted two federal laws and a resolution of the federal government. More decrees suspending regional legal acts soon followed: against Adygeia, on 7 June; Tver' on 12 June; Tula on 12 August; Ingushetia on 1 September; and Adygeia again on 9 September.[37]

[34] No. 800, 5 May 2000, 'O postanovlenii glavy administratsii Amurskoi oblasti ot 23 iunia 1999 g., No. 365 "Ob organizatsii propuska grazhdan Rossiiskoi Federatsii v torgovyi kompleks g. Kheikhe (KNR)"', SZRF, No. 19, 8 May 2000, item 2064, p. 4210.

[35] 'Russia's Putin suspends decrees by Ingush president, Amur Region governor', ITAR-TASS news agency, Moscow, in English 1212 gmt, 11 May 2000, reported by BBC Monitoring.

[36] No. 851, 15 May 2000, 'O postanovlenii glavy administratsii Smolenskoi oblasti ot 26 iiunia 1998 g. No. 271 "O vzimanii platezhei za zagriaznenie okruzhaiushchei prirodnoi sredy ot inostrannykh iuridicheskikh lits i grazhdan, ekspluatiriushchikh avtotransportnyie sredstva na avtodorogakh Smolenskoi oblasti"', SZRF, No. 21, 22 May 2000, item 2164, p. 4387. Rossiiskaia gazeta, 18 May 2000, 4.

[37] No. 1055, 7 June 2000, 'Ob ukazakh Prezidenta Respubliki Adygeia ot 8 oktiabria 1997 g. No. 246 "O nomenklature kadrov Prezidenta Republiki Adygeia i Kabineta Ministrov Respubliki Adygeia" i ot 4 iiunia 1999 g. No. 111 "O vnesenii izmenenii i dopolnenii v Ukaz Prezidenta Respubliki Adygeia" ot 8 oktiabria 1997 g. No. 246 "O nomenklature kadrov Prezidenta Respubliki Adygeia i Kabineta Ministrov Respubliki Adygeia"', SZRF, No. 24, 12 June 2000, item 2544, p. 4971. The Adygeia decrees enumerated state posts to be filled by the nomination of the President of Adygeia.

No. 1101, 12 June 2000, 'O priostanovlenii deistviia postanovleniia gubernatora Tverskoi oblasti ot 28 sentiabria 1999 g. No. 856 "O tarifakh na elektricheskuiu energiiu dlia naseleniia oblasti"', SZRF, No. 25, 19 June 2000, item 2676, p. 5122. This decree established tariffs on electric energy for the population of the oblast.

No. 1500, 12 August 2000, 'O priostanovlenii deistviia postanovleniia gubernatora Tul'skoi oblasti ot 12 aprelia 2000 g. No. 137 "Ob uporiadochenii litsenzirovaniia deiatel'nosti po zagotovke, pererabotke i realizatsii loma tsvetnykh i chernykh metallov"', SZRF, No. 34, 21 Aug. 2000, item 3436, p. 6913. This decree regulated licensing of the procurement, stock-piling and use of scrap ferrous and non-ferrous metals in the oblast.

No. 1605, 1 September 2000, 'O priostanovlenii deistviia Ukaza Prezidenta Respubliki Ingushetia ot 26 aprelia 1999 g. No. 102 "O nekotorykh merakh po regulirovaniiu protsessa migratsii v Respublike Ingushetia"', SZRF, No. 36, 4 Sep. 2000, item 3635, p. 7190. This degree concerned migration and residency policies in the republic.

No. 1620, 9 September 2000, 'O priostanovlenii deistviia Ukaza Prezidenta Respubliki Adygeia ot 30 maia 1994 g. No. 83 "O merakh po ogranicheniiu migratsii v Respubliku Adygeia"', SZRF, No. 38, 18 Sep. 2000, item 3777, p. 7682. This decree concerned republican procedures for the acquisition of rights of residence in the republic.

This was Putin's first expression of the refrain of his federal reforms, the strengthening of the president's 'vertical powers' in the Federation. Putin based these powers on four articles of the federal constitution. Article 90 gives the president expansive powers to enact gap-filling decrees (*ukazy*) and orders (*rasporiazheniia*) on any subject not otherwise prohibited by or contradicting the Constitution and/or federal law.[38] Putin's decrees, however, were of a special type made in reliance on a relatively untested article of the Constitution: Article 85, §2. Pending ultimate resolution of the issue by an appropriate court, the federal executive has the power to suspend the acts of executive organs of state power *on all levels of government* for violation of the Constitution, federal law, or presidential decrees.[39] This quasi-judicial power is the practical expression of the authority expressed in two other articles: Article 77, §2 and Article 80, §2. The former provides the specific philosophical backing for the 'vertical power,' providing that 'federal organs of executive power and the organs of executive power of the subjects of the Russian Federation *shall form a unified system of executive power* in the Russian Federation'. The latter article names the president as 'guarantor of the Constitution of the Russian Federation'. Neither the legislative branch nor the judicial branch of the federal government is given that powerfully symbolic—and vague—authority.

Together, these articles give the president extraordinary implicit powers well beyond those powers specifically enumerated in the Constitution and which have led some political scientists to label the Russian system one of 'super-presidentialism'. As Danilenko and Burnham, two respected legal scholars, have noted, 'Although the Constitution does not place the President above the three main branches of government, some commentators argue that he may act (as the French President does) as "an arbiter" among the legislative, executive and judicial branches of government'.[40]

Although the Constitutional Court has ruled that the President has the constitutional power to issue temporary decrees to fill gaps in federal law, the opinion was not unanimous.[41] As Justice Luchin noted in a powerful dissent:

[38] *Konstitutsiia Rossiiskoi Federatsii*, Art. 90. Upon promulgation of a federal law previously subject to a presidential decree, the latter loses force to the former.

[39] *Konstitutsiia Rossiiskoi Federatsii*, Art. 85, §2: 'The president of the Russian Federation shall have the right to suspend the acts of organs of executive power of subjects of the Russian Federation in the case of conflict of these acts with the Constitution of the Russian Federation, federal laws, international responsibilities of the Russian Federation or violations of rights and freedoms of the person and citizen, pending resolution of this question by the appropriate court'.

[40] Gennady M. Danilenko & William Burnham, *Law and Legal System of the Russian Federation* (New York: Juris, 1999), 156.

[41] Postanovlenie Konstitutsionnogo suda Rossiiskoi Federatsii, 'Delo o proverke konstitutsionnosti polozhenii Ukaza Prezidenta Rossiiskoi Federatsii "O merakh po ukrepleniiu edinoi sistemy

This 'self-regulation', not knowing any kind of limitation, is dangerous and incompatible with the principle of the division of powers and other values of a rule-of-law state. The President may not decide any kind of questions if they do not flow from his authority as provided in the Constitution. He is not able to lean on his so-called 'latent (implied)' authorities. Use of them in the absence of a stable constitutional legal order or legality is fraught with negative consequences: the weakening of the mechanism of checks and balances, the strengthening of one branch of power at the expense of another, the beginning of confrontation between them.[42]

While lacunae in federal law are a serious problem and revision of certain parts of the federal constitution is obviously important, caution must be taken not to further aggravate existing problems. The federal executive's power to suspend acts of regional executive branches is an extraordinary encroachment on two core features of federal government. First, it fundamentally weakens the distinction between federal and regional government. No proponent of sustainable federal government in Russia could sensibly advocate *further* decentralization of authority, but care must be taken not to fall victim to the dangers of *over*-centralization of power in Russia in response to this debilitating deflation of federal power. This is precisely the view Putin advocates in his appeal for the 'strengthening of the vertical' of executive power. All executive branches, at every level of government, would fall subject to the will of the federal executive branch. Second, having weakened the separation of powers between federal government and the constituent subjects of the federation, Article 85 encroaches on the division of powers between the executive branch and the judicial branch of government, on all levels. The president, by suspending the legal force of a decree or resolution of a different executive authority, undertakes an act of legal judgment that the Russian Constitution accords, rightly, to the judicial branch. While suspensive decrees may ultimately be overruled by 'an appropriate court', the initial judgment of (and penalty for) unconstitutionality is made, not by the court, but by the executive. That judgment, lodged in tersely worded decrees is extremely conclusory: no explanation or rationale is provided. Even the institution of the procuracy does not have the authority to pronounce on the constitutionality of an act before resolution in the courts.

ispolnitel'noi vlasti v Rossiiskoi Federatsii"', 30 April 1996, *Vestnik Konstitutsionnogo Suda Rossiiskoi Federatsii*, No. 3 (1996), p. 15.

[42] Osoboe mnenie sud'i Konstitutsionnogo Suda Rossiiskoi Federatsii V.O. Luchina, 'Delo o proverke konstitutsionnosti polozhenii Ukaza Prezidenta Rossiiskoi Federatsii "O merakh po ukrepleniiu edinoi sistemy ispolnitel'noi vlasti v Rossiiskoi Federatsii"', 30 April 1996, *Vestnik Konstitutsionnogo Suda Rossiiskoi Federatsii*, No. 3 (1996), p. 24.

One month after Putin's initial reform package, the federal Constitutional Court issued an opinion (*opredelenie*) on the constitutions of Adygeia, Bashkortostan, Ingushetia, Komi, North Ossetia, and Tatarstan.[43] This highly critical document rejected the claims to sovereignty (several of which bordered on the doctrine of nullification, as noted in Chapters One and Seven) repeatedly made by these republics. The supremacy of the federal constitution was (again) reasserted over all other constitutions and charters, including those predating the 1993 federal constitution. The 'treaty-constitutional' federalism favored by the regions was categorically rejected. This opinion specifically noted that subjects of the Federation

...may not change the priorities established by the Constitution of the Russian Federation for the action of laws and other federal normative legal acts, limit their application, suspend their activity, or introduce any kind of procedures or mechanisms for the settlement of legal conflicts that constrain the action of these acts that is not foreseen by the Constitution of the Russian Federation or by federal laws.[44]

In other words, while the Federal President possessed the power to suspend regional executive acts deemed by him to conflict with the federal Constitution *prior to any judicial determination of that fact*, regional elites did *not* possesses a parallel power to suspend federal acts deemed by them to be in conflict with the federal constitution. For those who saw executive political pressure behind pronouncements of the Court,[45] this opinion signalled that a battle of decrees would not be tolerated. Only the federal president had that power.

Another Constitutional Court decision (*postanovlenie*) against the Republic of Altai, announced a few days earlier, held that republic's constitution to

[43] Opredelenie Konstitutsionnogo Suda Rossiiskoi Federatsii po zaprosu gruppy deputatov Gosudarstvennoi Dumy o proverke sootvetstviia Konstitutsii Rossiiskoi Federatsii otdel'nykh polozhenii konstitutsii Respubliki Adygeia, Respubliki Bashkortostan, Respubliki Ingushetiia, Respubliki Komi, Respubliki Severnaia Osetiia-Alaniia i Respubliki Tatarstan, 27 June 2000. Opinions and decisions of the Court have slightly different values as precedent. With regard to the subjects discussed above, however, there seems to be little practical difference.

[44] Opredelenie Konstitutsionnogo Suda Rossiiskoi Federatsii, 27 June 2000. The constitutional provisions of the republics of Komi and Adygeia were singled out for this violation.

[45] As Robert Sharlet reports, Chief Justice Marat Baglai 'enlisted enthusiastically in the campaign to control regional legal separatism'. There are many reasons why the Court, which has not always enjoyed cordial relations with the Executive Branch, found common cause with President Putin on federal questions. Indeed, the Court had consistently (but futilely) opposed doctrines of nullification, 'treaty-based' federalism and other forms of regional malfeasance. One reason worth noting, however, is the incentive provided by Putin's Kremlin, which pushed hard for the passage of a new law in early 2001 'extending court justices' term of office, as well as lifting the mandatory retirement age, [which] was tailored to fit Chief Justice Baglai, its chief near-term beneficiary'. Robert Sharlet, 'Putin and the Politics of Law in Russia', 17 *Post-Soviet Affairs*, 3 (2001): 218, 220.

be riddled with violations of federal law, especially regarding sovereignty. According to the Court:

The Constitution of the Russian Federation binds the sovereignty of the Russian Federation, its constitutional-legal status and authority, and also the constitutional-legal status and authority of the republics that compose the Russian Federation, not by their will on the basis of a treaty, but by the will of the multi-national Russian people—the carriers and sole source of power in the Russian Federation, which, realizing the principles of equality under the law and the self-determination of peoples, constitutes the rebirth of Russia's sovereign statehood as a historically fully developed state entity in its present federal structure. . . .

Recognition then of sovereignty for republics, when all other subjects of the Russian Federation do not possess it, would violate the constitutional equality under the law of subjects of the Russian Federation; its realization is made impossible in principle, in so far as subjects of the Russian Federation, not possessing sovereignty, by their own status may not be equal under the law with sovereign states.[46]

Large portions of this ruling were reprinted verbatim in the Constitutional Court's opinion later that month. It foreshadowed with one republic the sweeping denunciation of regional claims to sovereignty made subsequently against six others and, by implication, all republics. The rulings of the Court—a court of discretionary jurisdiction—at such a charged moment in Russian federal politics was considered by some to be more political warning than legal ruling. Putin's representative to the Court, Mikhail Mitiukov, asserted that the Altai decision 'gives a juridical stamp to the initiatives of the President . . . [for] the strengthening of a federal state and guarantees of the conformity of regional legislation to federal law. . . . The essence of this document, in my view, is that it puts an end to the so-called ideology of sovereignization of the subjects of the Federation. Their sovereignty is not boundless'.[47]

Not all regional observers shared this view. A senior official of the Permanent Mission of the Republic of Bashkortostan in Moscow observed shortly after the decision: 'In Russia, the political process is more important than the law itself. So the agreements of our president with the Russian Federation president are more important than the law. The Constitutional Court of Russia is just a body, highly respected, but just a body of the

---

[46] Postanovlenie Konstitutsionnogo Suda Rossiiskoi Federatsii po delu o proverke konstitutsionnosti otdel'nykh polozhenii Konstitutsii Respubliki Altai i Federal'nogo zakona, 'Ob obshchikh printsipakh organizatsii zakonodatel'nykh (predstavitel'nykh) i ispolnitel'nykh organov gosudarstvennoi vlasti sub'ektov Rossiiskoi Federatsii', 7 June 2000 g., *Rossiiskaia gazeta*, 21 June 2000, 5.

[47] Aleksandr Shinkin, 'Altai perebral suvereniteta', *Rossiiskaia gazeta*, 10 June 2000, 3.

Russian Federation. It has nothing to do with the Republic of Bashkortostan—we have our own Constitutional Court'.[48] In Tatarstan, Tatar nationalists presented that republic's parliament and president with a bill declaring the decision invalid on its territory.[49]

That attitude would radically change as the presidential envoys flexed their muscles and Putin's other proposals became federal law. Putin's *ukazy* quickly captured the attention of regional executives, who leapt to amend controverted laws and decrees and, in some cases, even constitutions. Days after the opinion of the Constitutional Court was delivered, the republic of Tyva, neither named in the cases before the Constitutional Court nor targeted by Putin's executive decrees, announced the completion of a massive amendment of its constitution.[50] In Kalmykia, President Kirsan Ilyumzhinov announced the total compliance of his republic with federal law.[51]

In less than two months, Putin and the Court had threatened the constitutionality of legal activity in a dozen subjects of the Federation, eight of which were republics. Extension of the 'executive power vertical' would not stop there. In conjunction with Putin's next wave of legislative reforms, soon all the republics and regions of the Russian Federation would be pressed by Putin's presidential envoys, the federal inspectors they appointed, and the procuracy and Ministry of Justice to bring their laws and government activity into conformity with federal norms. In September 2001, a new federal presidential commission charged with the (seemingly perennial) task of demarcating federal and regional authority intensified scrutiny of bilateral treaties. With over two score treaties and more than 500 agreements still considered valid by at least one of the signatory-governments to them, the Kremlin announced a deadline: there would be a 'unified consti-

[48] Author's interview, Moscow, 14 July 2000. This view was supported at much higher levels as well. 'President Rakhimov referred to the determination as a political act, not a legal act. Ildus Adigamov, the president of the republic's constitutional court, stated that in the current situation the main task of his institution was to uphold the basic law of the republic'. Igor Rabinovich, 'Bashkortostan Ignores Court Ruling', 5 *EastWest Institute Russian Regional Report*, 36, 4 Oct. 2000.

[49] Boris Bronshtein, 'Vosstanovit' nezavisimost", *Izvestia* (online), 9 Aug. 2000. *See also* Vera Postnova, 'Vnov' obretennaia gosudarstvennost", *Nezavisimaia gazeta*, 28 June 2000, 4.

[50] Petr Akopov, 'Snova v odnoi sviazke: Tuva otkazyvaetsia ot prava na otdelenie', *Izvestiia*, 1 July 2000, 2. 26 amendments to 15 articles of the Constitution were accepted. The most outrageous violation of federal law—Tyva's constitutional assertion of the right to secession—was left unchanged. Amendment of that article requires a referendum. Efforts continued to patch the old constitution, resulting in over 60 amendments. Finally, a referendum held 6 May 2001 led to the adoption of a new constitution.

[51] Lidiia Andrusenko, 'Kalmykiia sdalas' dobrovol'no: Respublikanskie zakony priveli v sootvetstvie s Konstitutsiei RF', *Nezavisimaia gazeta*, 10 June 2000, 3. Iliumzhinov announced at a press conference that this step was taken to demonstrate complete support for the President's reforms.

tutional space' in the Russian Federation by 24 July 2002.[52] Just how bilateral treaties, which had taken years to negotiate, would be unravelled in a few months was not clear. Since treaties had never been ratified, one Kremlin official declared them to occupy the bottom rung of the hierarchy of laws; presumably, there would be no problem, then, in discarding them.[53] This was, of course, always the great risk carried by these documents, the product of highly personalized political relations unsupported by ratification or other procedures that would have strengthened their legal force.

There was, however, some risk to the steady stream of cancelled decrees, judicial determinations, sabre-rattling commissions, and strict deadlines. To be sure, from the point of view of a transition to democracy, many of the regional decrees that Putin suspended were clear abuses of power. As the previous chapter argued, many of these presidents and governors have had little interest in the development of democratic structures beyond the Potemkin villages they construct in (often futile) attempts to attract investment. But, from the point of view of federal development, Putin's cure seemed at times to risk side-effects as unappealing as the disease. In an attempt to deal with long-term violations of the law, Putin sought to solve the problem through his 'dictatorship of law'. But would his dictatorship know when to stop? Or, a victim of their own success, would federal authorities continue to strengthen the 'executive vertical' with ever increasing centralization of authority?

2.3 Putin's Legislative Reforms

Having established his federal districts in mid-May, sweeping legislative reforms followed in June. Putin sought the following: (1) to oust regional executives and parliament chairmen from their dual positions as members of the upper chamber of the Federal Assembly, the Federation Council; and (2) having weakened their influence on federal law-making (and removed their senatorial immunity from prosecution), to force regional laws and law-makers into conformity with federal norms by threat of dismissal from

[52] Dar'ia Zhdanova, 'Gubernatorov snova prizyvaiut delit'sia s tsentrom', *Nezavisimaia gazeta*, 20 Sept. 2001, 2. It might have been hard for some regions to take this deadline seriously. Previous 'strict deadlines' had pockmarked the Yeltsin years. The Putin administration had already changed the deadline at least twice. Julie A. Corwin, 'Power Sharing Agreements to be Fixed—Or Else', 5 *RFE/RL Newsline*, 194, Part 1 (12 Oct. 2001).

[53] Dmitrii Kozak, head of the presidential commission, declared the hierarchy to be: Federal Constitution, federal laws, presidential decrees, resolutions of the government. By the time of his announcement, the deadline for legal conformity had again been moved forward. Julie A. Corwin, 'Kozak Gives Regions Deadline to Fix Agreements', 3 *RFE/RL Russian Federation Report*, 29 (17 Oct. 2001).

their regional positions for repeated malfeasance.[54] The Federation Council, predictably, refused to drink the hemlock that Putin offered. Nor was it willing to permit federal condemnation of regional politicians (who, if the first reform succeeded in removing their immunity as senators, could well include themselves). While, in the latter case, the Duma was able to override (with the required two-thirds majority) the upper chamber's veto, a special conciliation commission had to be established to pass a substantially amended Federation Council reform: the hemlock was sweetened and its drinking postponed. Putin achieved his objectives through a combination of strong political pressure (his public approval ratings were at record levels) and a willingness to offer the occasional political compromise. A third 'reform'— extending to regional elites a power to dismiss local self-government officials that paralleled the power Putin would hold over regional executives and legislatures—provoked comparatively less controversy. It was, and was widely held to be, a sop to regional power aimed to make passage of Putin's other reforms more palatable. Putin's new power to dismiss regional execu- tives and legislatures was circumscribed in most cases by the multi-staged involvement of the judiciary. When the dust had cleared, however, Putin's presidential powers had grown significantly and federal authority, if not immediately strengthened, had been positioned to reassert itself on a new political playing field.

Putin understood that his fundamental changes could not be enacted by presidential decree. At the very least, these reforms required legislative action. Some critics argued that even promulgation as federal laws was inadequate for the scale of the reforms proposed—constitutional amend- ment was needed. In the end, Putin succeeded in winning support in the legislative branch both for the substance of his reforms and for the suffi- ciency of ordinary law for their adoption.

Putin's apparent victory in the Federal Assembly presents serious prob- lems of executive overreach, threatening an already fragile balance of powers (not only between branches of government but also between federal and regional levels of government). On the eve of the introduction of his reforms, Putin shared his objectives on national television: 'The general aim of these draft laws is to make both the executive and legislative power really work, bring a true meaning to the constitutional principle of division between the two branches of power and consolidate the vertical structure of executive power'.[55] Putin's Orwellian 'true meaning' of the separation of powers meant 'consolidation' and a 'vertical' executive power extending from the Moscow

---

[54] Original proposals (*zakonoproekty*) were published in *Nezavisimaia gazeta*, 20 May 2000, 4–5.

[55] Russian Public TV, Moscow, in Russian 1700 gmt, 17 May 2000, reported by BBC Monitoring. Reprinted in *Rossiiskaya gazeta*, 19 May 2000, 3.

Kremlin to local organs of self-government! As one respected legal scholar observed, Putin's federal reforms 'unwittingly unleashed a war', the resolution of which would neither be quick or predictable.[56]

Reform No. 1: Perestroika at the Federation Council

The first and most dramatic reform on Putin's agenda was the *perestroika* (restructuring) of the upper chamber of the Federal Assembly, the Federation Council. The Russian parliament is a bicameral legislature: 450 deputies sit in the lower chamber (the Duma); in the upper chamber (the Federation Council) sit 178 senators. Virtually all federal systems operate bicameral systems,[57] and it is not difficult to understand why. The sometimes competing, sometimes complementary impulses of federalism in a polity (outlined in Chapter Two) naturally suggest more than one collection of law-makers who, although chosen according to different principles of representation, are united under one legislative roof. Both houses are required to make law. Madison famously outlined the benefits of an upper chamber in *The Federalist Papers*, No. 62 as an 'impediment . . . against improper acts of legislation' by passing bills twice through deliberative bodies organized to represent different interests; the senate also acts as a shield against 'the impulse of sudden and violent passions, . . . seduced by factious leaders into intemperate and pernicious resolutions'. A bicameral legislature acts as a bulwark against what Tsebelis and Money have described as three tyrannies: Publius' classic protection against a 'tyranny of the majority' in the veto one chamber holds *vis-à-vis* the other; a protection against the 'tyranny of the minority' by demanding a more complex assent to legislation than a simple, unicameral majority;[58] finally protection against, the 'tyranny of the individual', who by the power to set an agenda can control the outcome, made more difficult because of the plurality of agendas.[59]

---

[56]   Vil'yam Viktorovich Smirnov, political scientist and academic lawyer, head of the Department of Political Science, Institute of State and Law of the Russian Academy of Sciences, Moscow. Author's interview, Moscow, 13 July 2000.

[57]   Only the Federated States of Micronesia and the United Arab Emirates are federal systems with unicameral legislatures. The assertion of federalism in the U.A.E.—a loose collective of 7 emirates with sultanistic governmental systems—is, at the very least, suspect. George Tsebelis & Jeannette Money, *Bicameralism* (Cambridge University Press, 1997), 6.

[58]   As Tsebelis & Money summarize this argument, 'majority rule in unicameral legislatures means that slightly more than one-quarter of the voters can prevail in having their preferences implemented—one-half of the representatives in the legislature, representing one-half of the voters in their constituencies. In bicameral systems, the presence of two legislative houses requires a broader constituency base to support any legislation'. Tsebelis & Money, 36.

[59]   By controlling the order of choices available on the legislative agenda, outcomes of voting can also be controlled. This device, as well as more complex 'vote cycling' (e.g. Condorcet's famous paradox) are both analysed from the perspective of unicameral and bicameral legislatures by Tsebelis & Money.

Since 1995, the Council had been comprised of senators sitting *ex officio*: the respective head of the executive branch (president or governor) and legislative branch (speaker or chairman of each region).[60] This was not always the case. The Russian Federation's first legislature was the Supreme Soviet, a holdover from the (then still existing) Soviet Union. This body was constituted from a much larger Congress of People's Deputies, directly elected for the first time in March 1990. Boris Yeltsin was elected chairman of the new Parliament and quickly fostered its self-image as a populist body demanding ever-increasing powers from Gorbachev's central authority. A year later, when Yeltsin traded his post as head of the legislative branch to become Russia's first president, Yeltsin was himself forced to confront the riotous legislature he had created. A paralysing conflict between Yeltsin and the Supreme Soviet resulted in the October 1993 storming of the White House, the Parliament's home, and adoption of Yeltsin's new Constitution, which established a bicameral legislature. The Federation Council was directly elected in its entirety in 1993, with two seats chosen (and rarely more than two or three candidates to chose from) on a first-past-the-post basis for each of the eighty-nine constituencies. Interestingly, however, Yeltsin's Constitution did not explicitly demand *election* of the upper chamber, as it did for the lower chamber (the Duma) of the Federal Assembly. The 'manner of formation' of the Federation Council was left to be established by federal law.[61] With much effort, and only after the Duma overrode the veto of its sister chamber, a new law established the *ex officio* scheme of appointment employed from 1995 until 2000.[62]

Initially, the bargain must have seemed irresistible to Yeltsin. Having forcefully dispatched his enemies in the old parliament, Yeltsin's new law filled the upper chamber with a majority of men who owed their regional positions to appointment by him. Yeltsin also hoped for a less cantankerous body of law-makers, who by the very nature of their dual appointment, would behave more like a part-time legislature. The perks of office (e.g. apartments in Moscow) controlled by the Kremlin's state property administration further ensured a more passive upper chamber. As Yeltsin soon learned, however, he could not buy the love of the Federation Council. As more and more governors and republican presidents won election to their regional executive positions, their allegiance to Yeltsin waned. Local constituencies gave regional elites the luxury of characterizing the centre as

[60] *See* Stephen White, Richard Rose & Ian McAllister, *How Russia Votes* (Chatham, NJ: Chatham House, 1997), 31, 107–9, 125–6.

[61] Art. 96, §2, *Konstitutsiia Rossiiskoi Federatsii* (1993).

[62] Federal'nyi zakon 'O poriadke formirovaniia Soveta Federatsii Federal'nogo Sobraniia Rossiiskoi Federatsii', (No. 192-FZ, 5 December 1995), *SZRF*, No. 50 (11 Dec. 1995), item 4869, p. 8967.

stingy adversary, in much the same manner that Yeltsin had attacked Gorbachev. No longer beholden to their patron, governors, and presidents took seriously their roles as senators, sometimes to the visible frustration of President Yeltsin.

Putin immediately recognized the problem such a chamber posed for his efforts to strengthen federal executive power. Any attempt to weaken regional autonomy or limit regional jurisdiction would be opposed by senators whose personal power was decreased. Efforts to force out of office the most recalcitrant and rebellious governors and presidents would by stymied by the senatorial immunity from prosecution regional executives enjoyed. Reform would have to be multi-staged, beginning with a change of faces.[63]

The initial proposal from the Kremlin was draconian: senators were to be elected by each region's legislature. Although the regional executive had the power to nominate his representative, the advice and consent of the regional legislature was required for both senatorial appointments. The post of senator was explicitly defined as a 'professional-permanent' position, which meant that members of the Federal Duma, regional legislatures, local self-government, elected state or municipal officials and 'category A' state officials were expressly prohibited from service. Election of new senators to the reformed upper chamber would be completed no later than 1 April 2001. Regional heads of executive and legislative branches would enjoy, at most, a nine-month grace period of immunities and privileges.

As expected, the Federation Council expressed strong opposition, voting 129 to 13 against reform.[64] The Duma, therefore, became a critical player, where 300 votes (out of 450 deputies) would be required to override the

[63] Arguably, the governor of Primorskii Krai, Yevgenii Nazdratenko, was the first, albeit indirect, victim of this law. Nazdratenko, who defied Yeltsin's repeated efforts to remove him from his corrupt, personal fiefdom in the Far East, abruptly agreed to resign (despite recent statements to the contrary) following a phone call from Putin and a personal visit by the head of the Kremlin's Control Department (GKU), Yevgenii Lisov. What transpired in those conversations is unknown, but it is not unreasonable to speculate that the new consequences of remaining in office were made clear to the wayward governor. Julie A. Corwin 'Putin Makes Far East Governor An Offer He Can't Refuse', 5 *RFE/RL Newsline*, 25, Part I, 6 February 2001. A few weeks later, Putin appointed Nazdratenko Chairman of the Federal State Fisheries Committee, suggesting a carrot as well as stick approach. 6 *EastWest Institute Russian Regional Report*, 8, 28 Feb. 2001.

[64] Criticism of the bill by senators was particularly harsh. Even Novgorod Governor Mikhail Prusak, described as 'slavishly supportive' of Putin, reminded the new president that he 'was elected with the governors' help' and should therefore avoid 'confrontation between the president and the governors'. Julie A. Corwin, 'Senators Reject Bill Disbanding Upper House', 4 *RFE/RL Newsline*, 125, Part I (28 June 2000). Republic of Chuvashia President Nikolai Fedorov (a former federal Minister of Justice) declared that the bill was no less than a 'destruction of the system of checks and balances, and is very dangerous for democracy'. 5 *EastWest Institute Russian Regional Report*, 29 (26 July 2000).

upper chamber's veto.[65] Although Putin had achieved this support in the Duma's first three votes, his margin was extremely narrow. He was quick to signal that his bill was not engraved in stone; he was willing to compromise.[66] Senators could remain in office for the full length of their terms—1 January 2002 at the very latest—in what was termed a 'soft rotation' from power. A joint conciliatory commission of senators and Duma deputies hammered out further compromises, though it worked under the shadow of the Duma's override powers.[67] Under pressure, the commission took less than a fortnight to arrive at a compromise: senatorial appointments by regional executives would stand *unless* their legislatures rejected the candidate by a two-thirds special majority. Regional executives could, with the same limitation, recall their representative. With these additional amendments, and the Duma's super-majority the sword of Damocles hanging over their heads, the senators accepted the reform as a *fait accompli*.[68]

From the point of view of Putin's attempts to strengthen federal authority, reform of the Federation Council was obviously important. Most crucially, Putin removed regional elites from their dual posts as federal senators without serious revolt, stripping them in the process both of immunity against federal prosecution and influence over federal policy-making. Many observers feared that this was only the first step in a process that would strip the Council of its competences, reducing an important check on both the executive branch and the lower chamber of the parliament as well. Some, viewing Putin's reforms as a complete package, saw sinister connections between the reformation of the upper chamber and the creation of governors-general, transforming federal governance into an executive capped pyramid.[69] Egor Stroev, Chairman of the Federation Council, expressed his fear that Putin's so-called reform was the first stage in the 'dismantling' of the

[65] Art. 105, §5 of the Constitution requires a vote of two-thirds of the total number of Duma deputies to override a veto by the Federation Council.

[66] Anna Kozyreva, 'V poiskakh kompromissa', *Rossiiskaia gazeta*, 1 July 2000, 1–2.

[67] Anna Kozyreva, 'L'vinaia dolia popravok', *Rossiiskaia gazeta*, 12 July 2000, 1–2. One of the most contested amendments was to give regional executives the right to recall their representatives from the Federation Council without the agreement of the regional legislature. Ol'ga Tropkina, 'Soglasitel'naia komissiia k soglasiiu ne prishla', *Nezavisimaia gazeta*, 15 July 2000, 1. *See also* Svetlana Sukhova, 'Zakon samosokhraneniia', *Segodnia*, 18 July 2000, 1.

[68] In February 2001, Putin signed another law that received strong support in the Federation Council, for obvious reasons: it lifted the limit on terms in office for regional governors and presidents, permitting an incumbent executive to run for a third term (and in some cases, even a fourth term). No. 3-FZ, 8 February 2001, 'O vnesenii dopolneniia v Federal'nyi zakon "Ob obshchikh printsipakh organizatsii zakonodatel'nykh (predstavitel'nykh) i ispolnitel'nykh organov gosudarstvennoi vlasti sub"ektov Rossiiskoi Federatsii"', *SZRF*, No. 7, 12 Feb. 2001, item 608, p. 1784.

[69] Natal'ia Kalashnikova & Svetlana Sukhova, 'Vsia vlast' Sovetam bezopasnosti!' *Segodnya*, 26 May 2000, 1.

upper chamber; the result, he warned, would weaken the parliament as a federal representative organ for regional interests, and thus, the prospects for federalism and democracy in Russia: 'there will result a serious weakening of the federal bases of Russian statehood, for a democratic federation with a unicameral parliament is nonsense'.[70] One outspoken critic of the reform in the Federation Council, President of Chuvashia Nikolai Fedorov, threatened to challenge the reform in the Constitutional Court, contending that 'all honest lawyers admit that these reforms and laws are essentially revising the existing constitutional structure of the Russian Federation ...'.[71]

In an effort to appease the soon-to-be ex-senators, Putin created a new forum in which they could sit. In early September 2000, as he had hinted throughout the summer, Putin formed a 'State Council'.[72] This body was directly subordinated to the executive branch, having been created by presidential decree.[73] Its composition included all eighty-nine regional executives. A smaller presidium comprised of the seven regional executives chosen by the President on a six-month rotating basis, ensured that the reform would be tempered with the promise of the president's ear.[74] At its first meeting the Presidium established for itself monthly meetings with the president, while the Council would meet in plenary sessions only four times a year. While Putin made assurances that the State Council was merely an advisory body (though given the president's extensive decree powers, such a role was not to be downplayed), some suggested that its establishment presaged a transfer of competence from the Federation Council, a move that virtually all critical analysts agreed would require constitutional amendment.[75]

[70] Egor Stroev, 'Ne Navredi: Razmyshleniia o reforme gosudarstvennogo ustroistva Rossii', *Nezavisimaia gazeta*, 6 June 2000, 1, 8.

[71] *Radio Free Europe/Radio Liberty Newsline*, Vol. 4, No. 148, Part I, 3 Aug. 2000. In the end, Fedorov's threatened appeal to the Constitutional Court was abandoned when the Federation Council's Committee on Constitutional Legislation, with whom the appeal was to be made, decided not to take up the case.

[72] Speculation about the creation of (and strategic implications of creating) such a body in the light of Putin's reforms began as early as May. See Svetlana Sukhova, 'Gossovetskaia vlast"', *Segodnya*, 24 May 2000, 1. Hints were also made that immunity might vest in membership (though ultimately this was not made part of Putin's *ukaz*). *See* Natal'ia Kalashnikova & Svetlana Sukhova, 'Vsia vlast' Sovetam bezopasnosti!' *Segodnya*, 26 May 2000, 1.

[73] No. 1602, 1 Sep. 2000, 'O Gosudarstvennom sovete Rossiiskoi Federatsii', *SZRF*, No. 36, 4 Sept. 2000, item 3633, p. 7186.

[74] The members of the first Presidium were: Tyumen Oblast Governor Leonid Roketskii, Tomsk Oblast Governor Viktor Kress, Moscow Mayor Yurii Luzhkov, Khabarovsk Krai Governor Viktor Ishaev, Dagestan State Council Chairman Magomedali Magomedov, Tatarstan President Mintimer Shaimiev, and St. Petersburg Governor Vladimir Yakovlev. Each executive was chosen from a different federal district, as became the rule. Julie A. Corwin, 'State Council Presidium Holds First Meeting', *RFE/RL Newsline*, 190, Part I, 2 Oct. 2000.

[75] According to the powerful governor of St. Petersburg and a member of the new Presidium (and one of Putin's adversaries), Vladimir Yakovlev: 'Our conversations with Mr Putin have confirmed that in order for the State Council to be legitimate, we have to change the constitution. A number of the functions of the Federation Council may be transferred to it'. Andrew Jack, 'Council of Russia's governors to gain new powers', *Financial Times*, 28 Sept. 2000.

Beyond the substantive questions of competences and personnel, reform of the Federation Council raised procedural questions that touched not only on federal development, but on the transition from authoritarianism. An optimist would contend that Russia's constitutional system had functioned well: following the legitimate legislative initiative of a new president, disagreement in the legislative branch was expeditiously resolved in a conciliatory commission, compromise legislation worked out, and a law passed by large majorities in both houses. Threats to take the political battle to the Constitutional Court quickly lost support.[76] On the other hand, the pressure placed on the Federation Council, operating under the shadow of the Duma's supermajority and the untested rule-of-law credentials of Vladimir Putin, meant that conciliation on such a fundamental issue was hardly genuine. Senators accepted the reforms grudgingly, still under the threat of a Duma override, and with the feeling that they had little choice but to accede to the demands of a powerful new president.

A timeline of this legislative action is presented in Table 8.3.

Table 8.3   Timeline of Legislative Action

Date	Reform 1: Federation Council	Reform 2: Dismiss regional executives and legislatures	Reform 3: Dismiss local self-government
19 May	Duma receives bill	Duma receives bill	Duma receives bill
31 May	Duma approves bill in 1st reading		
23 June	Duma approves bill 2nd Reading: 302-86-5 3rd Reading: 308-86-3		
28 June	**Fed. Council VETO, 129–13**		
30 June		Duma approves bill 3rd Reading: 339-9-3	
7 July	Fed. Council votes to participate in conciliatory commission with Duma.	**Fed. Council VETO, 83-16-9**	Duma approves bill 3rd Reading: 334-27-3
19 July	Duma approves compromise bill, in three readings: 307-88-5	Duma overrides Fed. Council veto, 361-35-8	
26 July	Fed. Council accepts compromise bill, 119-18-4		
29 July		Putin signs into law	
4 Aug.			Putin signs into law
5 Aug.	Putin signs into law		

Sources: Vote tallies reported in *RFE/RL Newsline*, Vol. 4, Part I, No. 123 (26 June 2000); No. 125 (28 June); No. 127 (30 June); No. 130 (10 July); No. 137 (19 July); No. 142 (26 July).

[76] Ol'ga Tropkina, 'Sovet Federatsii ne speshit obrashchat'sia v KS', *Nezavisimaia gazeta*, 20 Oct. 2000, 3.

Implementation of the reform of the Federation Council moved slowly. Under the compromise known as the 'soft rotation', regional executives and chairs of regional legislatures sitting *ex officio* in the Federation Council had until 1 January 2002 to comply with the new law. According to the Federation Council website, as of 2 November 2001, only 85 senators (of 178) were working in the Federation Council on a 'permanent' basis, as prescribed by the new law.[77] Only 15 of these new members were from republics.[78] In 9 republics, no changeover had been accomplished at all. In only three republics (Marii El, Udmurtia, and Khakassia) had both senators been newly selected according to the law.

Reform No. 2: Federal Influence over Regional Legislatures and Executives

Regional executive and legislative branches of government were also targets of reform from above. Putin wanted to install the mechanisms that would give him real power according to his formula for 'strengthening of the executive vertical'. His draft legislation amended a 1999 law that had attempted to standardize baseline principles for regional legislative and executive structures (e. g. maximum lengths of legislative terms, deputies' immunities, use of official seals, procedural regularity, etc.), often merely by repetition or elaboration of principles set in the constitution (e.g. elections, jurisdictional competences, guarantee of control by legislatures of expenses required for their operation, etc.).[79] Among its most significant provisions, Yeltsin's old law appears to have outlawed the not uncommon republican practice of permitting members of republican legislatures simultaneously to hold official positions as executive heads of local administrations (a post akin to mayor of a district)—though this prohibition has been observed mainly in the breach by the republics.[80]

Putin amended this law to give the federal executive the power to dismiss regional legislatures and executives for extended and/or gross violations of federal law. Announcement of such an extraordinary power sent shock waves through opposition circles, who predicted a flagrant violation of the separation of powers. The actual legislation, however, was less extreme than

[77] http://www.council.gov.ru/sostav/members/spisok.htm

[78] Republican presidents Dzharimov (Adygeia), Rakhimov (Bashkortostan), Magomedov (Dagestan), Aushev (Ingushetia), Kokov (Kabardino-Balkaria), Ilumzhinov (Kalmykia), Semenov (Karachaevo-Cherkessia), Katanandov (Karelia), Merkushkin (Mordova), Nikolaev (Sakha-Yakutia), Dzasokhov (North Osetia-Alania), and Oorzhak (Tyva) continued to sit *ex officio* in the Federation Council.

[79] No. 184-FZ, 6 October 1999, 'Ob obshchikh printsipakh organizatsii zakonodatel'nykh (predstavitel'nykh) i ispolnitel'nykh organov gosudarstvennoi vlasti sub"ektov Rossiiskoi Federatsii', *SZRF*, No. 42, 18 Oct. 1999, item 5005, p. 9417.

[80] *See* Art. 12, §1. The negative ramifications of such a practice from the comparative perspective of representative democracies, as well as federalism, are analysed in Ch. 6.

what had been imagined, thanks mainly to the cumbersome and lengthy procedure through which this power could be realized. Although the law gave the president a considerable power to threaten regional politicians with dismissal, the law's procedures—if followed as outlined in the law—provided numerous opportunities over a long period of time and multiple stages of action by which those threatened could avoid fulfilment of the threat. Legislatures and executives were given six months to put their legal houses in order, after which time normative legal acts recognized by courts to contradict federal law would be susceptible to the provisions of the new law.[81] Analysis of these procedures is provided in Table 8.4.

The involvement of multiple authorities and deliberately long periods for compliance limit the severity of this reform. The strongest potential bulwark against abuse of this new power, however, is the involvement of the judicial branch at the initial stages of the process. The judiciary's role as shield against the executive's sword or the legislature's purse, and the invaluable institution of the rule of law for democracies, is discussed in Chapter Two. The authority of the court to demand the *rational* use of power—to demand *reasons* behind executive action—and to command adherence by *political* actors to *legal* principles (in other words, to establish and protect Cass Sunstein's 'republic of reasons' in a deliberative democracy) is extraordinarily important. Although predictions are always hazardous, the role of the judiciary in this process may well turn out to be what preserves the legal integrity—and prevents the capricious use of—this new law.

Nevertheless, a grant of power to the federal executive to initiate a process of dismissal of popularly elected officials and even whole legislatures for derogation from the constitutional order is an extraordinary authority in a federal system. By 'strengthening the vertical of executive power', this law emasculates the separation of powers between the federal and regional governments. Regional executives receive their mandate to govern in popular elections, not by commission from the federal executive. To subject them to discharge—either by the initiative of a federal executive *ukaz* or, worse, on the mere accusation (*not*, it must be emphasized, upon conviction) of the federal procurator—is as much a threat to the separation between regional and federal administration as it is to the political life of the official. Regional legislatures also receive, collectively, an electoral mandate that is entirely separate from that of the federal legislature that is now empowered to dissolve them, impliedly on a theory of collective culpability of all deputies for violating as a body the constitutional order. Those deputies who vote 'correctly' are not saved from the fate that awaits their stubborn colleagues.

[81] Art. 2 of federal law No. 106-FZ of 29 July 2000.

Table 8.4   Procedures for the Dismissal of Regional Executives and Legislatures Established by Federal Law no. 106-FZ, 29 July 2000

Article 3: Range of Potential Violations

'Organs of state power of subjects of the RF are responsible for violation of the RF Constitution, federal constitutional laws and federal laws, and also guarantee conformity with the RF Constitution, federal constitutional laws and federal laws... [of their constitutions, charters, laws and other normative legal acts].

[Organs of state power of subjects of the RF are responsible for]... normative legal acts that contradict the RF Constitution, federal constitutional law and federal law and that entail massive and flagrant violation of the rights and freedoms of man and citizen, a threat to the unity and territorial integrity of the Russian Federation, the national security of the Russian Federation and its defence capacity, [and] the unity of the legal and economic space of the Russian Federation,...'

Article 9, §4: Procedure for Dismissal of Regional Legislatures for Violation of Article 3	Article 29: Procedure for Dismissal of Regional Executives for Violation of Article 3
1. The 'appropriate' court establishes the existence of a violation;	1. The 'appropriate' court establishes the existence of a violation; or, the President issues an *ukaz* suspending action of a normative legal act of the executive or an organ of the executive branch;
2. Legislature fails to comply with court decision within six months (or other term set by court);	
3. Obstacles to the realization of federal law continue to exist;	2. Executive has two months (or other term set by the court) to comply with the court's decision; or two months to comply with the presidential *ukaz* or appeal to the appropriate court for resolution of the dispute;
4. President issues a warning to legislature in the form of an *ukaz* within one year of court decision;	
5. Legislature has three months to comply with court decision (and presidential warning);	3. President must issue a warning (in form of *ukaz*) to the executive within six months of the court's opinion or the president's first (suspensive) *ukaz*;
6. President introduces bill to Federal Duma for dissolution of legislature;	4. Executive has one month from issuance of warning to enact measures to correct the reason for the warning;
7. Duma required to examine bill within two months;	5. President may then dismiss the executive with an *ukaz*, which enters into force ten days after publication;
8. Legislature dissolved upon passage of federal law by Duma.	6. The dismissed executive may appeal the *ukaz* to the RF Supreme Court within that ten day period; the Supreme Court should consider the complaint and accept a decision within ten days.

OR

In accord with criminal procedural legislation, upon presentation by the Procurator-General of an accusation against the regional executive for perpetration of a grave or especially grave crime, the President may temporarily discharge the executive from his office.

This is not to say that violation of the supremacy of the federal constitution or federal law is tolerable;[82] nor does it diminish the flagrant disregard for federal legal authority that has been the rule and not the exception
in post-Soviet Russia. These dangers (in the form of philosophies of state
sovereignty and 'treaty-constitutional' conceptions of the federal compact,
support for the principle of nullification, secessionism, or simple nonfeasance) have been recurring themes of this book, as has been the fundamental
importance of acceptance of rule-of-law principles in any federal system. But
the powers granted the federal authorities by this reform are so extreme on
the continuum of federal systems as to be virtually off the register.

An underlying acceptance of the role of the rule of law (and by extension
courts in general) as a neutral arbiter, rather than political weapon, is profoundly lacking in Putin's reforms. The destructive double legacy of Soviet
conceptions of law as a political tool or weapon and federalism as a mere
administrative device for centralization, is glaringly apparent in the perceived
need for federal dismissal of regionally elected officials and legislatures. The
experience of other federations has generally led to an acceptance, even in the
most politically charged moments, of the rule of law (interpreted by courts of
law) as the unshakeable bedrock for the 'rules of the game'. In the United
States, for example, dismissal of *state* officials by federal authorities (either
executive or legislative) for violation of the federal constitution is simply
unimaginable.[83] While it was conceivable that a federal executive could
enforce Supreme Court-ordered integration of public schools in the 1950s,
for example, there could be no serious discussion of a federally sponsored
eviction of elected state governors who, in every imaginable way, sought to
defy the Court, the Congress and the President.[84] Nor was there room to
imagine that the angry legislative resolutions passed by many southern states
reacting against the opinion of the Court could be grounds for federally
ordered dissolution of those elected bodies. The Court, and the country as a

---

[82]   Oliver Wendell Holmes' famous comment is *à propos*: 'I do not think the United States would
come to an end if we lost our power to declare an Act of Congress void. I do think the Union
would be imperiled if we could not make that declaration as to the laws of the several States'.
Quoted in Gerald Gunther & Kathleen M. Sullivan, *Constitutional Law*, 13th Ed. (Westbury, NY:
Foundation Press, 1997), 65.

[83]   While impeachment has sometimes been used to remove executive officials from office, this
function has been rare in the United States. Impeachment has predominantly been used to unseat
judges. In either case, this is done by and at the behest of the legislature (not the executive) sitting
as a *court* of impeachment (not, in principle, as a political body) to decide a violation of the law of
its own jurisdiction (state or federal).

[84]   Even when in 1957, Arkansas Governor Orval E. Faubus openly defied court-ordered school
desegregation with the use of Arkansas national guardsmen, his flagrantly unconstitutional act was
not met by then President Eisenhower with efforts to seek his dismissal. Nor could this have been
attempted by the federal Chief Executive against a state governor with an electoral mandate.
Eisenhower responded by calling out U.S. soldiers, whose forceful presence was used to accomplish
the federal courts' orders.

federal system, relied on the authority of the judiciary (remarkably, even when federal relations were at their most strained) to declare the rule for all and leave to the executive branch its enforcement.

There are still other considerable grounds for serious concerns about abuse of presidential discretion. The rather vague power of the President to *temporarily* discharge regional executives is extremely severe.[85] Only an *accusation* (*not* a conviction, or even a scheduled trial) is required for exercise of this power. An order by an 'appropriate' court is not required at any stage of its use. Nothing is said about what stage in the criminal investigative process the 'temporary' discharge terminates. Given that the period of time between accusation and trial can extend to years (and that, even following an acquittal, reinvestigation, and retrial is permitted by the Constitution), a regional executive may be confronted with an interminable 'temporary' suspension from office. Furthermore, no limitations are put on the exercise of this power, for example, in the final days of a gubernatorial election, or even to disqualify an incumbent executive as a candidate in the next elections. The new law does not specify what constitutes a 'grave' or 'especially grave' crime. There is also no built-in waiting period for the exercise of this power, as adopted for the other mechanisms for dismissal provided in this law. This is the power that regional executives truly feared,[86] especially as their senatorial immunities were taken away by the law on the Federal Assembly.[87]

---

[85]   Art. 29, §4 of the revised law, No. 184-FZ of 6 October 1999 (explicated in Art. 1, §6 of Putin's reform legislation, No. 106-FZ of 29 July 2000).

[86]   The fear may well be justified. One week after the law entered into effect (a 6-month delay was built into the law signed 29 July 2000), Putin seemed to have won a prize that had eluded his predecessor for years—the resignation of Primorskii Krai governor Evgenii Nazdratenko. Though it is unclear whether Putin specifically threatened the governor with use of *this* law, its sudden presence in Putin's arsenal of powers certainly was known to all parties. David Filipov, 'Russians Still Shiver As Governor Is Ousted', *Boston Globe*, Feb. 6, 2001, A9. According to Radio Free Europe, the day before Nazdratenko's resignation (for health reasons many disputed), Putin phoned Nazdratenko, and the head of the Kremlin's State Control Department, Yevgenii Lisov, personally visited Nazdratenko. Paul Goble & Julie A. Corwin, 'Putin Sacks Energy Minister, Makes Far East Governor An Offer He Can't Refuse', 5 *RFE/RL Newsline*, 25, Part I, 6 Feb. 2001.

[87]   Why wasn't a conciliation commission established to whittle away the harshest features of this reform, as had been accomplished with the reform of the Federation Council itself? One factor may have been the different vote tallies in the Duma between the two pieces of legislation. Art. 105, §5 of the Russian Constitution grants the Duma the power to adopt a federal law over a Federation Council veto by a vote of two-thirds the total number of the lower chamber's 450 deputies (i. e. 300 deputies). Whereas the third reading of the bill on the composition of the Federation Council passed in the Duma with only 308 votes, and approval of its compromise version passed with only 307 votes, the Duma passed the bill on dismissal of regional executives and legislatures by a solid 361 votes, well over the margin necessary to defeat a veto by the upper chamber.

Reform No. 3:   Federal Influence over Local Self-government

As noted above, Yeltsin rapidly lost the power to appoint and dismiss regional executives as increasing numbers of regional politicians won popular mandates in open (if not always contested) elections. This was not the case for the relationship between regional executives and the heads of local self-government, the lowest level of government in the regions. In many cases, heads of local self-government were appointed by the executive, responsive (because responsible) to their political patrons rather than to political parties or the electorate. Frequently, heads of local executive administrations served *ex officio* as deputies in regional legislatures, according to the same formula by which the Federation Council had formerly been composed. When these local executives owed their posts to the governor or president of the region, the result was a flagrant violation of the principle of separation of powers. As noted above, this practice was outlawed in the Yeltsin administration, though compliance seems to have been negligible in the absence of strong enforcement.

Putin sought to change this practice, again by submitting a Yeltsin-era law to amendment.[88] These amendments did to local self-government what Putin's strengthening of the executive 'vertikal' did to the relationship between the federal executive branch and the executive and legislative branches of regional governments.[89] Upon a finding by a court (*which* court is unspecified) that a normative legal act promulgated by a local representative or administrative body contradicts either federal or regional laws, or otherwise amounts to a 'violation (disparagement)' of human or civil rights 'or offensive of anther injury', those organs are required to revoke the act and publish the ruling of the court. In the event of non-compliance with the judicial order, the representative organ is subject to dismissal and the head of the administrative body subject to early discharge from duty. The procedure for discharge is also similar, although the required preliminary written warning could come either from the initiative of the regional legislature (to warn the local representative organ), or by the regional executive (to warn both the representative and executive local organs). Following issuance of the warning, the local organs at risk of dismissal have one month to comply with the original court order; after that time, but within six months of the

[88] That law was No. 154-FZ, 28 August 1995, 'O obshchikh printsipakh organizatsii mestnogo samoupravleniia v Rossiiskoi Federatsii', *SZRF*, No. 35 (1995), item 3506; with amendments found at No. 12 (1997), item 1378.

[89] This reform was made law by No. 107-FZ, 4 August 2000, 'O vnesenii izmenenii i dopolnenii v Federal'nyi zakon "Ob obshchikh printsipakh organizatsii mestnogo samoupravleniia v Rossiiskoi Federatsii"', *SZRF*, No. 32, 7 Aug. 2000, item 3330, p. 6243.

court order, the local representative body may be dismissed by the regional legislature (by passage of a law), and the local executive body may be dismissed by the regional executive (by issuance of an *ukaz*). If the regional power lay dormant, three months after the court order, the President of the Russian Federation may introduce legislation to the State Duma to dismiss the representative organ, and on his own authority dismiss the local executive. New elections would be triggered immediately by any dismissals.[90] As before, courts have the ultimate authority to review dismissals (where citizens who could claim that the dismissal worked a violation of their rights or legal interests would have standing to appeal dismissals). A six-month grace period was established, as in the other reform, before retroactive enforcement of decisions by courts on existing violations would commence.

While supporting the procedure for dismissal with judicial orders on either side could potentially de-politicize disputes by maintaining rule-of-law standards for judgment of local authorities and abuses of administrative discretion, the new procedure presents several problems as well. The same criticism of Russia's courts, slowly emerging from their traditional place under the thumb of political powers, could be laid before this 'reform'. In other governmental systems, violations of the law by officials of the executive branch result in orders to comply with law or be impeached. In the United States, impeachment has predominantly settled on the removal of corrupt judges, although in its original conception (deeply influenced by the English common law tradition) impeachment was put forward also as a means to restrain abuses of power by the chief executive and his appointed officials.[91] Usually, impeachment is by a legislature (or some part of it) sitting as a court of impeachment. The point is that the procedure is a judicial one, with all the attendant safeguards and rules of evidence. Under Putin's law, impeachment is by decree of the next higher executive in the chain of command.

Another problem is the use of a power to dissolve legislatures as an impeaching device. 'Aggrandizement of the legislative at the expense of the other departments' was a serious enough concern for James Madison to

---

[90] The treatment of heads of *municipal* administrative organs is exceptional. Regional executives and the RF President both have power to issue an *ukaz* of dismissal and to appoint temporary acting heads of those organs in the interim before elections, unless the charter of the municipality prescribed a different procedure. Proposals for dismissal of such officials by the President of the Russian Federation may be introduced by the legislature of the region, the regional executive, the RF Government and the RF Procurator-General.

[91] Raoul Berger, *Impeachment: The Constitutional Problems* 2nd ed. (Cambridge, MA: Harvard University Press, 1999), 4–5.

devote several articles of *The Federalist Papers* to its attention.[92] But his solutions—bicameralism, an executive veto, and the competing interests of different constituencies in a 'compound republic', i. e. federalism itself—did not include the power of the executive and judicial branches to discharge the legislative branch from power.[93] The legislature, as a body, was not subject to discharge by the executive, even if it passed legislation declared by the Supreme Court to be in flagrant and gross violation of the Constitution. The solution to the problem of how to deal with a recalcitrant parliament that persisted in passing unconstitutional legislation was either to rely on popular displeasure at election time or to rely on the executive branch to refuse to implement the law declared by the judiciary to be unconstitutional.

The Russian tradition has pointed in the opposite direction, and it is to this legacy that the source of the idea of prorogation-as-impeachment might be attributed. One of the most debilitating legacies of the Soviet era has been the continued approach to law as a political weapon rather than as an administrative tool: law is a means to crush opponents when in power, to weaken them when in opposition. Yeltsin's baptism by parliamentary fire in 1992–3 showed the depths to which such thinking could sink. The remedy there was executive dissolution of the Parliament,[94] followed by the use of the military to shell parliamentary opponents (who themselves had declared the executive power null and void due to misuse) into submission. Putin has characterized his own 'reforms' as *restoration* of the vertical executive power, indicating that for him, autonomy from central control is an aberration to be corrected.[95]

3. POLITICAL PALIMPSESTS: REFORM OF REPUBLICAN CONSTITUTIONS

As part of his campaign to strengthen the vertical of executive power, Putin demanded the conformity of regional constitutions and laws to federal laws.

---

[92] *See*, in particular, No. 48, 49, and especially 51.   [93] *The Federalist, No. 51.*

[94] This was the infamous *Ukaz* No. 1400, 21 September 1993, 'O poetapnoi konstitutsionnoi reforme v Rossiiskoi Federatsii', *Sobranie Aktov Prezidenta i Pravitel'stva Rossiiskoi Federatsii*, No. 39, 27 Sept. 1993, item 3597, p. 3912.

[95] Addressing the nation on 17 May, Putin expounded: 'If the head of a territory can be dismissed by the country's president under certain circumstances, he should have a similar right in regard to authorities subordinate to him. Today, this is not just a right thing to do, but simply necessary in order to restore the functional vertical structure of executive power in the country. For a long time now the federal parliament, the government and even the president have not been able to achieve even simple but absolutely necessary things because they lacked such tools: to observe the citizens' rights and implement Russian state legislation with equal precision throughout Russia, in its most remote parts as well as in Moscow. This is what the dictatorship of law means. It would mean we are living in one strong country, one single state called Russia'.

This was, by any comparison with other federal systems, an eminently reasonable demand. The Russian Federal Constitution expressed the supremacy of federal law over the laws of constituent units of the Federation. In this sphere, Putin was battling not Soviet legacies, but the legacy of his predecessor Boris Yeltsin. As has been discussed in earlier chapters, beginning with his campaign for political advantage over Mikhail Gorbachev, Yeltsin relied on a rhetoric of sovereignty and autonomy ill-suited for the federal system he was attempting to craft. Regional politicians seized on this vocabulary when Yeltsin urged them to 'take all the sovereignty you can swallow', and found themselves unwilling to drop such habits of thought when Yeltsin sought to reassert federal control.

Putin's reforms sought to undo this legacy. The Federation Council reform deprived regional political elites of seats and voices in the federal capital. This reform also deprived regional executives and heads of legislatures of their senatorial immunity. This deprivation gave the second reform—federal power to dissolve and dismiss wayward legislatures and executives—that much more sting. The third reform established the same power over local self-government. Faced with rising tallies of regional constitutions, charters, laws, and decrees that violated federal law, Putin's reforms laid a new foundation on which to command compliance—which his new governors-general could confirm and, if need be, compel.

The post-Soviet researcher now has an extraordinary collection of public documents available for analysis. A burst of constitutional reform resulted in the regions, and especially the republics, where violations were the most frequent and flagrant. The rush to reform generated a tremendous amount of legislative activity for comparison and analysis.[96] In some cases, three sets of constitutions could be compared: Soviet, Yeltsin and Putin-era legal documents, exposing the frameworks and follies of a decade of constitution-making. Republican reaction to Putin's threatening reforms produced constitutional palimpsests: documents that have been written, imperfectly erased, and written over again, with the result that the original work often remains visible underneath more recent revisions. Two examples are briefly examined below: one from relatively pro-federal Mordova, one from the rebellious republic of Bashkortostan.

---

[96] No less a bounty of documents awaits the researcher interested in sub-constitutional legal reform. Following the passing of a 1 January 2001 deadline for regional laws to be made compliant with federal ones, President Putin claimed that 60 constitutions and over 2,300 regional laws had been made to conform with federal law. Paul Goble, 'Putin Calls for Prosecutors to Shift Approach', 5 RFE/RL Newsline, 8, Part I (12 Jan. 2001).

3.1 The Constitutions of the Republic of Mordova

Consider three preambles for the constitution of the Republic of Mordova (Table 8.5). Some changes are obvious. The 'soviet' and 'socialist' appellations of the first revision are deleted from the later drafts.[97] A more subtle change is between the 1995 version—stating support for the maintenance of a federation while expressing a more direct connection to the people of Mordova—and the version revised under pressure from Putin. In the 2000 version, primacy of place is given not to the people of Mordova but to the people of the Russian Federation, who incidentally 'live' in this republic. Allegiance, it would seem, is based solely on citizenship (federal), not residency (Mordovan).

More substantive changes are detectable in other parallel provisions of these constitutions. For example, those pertaining to the supremacy of laws (Table 8.6). Again, the soviet-era terminology and principles of democratic centralism are erased early in the process of revisions, as the vocabulary is shaped by practice: 'social organizations' give way to organs of local self-government. Subtle changes speak volumes. In 1995, in the height of legal flux in the regions, the hierarchy of law from the vantage point of constitutional engineers sitting in the Mordovan capital of Saransk was: federal constitution, republican constitution, federal law, republican law. The latest revision reflects the victory of Moscow's point of view: federal constitution, federal law, republican constitution, republican law. Similar changes are made to key constitutional provisions for the control of land and natural

Table 8.5   Preambles of Three Mordovan Constitutions, 1990–2000

Late Soviet Constitution	1995 Constitution	2000 Revised Constitution
The Supreme Soviet of the Mordova Soviet Socialist Republic, realizing responsibility for the fate of the multinational people of the republic, . . . declares its resolve to create a democratic rule-of-law state in the RSFSR and a renewed USSR.	We, the plenipotentiary representatives of the multinational people of the Republic of Mordova, . . . confirming our striving for the preservation of the integrity of the Russian Federation, . . . supporting the principles of a democratic, rule-of-law society. . .	We, the plenipotentiary representatives of the multinational people of the Russian Federation, living in the Republic of Mordova, . . . proclaiming the principles of a democratic, rule-of-law society. . .

[97] This author's official copy of the Soviet-era Mordovan Constitution (provided by the Mordovan 'embassy' in Moscow in 1994) is undated, but was almost certainly promulgated in late 1990 or early 1991, as reference to the 'renewed' USSR—the focus of Gorbachev's last 18 months in office and a common refrain in republican declarations of sovereignty—strongly suggests.

Table 8.6   Supremacy of Law in Three Mordovan Constitutions, 1990–2000

Late Soviet Constitution	1995 Constitution	2000 Revised Constitution
Organization and activity of the Soviet state is constructed according to the principle of democratic centralism . . . (Art. 3); State and social organizations, officials must observe the Constitution of the [U]SSR, RSFSR Constitution, Constitution of the Mordova SSR, and also the laws of the USSR, RSFSR and Mordova SSR, . . . (Art. 4, §2)	Organs of state power, organs of local self-government, officials, citizens and their associations must observe the Constitution of the Russian Federation, Constitution of the Republic of Mordova, federal laws and laws of the Republic of Mordova. (Art. 4, §3)	Organs of state power, organs of local self-government, officials, citizens and their associations must observe the Constitution of the Russian Federation, federal laws, the Constitution of the Republic of Mordova, and laws of the Republic of Mordova. (Art. 4, §3)

resources in the republic (Article 8, §3 in the 1995 and 2000 redactions) and the right to possession, use and disposal of property (Article 35, §2 in the 1995 and 2000 redactions). Federal power is ascendant.

3.2   The Constitutions of the Republic of Bashkortostan

The Republic of Mordova, never a trouble-maker for federal authorities, was quick to comply with demands for legal conformity. The Republic of Bashkortostan, however, seized the opportunity to turn nonfeasance into malfeasance: while the most glaring violations of the federal constitution were removed from the republic's constitution, still more problematic features remained, and in some cases, were added to the new version, both approved by the legislature and signed by the president on 3 November 2000.[98] As the history of Russia's federal development demonstrates, Bashkortostan has been a thorn in the side of federal officials from the very beginning. Bashkortostan was one of the first republics to declare sovereignty in 1990. In 1992, Bashkortostan used the added pressure on federal authorities created by Tatarstan's refusal to sign the Federation Treaty to

---

[98] No. 94-z, Zakon Respubliki Bashkortostan 'O vnesenii izmenenii i dopolnenii v Konstitutsiiu Respubliki Bashkortostan', passed by the State Assembly of the Republic of Bashkortostan, and signed by the President of the Republic, on 3 November 2000. The law entered into force on 23 November 2000. A copy of this law was provided by the Plenipotentiary Representation of the Republic of Bashkortostan in Moscow (Vx. No. 164, 8–11–2000) to Mr David Hoffman, to whom the author is very grateful.

win for itself an eleventh hour special appendix of privileges and exceptions. Bashkortostan, again profiting from the tension Tatarstan injected into federal politics, negotiated one of the earliest bilateral treaties—winning for itself considerable promises of autonomy. Emboldened by such victories, Bashkir President Murtaza Rakhimov continued to press his hand, building a personal autocracy at the base of the Ural Mountains, placing family and friends at the head of key republican industries and political institutions, and with increasing flagrancy, defying federal authority.

Demands by the new federal president and his governor-general (in this case, Sergei Kirienko) to reform were met first by stubborn refusal. Following a Constitutional Court determination that the republic's constitution violated federal law, Rakhimov grumbled that the determination was a political, not a legal act; his republic's chief justice quibbled with the procedures of the federal Court.[99] Using the ten-year anniversary celebrations of Bashkortostan's Declaration of Sovereignty as a platform, Rakhimov criticized the federal government, explaining that republican laws had resolved urgent problems in the republic that Moscow had been too slow or timid to confront.[100]

Bashkortostan's new preamble set the tone for the confrontational document it introduced. In many ways, the new version is even more forceful than the old. As Table 8.7 shows, nothing was removed from the first preamble, but much was added. The 1993 Constitution explicitly referred to the republican referendum to confirm the 'treaty character' of the republic's relations with Moscow. This reference was not to a bilateral treaty (not signed until August 1994) but to the 1992 Federation Treaty. That document had just been superceded by the Federal Constitution adopted twelve days before the Bashkir Constitution, on 12 December 1993. Bashkir elites, like many of their republican peers, were furious that the much more republican-friendly Treaty had essentially been made null-and-void by Yeltsin's Constitution. The Russian Federation Constitution was not even acknowledged in the republican preamble. The new preamble goes much further. Not only is the referendum mentioned, but the treaty-basis for Bashkir-Russian relations is traced back to the 16th century! Explicit reference is made not only to the republic's Declaration of Sovereignty (a feature of the old preamble), but to the 'generally recognized' principle of self-determination of peoples in the

[99] Igor Rabinovich, 'Bashkortostan Ignores Court Ruling', 5 *EastWest Institute Russian Regional Report*, 36, 4 Oct. 2000.

[100] Igor Rabinovich, 'Leaders of National Republics Criticize Kremlin', 5 *EastWest Institute Russian Regional Report*, 39, 23 Oct. 2000. Rakhimov shared the stage in Ufa with Tatarstan President Shaimiev and Ingushetia President Aushev, whose speeches were even more critical of the federal government.

Table 8.7   Preambles of the 1993 and 2000 Bashkir Constitutions Compared

24 December 1993 Constitution	23 November 2000 Constitution
[1] We, the multi-national people of the Republic of Bashkortostan,	[1] We, the multinational people of the Republic of Bashkortostan,
[2] UNITED by a common fate on our land,	[2] UNITED by a common fate on our land,
[3] SHOWING respect for the rights and freedoms of man and citizen, of all peoples,	[SEE BELOW, CLAUSE SEVEN]
[4] RECOGNIZING the responsibility for our Motherland before current and future generations,	[SEE BELOW, CLAUSE EIGHT]
	[3] NOTING that Bashkortostan in the XVI century voluntarily, on a treaty basis, united with Russia and the Bashkir Autonomous Republic was formed in 1919 in the composition of the RSFSR on the basis of the Agreement of the Central Soviet Power of Russia with the Bashkir government as the Soviet Autonomy of Bashkiriia as a result of the realization of the right of the Bashkir nation to self-determination,
[5] BEING LED by the Declaration of State Sovereignty of the Republic of Bashkortostan,	[4] EMANATING from the generally recognized principles of equal rights and self-determination of peoples in the Russian Federation, and also the Declaration of State Sovereignty of the Republic of Bashkortostan,
[6] PROCEEDING from the results of the republican referendum of 25 April 1993, which confirmed the treaty character of relations of the Republic of Bashkortostan and the Russian Federation,	[5] BEARING in mind the results of the republican referendum of April 1993, which confirmed the treaty character of relations of the Republic of Bashkortostan and the Russian Federation,
	[6] BEING FOUNDED on the Treaty of the Russian Federation and the Republic of Bashkortostan 'On the demarcation of subjects of jurisdiction and joint delegation of authority between organs of state power of the Russian Federation and organs of state power of the Republic of Bashkortostan',
[SEE ABOVE, CLAUSE THREE]	[7] SHOWING respect for the rights and freedoms of man and citizen, of all peoples,
[SEE ABOVE, CLAUSE FOUR]	[8] RECOGNIZING the responsibility for our Motherland before current and future generations,
[7] DECLARING its resolve to create a democratic, rule-of-law state,	[9] DECLARING its resolve to create a democratic, rule-of-law state,
[8] ACCEPT in the person of our plenipotentiary representatives the present Constitution of the Republic of Bashkortostan.	[10] ACCEPT in the person of our plenipotentiary representatives the present Constitution of the Republic of Bashkortostan.

Russian Federation.[101] The 1994 bilateral treaty is explicitly mentioned by its lengthy formal title, while reference to the federal constitution is conspicuous by its continued absence.

The 'treaty character' of relations is the underlying theme woven into virtually every part of the new constitution. Perhaps the most radical change between the two documents is the insertion of the complete text of the republic's bilateral treaty into the fundamental law of Bashkortostan, confusingly preceding 'Section One' of the Constitution, on the 'fundamentals of the constitutional order'. This is an extraordinary addition to the Constitution! By virtue of the approval of the republican constitution by the Bashkir legislature, Bashkortostan's treaty would appear to enjoy a status no other bilateral treaty to date enjoys—formal legislative approval. The bilateral treaty is now elevated (at least in the eyes of republican authorities) to the level of constitutional law.

The republic's struggle between concessions to federal authority and assertions of its own autonomy continued in the 'first' (after the reproduced treaty) section of the Constitution, 'Fundamentals of the Constitutional Order'. As shown in Table 8.8, Bashkortostan redacted some, but not all, of its assertions of sovereignty from the text. In Article One, defining the state, the draftsmen of the new edition cling to the word 'sovereignty', but remove it from its lead position, tacking on to the first clause the formulaic phrase used in most other republican constitutions to denote membership in the Russian Federation. Sovereignty is similarly abridged in the assertion of jurisdictional competence and policy-making. While the republic's authority to conduct its own foreign policy is conspicuously deleted from the new text, a lengthy description of the republic's adherence to international legal principles is clumsily added to the section. Again asserting the 'inalienable right to self-determination', the addition of Article Sixteen seems as much an assertion of the republic's interest in participation in the community of sovereign states as it is an announcement to federal authorities of republican expectations for these principles to govern *their* relations. Articles 16, 17, and 18 (on defence and conscription) seem crafted to limit the effect of the deletion of identical articles in the old Chapter VII, 'The Republic of Bashkortostan—a Sovereign State', as well as the deletion of other articles covering treaty relations, principles of budget negotiations, and international relations.

---

[101] As discussed in Ch. 2, the principle of self-determination of peoples is *not* generally recognized in international law, including the founding documents of the United Nations. It may be argued that, as the assertion to this right has been deleted from the body of the Constitution (the old Art. 69), its appearance in the preamble (traditionally *not* the repository of justiciable claims) is a lessening of the power of that assertion. However, this argument is mitigated by the appearance of the claim in the newly minted Art. 16, §3.

Table 8.8   Sovereignty and Federal Relations in Bashkortostan's Two Constitutions

Subject	1993 Constitution	2000 Constitution
Definition of the State (Article 1)	The Republic of Bashkortostan is a sovereign, democratic, rule-of-law state, . . .	The Republic of Bashkortostan is a democratic, rule-of-law sovereign state in the composition of the Russian Federation, . . .
	The Republic of Bashkortostan possesses the highest power on its territory,	Sovereignty in the RB is expressed in the possession of all fullness of state power (legislative, executive, and judicial) outside the boundaries of jurisdiction of RF and authority of the RF on subjects of joint jurisdiction of RF and the RB.
	independently determines and conducts domestic and foreign policy,	The RB independently determines and conducts domestic policy and participates within the limits of its authority in international relations. . . .
	accepts the Constitution of the Republic of Bashkortostan and republican laws, which have supremacy on its entire territory.	The RB has its own Constitution and legislation. Laws of RB, accepted on subjects of jurisdiction of the RB and authority of the RB on sujects of joint jurisdiction of the RF and RB, possess supremacy on the whole territory of the RB.
Location and Defence of Sovereignty	The bearer of sovereignty and the sole source of state power in the Republic of Bashkortostan is its multi-national people. (Art. 3)	The sole source of state power in the Republic of Bashkortostan is its multi-national people. (Art. 3)
		The international activity of the RB is based on the recognition of principles of respect for state sovereignty and the equality of all countries, the inalienable right to self-determination, equal rights and non-interference in domestic affairs, respect for territorial integrity and inviolability of existing borders, rejection of the use of force and threat of force, of economic and every other method of pressure, peaceful regulation of conflicts, respect for the rights and freedoms of man, including the right of national minorities, conscientious

Table 8.8 (contd.)

Subject	1993 Constitution	2000 Constitution
		fulfillment of responsibilities and other generally recognized principles and norms of international law. (Art. 16, §3)
Federal Relations (Article 5)	The Republic of Bashkortostan is an independent subject of the renewed Russian Federation. The RB enters into the composition of the RF on a voluntary and equal-rights basis. Relations of the RB and the RF are determined by the Treaty on the bases of inter-state relations of the RF and the RB, by other bilateral treaties and agreements. Laws of the RF, which are accepted on questions voluntarily transferred by the RB to the jurisdiction of the RF are binding on the territory of the RB.	The Republic of Bashkortostan is a full-rights subject of the Russian Federation. The RB enters into the composition of the RF on a voluntary and equal-rights basis. Relations between organs of state power of the RB and organs of state power of the RF are determined by the Constitution of the RB, Constitution of the RF and the Treaty on demarcation of subjects of jurisdiction and joint delegation of authority between organs of state power of the RF and organs of state power of the RB, with other bilateral treaties and agreements.

As discussed in Chapter Seven, the creation of special rights to citizenship in some republics presents particular problems for federalism as well as democracy in the Russian Federation. Dualist conceptions of distinctive rights of citizenship (as opposed to mere residency) in select parts of a federation threaten the existence of a unified legal and economic space that is a prime advantage of federal governance. When this citizenship is predicated on ethnic or other particular qualities, additional problems may be presented for rights of franchise and social entitlements from the state. Bashkortostan is one of the republics that issued its own citizenship early in the development of its republican institutions. Along with Tatarstan, it has engaged in a long-running battle with federal authorities over the issuance of multiple foreign passports or, alternatively, inserts in the official languages of the republics noting dual citizenship, federal and republican.

The new redaction of the Constitution leaves open the possibility of republican citizenship (Art. 4, Art. 25)[102] but states categorically that all

---

[102] Article 4 categorically begins 'The Republic of Bashkortostan has its own citizenship' but then establishes the 'unity' (edinye) of federal and Bashkir citizenship. Art. 25 prohibits the limitation of rights and duties of Bashkir and federal citizenship in the event of possession by a citizen of dual citizenship. The first constitution's articles on republican and dual citizenship implied the legal capacity of the republic to create such citizenship by law or international treaty (Arts. 22 and 23, 1993 Constitution).

citizens of the Russian Federation enjoy the full protection and benefits of federal and republican constitutions in Bashkortostan (Art. 24). Those articles guaranteeing civil and political rights that formerly began with the phrase 'Citizens of the Republic of Bashkortostan have the right' are now revised to imply that such rights are available to all people in the republic, regardless of Bashkir (or even, arguably, federal) citizenship.[103] One month after the adoption of these provisions, Tatar President Shaimiev, Bashkir President Rakhimov and governor-general Sergei Kirienko of the Volga District hammered out an agreement on the matter, ending a three-year suspension by the republics of the issuance of new federal passports.[104] In keeping with the ambivalence of the new constitution, the agreement permits the insertion of supplemental pages giving the bearer's data in Bashkir or Tatar (though it remains unclear whether these data will include nationality). Whether or not these supplements constitute the physical manifestation of republican citizenship is equally unclear, though in combination with the above constitutional provisions, they were evidently satisfactory enough to the two famously stubborn republican leaders.

Perhaps the most vexing characteristic of federal-Bashkir relations, disregard for the supremacy of federal laws, is not resolved by the new RB Constitution. 'In the event of a contradiction', reads the final clause of Article 117 on the hierarchy of laws in the republic, 'between a law of the Republic of Bashkortostan, accepted in conformity with part two of the present article, and federal law [i. e. either on subjects of RB jurisdiction or subjects of RB authority in areas of joint jurisdiction between the RF and the RB], the law of the Republic of Bashkortostan has effect'. There seems to be little change from the categorical assertion of the previous constitution that laws of the republic 'possess supremacy' on the entire territory of the republic (Art. 128, 1993 Constitution).

---

[103] Although the retention of the old chapter heading ('Civil and Political Rights of Citizens') might suggest that rights are so restricted, the redaction of the phrase 'RB citizens' from the following articles implies a more general interpretation. Those articles are No. 33 (freedom to move one's domicle), 34 (freedom of thought and speech), 35 (freedom of conscience), 36 (freedom of choice of language, but *not* freedom of choice of national membership—reserved only for RB citizens), 41 (freedom of association—but *not* the freedom to peaceably assemble, guaranteed by Art. 40 only to RB citizens), and 42 (right of appeal). Similar revisions have been made to most of the rights categorized under the chapter heading 'Economic, Social and Cultural Rights' (although these are mostly aspirational rights, e. g. rights to rest, medical aid, a clean environment, a home, etc.) and to procedural guarantees (e. g. rights to qualified legal aid).

[104] Liz Fuller, 'Tatarstan, Bashkortostan Resolve Passport Dispute with Moscow', 4 *RFE/RL Newsline*, 244, Part I, 19 Dec. 2000.

These and other revisions of the Bashkir constitution received mixed reaction by federal authorities. Shortly after its adoption, governor-general Sergei Kirienko made his first trip to Bashkortostan, to participate in the tenth anniversary celebrations of the republic's declaration of sovereignty. In a sudden spurt of activity, Kirienko and RF Minister of Justice Yurii Chaika balanced criticism of the Bashkir legal order (still one of the most egregious violators of federal legislation) with the appointment of a former republican minister as federal inspector for the republic, and the agreed abolition of the republican Ministry of Justice, clearing the way for a branch of the federal ministry to oversee legislation, a function it lost in the mid 1990s when Bashkortostan stopped sending draft legislation to Moscow for analysis.[105] Nevertheless, just two months later, Aleksandr Zvyagintsev, the deputy procurator-general for the Volga federal district (perhaps responding to accusations of 'professional idiocy' laid at the feet of federal authorities by the head of the RB presidential analytic department, Amir Yuldashbaev) declared the Bashkir constitution still to be in violation of federal law.[106]

4. CONCLUSIONS

Putin's reforms were, more than anything else, a reaction to Yeltsin's federal legacy of weak federal institutions and lack of consensus on basic questions of sovereignty and inter-governmental relations in a federal state. Writing while Putin was still acting president, Vladimir Lysenko, the Deputy Chairman of the Duma's Committee on Federal and Regional Policy, described a model of centralization he called 'guided democracy, or a soft authoritarian regime—an attempt to consolidate power for the completion of economic reforms in the country by way of the creation of a regime of personal power of the president of the country and the limitation of a number of democratic institutions and procedures'.[107] In many ways, Lysenko's programme presaged Putin's federal reforms, including reform of the Federation Council,

---

[105] Igor Rabinovich, 'Kirienko Finally Visits Bashkortostan', 5 *EastWest Institute Russian Regional Report*, 42, 15 Nov. 2000. The new federal inspector, Rustem Khamitov, is the former RB Minister of Emergency Situations (until 1998); 'Kirienko Abolishes Bashkortostan Justice Agency', 1 *RFE/RL Security Watch*, 18, 20 Nov. 2000; Igor Rabinovich, 'Justice Minister Sets Up Office In Bashkortostan', 5 *EastWest Institute Russian Regional Report*, 44, 29 Nov. 2000.

[106] 5 *RFE/RL Newsline*, 5, Part I, 9 January 2001; 5 *RFE/RL Newsline*, 8, Part I, 12 Jan. 2001.

[107] This model was expounded as early as February 2000 in an unpublished paper prepared for Duma and Federation Council working groups. The author is grateful to Mikhail Stolyarov for a copy of this document. The model was eventually published in early April. Vladimir Lysenko, 'Federatsiia v nachale XXI veka', *Nezavisimaia gazeta*, 11 Apr. 2000, 8.

reform of the system of presidential representatives, and strengthening (i.e. centralization) of the power to enforce the supremacy of federal legal and economic (including budget and tax) systems. This approach, Lysenko asserted, was already slowly beginning to operate in Russia and should be encouraged: centralization of federal power and an even stronger president were prerequisites for a 'developed democracy', only after which could there be a return to decentralized federalism.[108]

Neither Lysenko nor Putin could provide satisfactory assurances that 'soft authoritarianism' (in Lysenko's phrase) or 'the dictatorship of law' and the 'strengthening of the vertical of executive federal power' (in Putin's words) would not be medicine worse than the disease. Is Russia doomed to decide between an increasingly centralized federal system and a system increasingly at risk of disintegration, as Riker predicted for all federal systems? On a more nuanced continuum of federal systems, which direction does Russia face? It is to these larger questions, that this book again returns in conclusion.

---

[108] Vladimir Lysenko, 'Federatsiia v nachale XXI veka', *Nezavisimaia gazeta*, 11 April 2000, 8. Lysenko argued that the strong president and centralized state he prescribed for Russia was of a 'European type', resembling the personal power of Charles de Gaulle, not some 'central Asian despotic regime.'

9

Conclusion

William Riker's classic exploration of federalism in the Handbook of Political Science opens with the observation, 'An initial difficulty in any discussion of federalism is that the meaning of the word has been thoroughly confused by dramatic changes in the institutions to which it refers'.[1] That statement encapsulates a key point of departure for the analysis of federalism in this book. It is also a clue to one of the core problems faced by political elites in the new Russian Federation—conflicting conceptions of what, exactly, it means to be 'federal'. Consensus about how to build (or rebuild) a new state order would be difficult for any polity to secure. Federalism is a complex political philosophy for the interaction of different levels of government that are somehow simultaneously decentralized and unified. Federalism is based upon a conception of sovereignty that is a radical departure from the traditional understanding of sovereignty as absolute and indivisible. For Russia, a multi-national state in transition from the debilitating legacy of Soviet power, these conceptual hurdles were monumental.

This book takes an insistently multi-disciplinary and comparative approach to these and other problems of Russian federalism. In place of a single definition or list of federal requirements, a continuum of federal possibilities has been examined. Acknowledging the enormous contribution (to theory and by empirical example) of the American case to the study of federalism, it is a poor methodology to utilize the American federation as if it were one of Plato's Forms. This is especially true in the study of federal approaches in multi-national states. Nevertheless, it is impossible to deny that the American experience has deeply influenced both political scientists and legal scholars. It is therefore that much more surprising, given the influence of the American democratic federal system on federal theory, that so many theorists have accepted the assertions of *non-democratic* regimes to be federations. In an earlier work, Riker asserted, 'Since the Soviet Union preserves all the features of federalism, the mere fact that its federalism fails to prevent tyranny should not lead to casting it out of the class of

[1] William H. Riker, 'Federalism', in Fred I. Greenstein & Nelson W. Polsby, eds. *Handbook of Political Science: Vol. Governmental Institutions and Processes* (Reading, MA: Addison-Wesley, 1975), 93.

federalisms.'[2] The Soviet Union, however, preserved *none* of the features of federalism. An important aim of this study has been to explain why the existence of 'tyranny' in a state is one of the clearest indications that, despite august constitutional assertions to the contrary, its political system cannot be considered federal. In particular, this book focuses on the relationship of federalism to sovereignty, democracy and the rule of law.

Building a federal system means creating a culture of legality. Unilateral declarations of sovereignty must eventually give way, if the federation is to survive, to consensus over how best to establish jurisdiction over an issue, what level of government shall possess what jurisdictional authority, and how best to handle the inevitable disputes that arise. Jurisdiction problems require juridical solutions. It is crucially important to develop a mindset that appreciates, responds to, and engages in the exercise of legal self-limitation. There must be a willingness to be bound by the rule of law. But how is a sense of legal constraint created among ruling elites? Acceptance of the *rule* of law requires acceptance of the *role* of law in the state and society. How is an appreciation developed for law as a mechanism for long-term dispute resolution, not as a short-term political tool? This is a question that will face Russia for a long time to come.

This book has focused on the institutional asymmetry of Russian federalism. There is nothing inherently pathological about asymmetry in federal systems; in fact, federations are often the product of regional disparities of all sorts. But asymmetry that is built into the constitutional structure of the state must be created and managed carefully, with particular attention to the democratic and rule-of-law prerequisites federalism requires. At several points in this book, Russia's federal transition has been compared—unfavourably—to the transition that occurred in Spain. Whereas Madrid co-ordinated lengthy, constitutionally entrenched, transparent and multi-lateral negotiations, Moscow relied on short-term, opaque, bilateral deals between executive branches that were either aconstitutional or brazenly anti-constitutional. The result for Russia was not a federal system in which institutional asymmetry was accepted (because mutually agreed upon), but one constantly challenged and, consequently, perpetually open to destabilizing renegotiation of the fundamental order.

It is a misuse of terms to characterize non-democratic regimes as federal systems, even if they appear to adopt various forms of decentralization or even devolution of power. The Soviet Union was no more a federal state than it was a democratic state, or one bound by the rule of law. Such a non-democratic regime, operating outside the rule of law, is really just a federal

---

[2]   William H. Riker, *Federalism: Origin, Operation, Significance* (Boston: Little, Brown, 1964), 40.

façade. That is not to say that institutions thus mis-labelled federal do not have profound and lasting effects on their respective political systems. In several instances, these states have exploded (or imploded, depending on the metaphors and conceptions of the analyst) into competing—sometimes warring—states.

I take issue with such characterizations but not with the underlying premise. Institutions do matter. Tremendously so, in fact. The break-up of Yugoslavia, like the break-up of Czechoslovakia and the Soviet Union had much to do with the institutional design of these complex state systems. My refusal to call these systems federal does not devalue or underestimate the influence of their institutional make-up. On the contrary, by making careful distinctions between federal and non-federal systems we may better understand why some 'federal' systems function better than others, particularly those that have their origins in preceding, radically different, political systems.

Rather than a federal political system, the Soviet Union was a highly centralized authoritarian (and sometimes totalitarian) regime that operated behind a federal façade. Like a Potemkin village, Soviet 'federalism' exhibited many of the structural manifestations common to federal systems. But these could not conceal a rigidly unitary state. The federal provisions of its successive constitutions were trumped by organizing principles that privileged a vanguard party with monopoly control over state (and societal) institutions and a governing position always superior to the rule of law. Ironically, it was precisely this façade nature of Soviet federalism, at least as much as its constitutionally enshrined formal provisions, which have helped to shape the new Russian Federation. The very lexicon that republican elites employed—sovereignty, self-determination, and federalism 'from the ground up'—owes much to Leninist and Stalinist doctrines that disingenuously used the same vocabulary to beguile from the true foundations for the Soviet state. Republican elites were forced by the weakening power of the Party on one side and the simultaneous growing importance of local constituencies on the other to develop strategies to maintain their authority. The 'Parade of Sovereignties' provided a powerful issue around which to unite and a foundation upon which new rules of the political game could be designed. Ethnically demarcated territorial units with traditions of privilege for their titular ethnic (and usually minority) populations provided the building blocks for constructing a new Russian Federation as the institutions of the old Soviet Union were being demolished.

The existing ethno-federal façade combined with the political machinations of Boris Yeltsin to result in a highly politicized environment in which the vocabulary and conceptions of Soviet federalism were uncritically deployed in open debates and closed negotiations. Yeltsin famously urged the republics to 'take as much sovereignty as you can swallow', with the intention of creating an environment that would weaken Mikhail Gorbachev's Union centre while strengthening Yeltsin's authority in the RSFSR. This strategy worked well in the short term, unleashing a flood of sovereign demands that overwhelmed the centre and temporarily cast Yeltsin as the marshal of a parade of sovereignties. But as Yeltsin's RSFSR emerged from the fading shadow of Soviet control to be the new 'centre', his promises and entreaties returned to haunt him. Republican elites, it seemed, actually expected their sovereign demands to be heeded in a 'renewed federation', and Yeltsin soon found himself in a position similar to the one in which he had cast his previous adversaries. Gorbachev was gone but the language and anti-centrist conceptions that were used to remove him and the system he represented were solidly established in the politics of the new Russian Federation.

The argument of this book has been that such strategies, however politically expedient at the moment, sowed the seeds for deeper problems, and made them that much harder to resolve in the future. Yeltsin's exhortation to 'take all the sovereignty you can swallow', like nontransparent bargaining games that followed, no doubt preserved Yeltsin's power *vis-à-vis* political opponents. But such politics did little to preserve federal cohesion (not to mention a federal consensus); in Yeltsin's own words, it could only 'paper over the cracks'.[3] These cracks expanded at the same time that they were being obscured. The short-term political advantages of conceptual confusion—in speeches, commissions and declarations—resulted in long-term hazards for what is most fundamental to federal cohesion: consensus on the basic 'rules of the game' and purpose of federal unity.

The institutional structure of this new federation, the 1992 Federation Treaty and 1993 Constitution, has been analysed in this book. The former document was a weak, vague and ambivalent political compromise. As republics began to adopt their constitutions and pass new laws, little attention seemed to be spared to ensure their conformity with the Federation Treaty. When pressed to explain these incongruities, republican elites reverted to the language of sovereignty and *snizu vverkh*, federalism built from the ground up. Taxes were withheld, court decisions ignored, federal presidential and parliamentary directives alike rejected by the leading republics as infringements on their sovereign rights. The origins of a doctrine of

[3] Daniel S. Treisman, *After the Deluge: Regional Crises and Political Consolidation in Russia* (Ann Arbor: University of Michigan Press, 1999), 47, 223, note 33.

nullification, inimical to federal theory, can already be seen at this early stage in Russia's federal development.

Yeltsin's federal Constitution, realized in no small part through violence, rescinded the Federation Treaty. A new clause in the Constitution reversed the previous presumption that republics possess all powers not explicitly granted the Federation by the Treaty, to one which left constituent units only the powers not claimed by federal authorities—few indeed. It is an academic but still disputed point whether the Constitution met the required participation threshold for passage in its 12 December 1993 referendum. It is clear, however, that the majority of republics, taken as complete units, either rejected the new Constitution (eight republics) or had voting levels too low to validate the result.

The institutional asymmetry already inherent in Russia's hierarchy of constituent units proliferated in a 'Parade of Treaties'.[4] Although various forms of asymmetry are common in federal systems, this book has examined the theoretical and empirical reasons why Russia's unique brand of bilateral institutional asymmetry is of serious concern. The effects of political brinkmanship and iterated, weakly constrained bargaining on federal structures have been examined. Particular attention has been drawn to the problems such inter-governmental relations cause for the development of a unified legal space and a stable fiscal system, especially taxation.

Would republics eventually have splintered the Russian Federation apart, succumbing to a 'bandwagon effect' of secession and incorporation of various regional associations? The public declarations and private negotiations of regional elites suggest that greater autonomy, not independence, was their primary objective. The federal government's fiscal appeasement strategy, expertly identified by Daniel Treisman, helped regions achieve this goal. Moscow adopted a strategy of rewarding threatening behaviour in order to avert a feared cascade of secession. Republican political elites, however, were not infrequently just as anxious that their bluffs might be called. Federal anxiety was manipulated to prevent a deluge of independence that both sides hoped would never come. Manipulation of the centre's fears of ethnic violence, nationalism, and separatism were arrows in republican quivers, weapons many republics (but by no means all) used masterfully to obtain precisely the fiscal largesse, political appeasement and greater institutional autonomy they desired. But the concomitant effect was to seriously weaken acceptance of the value of federal unity, *Bundestreue*, and respect for the rule of law to mediate disputes. Instead, law often became just another weapon in federal-regional disputes.

---

[4] Elena Tregubova, 'Boris El'tsin v Tatarii', *Segodnia*, 31 May 1994, 1.

Russia's unique structure of inter-governmental relations also has had an effect on the development of institutions *inside* the republics. These republican institutions have been examined in detail both because of their importance from a federal perspective and from the related standpoint of an ongoing transition from authoritarian rule. Republican elites, mostly *nomenklatura* incumbents, designed rules of the game that provided them with winning strategies to retain power but which have had a debilitating effect on the political development of their republics. Examination of presidential and parliamentary elections reveals some starkly undemocratic practices and very weakly developed democratic structures (e. g. extremely weak party systems). Problematic conceptions of citizenship have been explored and the maintenance of privileges—*de facto* and *de jure*—for the titular ethnic group has been revealed. This is particularly apparent in the ethnic composition of parliaments and local administrations. It also goes hand in hand with a blurring of the division of powers, most obvious in intra-bicameral systems but also existent elsewhere. So remote are many republics from completing a transition to democracy that a different analytical perspective—their varying transitions *from* authoritarianism—seems a more accurate approach to the classification of republican political systems.

The conceptualization of 'treaty-constitutional' federal relations is perilously close to doctrines of sovereignty and nullification that are direct opposites of the unity and multilateralism that most federal theorists accept to be at the core of federal theory. The over-centralization and authoritarianism of Soviet 'federalism' has given way to a new Russian federalism that approaches the other extreme. The republican conception that the Russian Federation is no greater than the sum of its parts, that federalism is only justified 'from the ground up,' and that the sovereignty that the republics have retained permits selective compliance with federal agreements is a significant threat to the stability and integrity of the Russian Federation. Russia's second president, Vladimir Putin, has responded at the other extreme. Declaring a 'dictatorship of law', the federal reforms that inaugurated his presidency were designed to 'strengthen the executive vertical' of power. Weak conceptual, democratic and rule-of-law foundations continue to threaten the new Russian state.

Bibliography

(1) Documents

(a) Constitutions

Konstitutsiia Respubliki Bashkortostan. Ufa: Respublikanskogo izdatel'stva 'Bashkortostan', 1994.

Konstitutsiia Respubliki Buriatia. Ulan-Ude: Komp'iuterno- izdatel'skii tsentr 'Buriatiia', 1994.

Konstitutsiia Karachaevo-Cherkesskoi Respubliki. Cherkessk: Karachaevo-Cherkesskoe gosudarstvennoe respublikanskoe knizhnoe izdatel'stvo, 1996.

Konstitutsiia Respubliki Khakasia. Abakan: Verkhovnyi Sovet Respubliki Khakasiia, 1995.

Konstitutsiia Respubliki Marii El. Ioshkar-Ola: Izdanie Verkhovnogo Soveta Respubliki Marii El, 1993.

Konstitutsiia (Osnovnoi zakon) Respubliki Sakha (Yakutia). Yakutsk: Natsional'naia izdatel'sko-poligraficheskaia kompaniia 'Sakapoligrafizdat', 1995.

Konstitutsiia Respubliki Severnaia Osetia-Alania. Vladikavkaz: Goskomizdat RSO-Alania, 1995.

Konstitutsiia Respubliki Tatarstan. Kazan: Tatarskoe knizhnoe izdatel'stvo, 1995.

Konstitutsii Respublik v sostave Rossiiskoi Federatsii. Parts 1 & 2. Moscow: Izdanie Gosudarstvennoi Dumy, Izvestiia, 1995.

Konstitutsiia Rossiiskoi Federatsii. Moscow: Izdatel'stvo 'Os'–89', 1998.

Proekty Konstitutsii Rossiiskoi Federatsii i analiticheskie materialy (v dvukh chastiakh). Moscow: Izdanie Verkhovnogo Soveta Rossiiskoi Federatsii, undated.

Stepnoe Ulozhenie (Osnovnoi Zakon) Respubliki Kalmykia. Elista: Kalmytskoe knizhnoe izdanie, 1994.

(b) Declarations of Sovereignty

'Deklaratsiia o Gosudarstvennom Suverenitete Bashkirskoi Sovetskoi Sotsialisticheskoi Respubliki' (Council of Ministers and Supreme Soviet drafts), *Sovetskaia Bashkiriia*, 10 August 1990, 2.

'Deklaratsiia o Gosudarstvennom Suverenitete Buriatskoi Sovetskoi Sotsialisticheskoi Respubliki' (Procuracy draft) *Pravda Buriatii*, 9 September 1990, 4.

'Deklaratsiia o Gosudarstvennom Suverenitete Buriatskoi Sovetskoi Sotsialisticheskoi Respubliki' (Council of Ministers draft), *Pravda Buriatii*, 3 October 1990, 3.

'Deklaratsiia o Gosudarstvennom Suverenitete Buriatskoi Sovetskoi Sotsialisticheskoi Respubliki' (Presidium Supreme Soviet draft), *Pravda Buriatii*, 6 October 1990, 1.

'Deklaratsiia o Gosudarstvennom Suverenitete Iakutskoi Sovetskoi Sotsialisticheskoi Respubliki' (Presidium Supreme Soviet draft), *Sotsialisticheskaia Iakutiia*, 2 September 1990, 2.

'Deklaratsiia o suverenitete IaASSR' (draft of N. Egorov) *Sotsialisticheskaia Iakutiia*, 15 September 1990, 2.

'Deklaratsiia o Gosudarstvennom Suverenitete Iakutskoi-Sakha Sovetskoi Sotsialisticheskoi Respubliki' *Sotsialisticheskaia Iakutiia*. 30 September 1990, 1.

Deklaratsiia o Gosudarstvennom Suverenitete Iakutskoi-Sakha Sovetskoi Sotsialisticheskoi Respubliki. Postoiannoe predstavitel'stvo Respubliki Sakha (Iakutiia) pri Prezidente Rossiiskoi Federatsii.

'Deklaratsiia o Gosudarstvennom Suverenitete Kalmytskoi ASSR' (Supreme Soviet draft) *Sovetskaia Kalmykiia*, 7 September 1990.

'Deklaratsiia o Gosudarstvennom Suverenitete Kalmytskoi ASSR' (Supreme Soviet draft) *Sovetskaia Kalmykiia*, 6 October 1990, 2.

Deklaratsiia o Gosudarstvennom Suverenitete Kalmytskoi Sovetskoi Sotsialisticheskoi Respubliki. Postoiannoe predstavitel'stvo Respubliki Kalmykiia pri Prezidente Rossiiskoi Federatsii.

'Deklaratsiia o Gosudarstvennom Suverenitete Karelskoi ASSR' *Leninskaia pravda (Karelskoi ASSR)*. 11 August 1990, 1.

'Deklaratsiia o gosudarstvennom suverenitete Komi Sovetskoi Sotsialisticheskoi Respubliki', *Krasnoe znamia*. 5 September 1990.

'Deklaratsiia o gosudarstvennom suverenitete Komi Sovetskoi Sotsialisticheskoi Respubliki' (drafts by Komi kotyr), *Krasnoe znamia*. 13 July 1990.

Deklaratsiia o Gosudarstvennom Suverenitete Komi Sovetskoi Sotsialisticheskoi Respubliki. Postoiannoe predstavitel'stvo Respubliki Komi pri Prezidente Rossiiskoi Federatsii.

Deklaratsiia o Gosudarstvennom Suverenitete Rossiiskoi Sovetskoi Federativnoi Sotsialisticheskoi Respubliki. Moscow: Priniata pervym S"ezdom narodnykh deputatov RSFSR, 12 June 1990.

'Deklaratsiia o Gosudarstvennom Suverenitete Tatarskoi Respubliki' (Citizens' Committee draft, Shtanin draft, and TOTs draft) *Sovetskaia Tatariia*. 8 August 1990, 2.

'Deklaratsiia o Gosudarstvennom Suverenitete Tatarskoi Sovetskoi Sotsialisticheskoi Respubliki' (Supreme Soviet draft) *Sovetskaia Tatariia*. 15 August 1990, 1.

'Deklaratsiia o Gosudarstvennom Suverenitete Tatarskoi Sovetskoi Sotsialisticheskoi Respubliki', *Sovetskaia Tatariia*. 31 August 1990, 1.

'Deklaratsiia o Gosudarstvennom Suverenitete Udmurtskoi Sovetskoi Sotsialisticheskoi Respubliki' (Supreme Soviet draft) *Udmurtskaia pravda*. 11 August 1990, 1.

(c) Stenographic Records and Gazettes

Pervyi s"ezd narodnykh deputatov SSSR, 25 maia–9 iiunia 1989 g. Stenograficheskii otchet. Vol. I. Moscow: Uzdannie Verkhovnogo Soveta SSSR, 1989

Vtoroi s"ezd narodnykh deputatov SSSR, 12–24 dekabria 1989 g. Stenograficheskii otchet. Vol. I. Moscow: Izdanie Verkhovnogo Soveta SSSR, 1990.

Chetvertyi s"ezd narodnykh deputatov SSSR, 17–27 dekabria 1990 g. Stenograficheskii otchet. Vol. 1. Moscow: Izdanie Verkhovnogo Soveta SSSR, 1991.

Stenograficheskii otchet, Zasedanie pervoe, Vtoraia sessia Verkhovnogo Soveta Tatar ASSR. August 1990.

Stenograficheskii otchet, Tret'ia sessia Verkhovnogo Soveta Bashkirskoi SSR (dvenadtsatyi sozyv), 10–13 oktiabria 1990 g., 23–24 octiabria 1990 g. Ufa: Izdanie Verkhovnogo Soveta Bashkirskoi SSR, 1991.

Vedomosti S"ezda narodnykh deputatov RSFSR i Verkhovnogo Soveta RSFSR. Moscow: Izdanie Verkhovnogo Soveta RSFSR, 1990.

Vedomosti S"ezda narodnykh deputatov Rossiiskoi Federatsii i Verkhovnogo Soveta Rossiiskoi Federatsii. Moscow: Izdanie Verkhovnogo Soveta RF, 1992.

Vneocheredniaia Vtoraia Sessiia Verkhovnogo Soveta Bashkirskoi ASSR Dvenadtsatogo Sozyva Zasedanie Pervoe (3 sentiabria 1990 g., utrenee), Stenograficheskii otchet Izdanie Verkhovnogo Soveta Bashkirskoi ASSR. Ufa, 1990.

(d) Treaties and Agreements

Publication of treaties and agreements was sporadic and uncomprehensive. No official gazette exists as the publication of record for these documents, although *Rossiiskie vesti* has on occassion printed some treaties (*dogovory*). Treaties and agreements are sometimes published in regional newspapers. These have been cited in footnotes. The best unofficial, though incomplete, compilation is by M.N. Guboglo, *Federalizm vlasti i vlast' federalizma* (full citation below). Photocopies and computer reproductions of treaties were provided to the author by a variety of sources, including the permanent representations of different republics in Moscow and authorities in the republics themselves. V.T. Andreevna, Director of the Programme for assistance to reform of legal education in Russia, of the Moscow branch of the Russian Science Fund, provided copies of agreements for Bashkortostan, Komi, and Tatarstan.

(e) Other Documents and Compilations

Abdulatipov, R.G. & L.F. Boltenkova (eds.) *Federativnyi dogovor: Dokumenty. Kommentarii.* Moscow: Izdatel'stvo 'Respublika', 1992.

Adrov, A.N., & S.M. Shakhrai (eds.) *Sbornik zakonodatel'nykh aktov RSFSR o gosudarstvennom suverenitete, soiuznom dogovore i referendume.* Moscow: 'Sovetskaia Rossiia' izdatel'stvo, 1991.

Aiupov, M.A., I.A. Adigamov, I.Sh. Muksinov, F.R. Muratshin, V.E. Safonov, & I.M. Iulbarisov (eds.) *Stanovlenie dogovornykh otnoshenii Respubliki Bashkortostan i Rossiiskoi Federatsii (1990–1996 g.) (Sbornik dokumentov).* Ufa: Izdatel'sko- poligraficheskii kompleks pri Sekretariate Gosudarstvennogo Sobraniia Respubliki Bashkortostan, 1997.

Doronchenkov, A.I. (ed.) *K Soiuzu suverennykh narodov: Sbornik dokumentov KPSS, zakonodatel'nykh actov, deklaratsii, obrashchenii i presidentskikh ukazov, posviashchennykh problema natsional'no- gosudarstvennogo suvereniteta.* Moscow: Institut teorii i istorii sotsializma TsK KPSS, 1991.

Goroda i raiony Respubliki Tatarstan v tsifrakh: Statisticheskii sbornik. Kazan': Goskomstat Rossiiskoi Federatsii, Gosudarstvennyi Komitet Respubliki Tatarstan po statistike, 1996.

Gosudarstvennyi komitet Rossiiskoi Federatsii po statistike. *Demograficheskii ezhegodnik Rossiiskoi Federatsii: 1993.* Moscow: Goskomstat, 1994.

Gosudarstvennaia Simvolika Respubliki Tatarstan. Kazan: Tatarskoe knizhnoe izdatel'stvo, 1995.

Guboglo, M.N. (ed.) *Federalizm vlasti i vlast' federalizma.* Moscow: IntelTekh, 1997.

Khakimov, Rafael. *Belaia kniga Tatarstana. Put' k suverenitetu (Sbornik ofitsial'nykh dokumentov) 1990–1995.* Kazan': 'Tatpoligraf', 1996.

Kodeks Respubliki Bashkortostan o vyborakh. Ufa: Redaktsionno- izdatel'skii otdel Sekretariata Gosudarstvennogo Sobraniia Respubliki Bashkortostan, 1997.

Real'nyi federalizm: Piat' let suvereniteta Respubliki Sakha (Iakutiia). Yakustk: 'Sakha- poligrafizdat', 1995.

Respublika Tatarstan v tsifrakh za 1995 god: Statisticheskii sbornik. Kazan': Goskomstat Rossiiskoi Federatsii, Gosudarstvennyi Komitet Respubliki Tatarstan po statistike, 1996.

Rossiiskie zakony. Sbornik tekstov. Moscow: Izdatel'stvo BEK, 1996.

Salikov, M.S. *Konstitutsionnoe pravo Rossiiskoi Federatsii: Sbornik sudebnykh reshenii.* Sankt-Peterburg: Paritet, 1997.

Sbornik zakonov SSSR i ukazov Prezidiuma Verkhovnogo Soveta SSSR 1938–1961 g. Moscow: Izdatel'stvo 'Izvestiia Sovetov Deputatov Trudiashchikhsiia SSSR', 1961.

XIX All-Union Conference of the CPSU, Documents & Materials. Report and Speeches by Mikhail Gorbachev, General Secretary of the CPSU Central Committee. Resolutions. Moscow: Novosti Press Agency, 1988.

Zakon Respubliki Bashkortostan O Konstitutsionnom Sude Respubliki Bashkortostan. Ufa: Redaktsionno-izdatel'skii otdel Sekretariata Gosudarstvennogo Sobraniia Respubliki Bashkortostan, 1997.

Zakon Respubliki Bashkortostan O Mestnom Samoupravlenii v Respublike Bashkortostan. Ufa: Redaktsionno- izdatel'skii otdel Sekretariata Gosudarstvennogo Sobraniia Respubliki Bashkortostan, 1998.

Zakon Komi Avtonomnoi Sovetskoi Sotsialisticheskoi Respubliki O Sobstvennosti v Komi ASSR. Syktyvkar: Komi knizhnoe izdatel'stvo, 1990.

(2) Interviews with the Author

The following interviews were conducted between 1995 and 2000.

(a) Republic of Bashkortostan

Y.S. Afanasiev, Specialist, Department for International and National Questions, Administration of the President. Ufa, 5 and 14 May 1997.

A.N. Arinin, RF Duma Deputy, Candidate for President. Ufa, 14 June 1998 (with Tomila Lankina).

D.D. Azamatov, Specialist, Administration of the President. Ufa, 16 June (with Tomila Lankina).

S. Fufaev, Journalist, Adviser to Arinin. Ufa, 14 June 1998 (with Tomila Lankina).

M.A. Gazizov, Specialist, Administration of the President. Ufa, 16 June (with Tomila Lankina).

V.S. Kalmatskii, Deputy Dean, Law Faculty, Bashkir State University. Ufa, 28 April 1997.

B.I. Kinziagulov, Chairman, Bashkir Central Election Commission. Ufa, 14 June 1998 (with Tomila Lankina).

R.Z. Mavliiarov, Specialist, Department for Currency Investment and Economic Expertise, Ministry of Foreign Affairs. Ufa, 12 and 14 May 1997.

M.P. Mirgaziamov, Former Chairman, Council of Ministers, Candidate for President. Ufa, 7 May 1997; 15 June 1998 (with Tomlia Lankina).

F.M. Raianov, Professor of Law, Law Faculty, Bashkir State University, Former Member of the Bashkir Constitutional Commission. Ufa, 30 April 1997.

V.K. Samigullin, Professor of Law, Law Faculty, Bashkir State University, Co-Drafter of Declaration of Sovereignty & Former Member of Bashkir Constitutional Commission. Ufa, 28 and 30 April 1997.

P.A. Samoilin, Correspondent, Radio Bashkortostan. Ufa, 14 June 1998 (with Tomlia Lankina).

Z.D. Yenikeev, Professor of Law, Law Faculty, Bashkir State University. Ufa, 29 April 1997.

Z.I. Yenikeev, Chairman, Legislative Committee on Local Power, National Affairs and Social & Religious Groups, State Assembly, Former Member of Bashkir Constitutional Commission and Bashkir Delegation to Federation Treaty Talks. Ufa, 6 and 8 May 1997.

(b) Republic of Kalmykiia

Z.K. Dordzhaeva, Chairman, Movement for Democratic Reforms. Elista, 29 June 1997.

K.N. Ilumzhinov, President of Kalmykiia. Elista, 30 June 1997 (with Andrew Kramer).

Iu.O. Oglaev, Chairman, General Committee for the Defense of the Constitution. Elista, 28 June 1997.

L.A. Iudina, Editor, *Sovetskaia Kalmykiia*. Elista, 30 June 1997 (with Andrew Kramer).

(c) Moscow

S. Chugrov, IMEMO. 27 June 1995; 30 June 1996.

A.R. Galliamov, Expert, Department for Consular and Protocol Services, Plenipotentiary Representative Office of Bashkortostan. Multiple meetings.

M. Harvey, Russian Foundation for Legal Reform. Multiple meetings.

D.E. Hoffman, Bureau Chief, *Washington Post*. Multiple meetings.

M.M. Kipkeev, Adviser, Permanent Representation of the Republic of Karachaevo-Cherkessia

B.V. Khylkhachiev, Former RF Duma Deputy, Founder: People's Party of Kalmykiia. 26 June 1997.

E.A. Omuku, Assistant to President Ilumzhinov, FIDE. 24 June 1997.

M. McFaul, Senior Consultant, Carnegie Center for International Peace. 18 July 1995.

N. Petrov, Senior Consultant, Carnegie Center for International Peace. 5 July 1996; 24 November 1998

E.V. Serova, Institute of Economic Problems of the Transition Period.

V.V. Smirnov, Institute of State and Law, 13 July 2000

M. Snowdon, Second Secretary Political/Internal Unit, U.S. Embassy. 2 June 1997.

D.I. Solov'ev, Chief Adviser on International and Economic Relations, Permanent Representation of the Republic of Sakha (Yakutia).

M.V. Stoliarov, First Deputy Representative, Plenipotentiary Representation of Tatarstan. Multiple meetings.

(d) Republic of Tatarstan

T. Akulov, Advisor to the President. Kazan', 13 June 1997.

M.V. Andreev, Legal Advisor, Dialogue-Investments. Multiple meetings.

V.A. Beliaev, 'Democratic Union'. Kazan', 2 June 1997 (with David Hoffman).

R.A. Bigmetov, Goskomstat. Kazan', 16 June 1997.

E.N. Chernobrovkina, Political Editor, *Vecherniaia kazan'*. Kazan', 23 June 1998 (with Tomila Lankina).

M.G. Galeev, Chairman, Committee on Economic Development, State Soviet. Kazan', 14 June 1997.

N.F. Galiullin, Deputy Director KamAZ Public Relations Centre. Naberezhnye Chelny, 4 June 1997 (with David Hoffman).

D.B. Izmagilov, Minsitry of Economics. Kazan', 13 June 1997.

R.S. Khakimov, Advisor to the President. Kazan', 31 May 1997 (with David Hoffman).

G.I. Kurdiukov, Professor of Law, Law Faculty, Kazan' State University. Multiple meetings.

I.M. Kostin, General Director, KamAZ Truck Factory. Naberezhnye Chelny, 4 June 1997 (with David Hoffman)

R.A. Saiakhov, Deputy Minister for Legislative Activity, Ministry of Justice. Kazan', 5 June 1997.

M.S. Shaimiev, President of Tatarstan. 3 June 1997 (with David Hoffman).

A.V. Shtanin, Chairman of Regional Cell 'Russia's Choice'. Kazan', 3 June 1997 (with David Hoffman)

I.T. Sultanov, 'Equality and Law'. Kazan', 1 June 1997 (with David Hoffman).

A.N. Tarkaiev, Chairman of Tatar Chamber of Commerce. Kazan', 31 May 1997 (with David Hoffman); 22 June 1998.

F.Iu. Urazaev, Tatar Public Centre. Kazan', 2 June 1997 (with David Hoffman).

R.G. Vagizov, Chairman, Committee on Legislation, Legality, Law and Order, and Deputies' Ethics, State Soviet. Kazan', 10 June 1997.

Z.L. Zaimullin, Tatar Public Centre. Kazan', 2 June 1997 (with David Hoffman).

B.L. Zheleznov, Professor of Law, Law Faculty, Kazan' State University. Kazan', 6 June 1997.

(e) Republic of Sakha

A.N. Alekseev, Parliament Deputy, Chairman, Sakha Communist Party. Yakutsk, 2 June 1998.

T.E. Andreeva, Institute of Problems of the Small Peoples of the North. Yakutsk, 3 June 1998.

A.I. Chemchoup, former Parliament Deputy. Yakutsk, 9 June 1998.

R.I. Donskoi, Institute of Problems of the Small Peoples of the North. Yakutsk, 3 June 1998.

A.N. Kim, President, Ayar-Jur International, Ltd. Yakutsk, 9 June 1998.

D.N. Mironov, Chairman of Constitutional Court. Yakutsk, 4 June 1998.

F.S. Tumusov, President, SAPI Corporation. Yakutsk, 8 June 1998.

U.A. Vinokurova, Parliament Deputy. Yakutsk, 1 June 1998.

E.P. Zhirkov, Head of Administration of the President. Yakusk, 5 June 1998.

(3) Primary Sources: Published Interviews, Memoirs, Collected Works

Aganbegyan, Abel. Transcript of interview by Brian Lapping Assoc. for the BBC television series *The Second Russian Revolution*. British Library of Politics and Economic Science [LSE].

Dobrynin, Anatoly. *In Confidence: Moscow's Ambassador to America's Six Cold War Presidents (1962–1986)*. New York: Times Books, 1995.

Dolgikh, Vladimir I. Transcript of interview by Brian Lapping Assoc. for the BBC television series *The Second Russian Revolution*. British Library of Politics and Economic Science [LSE].

Gorbachev, Mikhail. Memoirs. London: Doubleday, 1996.

—— *Zhizn' i reformy.* 2 vols. Moscow: Novosti, 1995.

—— *Perestroika: New Thinking for Our Country and the World*. London: Wm. Collins Sons, 1987.

—— *Izbrannie rechi i stat'i*. Vols. 3 & 4. Moscow: Izdatel'stvo politicheskoi literatury, 1987.

—— *Address at the United Nations, New York, December 7, 1988*. Moscow: Novosti Press Agency Publishing House, 1988.

—— 'The Ideology of Renewal for Revolutionary Restructuring'. *The Speech Made by the General Secretary of the CPSU Central Committee at the Plenary Meeting of the CPSU Central Committee, February 18, 1988*. Moscow: Novosti Press Agency, 1988.

—— 'On the Basis of Full Equality, Independence and Mutual Respect', *The Speech of the General Secretary of the CPSU Central Committee at the Skupstina of the Socialist Federal Republic of Yugoslavia, Belgrade, March 16, 1988*. Moscow: Novosti Press Agency, 1988.

—— *Izbrannie rechi i stat'i*. Vol. 5. Moscow: Izdatel'stvo politicheskoi literatury, 1988.

—— *The Nationalities Policy of the Party in Present- Day Conditions: Address and Report of the General Secretary of the CPSU Central Committee at the Plenary Meeting of the Central Committee, September 19, 1989*. Moscow: Novosti Press Agency Publishing House, 1989.

—— *Meaning of My Life. Perestroika*. Edinburgh: Aspect Publications Ltd., 1990.

—— Transcript of interview by Brian Lapping Assoc. for the BBC television series *The Second Russian Revolution*. British Library of Politics and Economic Science [LSE].

Grachev, Andrei S. *Final Days: The Inside Story of the Collapse of the Soviet Union*. Boulder, CO: Westview Press, 1995.

Khasbulatov, Ruslan. *The Struggle for Russia: Power & Change in the Democratic Revolution*. London: Routledge, 1993.

Kolbin, G.V. Transcript of interview by Brian Lapping Assoc. for the BBC television series *The Second Russian Revolution*. British Library of Politics and Economic Science [LSE].

Kol'tsov, P.S. 'A Law-Governed State in Russia? Yes! Interview with Boris Aleksandrovich Strashun', *Russian Politics and Law*, Vol. 32, No. 1 (1994): 37–55.

Lenin, V.I. *Sochineniia*. Vol. 22. Moscow: Gosudarstvennoe izdatel'stvo politicheskoi literatury, 1948.

—— *Polnoe sobranie sochinenie*. Vol. 24. Moscow: Gosudarstvennoe izdatel'stvo politicheskoi literatury, 1961.

Ligachev, Yegor. *Inside Gorbachev's Kremlin*. Boulder, CO: Westview Press, 1996.

Nikitinsky, Leonid. 'Interview with Boris Ebzeev, Justice of the Constitutional Court of the Russian Federation'. 6 *East European Constitutional Review*. No. 1 (1997): 83–8.

Nikolaev, Mikhail. *My Choice is Freedom and a Man*. Milan: Grafiche Jodice S.r.l., 1992.

Palazchenko, Pavel. *My Years with Gorbachev and Shevardnadze: The Memoir of a Soviet Interpreter*. University Park, PA: Pennsylvania State University Press, 1997.

Popov, Gavriil. *What is to be Done?* London: The Centre for Research into Communist Economies, 1992.

Ryzhkov, Nikolai I. Transcript of interview by Brian Lapping Assoc. for the BBC television series *The Second Russian Revolution*. British Library of Politics and Economic Science [LSE].

Shakhnazarov, Georgii. *Tsena svobody: Reformatsiia Gorbacheva glazami ego pomoshchnika*. Moscow: Rossika, 1993.

Shevardnadze, Eduard. Transcript of interview by Brian Lapping Assoc. for the BBC television series *The Second Russian Revolution*. British Library of Politics and Economic Science [LSE].

Sobchak, Anatoly. *For A New Russia*. London: Harper Collins, 1992.

Veber, A.B., V.T. Loginov, G.S. Ostroumov & A.S. Cherniaev (eds.) *Soiuz mozhno bylo sokhranit'*. Moscow: Izdatel'stvo 'Aprel'-85', 1995.

Volsky, Arkady. Transcript of interview by Brian Lapping Assoc. for the BBC television series *The Second Russian Revolution*. British Library of Politics and Economic Science [LSE].

Yeltsin, Boris. *The View from the Kremlin*. London: Harper Collins, 1994.

(4) Russian Sources on Russia and the Soviet Union

Beliaev, V.A. (ed.) *Aktual'nye problemy politicheskogo i sotsial'no-ekonomicheskogo razvitiia strany* (Tezisy povolzhskoi nauchno-prakticheskoi konferentsii) Kazan': 1993.

Chervonnaia, S.M. & M.N. Guboglo (eds.) *Probuzhdenie finno-ugorskogo severa: Tom 1. Natsional'nye dvizheniia Marii El.* Moscow: RAN Tsentr po izucheniiu mezhnatsional'nykh otnoshenii, iinstituta Etnologii i Antropologii im. N.N. Miklukho-Maklaia, 1996.

―――(eds.) *Probuzhdenie finno-ugorskogo severa: Tom 2. Natsional'nye dvizheniia Marii El.* Moscow: RAN Tsentr po izucheniiu mezhnatsional'nykh otnoshenii, instituta Etnologii i Antropologii im. N.N. Miklukho-Maklaia, 1996.

Drobizheva, L.M. (ed.) *Asimmetrichnaia federatsiia: vzgliad iz tsentra, respublik i oblastei.* Moscow: Izdatel'stvo Instituta sotsiologii RAN, 1998.

――A.R. Aklaev, V.V. Koroteeva and G.U. Soldatova. *Demokratizatsiia i obrazy natsionalizma v Rossiiskoi Federatsii 90-kh godov.* Moscow: Mysl', 1996.

Farukshin, M. Kh. 'Politicheskaia elita v Tatarstane: Vyzvovy vremeni i trudnosti adaptatsii', *Polis: politicheskie issledovaniia.* No. 6/24 (1994).

Golovanov, Leonid. 'Dogovor—ne sgovor', [Interview with Vladimir Lysenko]. *Rossiiskaia Federatsiia.* No. 15 (July 1999): 21–2.

Iliumzhinov, K.N. & K.N. Maksimov. *Kalmykiia na rubezhe vekov.* Moscow: Izdatel'stvo 'ZelO', 1997.

Iskhakov, D.M. (ed.) *Sovremennyi natsional'nye protsessy v respublike Tatarstan.* Kazan': Akademiia nauk Tatarstana, Institut iazyka, literatury, i istorii im. G. Ibralimova, 1994.

Iulcherin, Salavat (ed.) *Bashkortostan.* Ankara: EKA International, 1994.

Iuldashbaev, Bilal Khamitovich. *Bashkiry i Bashkortostan. XX vek. Etnostatistika.* Ufa: izdatel'stva 'Bashkortostan', 1995.

Ivanova, K.E. (ed.) *Ia tvoi syn, Sakha sire! Shtrikhi k portretu sovremennika.* Moscow: Izdatel'skii Dom XX vek, 1997.

Kataev, N.A. & V.K. Samigullin (eds.) *Problemy konstitutsionnogo razvitiya suverennoi respubliki* (materialy respublikanskoi nauchno-prakticheskoi konferentsii 24–25 marta 1992 g., gorod Ufa). Ufa: Izdanie Verkh. Soveta i Soveta ministrov Respubliki Bashkortostan, 1992.

Khachatrian, G.M. 'Sotsialisticheskii federalizm kak forma i printsip gosudarstvennogo edinstva narodov'. *Sovetskoe gosudarstvo i pravo.* No. 2 (1990): 13–20.

Kim, A.N. *Pravovye aspekty perekhodnogo perioda v respublike Sakha (Iakutiia).* Yakutsk: Sakhapoligrafizdat, 1996.

Kirpichnikov, Aleksei. 'Novaia tekhnologiia polnomochnogo predstavitelia: Sergei Mikhailovich Shakhrai protianul Kirsanu Nikolaevichu Iliumzhinonu ruku pomoshchi Borisa Nikolaevicha El'tsina'. *Itogi* (11 February 1997), 18.

' "Kruglyi stol" zhurnala "Sovetskoe gosudarstvo i pravo": demokratizatsiia sovetskogo obshchestva i gosudarstvenno-pravovye aspekty natsional'nykh otnoshenii v SSSR'. *Sovetskoe gosudarstvo i pravo.* No. 1 (1989), 30–48; No. 2 (1989), 18–33.

Kuzivanova, O. Yu. (ed.) *Aktual'nye problemy politiko-pravovogo, sotsial'no-ekonomicheskogo i kul'turnogo razvitiia evropeiskogo sevara Rossiiskoi Federatsii (istoriia i sovremennost').* Syktyvkar: Ministerstvo po delam natsional'nostei Respubliki Komi, 1995.

McFaul, Michael & Nikolai Petrov (eds.) *Politicheskii al'manakh Rossii 1997.* 2 Vols. Moscow: Moskovskii Tsentr Karnegi, 1998.

Mironov, Dmitrii N. *Konstitutsionno-pravovoi status respubliki sakha (iakutia) kak sub'ekta Rossiiskoi Federatsii.* Novosibirsk: 'Nauka' sibirskaia izdatel'skaia firma RAN, 1996.

Mukhametshin, F.M. & R.T. Izmailov (eds.) *Suverennyi Tatarstan.* Moscow: 'INSAN', 1997.

Muksinov, I. Sh. 'Sovetskii federalizm i kompleksnoe ekonomicheskoe i sotsial'noe razvitie soiuznoi respubliki'. *Sovetskoe gosudarstvo i pravo.* No. 10 (1989): 3–13.

Nad gnezdom Murtazy. Moscow: TOO 'IntelTex', 1998.

Pavlenko, Sergei P. 'Tsentr—Regiony: kto kogo?' *Mezhdunarodnaia zhizn'.* No. 4 (April 1993).

'Perestroika v pravovoi sisteme, iuridicheskoi nauke, praktike'. *Sovetskoe gosudarstvo i pravo.* No. 9 (1987): 17–43.

Programma kommunisticheskoi partii sovetskogo soiuza (XXII S''ezda KPSS), 'IV. Zadachi partii v *oblasti* natsional'nykh otnoshenii'. *Kommunist.* No. 16 (1961): 84–6.

Raianov, Fanis M. (ed.) *Sistema zakonodatel'stva Respubliki Bashkortostan: stanovlenie i dal'neishee razvitie (Materialy respublikanskoi nauchno-prakticheskoi konferentsii 27 fevralia 1996 g., g. Ufa).* Ufa: Izdanie Akademii nauk Respubliki Bashkortostan, 1996.

Raspredelenie naseleniia Bashkirskoi SSR po obshchestvennym gruppam, otrasliam narodnogo khoziaistva i istochnikam sredstv sushchestvovaniia po dannym Vsesoiuznoi perepisi naseleniia 1989 goda Ufa: Goskomstat RSFSR Bashkirskoe respublikanskoe upravlenie statistiki, 1991.

Samigullin, V.K. *Konstitutsiia Respubliki Bashkortostan (voprosy teorii).* Ufa: Bashkirskii Gosudarstvennyi Universitet, 1993.

Savitskii, V.M. 'Pravosudie i perestroika', in 'Perestroika v provovoi sisteme, iuridicheskoi nauke, praktike'. *Sovetskoe gosudarstvo i pravo.* No. 9 (1987): 29–35.

Semenov, P.G. 'Programma KPSS o razvitii sovetskikh natsional'no-gosudarstvennykh otnoshenii'. *Sovetskoe gosudarstvo i pravo.* No. 12 (1961): 15–25.

Shabaev, Yu.O. & M.N. Guboglo (eds.) *Shtrikhi etnopoliticheskogo razvitiia Respubliki Komi: Ocherki, dokumenty, materialy.* Vol. 1. Moscow: RAN Tsentr po izucheniiu mezhnatsional'nykh otnoshenii instituta etnologii i Antropologii im. N.N. Miklukho-Maklaia, 1994.

Simonov, Aleksei. *Delo No. 2: Respublika Kalmykiia protiv 'Sovetskoi Kalmykii'* (Moscow: Izdatel'stvo 'Prava cheloveka', 1997.

Sovet Evropy. *Konferentsiia po federalizmu: federativnoe ustroistvo Rossiiskoi Federatsii i realizatsiia printsipov pliuralisticheskoi demokratii, pravovogo gosudarstva i prav cheloveka.* Moscow, 15–18 fevralia 1994 g. Protokoly zasedanii.

Stoliarov, M.V. *Rossiia v puti: Novaia Federatsiia i Zapadnaia Evropa.* Kazan': Izdatel'stvo 'Fen', 1998.

Strashun, B.A. *Federal'noe konstitutsionnoe pravo Rossii: Osnovnye istochniki po sostoianiiu na 15 sentiabria 1996 goda.* Moscow: Izdatel'stvo NORMA, 1996.

Sukharev, A.I. (ed.) *Regional'naia politika Rossiiskoi Federatsii.* Saransk: NII regionologii, 1993.

Toropov, Dmitrii. *Spravochnik novykh partii i obshchestvennykh organizatsii Tatarstana.* Moscow: Informatsionno-ekspertnaia gruppa 'Panorama', iiun' 1992.

Tumusov, Fedot Semenovich. *Finansy respubliki: ot proshlogo k budushchemu.* Moscow: Moskovskaia tipografiia. No. 2 RAN, 1995.

Valeeva, Zilia R. (ed.) *Mezhdunarodnaia nauchno-prakticheskaia konferentsiia 'Federalizm—global'nye i rossiiskie izmereniia'.* Kazan': Tipografiia Tatarskogo gazetno-zhurnal'nogo izdatel'stva, 1993.

Zheleznov, Boris & Vasilii Likhachev. *Pravovoi status respubliki Tatarstan.* Kazan': Tatarskoe knizhnoe izdatel'stvo, 1996.

Zlatopol'skii, D.L. 'Natsional'naia gosudarstvennost' soiuznykh respublik: nekotorye aktual'nye problemy', *Sovetskoe gosudarstvo i pravo.* No. 4 (1989): 12–20.

The following periodicals were frequently consulted. Specific citations are in the footnotes.

Argumenty i fakty	*Rossiiskaia gazeta*
Izvestia	*Rossiiskie vesti*
Kommersant''-daily	*Segodnia*
Nezavisimaia gazeta	*Sovetskaia bashkiria*
Pravda	*Vechernaia kazan'*

(5) English Language Secondary Sources on Russia and the Soviet Union

Ahdieh, Robert B. *Russia's Constitutional Revolution: Legal Consciousness and the Transition to Democracy, 1985–1996.* University Park, PA: Pennsylvania State University Press, 1997.

Allworth, Edward (ed.) *Soviet Nationality Problems.* NY: Columbia University Press, 1971.

Argounova, Tanya. *Federal Relations Between Yakutsk and Moscow.* M.Phil. Thesis. Scott Polar Research Institute, University of Cambridge, June 1995.

Aslund, Anders. *Market Socialism or the Restoration of Capitalism?* Cambridge University Press, 1992.

Bahry, Donna. *Outside Moscow: Power, Politics & Budgetary Policy in the Soviet Republics*. New York: Columbia University Press, 1987.

Balzer, Marjorie Mandelstam & Uliana Alekseevna Vinokurova. 'Nationalism, Interethnic Relations and Federalism: The Case of the Sakha Republic (Yakutia)'. 48 *Europe-Asia Studies*. No. 1 (1996): 101–20.

Barry, Donald. 'The USSR: A Legitimate Dissolution'. 18 *Review of Central and East European Law*. No. 6 (1992): 527–33.

——(ed.) *Toward the 'Rule of Law' in Russia? Political and Legal Reform in the Transition Period*. Armonk, NY: M.E. Sharpe, 1992.

Begum, Anwara. *Inter-Republican Cooperation of the Russian Republic*. Aldershot, UK: Ashgate, 1997.

Beliaev, Sergei A. 'The Evolution in Constitutional Debates in Russian in 1992–1993: A Comparative Review'. 20 *Review of Central and East European Law*. No. 3 (1994): 305–19.

Berman, Harold J. *Justice in the USSR: An Interpretation of Soviet Law*. Cambridge, MA: Harvard University Press, 1966.

Bernhardt, Rudolf, Stefan Trechsel, Albert Weitzel & Felix Ermacora. 'Report on the conformity of the legal order of the Russian Federation with Council of Europe standards'. Doc. AS/Bur/Russia (1994), reprinted in 15 *Human Rights Law Journal* 7 (1994).

Bindig, Rudolf. 'Opinion on Russia's application for membership of the Council of Europe', Doc. 7463 (18 January 1996) Opinion by the Committee on Legal Affairs and Human Rights, Parliamentary Assembly of the Council of Europe, Strasbourg. Reprinted in 17 *Human Rights Law Journal* 3–6 (15 October 1996).

Blankenagel, Alexander. 'Local Self-Government vs. State Administration: The Udmurtia Decision'. 6 *East European Constitutional Review*. No. 1 (1997): 50–4.

Bradshaw, Michael J. 'Siberia Poses a Challenge to Russian Federalism'. 1 *RFE/RL Research Report*. No. 41 (1992): 6–14.

Bremner, Ian & Ray Taras (eds.) *Nations & Politics in the Soviet Successor States*. Cambridge University Press, 1993.

Brown, Archie (ed.) *New Thinking in Soviet Politics*. London: St. Antony's/Macmillan, 1992.

——*The Gorbachev Factor*. Oxford University Press, 1996.

——'Asymmetrical Devolution: The Scottish Case'. 69 *The Political Quarterly* 3 (1998): 215–23.

——'The Russian Crisis: Beginning of the End or End of the Beginning?' 15 *Post–Soviet Affairs*. No. 1 (1999): 56–73.

——(ed.) *Contemporary Russian Politics: A Reader*. Oxford University Press, 2001.

Brubaker, Rogers. 'Nationhood and the National Question in the Soviet Union and Post-Soviet Eurasia: An Institutionalist Account'. 23 *Theory and Society*. No. 1 (1994): 47–78.

Brubaker, Rogers. 'National Minorities, Nationalizing States, and External Home-lands in the New Europe'. 124 *Daedalus*. No. 2 (1995): 107–32.

Brudny, Yitzhak M. 'The Dynamics of "Democratic Russia", 1990–1993'. 9 *Post-Soviet Affairs*. No. 2 (1993): 141–70.

Brumberg, Abraham (ed.) *Chronicle of a Revolution: A Western-Soviet Inquiry into Perestroika*. New York: Pantheon, 1990.

Brzezinski, Zbigniew. 'Post-Communist Nationalism'. 68 *Foreign Affairs*. No. 5 (1989/90): 1–25.

Bunce, Valerie. *Subversive Institutions: The Design and the Destruction of Socialism and the State*. Cambridge University Press, 1999.

Butler, William E. *Russian Law: Historical and Political Perspectives*. Leyden: A.W. Sijthoff, 1977.

—— *Soviet Law.* 2nd Ed. London: Butterworths, 1988.

—— *Basic Documents on the Soviet Legal System.* 2nd Ed. London: Oceana, 1991.

—— *Collected Legislation of Russia*. New York: Oceana, May 1993.

—— *Russian Law.* Oxford University Press, 1999.

Cassese, Antonio. *Self-Determination of Peoples: A Legal Reappraisal*. Cambridge University Press, 1995.

Cohen, Stephen F. 'Russian Studies Without Russia', 15 *Post-Soviet Affairs*. No. 1 (1999): 37–55.

—— Katrina vanden Heuvel (eds.) *Voices of Glasnost: Interviews with Gorbachev's Reformers*. New York: Norton, 1989.

Conquest, Robert. *The Nation Killers: The Soviet Deportation of Nationalities*. London: Macmillan, 1970.

Daniels, Robert V. (ed.) *A Documentary History of Communism in Russia: From Lenin to Gorbachev*. Hanover, NH: University Press of New England, 1993.

Danilenko, Gennady M. & William Burnham. *Law and Legal System of the Russian Federation*. Parker School of Foreign and Comparative Law, Columbia University. Juris, 1999.

Dawisha, Karen & Bruce Parrott (eds.) *Democratic Changes and Authoritarian Reactions in Russia, Ukraine, Belarus, and Moldova*. Cambridge University Press, 1997.

Denber, Rachel (ed.) *The Soviet Nationality Reader: The Disintegration in Context*. Boulder, CO: Westview, 1992.

Duncan, W. Raymond & G. Paul Holman Jr. (eds.) *Ethnic Nationalism and Regional Conflict: The Former Soviet Union and Yugoslavia*. Boulder, CO: Westview, 1994.

Emizet, Kisangani N. & Vicki L. Hesli. 'The Disposition to Secede: An Analysis of the Soviet Case'. 27 *Comparative Political Studies*. No. 4 (1995): 493–536.

Feldbrugge, F.J.M. (ed.) *The Constitutions of the USSR and the Union Republics: Analysis, Texts, Reports*. Alphen aan den Rijn, The Netherlands: Sijthoff & Noordhoff, 1979.

—— Russian Law: The End of the Soviet System and the Role of Law. Dordrecht, The Netherlands: Martinus Nijhoff, 1993.

—— 'The Elections in Chechnia in the Framework of Russian Constitutional Law'. 23 Review of Central and East European Law. No. 1 (1997): 1–7.

Finer, S.E., Vernon Bogdanor & Bernard Rudden (eds.) Comparing Constitutions. Oxford: Clarendon Press, 1995.

Fish, M. Stephen. Democracy from Scratch: Opposition and Regime in the New Russian Revolution. Princeton, NJ: Princeton University Press, 1995.

Friedgut, Theodore H. & Jeffrey W. Hahn (eds.) Local Power and Post-Soviet Politics. Armonk, NY: M.E. Sharpe, 1994.

Furtado, Charles F. & Henry R. Hottenbach (eds.) 'The Ex-Soviet Nationalities Without Gorbachev'. 20 Nationalities Papers (1992): 1–124.

Furtado, Charles F., Jr. & Andrea Chandler (eds.) Perestroika in the Soviet Republics: Documents on the National Question. Boulder, CO: Westview, 1992.

Gellner, Ernest. 'Home of the Unrevolution'. 122 Daedalus. No. 3 (1993): 141–254.

Gelman, Vladimir. 'Regime Transition, Uncertainty and Prospects for Democratisation: The Politics of Russia's Regions in a Comparative Perspective'. 51 Europe-Asia Studies. No. 6 (1999): 939–956.

Ginsburgs, George, Donald D. Barry, & William B. Simons (eds.) The Revival of Private Law in Central and Eastern Europe: Essays in Honor of F. J. M. Feldbrugge. The Hague: Martinus Nijhoff, 1996.

Gleason, Gregory. Federalism and Nationalism: The Struggle for Republican Rights in the USSR. Boulder, CO: Westview, 1990.

—— 'The Federal Formula and the Collapse of the USSR'. 22 Publius (1992): 141–63.

Goble, Paul. 'Ethnic Politics in the USSR'. 38 Problems of Communism. No. 4 (1989): 1–14.

Gorenburg, Dmitry 'Nationalism for the Masses: Popular Support for Nationalism in Russia's Ethnic Republics'. 53 Europe-Asia Studies. No. 1 (2001): 73–104.

—— 'Regional Separatism in Russia: Mobilisation or Power Grab?' 51 Europe-Asia Studies. No. 2, (1999): 245–74.

Gsovski, Vladimir. Soviet Civil Law. 2 Vols. Ann Arbor, MI: University of Michigan Law School, 1948.

Hahn, Jeffrey W. 'Regional Elections and Political Stability in Russia'. 38 Post-Soviet Geography and Economics. No. 5 (1997): 251–63.

Hajda, Lubomyr & Mark Beissinger (eds.) The Nationalities Factor in Soviet Politics and Society. Boulder, CO: Westview, 1990.

Hanson, Philip. Regions, Local Power and Economic Change in Russia. London: Royal Institute of International Affairs, 1994.

Hanauer, Laurence S. 'Tatarstan and the Prospects for Federalism in Russia: A Commentary'. 27 Security Dialogue. No. 1 (March 1996): 81–6.

Hazard, John N., William E. Butler & Peter B. Maggs. *The Soviet Legal System.* 3rd Ed. Dobbs Ferry, NY: Oceana, 1977.

Hill, Fiona. *'Russia's Tinderbox': Conflict in the North Caucasus and its Implications for the Future of the Russian Federation.* Harvard University, John F. Kennedy School of Government Strengthening Democratic Institutions Project, September 1995.

Hill, Ronald J. *Soviet Politics, Political Science and Reform.* White Plains, NY: M.E. Sharpe, 1980.

Hodnett, Grey. 'The Debate over Soviet Federalism'. 18 *Soviet Studies.* No. 4 (1967): 458–81.

Hoffmann, Erik P. 'Challenges to Viable Constitutionalism in Post-Soviet Russia'. 7 *The Harriman Review.* No. 10–12 (1994): 19–56.

Hosking, Geoffrey A., Jonathan Aves & Peter J.S. Duncan. *The Road to Post-Communism: Independent Political Movements in the Soviet Union, 1985–1991.* London: Pinter, 1992.

Hough, Jerry F. *The Soviet Prefects: The Local Party Organs in Industrial Decision-making.* Cambridge, MA: Harvard University Press, 1969.

Hughes, James 'Regionalism in Russia: The Rise and Fall of Siberian Agreement'. 46 *Europe-Asia Studies.* No. 7, (1994): 1133–61.

—— 'Moscow's Bilateral Treaties Add to Confusion'. 2 *Transition.* No. 19 (1996): 39–43.

—— 'Sub-national Elites and Post-communist Transformation in Russia: A Reply to Kryshtanovskaya and White'. 49 *Europe-Asia Studies.* No. 6 (1997): 1017–36.

—— 'Institutional Design and Political Stability: Asymmetric Federalism in Russia's State of Transition'. Paper prepared for the ESRC Research Seminar on Regional Transformations in Russia, London School of Economics, 21 October 1998.

Huttenbach, Henry R. (ed.) *Soviet Nationalities Policies: Ruling Ethnic Groups in the USSR.* London: Mansell, 1990.

'Interethnic Contradictions in Russia: The Strategy of Parties and Social Movements (A Roundtable)'. 32 *Russian Politics and Law.* No. 5 (1994): 6–31.

Kahn, Jeff. 'The Parade of Sovereignties: Establishing the Vocabulary of the New Russian Federalism'. 16 *Post-Soviet Affairs* 1 (2000): 58–89.

Kaiser, Robert. *The Geography of Nationalism in Russia and the USSR.* Princeton, NJ: Princeton University Press, 1994.

Kempton, Daniel R. 'The Republic of Sakha (Yakutia): The Evolution of Centre-Periphery Relations in the Russian Federation'. 48 *Europe-Asia Studies.* No. 4 (1996): 587–613.

Khakimov, Raphael S. 'Prospects of Federalism in Russia: A View from Tatarstan'. 27 *Security Dialogue.* No. 1 (1996): 69–80.

Khazanov, Anatoly. 'The Collapse of the Soviet Union: Nationalism During Pere-stroika and Afterwards'. *Nationalities Papers.* Vol. 22, No. 1 (1994): 157–74.

Kux, Stephen. 'Soviet Federalism'. 39 *Problems of Communism.* No. 2 (1990): 1–20.

Lapidus, Gail W. (ed.) *The New Russia: Troubled Transformation*. Boulder, CO: Westview, 1995.

—— 'Asymmetrical Federalism and State Breakdown in Russia', 15 *Post-Soviet Affairs*. No. 1 (1999): 74–82.

—— with Philip Goldman (eds.) *From Union to Commonwealth: Nationalism & Separatism in the Soviet Republics*. Cambridge University Press, 1992.

Lieven, Anatol. *The Baltic Revolution: Estonia, Latvia, Lithuania and the Path to Independence*. 2nd Ed. New Haven: Yale University Press, 1994.

—— *Chechnya: Tombstone of Russian Power*. New Haven: Yale University Press, 1998.

Lowenhardt, John. *The Reincarnation of Russia: Struggling with the Legacy of Communism, 1990–1994*. Harlow, Essex: Longman, 1995.

Lukin, Alexander V. *'Democratic' Groups in Soviet Russia (1985–1991): A Study in Political Culture*. D.Phil. Dissertation. Oxford: Faculty of Social Studies, Trinity Term 1997.

Lukin, Alexander. *The Political Culture of the Russian 'Democrats'*. Oxford University Press, 2000.

Lynn, Nicholas J. & Alexei V. Novikov. 'Refederalizing Russia: Debates on the Idea of Federalism in Russia'. *Publius*. Vol. 27, No. 2 (1997): 187–203.

Malik, Hafeez. 'Tatarstan's Treaty with Russia: Autonomy or Independence'. 18 *Journal of South Asian and Middle Eastern Studies*. No. 2 (1994): 1–36.

Mann, Dawn. 'Leadership of Regional Communist Party Committees and Soviets'. *Report on the USSR* (21 December 1990).

McAuley, Alastair. (ed.) *Soviet Federalism, Nationalism and Economic Decentralization*. Leicester, UK: Leicester University Press, 1991.

—— 'The Determinants of Russian Federal-Regional Fiscal Relations: Equity or Political Influence?' 49 *Europe-Asia Studies*. No. 3 (1997): 431–44.

McAuley, Mary. *Russia's Politics of Uncertainty*. Cambridge University Press, 1997.

McFaul, Michael. *Russia's 1996 Presidential Election: The End of Polarized Politics*. (Stanford: Hoover Institution Press, 1997.

—— Nikolai Petrov. 'Russian Electoral Politics After Transition: Regional and National Assessments'. 38 *Post-Soviet Geography and Economics*. No. 9 (1997): 507–549.

Melvin, Neil J. 'The Consolidation of a New Regional Elite: The Case of Omsk, 1987–1995'. 50 *Europe-Asia Studies*. No. 4 (1998): 619–50.

Middleton, Joseph. 'The New Russian Law on Electoral Rights'. 7 *East European Constitutional Review*. No. 3 (1998): 59–63.

Miller, John. *Mikhail Gorbachev and the End of Soviet Power*. London: St. Martin's Press, 1993.

Miller, John H. 'Cadres Policy in Nationality Areas: Recruitment of CPSU First and Second Secretaries in Non-Russian Republics of the USSR'. 29 *Soviet Studies*. No. 1 (1977): 3–36.

Motyl, Alexander J. (ed.) *Thinking Theoretically About Soviet Nationalities: History and Comparison of the USSR*. New York: Columbia University Press, 1995.

Nahaylo, Bohdan & Victor Swoboda. *Soviet Disunion*. New York: Free Press, 1989.

Ordeshook, Peter C. 'Russia's Party System: Is Russian Federalism Viable?' 12 *Post-Soviet Affairs*. No. 3 (1996): 195–217.

Organization for Economic Co-operation and Development. *OECD Economic Surveys: The Russian Federation*. Paris: OECD, 1995.

Pipes, Richard. *The Formation of the Soviet Union—Communism & Nationalism: 1917–1923*. Cambridge, MA: Harvard University Press, 1964.

Pomeranz, William E. 'Judicial Review and the Russian Constitutional Court: The Chechen Case'. 23 *Review of Central and East European Law*. No. 1 (1997): 9–48.

Pravda, Alex (ed.) *The End of the Outer Empire: Soviet-East European Relations in Transition, 1985–1990*. London: Sage, 1992.

Raviot, Jean-Robert. 'Types of Nationalism, Society, and Politics in Tatarstan'. 32 *Russian Politics and Law*. No. 2 (1994): 54–83.

Remington, Thomas F. 'Federalism & Segmented Communication in the USSR'. 15 *Publius* (1985): 113–32.

Remnick, David. *Resurrection: The Struggle for a New Russia*. New York: Random House, 1997.

Reynolds, Sarah J. 'First Steps: Voluntary Union, Constitutional Equality, and the Nature of the Federation'. 33 *Statutes and Decisions: The Laws of the USSR and Its Successor States*. No. 6 (1997): 3–22.

Rezun, Miron (ed.) *Nationalism and The Breakup of an Empire: Russia and Its Periphery*. Westport, CT: Praeger, 1992.

Roeder, Philip G. 'Soviet Federalism & Ethnic Mobilization'. 43 *World Politics*. No. 2 (1991): 196–232.

Roxburgh, Angus. *The Second Russian Revolution*. London: BBC Books, 1991.

Rudden, Bernard. 'Civil Law, Civil Society, and the Russian Constitution'. 110 *The Law Quarterly Review* (January 1994): 56–83.

Rumyantsev, Oleg G. 'The Present and Future of Russian Constitutional Order'. 8 *Harriman Review*. No. 2 (1995): 21–35.

Russell, John. 'Improbable Unions: The Draft Union Treaties in the USSR, 1990–1991'. 22 *Review of Central and East European Law*. No. 4 (1996): 389–416.

Rutland, Peter. 'Tatarstan: A Sovereign Republic Within the Russian Federation'. 1 *OMRI Russian Regional Report*. No. 5 (25 September 1996), Part I.

—— 'Putin's Path to Power'. 16 *Post-Soviet Affairs*. No. 4 (2000): 313–54.

Rywkin, Michael. *Moscow's Lost Empire*. Armonk, NY: M.E. Sharpe, 1994.

Semonov, G. 'Establishing More Rational Relations Between Federal and Regional Budgets: Ways of Updating the Tax-Budget Mechanism'. 36 *Russian Social Science Review*. No. 5, (1995).

Sergeyev, Victor & Nikolai Biryukov. *Russia's Road to Democracy: Parliament, Communism and Traditional Culture*. Aldershot, UK: Edward Elgar, 1993.

Severtsov, Peter. *Kirsan: The Universal President. Kirsan Ilyumzhinov's Story in Comics*. Moscow: Zarealye, 1996.

Seymour, James D. 'The Rights of Ethnic Minorities in China: Lessons of the Soviet Demise'. 11 *Am Asian R* (Summer 1993): 44–56.

Sharlet, Robert. *Soviet Constitutional Crisis: From De-Stalinization to Disintegration*. London: M.E. Sharpe, 1992.

—— 'The Prospects for Federalism in Russian Constitutional Politics'. 24 *Publius*. No. 2 (1994): 115–27.

—— 'Putin and the Politics of Law in Russia'. 17 *Post-Soviet Affairs*. No. 3 (2001): 195–234.

Shaw, Denis, J.B. 'Russian Federation Treaty Signed'. 33 *Post-Soviet Geography*. No. 6 (1992): 414–17.

—— 'Geographic and Historical Observations on the Future of a Federal Russia'. 34 *Post-Soviet Geography*. No. 8 (1993): 530–40.

Sheehy, Ann. 'Moves to Draw up New Union Treaty'. *Report on the USSR*. No. 27 (6 July 1990).

—— 'Fact Sheet on Declarations of Sovereignty'. *Report on the USSR* (9 November 1990).

—— 'The Draft Union Treaty: A Preliminary Assessment'. 2 *Report on the USSR*. No. 51 (21 December 1990).

—— 'Russia's Republics: A Threat to its Territorial Integrity?' 2 *RFE/RL Research Report*. No. 20 (14 May 1993).

—— 'Kalmyk President Renounces Sovereignty of Republic'. 3 *RFE/RL Research Report*. No. 22 (3 June 1994): 16–20.

Shtromas, Alexander. 'The Building of a Multi-National Soviet "Socialist Federalism": successes and failures'. 13 *Can R Studies Nationalism* (Spring 1986): 79–97.

Slider, Darrell. 'Privatisation in Russia's Regions'. 10 *Post-Soviet Affairs*. No. 4 (1994): 367–96.

—— 'Elections to Russia's Regional Assemblies'. 12 *Post-Soviet Affairs*. No. 3 (1996): 243–64.

—— 'Russia's Market-Distorting Federalism'. 38 *Post-Soviet Geography and Economics*. No. 8 (1997): 445–60.

Smith, Graham. 'Russia, Multiculturalism and Federal Justice'. 50 *Europe-Asia Studies*. No. 8 (1998): 1393–411.

Sobell, Vladimir. *The New Russia: A Political Risk Analysis*. London: The Economist Intelligence Unit, 1994.

Solnick, Steven L. 'Federal Bargaining in Russia'. 4 *East European Constitutional Review*. No. 4 (1995): 52–8.

Solnick, Steven L. 'The Political Economy of Russian Federalism: A Framework for Analysis'. 43 *Problems of Post-Communism*. No. 6 (1996): 13–25.

—— 'Statebuilding, Asymmetries and Federal Stability in Russia'. Paper prepared for the Workshop on Democracy, Nationalism, and Federalism. Oxford University, 6–7 June 1997.

Solomon, Peter H. Jr. (ed.) *Reforming Justice in Russia, 1864–1996: Power, Culture, and the Limits of Legal Order*. Armonk, NY: M.E. Sharpe, 1997.

Stoner-Weiss, Kathryn. *Local Heroes: The Political Economy of Russian Regional Governance*. Princeton, NJ: Princeton University Press, 1997.

—— 'Central Weakness and Provincial Autonomy: Observations on the Devolution Process in Russia'. 15 *Post-Soviet Affairs*. No. 1 (1999): 87–106.

Subtelny, Orest. 'American Sovietology's Greatest Blunder: The Marginalization of the Nationality Issue'. 22 *Nationalities Papers*. No. 1 (1994): 141–56.

Suny, Ronald Grigor. *The Revenge of the Past: Nationalism, Revolution, and the Collapse of the Soviet Union*. Stanford: Stanford University Press, 1993.

Taagepera, Rein. *The Finno-Ugric Republics and the Russian State*. London: C. Hurst, 1999.

Teague, Elizabeth. 'Russia and Tatarstan Sign Power-sharing Treaty'. 3 *RFE/RL Research Report*. No. 14 (1994): 19–27.

Tishkov, Valery. *Ethnicity, Nationalism and Conflict In and After the Soviet Union: The Mind Aflame*. London: Sage, 1997.

Tolz, Vera. 'Regionalism in Russia: The Case of Siberia'. 2 *RFE/RL Research Report*. No. 9 (26 February 1993).

—— 'Drafting the New Russian Constitution'. 2 *RFE/RL Research Report*. No. 29 (16 July 1993).

Treisman, Daniel. 'Moscow's Struggle to Control Regions Through Taxation'. 2 *Transition*. No. 19 (20 September 1996): 45–9.

—— 'Russia's "Ethnic Revival": The Separatist Activism of Regional Leaders in a Postcommunist Order'. 49 *World Politics*. No. 2 (1997): 212–49.

—— 'Fiscal Redistribution in a Fragile Federation: Moscow and the Regions in 1994'. 28 *British Journal of Political Science*. No. 1 (1998): 185–200.

—— 'Deciphering Russia's Federal Finance: Fiscal Appeasement in 1995 and 1996'. 50 *Europe-Asia Studies*. No. 5 (1998): 893–906.

Treisman, Daniel S. *After the Deluge: Regional Crises and Political Consolidation in Russia*. Ann Arbor, MI: University of Michigan Press, 1999.

Uibopuu, Henn-Jüri. 'Soviet Federalism under the New Soviet Constitution'. 5 *Review of Socialist Law*. No. 2 (1979): 171–85.

Unger, Aryeh L. *Constitutional Development in the USSR: A Guide to the Soviet Constitutions*. New York: Pica Press, 1981.

Vasilyeva, Olga. 'Has Ethnic Federalism a Future in Russia'. *New Times* (Moscow). (1995): 34–7.

Walker, Edward W. 'Federalism—Russian Style: The Federation Provisions in Russia's New Constitution'. 42 *Problems of Post-Communism*. No. 4 (1995): 3–12.

—— 'The Dog That Didn't Bark: Tatarstan and Asymmetrical Federalism in Russia'. UC Berkeley: Unpublished paper, 27 November 1996.

White, Stephen. *After Gorbachev.* Cambridge University Press, 1993.

—— Richard Rose & Ian McAllister. *How Russia Votes.* Chatham, NJ: Chatham House Publishers, 1997.

'World Status: A Federal Russia?' *Energy Economist* (May 1991): 15–22.

Yavlinsky, Grigory. 'An Uncertain Prognosis'. 8 *Journal of Democracy.* No. 1 (1997): 3–11.

Zile, Zigurds L. *Ideas and Forces in Soviet Legal History: A Reader on the Soviet State and Law.* Oxford University Press, 1992.

Zolotukhin, B.A., *et al.* 'The Conception of Judicial Reform in the RSFSR'. 30 *Statutes and Decisions: The Laws of the USSR and its Successor States.* No. 2 (1994): 9–90.

Zubov, Andrei. 'A Postscript to the Epoch of Ethnic Revolutions: Soviet Practice of the Contemporary Theory of Ethnic Movements'. 32 *Russian Politics and Law.* No. 4 (1994): 6–38.

The following periodicals and computer digests were frequently consulted. For specific citations, see footnotes.

Computer digests:	*EWI Russian Regional Report*	*Jamestown Foundation Prism*
	OMRI Daily Digest	*RFE/RL Newsline*
	OMRI Russian Regional Report	*RFE/RL Russian Federation*
Periodicals and	*The Economist*	*The New York Times*
newspapers:	*Financial Times*	*The Times* (London)
	Guardian	*Washington Post*
	Independent	*International Herald Tribune*

Translation services: Current Digest of the Soviet Press; Current Digest of the Post-Soviet Press; Foreign Broadcast Information Service

(6) Federal and Democratic Theory

Agranoff, Robert. 'Federal Evolution in Spain'. 17 *International Political Science Review.* No. 4 (1996): 385–401.

—— Juan Antonio Ramos Gallarin. 'Toward Federal Democracy in Spain: An Examination of Inter-governmental Relations'. 27 *Publius.* No. 4 (1997): 1–38.

Alexander, Yonah & Robert A. Friedlander. *Self-Determination: National, Regional, and Global Dimensions.* Boulder, CO: Westview, 1980.

Bahro, Horst, Bernhard H. Bayerlein & Ernst Veser. 'Duverger's concept: Semi-Presidential government revisited'. 34 *European Journal of Political Research*. No. 2 (1998): 201–24.

Baker, J. Wayne. 'The Covenantal Basis for the Development of Swiss Political Federalism: 1291–1848'. 23 *Publius*. No. 2 (1993): 19–41.

Banning, Lance. *Jefferson and Madison: Three Conversations from the Founding*. Madison, WI: Madison House, 1995.

Berger, Raoul. *Impeachment: The Constitutional Problems*. 2nd Ed. Cambridge, MA: Harvard University Press, 1999.

Bermann, George A. 'Taking Subsidiarity Seriously: Federalism in the European Community and the United States'. 94 *Columbia Law Review*. (1994): 332–546.

Berneri, C. *Peter Kropotkin: His Federalist Ideas*. London: Freedom Press, 1943.

Bickel, Alexander M. *The Least Dangerous Branch: The Supreme Court at the Bar of Politics*. 2nd Ed. New Haven, CT: Yale University Press, 1986.

Blank, Stephen and Guy Stanley. 'Is Canadian Federalism a Model for Europe and the Soviet Union?' 4 *International Economist* (October–November 1990): 73–5.

Blaustein, Albert P. & Gisbert H. Flanz (eds.) *Constitutions of the Countries of the World: Spain*. Dobbs Ferry, NY: Oceana, 1997.

Bogdanor, Vernon. *Devolution in the United Kingdom*. Oxford University Press, 1999.

—— David Butler (eds.) *Democracy and Elections: Electoral Systems and their Political Consequences*. Cambridge University Press, 1983.

Bowman, Ann O'M. & Michael A. Pagano (eds.) 'Symposium: Federalism and the Collapse of Communism'. 24 *Publius* (1994): 81–127.

Brubaker, Rogers. *Nationalism Reframed: Nationhood and the National Question in the New Europe*. Cambridge University Press, 1996.

Buchanan, James M. 'Federalism as an Ideal Political Order and an Objective for Constitutional Reform'. 25 Publius. No. 2 (1995): 19–27.

Burgess, Michael. *Federalism: A Dirty Word? Federalist Ideas and Practice in the British Political Tradition*. Federal Trust for Education & Research, Federal Trust Working Papers, No. 2, June 1988.

—— Alain-G. Gagnon (eds.) *Comparative Federalism and Federation: Competing Traditions and Future Directions*. New York: Harvester Wheatsheaf, 1993.

Butler, David & Austin Ranney (eds.) *Referendums Around the World: The Growing Use of Direct Democracy*. Washington D.C.: American Enterprise Institute, 1994.

Calhoun, John C. *Reports and Public Letters of John C. Calhoun*, 7 Vols. Edited by Richard K. Cralle. New York: D. Appleton & Co., 1856.

Channing-Pearce, Melville (ed.) *Federal Union: A Symposium*. Great Britain, 1940. Reprint, London: Lothian Foundation Press, 1991.

Cicero. *The Republic and the Laws* (Trans. by Niall Rudd). Oxford University Press, 1998.

Coakley, John. 'Approaches to the Resolution of Ethnic Conflict: The Strategy of Non-territorial Autonomy'. 15 *International Political Science Review*. No. 3 (1994): 297–314.

Commager, Henry Steele (ed.) *Documents of American History.* 9th Ed., 2 Vols. Englewood Cliffs, NJ: Prentice-Hall, 1973.

Cox, Robert Henry & Erich G. Frankland. 'The Federal State & the Breakup of Czechoslovakia: An Institutional Analysis'. 25 *Publius.* No. 1 (1995): 71–88.

Croley, Steven P. 'The Majoritarian Difficulty: Elective Judiciaries and the Rule of Law'. 62 *University of Chicago Law Review* (1995): 689–794.

Dahl, Robert A. *A Preface to Democratic Theory.* Chicago: University of Chicago Press, 1956.

—— *Polyarchy: Participation and Opposition.* New Haven, CT: Yale University Press, 1971.

—— *Dilemmas of Pluralist Democracy: Autonomy vs. Control.* New Haven, CT: Yale University Press, 1982.

—— *Democracy, Liberty, and Equality.* Oslo: Norwegian University Press, 1986.

—— *Democracy and its Critics.* New Haven: Yale University Press, 1989.

—— *After the Revolution? Authority in a Good Society.* Rev. Ed. New Haven, CT: Yale University Press, 1990.

—— Edward R. Tufte. *Size and Democracy.* Stanford, CA: Stanford University Press, 1973.

Derbyshire, J. Denis and Ian Derbyshire. *Political Systems of the World.* Oxford: Helicon, 1996.

Dicey, A.V. *Introduction to the Study of the Law of the Constitution.* 10th Ed. London: Macmillan, 1967.

DiPalma, Giuseppe. *To Craft Democracies: An Essay on Democratic Transitions.* Berkeley: University of California Press, 1990.

Duchacek, Ivo D. *Power Maps: Comparative Politics of Constitutions.* Santa Barbara, CA: Clio Press, 1973.

—— *Comparative Federalism: The Territorial Dimension of Politics.* Lanham, MD: University Press of America, 1987.

Duverger, Maurice. 'A New Political System Model: Semi-Presidential Government'. 8 *European Journal of Political Research.* No. 2 (1980): 165–87.

Elazar, Daniel J. *Exploring Federalism.* Tuscaloosa: University of Alabama Press, 1987.

—— (ed.) *Constitutional Design and Power-Sharing in the Post-Modern Epoch.* New York: University Press of America, 1991.

—— 'From Statism to Federalism: A Paradigm Shift'. 25 *Publius.* No. 2 (1995): 5–18.

Elster, Jon & Rune Slagstad (eds.) *Constitutionalism and Democracy.* Cambridge University Press, 1988.

Esman, Milton J. (ed.) *Ethnic Conflict in the Western World.* Ithaca, NY: Cornell University Press, 1977.

European Commission for Democracy through Law. *The Modern Concept of Confederation*. Proceedings of the UniDem Seminar organized in Santorini on 22–25 September 1994 in co-operation with the Ministry of Foreign Affairs of Greece. No. 11: Science and Technique of Democracy Collection, Council of Europe, 1995.

Fehrenbacher, Don E. *Constitutions and Constitutionalism in the Slaveholding South*. Athens, GA: University of Georgia Press, 1989.

Finer, S.E. *The History of Government: Vol. 3. Empires, Monarchies and the Modern State*. Oxford University Press, 1997.

Forsyth, Murray (ed.) *Federalism and Nationalism*. Leicester, UK: Leicester University Press, 1989.

Franck, Thomas M. (ed.) *Why Federations Fail: An Inquiry into the Requisites for Successful Federalism*. New York: New York University Press, 1968.

—— 'The Emerging Right to Democratic Governance'. 86 *American Journal of International Law*. No. 1 (1992): 46–91.

Friedrich, Carl J. *Trends of Federalism in Theory and Practice*. London: Frederick A. Praeger, 1968.

Goldwin, Robert A., Art Kaufman & William A. Schambra (eds.) *Forging Unity Out of Diversity: The Approaches of Eight Nations*. Washington, D.C.: American Enterprise Institute, 1989.

Golub, Jonathan. 'Sovereignty and Subsidiarity in EU Environmental Policy'. 44 *Political Studies*. No. 4 (1996): 686–703.

Goodin, Robert L. & Hans-Dieter Klingemann (eds.) *A New Handbook of Political Science*. Oxford University Press, 1996.

Grodzins, Morton. *The American System: A New View of Government in the United States* (Edited by Daniel J. Elazar). Chicago: Rand McNally, 1966.

Gunlicks, Arthur B. 'German Federalism After Unification: The Legal/Constitutional Response'. 24 *Publius*. No. 2 (1994): 81–98.

Gunther, Gerald & Kathleen M. Sullivan. *Constitutional Law*. 13th Ed. Westbury, NY: Foundation Press, 1997.

Hamilton, Alexander, James Madison, & John Jay. *The Federalist* (Edited by Christopher Bigsby). London: J.M. Dent, 1992.

Harris, D.J. (ed.) *Cases and Materials on International Law*. 5th Ed. London: Sweet & Maxwell, 1998.

Hayden, Robert M. 'Constitutional Nationalism in the Formerly Yugoslav Republics'. 51 *Slavic Review*. No. 4 (1992): 654–73.

Hayward, Jack, Brian Barry & Archie Brown (eds.) *The British Study of Politics in the Twentieth Century*. Oxford: The British Academy in association with Oxford University Press, 1999.

Held, David (ed.) *States and Societies*. Oxford: Blackwell, 1983.

Hicks, Ursula K. *et al*. *Federalism and Economic Growth in Underdeveloped Countries*. London: Allen & Unwin, 1961.

Hills, Roderick M., Jr. 'The Political Economy of Cooperative Federalism: Why State Autonomy Makes Sense and "Dual Sovereignty" Doesn't'. 96 *Michigan Law Review*. (1998): 813–944.

Hinsley, F.H. *Sovereignty.* Cambridge University Press, 1986.

Hirschman, Albert O. *Exit, Voice and Loyalty: Responses to Decline in Firms, Organizations, and States.* Cambridge, MA: Harvard University Press, 1970.

Kant, Immanuel. *Eternal Peace*, 1795 (Trans. by W. Hastie). *Eternal Peace and Other International Essays.* Boston: The World Peace Foundation, 1914.

Kincaid, John. 'Values and Value Trade-offs in Federalism'. 25 *Publius.* No. 2 (1995): 29–43.

King, Preston & Andrea Bosco (eds.) *A Constitution for Europe: A Comparative Study of Federal Constitutions & Plans for the United States of Europe.* London: Lothian Foundation Press, 1991.

Kymlicka, Will. *Multicultural Citizenship: A Liberal Theory of Minority Rights.* Oxford: Clarendon Press, 1995.

——(ed.) *The Rights of Minority Cultures.* Oxford University Press, 1995.

Lakoff, Sanford. 'Between Either/Or and More or Less: Sovereignty Versus Autonomy Under Federalism'. 24 *Publius.* No. 1 (1994): 63–78.

Laski, Harold J. 'The Obsolescence of Federalism'. 98 *The New Republic* (3 May 1939): 367–9.

Lehmbruch, Gerhard. 'Consociational Democracy and Corporatism in Switzerland'. 23 *Publius.* No. 2 (1993): 43–60.

Lenaerts, Koen. 'Constitutionalism and the Many Faces of Federalism'. 38 *American Journal of Comparative Law* (1990): 205–63.

Lijphart, Arend. 'Consociation and Federation: Conceptual and Empirical Links'. 12 *Canadian Journal of Political Science.* No. 3 (1979): 499–515.

——*Democracies: Patterns of Majoritarian and Consensus Government in Twenty-One Countries.* New Haven, CT: Yale University Press, 1984.

—— 'The Puzzle of Indian Democracy: A Consociational Interpretation'. 90 *American Political Science Review.* No. 2 (1996): 258–68.

——*Electoral Systems and Party Systems: A Study of Twenty-Seven Democracies, 1945–1990.* New York, Oxford University Press, 1994; reprint, OUP, 1998.

Linz, Juan J. 'Democracy, Multinationalism and Federalism'. Paper presented at the International Political Science Association Meeting in Seoul, Korea, August 1997.

——H.E. Chehabi (eds.) *Sultanistic Regimes.* Baltimore, MD: Johns Hopkins University Press, 1998.

——Alfred Stepan. 'Political Identities and Electoral Sequences: Spain, the Soviet Union, and Yugoslavia'. 121 *Daedalus.* No. 2 (1992): 123–39.

—— ——*Problems of Democratic Transition and Consolidation: Southern Europe, South America, and Post-Communist Europe.* Baltimore, MD: Johns Hopkins University Press, 1996.

—— Arturo Valenzuela (eds.) *The Failure of Presidential Democracy: Comparative Perspectives*. Vol. 1. Baltimore, MD: The Johns Hopkins University Press, 1994.

Livingston, William S. *Federalism and Constitutional Change*. Oxford: Clarendon Press, 1956.

Mai, Angelo. *M. Tulli Ciceronis de re publica quae supersunt*. Rome: Vatican, 1822.

Malfliet, Katlijn & Liliana Nasyrova (eds.) *Federalism: Choices in Law, Institutions and Policy. A Comparative Approach with Focus on the Russian Federation*. Leuven, Belgium: Garant, 1998.

March, James G. & Johan P. Olsen, 'The New Institutionalism: Organizational Factors in Political Life'. 78 *American Political Science Review*. No. 3 (1984): 734–49.

Marriott, Sir J.A.R. *Federalism and the Problem of the Small State*. London: Allen & Unwin, 1943.

Massey, Calvin R. 'State Sovereignty and the Tenth and Eleventh Amendments'. 56 *University of Chicago Law Review* (1989): 61–151.

McWhinney, Edward. *Federal Constitution-Making for a Multi-National World*. Leyden: A.W. Sijthoff, 1966.

Miller, Arthur H., Charles Tien & Andrew A. Peebler. '*The American Political Science Review* Hall of Fame: Assessments and Implications for an Evolving Discipline'. *PS: Political Science and Politics* (March 1996): 73–83.

Mogi, Sobei. *The Problem of Federalism*. 2 Vols. London: Allen & Unwin, 1931.

Newton, K. 'Is Small Really So Beautiful? Is Big Really So Ugly? Size, Effectiveness, and Democracy in Local Government'. 30 *Political Studies*. No. 2 (1982): 190–206.

Peters, B. Guy. *Institutional Theory in Political Science: The 'New Institutionalism'*. London: Pinter, 1999.

Premdas, Ralph R., S.W.R. de A. Samarasinghe & Alan B. Anderson (eds.) *Secessionist Movements in Comparative Perspective*. London: Pinter, 1990.

Rabushka, Alvin & Kenneth A. Shepsle. 'Political Entrepreneurship and Patterns of Democratic Instability in Plural Societies'. 12 *Race: The Journal of the Institute of Race Relations*. No. 4 (1971): 461–76.

Randall, Stephen J. & Roger Gibbins (eds.) *Federalism and the New World Order*. Calgary: University of Calgary Press, 1994.

Rao, M. Govinda & François Vaillancourt. 'Interstate Tax Disharmony in India: A Comparative Perspective'. 24 *Publius*. No. 4 (1994): 99–114.

Riker, William H. *Federalism: Origin, Operation, Significance*. Boston: Little, Brown, 1964.

—— 'Six Books in Search of a Subject or Does Federalism Exist and Does it Matter?' 2 *Comparative Politics*. No. 1 (1969): 135–46.

—— 'Federalism', in Fred I. Greenstein & Nelson W. Polsby (eds.) *Handbook of Political Science: Vol. 5. Governmental Institutions and Processes*. Reading, MA: Addison-Wesley, 1975.

—— *The Development of American Federalism*. Norwell, MA: Kluwer Academic, 1987.

Rose-Ackerman, Susan. 'Does Federalism Matter? Political Choice in a Federal Republic'. 89 *Journal of Political Economy*. No. 1 (1981): 152–65.

Saunders, Cheryl. 'Constitutional Arrangements of Federal Systems'. 25 *Publius*. No. 2 (1995): 61–79.

Shugart, Matthew S. & John M. Carey. *Presidents and Assemblies: Constitutional Design and Electoral Dynamics*. Cambridge University Press, 1992.

Simpson, Alex. *A Treatise on Federal Impeachments*. Law Association of Philadelphia, 1916.

Smith, Anthony D. *Nations and Nationalism in a Global Era* Cambridge: Polity Press, 1995.

Smith, Graham (ed.) *Federalism: The Multiethnic Challenge*. London: Longman, 1995.

Souza, Celina. *Constitutional Engineering in Brazil: The Politics of Federalism and Decentralisation*. New York: St. Martin's Press, 1997.

—— 'Federalism, Decentralisation and Constitutional Reform in the Context of Regional Inequality: The Case of Brazil', Paper presented at the Institute of Latin American Studies, University of London, 13–14 February 1997.

Stein, Eric. *Czecho/Slovakia: Ethnic Conflict, Constitutional Fissure, Negotiated Breakup*. Ann Arbor, MI: University of Michigan Press, 1997.

Stepan, Alfred (ed.) *Authoritarian Brazil: Origins, Policies, and Future*. New Haven: Yale University Press, 1973.

—— *The State and Society: Peru in Comparative Perspective*. Princeton, NJ: Princeton University Press, 1978.

—— 'Toward a New Comparative Analysis of Democracy and Federalism: Demos Constraining and Demos Enabling Federations'. Paper prepared for the International Political Science Association, XVII World Congress, Seoul, Korea, 17–22 August 1997.

—— (ed.) *Democratizing Brazil: Problems of Transition and Consolidation*. Oxford University Press, 1989.

—— 'Russia's Federalism in Comparative Perspective: Reflections on Power Creation and Power Deflation'. Part II of paper for AAASS conference in Boca Raton, FL, 24–27 September, 1998.

—— 'Russian Federalism in Comparative Perspective'. 16 *Post-Soviet Affairs*. 2 (2000): 133–76.

—— 'Brazil: The Burden of the Past; The Promise of the Future'. 129 *Daedalus*. 2 (2000): 145–69.

—— *Arguing Comparative Politics*. Oxford University Press, 2001.

—— Cindy Skach. 'Constitutional Frameworks & Democratic Consolidation: Parliamentarism versus Presidentialism'. 46 *World Politics*. No. 1 (1993): 1–22.

Sunstein, Cass R. 'Constitutionalism and Secession'. 58 *University of Chicago Law Review*. No. 2 (1991): 633–70.

—— *The Partial Constitution*. Cambridge, MA: Harvard University Press, 1993.

Tarlton, C.D. 'Symmetry and Asymmetry as Elements of Federalism: A Theoretical Speculation'. 27 *Journal of Politics* (1965): 861–74.

Tribe, Laurence H. *American Constitutional Law.* 3rd Ed., Vol. 1. New York: Foundation Press, 2000.

Tsebelis, George & Jeannette Money. *Bicameralism.* Cambridge University Press, 1997.

Tummala, Krishna K. 'The Indian Union and Emergency Powers'. 17 *International Political Science Review.* No. 4 (1996): 373–84.

Verney, Douglas V. 'Federalism, Federative Systems, and Federations: The United States, Canada, and India'. 25 *Publius.* No. 2 (1995): 81–97.

Weber, Cynthia. *Simulating Sovereignty: Intervention, The State, and Symbolic Change.* Cambridge University Press, 1995.

Weber, Max. *Economy and Society* (Edited by Guenther Roth & Claus Wittich). Berkeley, CA: University of California Press, 1978.

Wheare, K.C. *Federal Government.* 4th Ed. London: Oxford University Press, 1963.

Whittington, Keith E. 'The Political Constitution of Federalism in Antebellum America: The Nullification Debate as an Illustration of Informal Mechanisms of Constitutional Change'. 26 *Publius.* No. 2 (1996): 1–24.

Statutes, Decrees and Constitutional Court Decisions

Laws

– 1957 –

'Ob otnesenii k vedeniiu soiuznykh respublik zakonodatel'stva ob ustroistve sudov soiuznikh respublik, priniatiia grazhdanskogo, ugolovnogo i protsessual'nykh kodeksov' and 'Ob otnesenii k vedeniiu soiuznykh respublik razresheniia voprosov oblastnogo, kraevogo administrativno-territorial'nogo ustroistva' zakony ot 11 fevralia 1957 g. (Vedomosti Verkhovnogo Soveta SSSR, 1957 g., No. 4) in *Sbornik zakonov SSSR i ukazov Prezidiuma Verkhovnogo Soveta SSSR 1938–1961 g.* (Moskva: Izdatel'stvo 'Izvestiia Sovetov Deputatov Trudiashchikhsiia SSSR', 1961), 42–43.

– 1990 –

No. 1407-I, 3 April 1990, 'O pravovom rezhime chrezvychainogo polozheniia', *Vedomosti S"ezda narodnykh deputatov SSSR i Verkhovnogo Soveta SSSR*, No. 15 (1990), item 250. (Law establishing legal restrictions during declared 'extraordinary situations')

No. 1409-I, 3 April 1990, 'O poriadke resheniia voprosov, sviazannykh s vykhodom soiuznoi respubliki iz SSSR', *Vedomosti S"ezda narodnykh deputatov SSSR i Verkhovnogo Soveta SSSR*, No. 15 (1990), item 252. (Law establishing procedures for secession from USSR)

No. 1457-I, 26 April 1990, 'O razgranichenii polnomochii mezhdu Soiuzom SSR i sub' ektami federatsii'', *Vedomosti S"ezda narodnykh deputatov SSSR i Verkhovnogo Soveta SSSR*, No. 19 (1990), item 329. (Law outlining demarcation of subjects of jursidiction between Union authorities and subjects of the federation)

Zakon 'Ob obespechenii ekonomicheskoi osnovy suvereniteta RSFSR', *Vedomosti S"ezda narodnykh deputatov RSFSR v Verkhovnogo Soveta RSFSR*. No. 22 (1 November 1990), (Law on the economic bases of sovereignty).

– 1992 –

Zakon RF, 3 July 1992, 'Ob ustanovlenii perekhodnogo perioda po gosudarstvenno-territorial'nomu razgranicheniiu v Rossiiskoi Federatsii', *Vedomosti S"ezda narodnykh deputatov RF i Verkhovnogo Soveta RF.* No. 32 (13 August 1992), item 1868, 2397–2398.

– 1994 –

No. 56-FZ, 6 December 1994, 'Ob osnovnykh garantiiakh izbiratel'nykh prav grazh-dan Rossiiskoi Federatsii', *Sobranie zakonodatel'stva Rossiiskoi Federatsii*, No. 32, item 3406, p. 4855. (Law on electoral rights)

– 1995 –

No. 154-FZ, 28 August 1995, 'O obshchikh printsipakh organizatsii mestnogo samou-pravleniia v Rossiiskoi Federatsii', *Sobranie zakonodatel'stva Rossiiskoi Federatsii*, No. 35 (1995), item 3506; No. 12 (1997), item 1378. (Law on general principles of organiza-tion of local self-government)

No. 192-FZ, 5 December 1995, 'O poriadke formirovaniia Soveta Federatsii Feder-al'nogo Sobraniia Rossiiskoi Federatsii', *SZRF*, No. 50, 11 December 1995, item 4869, p. 8967. (Formalizes selection of Federation Council senators: *ex officio* heads of regional executive and legislative branches)

– 1999 –

No. 119-FZ, 24 June 1999, 'O printsipakh i poriadke razgranicheniia predmetov vedeniia i polnomochii mezhdu organami gosudarstvennoi vlasti Rossiiskoi Feder-atsii I organami gosudarstvennoi vlasti sub"ektov Rossiiskoi Federatsii', *SZRF* No. 26, 28 June 1999, item 3176, pp. 5685–5692.

No. 184-FZ, 6 October 1999, 'Ob obshchikh printsipakh organizatsii zakonoda-tel'nykh (predstavitel'nykh) i ispolnitel'nykh organov gosudarstvennoi vlasti sub"-ektov Rossiiskoi Federatsii', *Sobranie Zakonodatel'stva Rossiiskoi Federatsii*. No. 42, 18 October 1999, item 5005, p. 9417. (Establishing by law the general principles for executive and legislative branches of regional government)

– 2000 –

No. 106-FZ, 29 July 2000, 'O vnesenii izmenenii i dopolnenii v Federal'nyi zakon "Ob obshchikh printsipakh organizatsii zakonodatel'nykh (predstavitel'nykh) i ispolnitel'nykh organov gosudarstvennoi vlasti sub"ektov Rossiiskoi Federatsii"', *SZRF*, No. 31, 31 July 2000, item 3205, p. 6075. (Creates Presidential power to dismiss regional executives and legislatures for violation of Constitution and federal law)

No. 107-FZ, 4 August 2000, 'O vnesenii izmenenii i dopolnenii v Federal'nyi zakon "Ob obshchikh printsipakh organizatsii mestnogo samoupravleniia v Rossiiskoi Federatsii"', *SZRF*, No. 32, 7 August 2000, item 3330, p. 6243. (Creates federal and regional executive power to dismiss heads of local self-government)

No. 113-FZ, 5 August 2000, 'O poriadke formirovaniia Soveta Federatsii Federal'nogo Sobraniia Rossiiskoi Federatsii', *SZRF*, No. 32, 7 August 2000, item 3336, p. 6249. (Restructures Federation Council)

– 2001 –

No. 3-FZ, 8 February 2001, 'O vnesenii dopolneniia v Federal'nyi zakon "Ob obshchikh printsipakh organizatsii zakonodatel'nykh (predstavitel'nykh) i ispolnitel'nykh organov gosudarstvennoi vlasti sub"ektov Rossiiskoi Federatsii"', *SZRF*, No. 7, 12 February 2001, item 608, p. 1784.

Decrees

– 1988 –

No. 9836-XI, 26 november 1988, Ukaz Prezidiuma Verkhovnogo Soveta SSSR 'O nesootvetstvii Zakona Estonskoi SSR "O vnesenii izmenenii i dopolnenii v Konstitutsiiu (Osnovnoi Zakon) Estonskii SSR" i Deklaratsii Verkhovnogo Soveta Estonskoi SSR o suverenitete Estonskoi SSR, priniatykh 16 noiabria 1988 goda, Konstitutsii SSSR i zakonam SSSR'. *Vedomosti Verkhovnogo soveta soiuza sovetskikh sotsialisticheskikh respublik* No. 48 (30 November 1988), item 720, p. 803. (Denouncing alteration of the Estonian constitution and adoption of Estonian Declaration of Sovereignty)

– 1992 –

No. 1622, 23 December 1992, 'O merakh po realizatsii Federativnogo dogovora v Respublike Komi', *Vedomosti S"ezda narodnykh deputatov RF i Verkhovnogo Soveta RF*, No. 52 (31 December 1992), item 3139, p. 3847–3849. (Providing special dispensations to the Komi Republic regarding the Federation Treaty)

– 1993 –

No. 1400, 21 September 1993, 'O poetapnoi konstitutsionnoi reforme v Rossiiskoi Federatsii', *Sobranie Aktov Prezidenta i Pravitel'stva Rossiiskoi Federatsii*, No. 39, 27 September 1993, item 3597, p. 3912. (Dissolution of Parliament)

– 1997 –

No. 696, 9 July 1997, 'O polnomochnom predstavitele Prezidenta Rossiiskoi Federatsii v regione Rossiiskoi Federatsii', *SZRF*, No. 28, 14 July 1997, item 3421, p. 5549.
(Yeltsin's creation of the office of presidential representative)

– 2000 –

No. 790, 5 May 2000, 'O postanovlenii Pravitel'stva Respubliki Ingushetiia ot 3
avgusta 1998 g., No. 204 "O merakh po ispolneniiu Ukaza No. 72 ot 28 fevralia
1997 g. Prezidenta Respubliki Ingushetiia, Postanovleniia Soveta Bezopastnosti
Respubliki Ingushetiia No. 4 ot 27 maia 1998 g." ', *SZRF*, No. 19, 8 May 2000, item
2060, p. 4208. (Cancellation of legal force of Republic of Ingushetia resolution as
unconstitutional)

No. 791, 5 May 2000, 'Ob Ukaze Prezidenta Respubliki Ingushetiia ot 16 sentiabria
1997 g. No. 229 "O merakh po uluchsheniiu sbora platezhei za potreblennye gaz i
elektroenergiiu" ', *SZRF*, No. 19, 8 May 2000, item 2061, p. 4209. (Cancellation of
legal force of Republic of Ingushetia resolution as unconstitutional)

No. 800, 5 May 2000, 'O postanovlenii glavy administratsii Amurskoi *oblasti* ot 23
iunia 1999 g., No. 365 "Ob organizatsii propuska grazhdan Rossiiskoi Federatsii
v torgovyi kompleks g. Kheikhe (KNR)" ', *SZRF*, No. 19, 8 May 2000, item 2064, p.
4210. (Cancellation of legal force of Amur Oblast Ukaz as unconstitutional)

No. 849, 13 May 2000, 'O polnomochnom predstavitele Prezidenta Rossiiskoi
Federatsii v federal'nom okruge', *SZRF*, No. 20, 15 May 2000, item 2112, p. 4318.
(Putin's creation of seven federal districts)

No. 851, 15 May 2000, 'O postanovlenii glavy administratsii Smolenskoi *oblasti* ot 26
iiunia 1998 g. No. 271 "O vzimanii platezhei za zagriaznenie okruzhaiushchei
prirodnoi sredy ot inostrannykh iuridicheskikh lits i grazhdan, ekspluatiriushchikh
avtotransportnyie sredstva na avtodorogakh Smolenskoi *oblasti*" ', *SZRF*, No. 21, 22
May 2000, item 2164, p. 4387. (Cancellation of legal force of Smolensk Oblast
resolution as unconstitutional)

No. 890, 18 May 2000, 'O polonomochnom predstavitele Prezidenta Rossiiskoi
Federatsii v Sibirskom federal'nom okruge', *SZRF*, No. 21, 22 May 2000. (Appointment of Drachevskii as governor-general in Siberian federal district)

No. 891, 18 May 2000, 'O polonomochnom predstavitele Prezidenta Rossiiskoi
Federatsii v Severo-Kavkazskom federal'nom okruge', *SZRF*, No. 21, 22 May
2000. (Appointment of Kazantsev as governor-general in N. Caucasus federal
district)

No. 892, 18 May 2000, 'O polonomochnom predstavitele Prezidenta Rossiiskoi Federatsii v Privolzhskom federal'nom okruge', *SZRF*, No. 21, 22 May 2000. (Appointment of Kirienko as governor-general in Volga federal district)

No. 893, 18 May 2000, 'O polonomochnom predstavitele Prezidenta Rossiiskoi Federatsii v Ural'skom federal'nom okruge', *SZRF*, No. 21, 22 May 2000. (Appointment of Latyshev as governor-general in Urals federal district)

No. 894, 18 May 2000, 'O polonomochnom predstavitele Prezidenta Rossiiskoi Federatsii v Tsentral'nom federal'nom okruge', *SZRF*, No. 21, 22 May 2000. (Appointment of Poltavchenko as governor-general in Central federal district)

No. 895, 18 May 2000, 'O polonomochnom predstavitele Prezidenta Rossiiskoi Federatsii v Dal'nevostochnom federal'nom okruge', *SZRF*, No. 21, 22 May 2000. (Appointment of Pulikovskii as governor-general in Far East federal district)

No. 896, 18 May 2000, 'O polonomochnom predstavitele Prezidenta Rossiiskoi Federatsii v Severo-Zapadnom federal'nom okruge', *SZRF*, No. 21, 22 May 2000. (Appointment of Cherkesov as governor-general in NW federal district)

No. 1055, 7 June 2000, 'Ob ukazakh Prezidenta Respubliki Adygeia ot 8 oktiabria 1997 g. No. 246 "O nomenklature kadrov Prezidenta Republiki Adygeia i Kabineta Ministrov Respubliki Adygeia" i ot 4 iiunia 1999 g. No. 111 "O vnesenii izmenenii i dopolnenii v Ukaz Prezidenta Respubliki Adygeia" ot 8 oktiabria 1997 g. No. 246 "O nomenklature kadrov Prezidenta Respubliki Adygeia i Kabineta Ministrov Respubliki Adygeia" ', *SZRF*, No. 24, 12 June 2000, item 2544, p. 4971. (Cancellation of legal force of Adygeia Republic Presidential Decree as unconstitutional)

No. 1101, 12 June 2000, 'O priostanovlenii deistviia postanovleniia gubernatora Tverskoi *oblasti* ot 28 sentiabria 1999 g. No. 856 "O tarifakh na elektricheskuiu energiiu dlia naseleniia *oblasti*" ', *SZRF*, No. 25, 19 June 2000, item 2676, p. 5122. (Cancellation of legal force of Tver' Oblast' gubernatorial decree as unconstitutional)

No. 1500, 12 August 2000, 'O priostanovlenii deistviia postanovleniia gubernatora Tul'skoi *oblasti* ot 12 aprelia 2000 g. No. 137 'Ob uporiadochenii litsenzirovaniia deiatel'nosti po zagotovke, pererabotke i realizatsii loma tsvetnykh i chernykh metallov" ', *SZRF*, No. 34, 21 August 2000, item 3436, p. 6913. (Cancellation of legal force of Tula Oblast' gubernatorial decree as unconstitutional)

No. 1602, 1 September 2000, 'O Gosudarstvennom sovete Rossiiskoi Federatsii', *SZRF*, No. 36, 4 September 2000, item 3633, p. 7186. (Establishing the State Council)

No. 1620, 9 September 2000, 'O priostanovlenii deistviia Ukaza Prezidenta Respubliki Adygeia ot 30 maia 1994 g. No. 83 "Omerakh po ogranicheniiu migratsii v Respubliku Adygeia" ', *SZRF*, No. 38, 18 September 2000, item 3777, p. 7682.

(Cancellation of legal force of Adygeia Republic Presidential Decree as unconstitutional)

– 2001 –

No. 97, 30 January 2001, 'O vnesenii dopolneniia i izmeneniia v Polozheniie o polnomochnom predstavitele Prezidenta Rossiiskoi Federatsii v federal'nom okruge, utverzhdennoe Ukazom Prezidenta Rossiiskoi Federatsii ot 13 maia 2000 g., No. 849', *SZRF*, No. 6, 5 February 2001, item 551, p. 1624 (Amendment of earlier decree on presidential representatives in the federal districts, subordinating *polpredy* to Chief of Staff of Presidential Administration)

No. 132, 7 February 2001, 'O priostanovlenii deistviia Ukaza Prezidenta Respubliki Ingushetiia ot 22 aprelia 2000 g. No. 76 "Ob uprazdnenii Gosudarstvennogo komiteta Respubliki Ingushetiia po sviazi" i postanovleniia Pravitel'stva Respubliki Ingushetiia ot 20 maia 2000 g. No. 192 "Ob uchrezhdenii gosudarstvennogo unitarnogo predpriatiia Upravlenie elektricheskoi sviazi Respubliki Ingushetia" ', *SZRF*, No. 7, 12 February 2001, item 627, p. 1812. (suspending Ingush decrees aimed at control of communications and electric links)

Cases of the Russian Federation Constitutional Court

Postanovlenie Konstitutsionnogo suda Rossiiskoi Federatsii, 'Delo o proverke konstitutsionnosti polozhenii Ukaza Prezidenta Rossiiskoi Federatsii "O merakh po ukrepleniiu edinoi sistemy ispolnitel'noi vlasti v Rossiiskoi Federatsii" ', 30 April 1996, *Vestnik Konstitutsionnogo Suda Rossiiskoi Federatsii*, No. 3 (1996), p. 15.

Postanovlenie Konstitutsionnogo Suda Rossiiskoi Federatsii po delu o proverke konstitutsionnosti Zakona Udmurtskoi Respubliki ot 17 aprelia 1996 goda 'O sisteme organov gosudarstvennoi vlasti v Udmurtskoi Respublike', 24 January 1997, *Vestnik Konstitutsionnogo Suda Rossiiskoi Federatsii*, No. 1 (1997), p. 2.

Postanovlenie Konstitutsionnogo Suda Rossiiskoi Federatsii po delu o proverke konstitutsionnosti statei 80, 92, 93 i 94 Konstitutsii Respubliki Komi i stat'i 31 Zakona Respubliki Komi ot 31 oktiabria 1994 goda 'Ob organakh ispolnitel'noi vlasti v Respublike Komi', *Rossiiskaia gazeta*. 31 January 1998, 4.

Postanovlenie Konstitutsionnogo Suda Rossiiskoi Federatsii po delu o proverke konstitutsionnosti otdel'nykh polozhenii Konstitutsii Respubliki Altai i Federal'nogo zakona 'Ob obshchikh printsipakh organizatsii zakonodatel'nykh (predstavitel'nykh) i ispolnitel'nykh organov gosudarstvennoi vlasti sub"ektov Rossiiskoi Federatsii', 7 June 2000, Vestnik *Konstitutsionnogo Suda Rossiiskoi Federatsii*, No. 5 (2000), p. 2.

Opredelenie Konstitutsionnogo Suda Rossiiskoi Federatsii po zaprosu gruppy deputatov Gosudarstvennoi Dumy o proverke sootvetstviia Konstitutsii Rossiiskoi Federatsii otdel'nykh polozhenii konstitutsii Respubliki Adygeia, Respubliki Bashkortostan, Respubliki Ingushetiia, Respubliki Komi, Respubliki Severnaia Osetiia-Alaniia i Respub liki Tatarstan, 27 June 2000, *Vestnik Konstitutsionnogo Suda Rossiiskoi Federatsii*, No. 5 (2000), p. 59.

Opredelenie Konstitutsionnogo Suda Rossiiskoi Federatsii po zaprosu Verkhovnogo Suda Kabardino-Balkarskoi Respubliki o proverke konstitutsionnosti punkta 'e' stat'i 81 Konstitutsii Kabardino-Balkarskoi Respubliki, stat'i 2 i punkta 3 stat'i 17 Zakona Kabardino-Balkarskoi Respubliki "O mestnom samoupravlenii v Kabardino-Balkarskoi Respublike," 2 November 2000, *Vestnik Konstitutsionnogo Suda Rossiiskoi Federatsii*, No. 2 (2001), p. 20.

Index

DATE DUE